Defining Engagement

Japan and Global Contexts, 1640–1868

Robert I. Hellyer

Published by the Harvard University Asia Center
and distributed by Harvard University Press
Cambridge (Massachusetts) and London, 2009

© 2009 by The President and Fellows of Harvard College

Printed in the United States of America

The Harvard University Asia Center publishes a monograph series and, in coordination with the Fairbank Center for Chinese Studies, the Korea Institute, the Reischauer Institute of Japanese Studies, and other faculties and institutes, administers research projects designed to further scholarly understanding of China, Japan, Vietnam, Korea, and other Asian countries. The Center also sponsors projects addressing multidisciplinary and regional issues in Asia.

Library of Congress Cataloging-in-Publication Data

Hellyer, Robert I.
    Defining engagement : Japan and global contexts, 1640–1868 / Robert I. Hellyer.
       p. cm. -- (Harvard East Asian monographs ; 326)
    Includes bibliographical references and index.
    ISBN 978-0-674-03577-5 (cloth : acid-free paper)
    1. Japan--Foreign relations—1600–1868. I. Harvard University. Asia Center. II. Title.
DS871.7.H454 2009
327.52009'03--dc22

2009045241

Index by David Prout
Maps by Bill Nelson

♾ Printed on acid-free paper

Last figure below indicates year of this printing

19 18 17 16 15 14 13 12 11 10 09

Defining Engagement

Japan and Global Contexts, 1640–1868

Harvard East Asian Monographs 326

To my father
Harold Jesse Hellyer
1934–1989

Acknowledgments

The idea for this book began in 1991 when I was sent, quite unexpectedly, to teach English on the island of Tsushima. Upon being accepted into the Japanese government's Japan Exchange and Teaching (JET) Program earlier that year, I had requested, because of my budding interest in Japanese history, to teach in Nagasaki, where I hoped to learn more about the history of that city. In a way my request was granted because I was dispatched to a part of Nagasaki *prefecture*: Tsushima. The island's natural beauty and the warmth of its people quickly assuaged my concerns about spending a year in such a remote location. And as I soon realized, I had been given a wonderful opportunity to learn firsthand about a place that offered an exciting and unique lens through which to consider the history of Japan.

That interest in Tsushima, and later in the Kyushu region overall, was supported and nurtured during my time as a graduate student at Stanford University, where I wrote the doctoral dissertation upon which this book is based. For helping me on the long road to completing that dissertation, I thank first my advisor, Peter Duus, who always took time to answer my questions and to give perspective in a challenging yet encouraging way. I especially appreciated his ability to help me move beyond merely the small story of the Kyushu region and to think more broadly about the history of Japan. James Ketelaar was equally supportive, continuing to read chapters and to offer valuable insights even after he moved to the University of Chicago midway through my graduate career. While at Stanford, my studies were made possible by a History

Department Graduate Fellowship as well as Mellon-Sawyer and Japan Fund grants. I also greatly benefited from the teaching of Harold Kahn, the late Jeffrey Mass, and of Key-Hiuk Kim, who by my good fortune taught a course on Korean history as a visiting professor. In addition, I valued being part of a strong community of graduate students which included at different times: Paul Atkins, Catherine Bae, Thomas Conlan, William Gardner, Angus Lockyer, Tobie Meyer-Fong, Greg Pflugfelder, Nancy Stalker, Bruce Suttmeier, and Shannon Sweeney. I offer special thanks to Robert Eskildsen, who constantly pushed me to rethink my ideas and more importantly to more effectively articulate them. His friendship and support, which included reading an early draft of this work, was instrumental in helping me complete this book.

During my graduate school days and after I also had the privilege of spending several extended periods as a visiting researcher at the Historiographical Institute, University of Tokyo. During my initial visit on a Ministry of Education fellowship, I received guidance first from Miyachi Masato, who kindly allowed me to attend his seminar on late Edo-period history and who freely offered his keen insights on my research and Japanese history in general. I could not have effectively researched the history of Tsushima without the unstinting assistance of Tsuruta Kei, and Yokoyama Yoshinori was generous with his wide knowledge of Satsuma and Ryukyu. Others who were also helpful during my visits were: Asami Masakazu, Gonoi Takashi, Hakoishi Hiroshi, Hoya Tōru, Ishida Chihiro, Kimura Naoki, Matsui Yōko, Nishizawa Mihoko, Ōhashi Akiko, Oka Mihoko, Ono Shō, Tanaka Yōko, the late Kanai Madoka, and the entire staff of the institute's library. I offer special thanks to Matsukata Fuyuko for her friendship and help and also thank Tomori Maiko and Yokoyama Yuriko for their tutoring in reading and analyzing Edo period sources. While at the University of Tokyo, I also benefited from attending the seminar of Hamashita Takeshi, who in subsequent years generously made time to meet and provide valuable advice. In addition, I appreciated the suggestions offered by Arano Yasunori, who invited me to participate in his engaging graduate seminar at Rikkyo University. Finally the Institute of Social Science, University of Tokyo, where I served on the faculty for two years, provided an extremely positive environment for furthering my research. I thank especially Nitta Michio and Hirashima Kenji for their help during my tenure there.

Acknowledgments

While teaching at Allegheny College, I was fortunate to receive research travel grants as well as funding from the Jonathan E. and Nancy L. Helmreich Research and Book Grant Fund to support additional research trips related to this book. I valued the encouragement and camaraderie offered by colleagues in the History Department—Sarah Buck, Paul Burton, Christopher Gill, Stephen Lyons, Kenneth Pinnow, Barry Shapiro, and Richard Turk—and from others throughout the college. I send particular thanks to Bruce Clayton and Paula Treckel for their advice and for providing models of consummate teacher-scholars.

I was subsequently privileged to spend an academic year as a postdoctoral fellow at the Reischauer Institute of Japanese Studies, Harvard University, where I was afforded time and invaluable access to Harvard's libraries to further develop this book. I benefited first from the support of Director Susan Pharr and Associate Director Ted Gilman and from the other postdoctoral fellows, Gina Cogan, Abby Margolis, Suzanne O'Brien, and David Odo. I received valuable suggestions and critiques from Mikael Adolphson, Harold Bolitho, Theodore Bestor, Dani Botsman, Albert Craig, Andrew Gordon, and Akira Iriye. I also thank the institute's staff members, Stacie Matsumoto, Margot Chamberlain, Mary Amstutz, and Ruiko Connor, for all their help.

From Wake Forest University, where I have taught since 2005, I received additional financial grants from the Archie Fund, the Department of History's Griffin Fund, and from the Publication and Research Fund. I thank all of my colleagues in the Department of History for their support and encouragement. I give special thanks to Simone Caron, who was helpful in uncountable ways, and to Paul Escott, Michele Gillespie, Jeffrey Lerner, Stephen Vella, and Alan Williams, whose kind words helped me push through the final stages in completing this book. Sarah Watts offered thoughtful insights and inspired me with her work ethic and passion for the study of history. I also thank Monique O'Connell for her suggestions, Qiong Zhang for sharing her knowledge of Chinese history, and Laura Gammons and Jing Wei for their cheerful help with administrative and computer matters.

Ronald Toby was extremely helpful especially at the initial stages of this project. Kären Wigen offered many useful suggestions, as did Jim Bartholomew. I owe much to David Howell, who gave advice on many occasions and generously took the time to read and offer comments on an entire draft of the manuscript. Among others who helped in different ways were: Akiyama Takayasu, Michael Auslin, Tirrell Black, Martha Buckingham, Wayne Combs, Mark Cosdon, Gilbert Dobbe, Haraguchi Izumi, the late Walter Jacobson, Mark Jones, Kimura Naoya, David Leheny, Robert MacDougall, Brent Malin, the Miyamoto family, Fred Notehelfer, Mark Ravina, Shibata Kaoru, Ryuto Shimada, Eric Tagliacozzo, Lee Taniguchi, Nobuko Toyosawa, and Scott Tritt. The entire Arai family, and most notably the late Arai Sayako, were also extremely generous to me during my time in Tokyo. Kenneth Pechter remained a supportive friend throughout the researching and writing of this book.

I also thank the two anonymous readers for Harvard University Asia Center who took the time to read this work and provide many useful suggestions which helped to improve it. Tachibana Atsushi, a friend from my time in Tsushima, Katsumori Noriko of the Kobe City Museum, and Shiraishi Megumi of the Historiographical Institute, University of Tokyo, were all helpful in securing images for this work. Great thanks go out to my editor, William M. Hammell, for his editorial assistance and for patiently guiding me through the publication process. My mother, Nancy I. Hellyer, kept her faith in me even during many trying moments and offered useful comments on an earlier draft. Always taking the time to listen to my often rambling ideas, my grandmother, Margaret D. Hellyer, was a wonderful sounding board and also generously added her comments to one of my drafts. I cannot forget the help of Connie Hellyer Conway, who drawing upon her fine editorial skills, pushed me to make important revisions that I would not have considered on my own. Finally I thank my wife, Miho, for her loving support which was instrumental in helping me to complete this book. I remain indebted to all those mentioned above but take full responsibility for any mistakes in this work.

Tokyo, Summer 2009

Contents

Figures, Maps, and Tables   xiii

Conventions   xv

Introduction   1
   International Relations and the Entrenched Ideology of Seclusion 6
   Japan and Early Modern Proto-Globalization 12
   The Domestic Parameters of the System of Foreign Relations 19

1 Interdependent Partners: The Shogunate, Satsuma, and Tsushima   25
   Foreign Relations in the Sixteenth and Early Seventeenth Centuries 30
   Satsuma and Tsushima in the New Tokugawa Foreign Relations Order 34

2 The Reaction against Globalization   49
   Restricting Silver 52
   The Domains and Tokugawa Currency Manipulations 59
   Localization 68
   Conclusions 71

3 Guarded Engagement   73
   1764 as a Trade Watershed 74
   The Local Impact 89
   Russian Probes 97
   The Reforms of Matsudaira Sadanobu 102
   Matsudaira and Foreign Trade 107
   The Presentation of Guarded Engagement 110
   Conclusions 114

4 Domestic Demand and Foreign Trade   116
    New Domestic Market Dynamics 121
    The Emergence of the Satsuma Entrepôt 125
    Reasserting Tokugawa Authority at Nagasaki 133
    *Tsushima: "We Are a Small Island Domain
        with Little Agricultural Production"* 139
    Maintaining the Outward Face of Guarded Engagement 145
    Conclusions 147

5 Local Japan Encounters the West   150
    Western Visits to Ryukyu and the Satsuma Response 152
    Divisions within Satsuma 159
    Nariakira in Control 162
    Tsushima and Western Visitors 168
    Conclusions 176

6 The Transition in Foreign Trade   178
    Tokugawa Trade Initiatives 180
    Satsuma's Domestic and Foreign Trade Ventures 186
    Godai Tomoatsu and Commercial Opportunism in Europe 200
    Conclusions 204

7 Defending the Domain and the Realm   207
    Ōshima Tomonojō and the Campaign for Bakufu Aid 218
    Bitter Factional Rivalry 227
    Ōshima and Tokugawa Initiatives 231
    Conclusions 233

   Conclusion: The End of Domain Agency
       and the Adoption of International Relations   235

Reference Matter

Works Cited   253
Index   271

Figures, Maps, and Tables

Figures

1	View of Kagoshima harbor and Sakurajima	35
2	Chinese ship carrying investiture mission	37
3	Arrival of investiture mission at Naha	37
4	Remains of the *funae* in Izuhara harbor, Tsushima	41
5	Japan House in Pusan harbor	43
6	Chinese Residence in Nagasaki harbor	57
7	Clearing-house and magistrate's office, Nagasaki	57
8	Diagram of thatched shelter for ginseng seedlings	69
9	Goods offloaded from Chinese merchant ship	77
10	Goods inspected at Chinese Warehouse	79
11	Goods placed in storage	79
12	Nikolai Rezanov received at Nagasaki, 1805	113
13	Grading of ginseng roots	119
14	Dejima and Marine Product Office and Warehouses	125
15	Marine cargo ships in harbor	135
16	Yamakawa harbor	155
17	Shimazu Nariakira (1809–58)	165
18	Shimazu Hisamitsu (1817–87)	192
19	Aerial view of Asō Bay, Tsushima	209
20	Imozaki, Asō Bay, Tsushima	211
21	"View of Sakurajima from the Harbor," 1872	239

Maps

1	Nansei [Southwest] Islands	3
2	Chosŏn Korea and Edo-period Tsushima	5
3	East and Southeast Asia in the seventeenth and eighteenth centuries	15
4	Honshu during the Edo period	29
5	Edo-period Kyushu and Nagasaki, circa 1800	33
6	Matsumae, Ezo, and Russian outposts in the late Edo period	99

Tables

1	Foreign Ships Reported Near or Landing in Tsushima and Korea, 1847–59	173
2	Russian and British Vessels at Tsushima, 1861	213

Conventions

Romanization

Japanese words, names, titles, and place names are spelled using the modified Hepburn system. Macrons are included for Japanese words, except for commonly used terms (such as shogun and Tokyo) that appear in standard, English dictionaries. Korean words and place names are romanized according to the McCune-Reischauer system. Chinese words, proper names, and place names are given in *pinyin*, except in cases, such as Amoy (Xiamen) and Canton (Guangzhou), where the older romanization is more familiar to English-language readers.

Proper Names

Chinese, Korean, and Japanese names appear in the original order, with the family name first, followed by the given name, except for citations in English-language works where the author's name appears in Western order.

Dates

All dates before 1 January 1873 (when Japan adopted the Gregorian calendar) are given according to the Japanese calendar. Exceptions are significant events widely chronicled according to their date on the Gregorian calendar, e.g., the opening of the ports of Nagasaki, Yokohama, and Hakodate to Western-style free trade on 1 July 1859.

Currency and Measures

During the Edo period, Japan had a multi-metal currency system, with silver used primarily in western Japan and on the Osaka market, with gold being standard in the east and Edo. While the Tokugawa set official conversion rates, in reality rates fluctuated based upon market conditions and varied by region. Copper coins were used throughout Japan for smaller market transactions.

CURRENCY WEIGHTS

mon: 0.1325 ounces or 3.75 grams of copper
monme: 0.1325 ounces or 3.75 grams of silver
kan: 8.72 pounds or 3.75 kilograms of silver
ryō: 0.63 ounces or 18 grams of gold (also referred to as *koban*)

The silver *kan*, used to measure values in foreign trade, consisted of 1,000 *monme* of silver coins or 1,000 *mon* of copper coins. While it is difficult to gauge the exact conversion rate, one *kan* equaled roughly 15 *ryō* of gold. The gold *ryō* equaled 50–60 *monme* of silver.

MEASURES

koku: 47.5 U.S. gallons (approximately 6 bushels) or 180 liters

The *koku* was used to measure especially rice, other grains, as well as the tonnage of ships. Because it was the staple crop, Japanese had begun to calculate taxes in rice in the sixteenth century. During the Edo period, the wealth of domains, the ranks of retainers, as well the stipends of samurai were calculated in *koku*.

kin: 1.32 pounds or 0.6 kilograms

The *kin* was used to measure bulk items such as copper bar and rods, marine products, and sugar.

Defining Engagement

Japan and Global Contexts, 1640–1868

Introduction

An outside view of Japan, presented by the governor of China's Fujian province, Xu Jiyu, offers a useful starting point to consider the actors in Japanese foreign relations in the mid-nineteenth century. In 1848, Xu published a collection of annotated maps of the world beyond China. In his section on the maritime provinces to the east, he wrote that Japan

is located in the Eastern Sea on three islands. The northern island is called Tui-ma-tao [Tsushima], which is across from the southern edge of Korea. It can be reached [from Korea] in one night. . . . The center island is called Ch'ang-ch'i [Nagasaki]. The land area is comparatively large and is opposite [the island of] P'u-t'o-shan, [Putuoshan Island in the Zhoushan Islands] off the coast of Chekiang [Zhejiang]. *China's merchant ships trade at this place.* The southern island is called Sa-szu-ma [Satsuma] and is opposite Wen [chou] and T'ai- [chou] in Chekiang. Its people are strong and healthy and their swords are the sharpest; horses are also raised. . . . In addition to these three islands there are numerous small ones. The king resides to the northeast of Nagasaki in a place called mi-yeh [?]-ku, meaning 'capital' in Japanese [*miyako*]. . . . The authority over state affairs resides with the generalissimo [shogun]. The king does not attend to such affairs, but only serves in a ceremonial capacity.[1]

---

1. Drake, *China Charts the World*, 73. For consistency, I use the pinyin of the governor's name, Xu Jiyu, although Drake uses the Wade-Giles spelling, Hsu Chi-Yü. The first ellipsis and most items in the brackets are original from Drake's translation. I added the second and third ellipses and for clarity, the "Putuoshan Island in the Zhoushan Islands," and "Zhejiang," the pinyin for Chekiang, in brackets.

Xu presents a surprising view of Japan's geography, which at that time was composed primarily of three main islands: Honshu, Kyushu, and Shikoku (the northern island of Hokkaido was fully incorporated into the Japanese state in the 1870s). For his sources, the governor exclusively utilized Chinese accounts of Japan published in the late seventeenth and early eighteenth centuries. He declined to use Western sources believing them based "on impressions only," given that Western merchant ships had seldom actually visited the waters around Japan.[2] As such, his description is revealing because it shows how Japan appeared from China, its most important trading partner during the Edo period (1603–1868).

Xu conceived of the port of Nagasaki in western Kyushu as the "central island" because Chinese merchant ships regularly called there in numbers that consistently eclipsed those of the Dutch East India Company (Vereenigde Oost-Indische Compagnie in Dutch, abbreviated as VOC). We can conclude that Xu dubbed as main islands the feudal domains of Satsuma, in southern Kyushu, and Tsushima, an island in the straits between Japan and Korea, because they were the only Japanese domains to be directly involved in Japanese-Chinese trade during the Edo period. Tsushima monopolized Japanese trade with Korea, and therefore the often more valuable Japanese-Chinese trade conducted through Korean intermediaries. For its part, Satsuma manipulated Japanese-Chinese trade flowing through the Ryukyu Kingdom (today's Okinawa prefecture). Finally Xu's seeming ignorance of the city of Edo (renamed Tokyo in 1868) is equally instructive. Because of the structure of Japanese foreign relations, it is understandable that Xu did not explicitly locate power and authority over foreign relations in the hands of the shogun, the leader of the Tokugawa shogunate (*bakufu*), Japan's central authority, based at Edo. Although the *bakufu* directly administered Nagasaki, the shogun and Tokugawa leaders did not dispatch envoys to China and other foreign lands and had only limited involvement in trade and related diplomatic contacts taking place at Satsuma and Tsushima. In the Edo-period system, Satsuma and Tsushima exercised control over a significant share of Japanese foreign

---

2. Ibid.

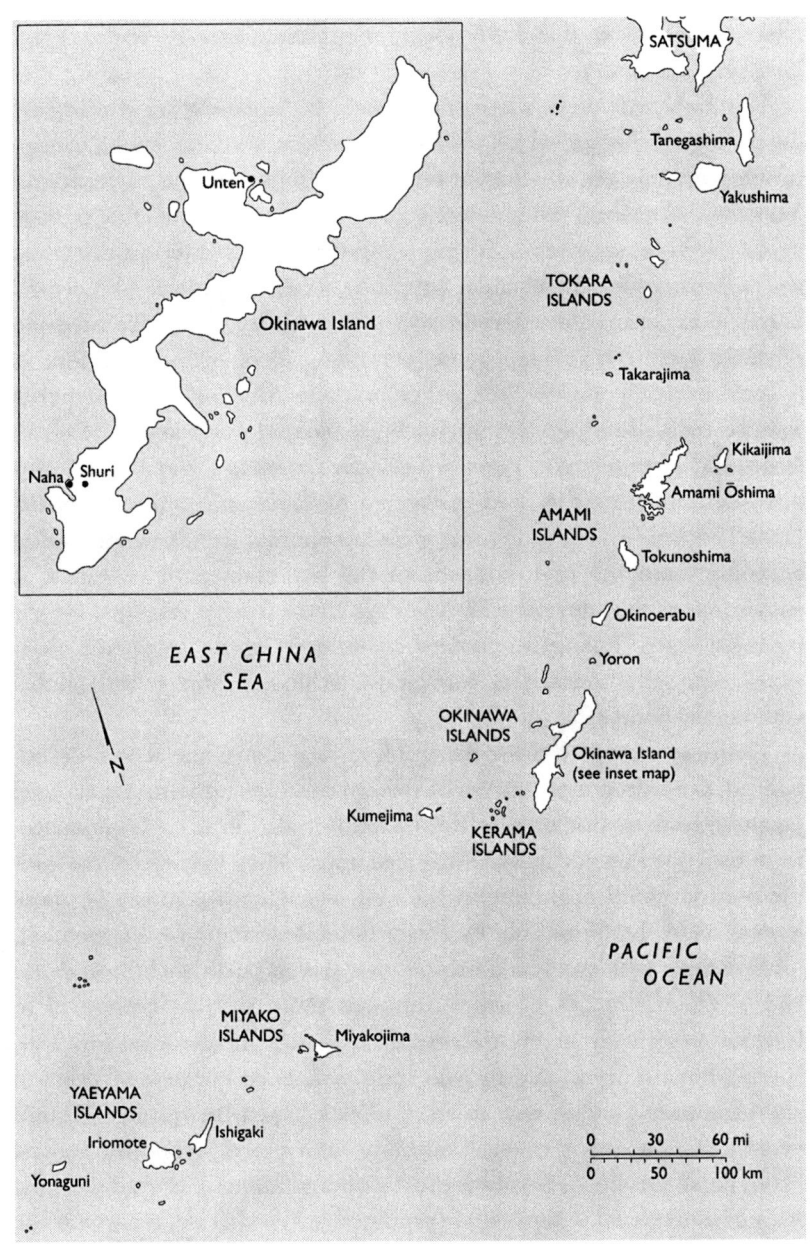

Map 1 The Nansei [Southwest] Islands.
The present name for the island groups extending from Kyushu to Taiwan.

relations, which in this study includes primarily foreign trade, diplomacy, and defense.

This book examines these three actors in Japan's foreign relations: the Tokugawa *bakufu*, which developed policies which created a foreign relations framework for the entire Japanese state, and the Satsuma and Tsushima domains, which maintained intercourse with the outside world based on an often changing combination of Tokugawa directives and politico-economic agendas particular to each domain. The central narrative exploring these three actors demonstrates that Japan's foreign relations were not defined by an overriding ideology of seclusion, as is conventionally argued, but rather by particular Tokugawa domestic agendas as well as political interchanges, shared goals and rivalries in trade, and disputes over defense between the *bakufu* and the two domains. As its secondary and connected narrative, this study considers Japan's interface with long-term global economic trends in the period spanning from the mid-sixteenth to the late nineteenth centuries. It shows that as they developed a larger system of foreign relations for the Japanese state, Tokugawa leaders consistently made pragmatic decisions, especially concerning foreign trade, in accordance with global commercial contexts.

Via these two narratives, the book argues that while it was decentralized, the Edo-period system of foreign relations nonetheless allowed Japanese leaders, not only in the *bakufu* but also in the two domains, to remain flexible and pursue nuanced approaches to intercourse with the outside world beginning in the mid-seventeenth century. Japanese leaders were therefore able to create rational systems of engagement, most notably with the China market, that served Japan well through the end of the eighteenth century. Although those systems continued to function effectively in the decades after 1800, the Satsuma and Tsushima domains were able to gain more influence because of political and economic factors, new military threats posed by visiting Western vessels, and Japan's particular interface with global economic trends. From those positions, Satsuma and Tsushima leaders jockeyed with the *bakufu* over coastal defense and competed, to varying degrees, with the Tokugawa regime to exploit existing commercial ties with China in particular, as all three actors simultaneously considered new engagement

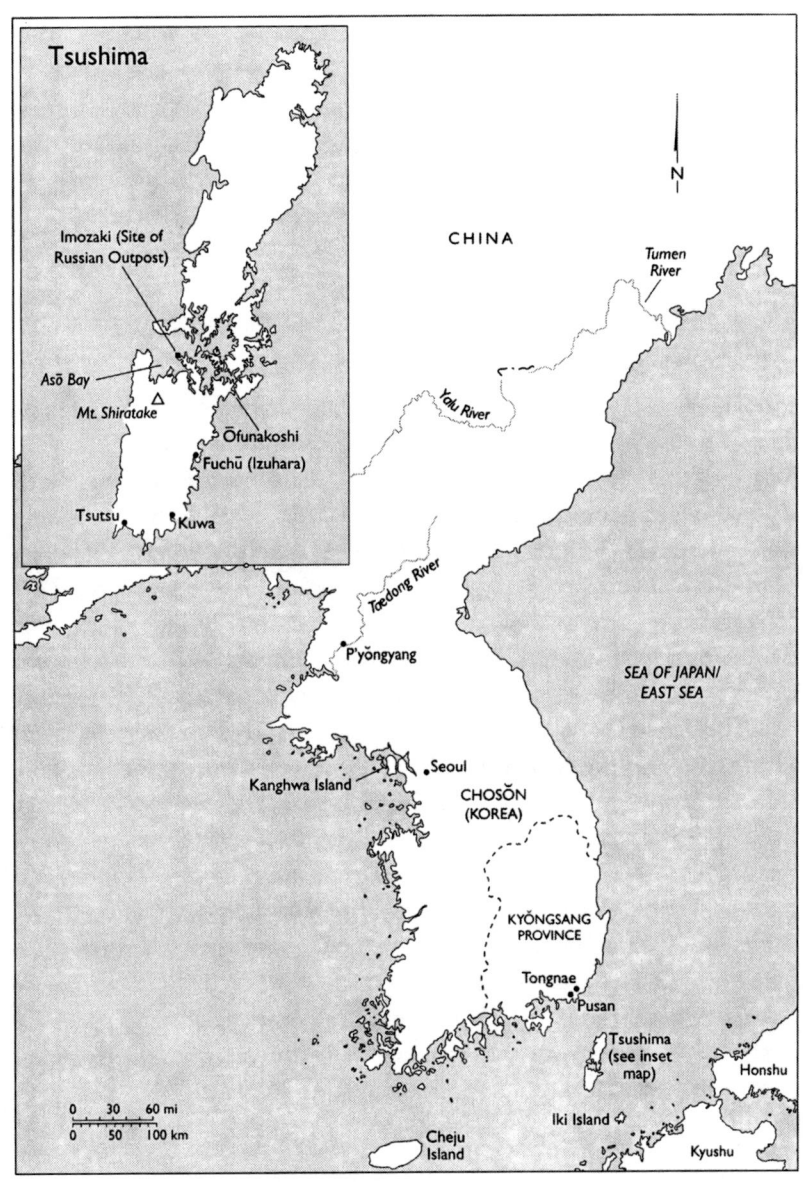

Map 2 Chosŏn Korea and Edo-period Tsushima

with Westerners. The domains were therefore integral players in Japan's larger shift from using early modern East Asian practices of foreign relations to the national adoption of international relations, not only in the centralization of foreign relations authority but also in the recasting of foreign trade, both of which were fully accomplished as Japan formed as a nation-state in the years following the Meiji Restoration of 1868.

International Relations and the Entrenched Ideology of Seclusion

The term "international relations" in this study refers to bilateral and multilateral intercourse among nation-states as practiced throughout much of the Western world since the eighteenth century and in East Asia since the closing decades of the nineteenth century. Its use underscores how fundamental aspects of interaction between states changed when the nation-state model gained global dominance over the course of the nineteenth century, creating veritable *inter national* relations. Nation-states, which developed first in eighteenth- and early nineteenth-century Europe, came to be defined by sovereignty, supreme authority within a territory, upon which leaders drew to establish systems of unified rule, centralized administration, and clearly demarked maritime and territorial borders. The strong central governments of nation-states assumed primary authority in defense and war as well as in foreign trade. They directly administered diplomatic ties with foreign states, which involved dispatching envoys to permanent embassies in foreign capitals. This interaction between nation-states helped to create international ties based upon an assumed equality among nations and governed by a framework of international law.[3] Through the wider use of international relations, Japan and its East Asian neighbors eventually developed a new normative framework for interaction, what can be termed an "international order," in the early 1880s.[4]

---

3. Discussion drawn partly from definitions of "international relations" and "sovereignty" offered by Berridge and James, *A Dictionary of Diplomacy*, 147, 248–49.

4. Hamashita, "Tribute and Treaties," 17–50 and especially Kim, *The Last Phase of the East Asian World Order*, 328–51, explore the process whereby Japan, Korea, and China developed a new "international order" for East Asia.

Aspects of nation-states and international relations can certainly be identified in Japan and other East Asian states and in foreign relations in the region during the early modern period—from the sixteenth century to the early nineteenth century. Yet to understand how early modern East Asian foreign relations functioned, we must be aware of several fundamental differences. First, that there was no presumed equality among states. Instead, the Chinese model of foreign relations, premised on a higher-and-lower, lord-vassal relationship, had broad influence. China, the dominant state in the region, portrayed itself as more civilized and powerful by receiving envoys, usually as part of a tribute mission, from states perceived as weaker and less civilized. Other East Asian states—for example, Korea in its relations with Tsushima—followed the Chinese model. Particularly in relations with China, the leaders of many states gladly accepted the subservient status of vassal because it provided prestige that enhanced the leader's position within his own state. This was certainly true for the Ryukyu Kingdom. Second, in early modern East Asia a central governing body did not necessarily hold complete authority over foreign relations. As this study will explore, in Japan, for example, local actors, Satsuma and Tsushima, accomplished foreign relations in conjunction with the central Tokugawa authority. Third, state borders, especially maritime ones, were not rigidly fixed and a ruler could assume the status of vassal to more than one overlord. This was the case with the Shō (the ruling house of Ryukyu) and the Sō (the ruling clan of Tsushima) and will be discussed in subsequent chapters. Finally, in early modern East Asia, foreign trade was entwined with diplomacy in ways not practiced in international relations. To enhance their domestic political positions, leaders often demanded that trade be conducted only if specific diplomatic protocols, usually based upon the Chinese tribute ideal of a superior state receiving envoys from a subservient other, were fulfilled.

By not taking into full consideration these particular aspects of East Asian foreign relations, many historians have approached Edo-period foreign relations based upon a set of assumptions, a key one being that the *bakufu*, as the central authority, held firm control over foreign trade and diplomacy. For example, in a persuasive recent study, Mark Ravina successfully challenges the previously accepted wisdom that the *bakufu* set policies for the entire Japanese realm in religion, defense, taxation, and commerce, which the lords were obliged to follow. In an important contribution to the study of Edo-period history, he instead portrays the *bakufu* as ruling in conjunction with the lords of the domains as part of a compound, feudal structure, in which local and larger state-wide concerns merged to create a functioning politico-economic system. Nonetheless, Ravina sees the *bakufu* as holding a monopoly in foreign relations, especially in diplomacy, where it "claimed the powers of a centralized state."[5]

Coupled with the perception of Tokugawa dominance is the still widely held view that seclusion defined Japanese engagement with the outside world during the late Edo period. Post-1945 studies concluded that Tokugawa leaders used their monopoly and ordered the lords to essentially close the Japanese realm when they expelled the Portuguese and limited foreign contacts in the 1630s, creating a stance that continued until the arrival of Commodore Matthew C. Perry and his flotilla of U.S. Navy warships in 1853.[6] Beginning in the 1970s, Japanese and American historians successively challenged this view by conclusively showing that *bakufu* leaders kept Japan diplomatically and commercially engaged, especially with neighboring East Asian states. In studies of foreign relations in the first century of the Edo period, Tashiro Kazui showed that Japanese trade with Korea and China continued to thrive and Ronald Toby illustrated that Tokugawa leaders aggressively pursued diplomacy with East Asian states.[7]

Yet while many scholars have identified active commercial and diplomatic agendas early in the Edo period, those examining the eighteenth and early nineteenth centuries often assume that Tokugawa leaders, firmly controlling foreign relations, came to be guided by what equates to an ideology of seclusion, implicitly making decisions based upon a shared consensus that intercourse with the outside world should at the very least be strictly limited. Even "enlightened" leaders like Shogun Yoshimune (r. 1716–45), who implemented sweeping reforms in the first half of the eighteenth century, are seen as conservative adherents to

---

5. Ravina, *Lord and Lordship in Early Modern Japan*, 23.
6. Sansom, *A History of Japan, 1615–1867*, 35–45.
7. Toby, *State and Diplomacy in Early Modern Japan*; Tashiro, *Kinsei Nitchō tsūkō bōeki-shi no kenkyū*.

seclusion policies. That subsequent Tokugawa leaders held the same stance is apparently confirmed by their rejection of proposals made by prominent intellectuals, many of whom had studied the Netherlands and its global trading activities. Honda Toshiaki, a mathematician–cum–self-styled political economist, is often seen as an especially prescient voice, more aware than *bakufu* leaders of looming demographic and economic problems that could be resolved by expanding trade with Western nations, the first being Russia, which made several overtures to open commercial and diplomatic ties in the decades around 1800.[8]

In a valuable study focusing on events in the 1820s, Bob Wakabayashi asserts that other more conservative intellectuals, in combination with Tokugawa edicts, helped to codify an ideology of seclusion in the late Edo-period polity. Wakabayashi believes that the conservative views of Aizawa Seishisai, a scholar from Mito domain (currently Ibaraki prefecture), were particularly influential because Aizawa persuasively presented Japan as the "divine realm" in his 1825 text *New Theses*. This powerful work helped Tokugawa leaders to conceive of Japan as the "Middle Kingdom" that superseded China's presentation of itself as the most civilized and powerful state in the world. Wakabayashi asserts that the timing of the publication of Aizawa's views was also especially significant as it came in the same year that the *bakufu* issued an order directing coastal domains to shell and repel all foreign ships arriving on Japanese shores. He concludes that in the decades after 1825, Tokugawa leaders committed to a more militant approach. Instead of simply turning away foreign visitors requesting the establishment of commercial and diplomatic ties, the Tokugawa now directed that force be used without hesitation to uphold "national isolation."[9]

Other historians have also identified an ideology of seclusion in nineteenth-century Japan, using it not only to frame the last decades of the Edo period but also to explain perceived stark differences between Japan and Western nations. As the story is often told, Britain, the United States, and other Western states, imbued with commercial vigor and technological innovation, expanded outward, while Japan, stagnating in its ideology and tradition, closed its borders and turned its back on

---

8. Howe, *The Origins of Japanese Trade Supremacy*, 67–71.
9. Wakabayashi, *Anti-Foreignism and Western Learning in Early Modern Japan*, 8–10.

foreign trade. The contrasting approaches set the stage for what Walter LaFeber, a prominent historian of American foreign relations, concludes was a collision between the irresistible force of the modern West against the immovable object of Japan. Like many before him, LaFeber sees this clash exemplified in the arrival of Commodore Perry near Edo in 1853. He asserts that from Perry's visit until the Meiji Restoration, "the relentless American determination to break feudal barriers and gain access for every individual—whether merchant, diplomat, or missionary—encountered a centuries-old and apparently immovable culture of Tokugawa Japan."[10]

In a more recent study, Michael Auslin effectively demonstrates that the leaders of the *bakufu* skillfully used negotiation to temper the diplomatic demands of Western nations in the 1850s and 1860s. Yet Auslin, too, sees Tokugawa leaders as focused on the defense of Japanese tradition. He paints them as interested not in trade but in protecting the "ideological, intellectual, and physical boundaries between themselves and Westerners."[11] Auslin concludes that while Tokugawa leaders could for a time successfully use negotiation as a tool against Western nations, in the end decisive Western military and economic power forced Tokugawa and later Meiji leaders to abandon tradition and to fully embrace international relations.

Without question, beginning in the late eighteenth century the Tokugawa regime assumed a strong and sometimes defiant stance against Western visitors that continued for decades. Moreover we cannot deny the importance of diplomatic intercourse between Tokugawa officials and Western envoys—interchange that certainly influenced the significant changes in Japanese foreign relations that occurred in the years surrounding the Meiji Restoration. It is also impossible to ignore that Western nations, which industrialized first, brought to Japan the treaty port system, the modern industrial structure, and, of course, the principles of international relations that Japan adopted after 1868 and continues to use today.

What this study aims to reconsider is the widely accepted wisdom that by the late eighteenth century, if not before, a single, powerful central

---

10. LaFeber, *The Clash*, 30–31.
11. Auslin, *Negotiating with Imperialism*, 9–10.

government, the Tokugawa *bakufu*, acted reflexively based upon an ideology of seclusion to protect Japanese tradition in the face of Western modernity. The influence of this interpretation of the late Edo period is important because the ideological label accentuates a negative perception of Japanese leaders, especially vis-à-vis their Western counterparts, to the point that the ideology of seclusion becomes what Clifford Geertz describes as a parodic paradigm: "I have a social philosophy, you have political opinions; he has an ideology."[12] Japanese leaders have become the "he," seeing the world through a rigid ideology, while their Western counterparts represent the "I" and "you," leaders acting flexibly and reasonably within sophisticated political systems that stimulated diverse opinions and philosophies and by consequence, a more informed understanding of the outside world. In addition, it is presumed that Western nations had already emerged as the centers of global economic power and had become more rational economic actors, especially in foreign trade. By contrast, Japanese leaders are viewed as failing to perceive the course of economic advancement emerging from Western nations. For example, they did not pursue foreign trade explicitly for capital accumulation, as Western nations did, and thus missed an opportunity to move Japan's economy toward industrialization.[13]

It follows that Japanese leaders were unable to institute significant changes without Western pressure. As a result, the story of late Edo foreign relations becomes one of Western nations, surging with economic and military power, dispatching envoys in an attempt to convince Japanese leaders to embrace economic rationality and consider expanding trade, especially with Western states, while adopting the tenets of international relations. Only through interaction with Western nations did Japan's leaders move to jettison their ideology of seclusion and begin to trade with the outside world and later adopt principles of international relations. Because of the presumed overwhelming sway of ideology, the actual actors in foreign relations, such as the Satsuma and Tsushima domains, are considered less significant than the scholars and ideologues who, while influencing discourse about interactions with the outside world, were not directly involved in foreign relations as they occurred at

---

12. Geertz, *An Interpretation of Cultures*, 194.
13. Hall, *Tanuma Okitsugu*, 18–20.

ground level—in the offices of Tokugawa and domain officials making decisions about coastal defense and diplomatic exchanges, or in the ports where foreign merchants were received and goods were imported and exported.

Overall this study demonstrates that because the system of foreign relations was divided among several actors—the *bakufu*, Tsushima, and Satsuma—it included multiple voices and agendas which went beyond a single and commonly held ideology of seclusion. Due in large part to this competitive political environment and because of conclusions born of an awareness of global commercial contexts, Japanese leaders made proactive decisions, especially concerning foreign trade. The logic and rationality inherent in their actions becomes clear if we consider both the global environments, and the particular agendas of the each actor, outlined in detail below.

Japan and Early Modern Proto-Globalization

Throughout the Edo period, we can identify points where Tokugawa leaders developed stances in tune with global commercial contexts, many of which emerged from world historians have termed "proto-globalization." Today we encounter daily references to globalization, which by undermining the importance of local and even national boundaries, is seen as having a pervasive influence on the contemporary human experience.[14] World historians have demonstrated that proto-globalization, a nascent form of today's globalization, emerged between 1600 and 1800 with the reconfiguration of state systems, along with the growth of finance, services, and pre-industrial manufacturing in Europe, Asia, and parts of Africa. Proto-globalization also included the incorporation of North and South America into global commercial networks.[15] The Americas became a fountainhead of new foodstuffs, such as the potato, manioc (cassava), and maize, which were adopted throughout the globe.[16] The region also emerged as a produc-

---

14. Scheuerman, "Globalization."
15. Hopkins, "Globalization: an Agenda for Historians," 6.
16. Maize, for example, was adopted in both the Venetian and Solomonic (Ethiopian) empires in the seventeenth century. See McCann, *Maize and Grace*, 59–93. For more on the flow of the potato in the early modern world, see Zuckerman, *The Potato*.

tion center for sugar, and more importantly, silver, mined in the mountains of South America and exported throughout the world. As scholars of world trade have shown, the flow of silver in early modern global trading networks illustrates the economic centers of power in the early modern world. They stress that much silver from South America, as well as from Japan, ended up in China, demonstrating that during this early globalization, China functioned as a center of the world economy. It absorbed a significant percentage of the world's silver largely because Europeans and Japanese alike used it to purchase tea, silk, porcelains, and medicines, all generally available only on the China market.[17]

With proto-globalization, the peoples of the Americas also found their economic lives defined by global markets instead of previously dominant local contexts. For example, Amerindians now labored in the silver mines of Potosí (in present-day Bolivia), which grew to a city of 150,000 by the 1570s. Their lives, connected to the global market, were in stark contrast to those of their ancestors just a generation before who had lived in the agrarian and largely self-contained economy of an Incan Empire that engaged in little intercourse with the outside world.[18]

While not as radically as Amerindians, in the sixteenth century Japanese commoners and the samurai elite alike were influenced by the new trading relationships and the concomitant cultural influences of proto-globalization. With Asian and European partners, Japanese merchants traded silver for Chinese silk, which supplied Japanese artisans crafting fine silkwares. Japanese merchants also ventured to Southeast Asia, where they established enclaves in port cities. New, thriving global trading networks brought European firearms, which samurai readily adopted, and Christianity, which achieved a foothold especially in Kyushu. The influence of European culture was also seen in new artistic trends such as the Nanban screens and paintings of the period, which depicted scenes of Iberian merchants and priests who were dubbed Nanban—"Southern Barbarians"—because they arrived in Japan from the south.

A similar process of deeper engagement with the outside world occurred simultaneously in Southeast Asia during what Anthony Reid

---

17. A prominent representation of this view is found in Frank, *ReOrient*.
18. Marks, *The Origins of the Modern World*, 78.

identifies as a "long sixteenth century" spanning from circa 1450 to 1680. Concomitant with expanded domestic and foreign trade, Southeast Asians entered an age of "globalized cosmopolitanism" during which they welcomed new religious and intellectual ideas from abroad, which were incorporated into their respective cultures and societies, notably in the performance traditions of state theater.[19]

Reid concludes that the increase in interaction with the outside world began to wane during the first half of the seventeenth century. Southeast Asian trading states faced serious setbacks resulting from intense competition from Portuguese merchants as well as from the VOC, which established monopoly control over the more lucrative exports. He believes that domestic strife proved even more costly. For example in Java, the "interior, rice-based regime" of Mataram quashed the influence of coastal cities, which through foreign trade had emerged as centers of a new cosmopolitan culture. Mataram later banned Javanese shipping, which the court feared might prove a threat to the king. Reid suggests that in turning away from foreign engagement, Mataram began a process that paralleled events in Japan in the 1630s. Namely he sees Mataram, and insular Southeast Asia overall, as entering an extended "reaction against globalization" during which "international trade was less rewarding, and many rulers urged their subjects not to plant pepper and cloves lest it bring them war and oppression." Reid argues that thereafter Southeast Asian states accordingly became more self-sufficient and less dependent on foreign trade, especially by promoting "localization," producing at home goods previously imported.[20]

We can also identify what equates to a "reaction against globalization" in the actions of Tokugawa leaders over the course of the seventeenth century. Beginning in the 1630s, the *bakufu* moved to reduce the cultural influences that had entered Japan during the period of generally free intercourse in the sixteenth century. Building upon the successful repression of Christianity within the realm, it cut ties with Portuguese merchants, who sought to bring their faith along with Chinese silk. In a series of edicts that Arano Yasunori and other historians have labeled

---

19. Reid, "Global and Local in Southeast Asian History," 7–11.
20. Ibid., 12–13, 19.

Map 3 East and Southeast Asia in the seventeenth and eighteenth centuries
Information about points in Southeast Asia drawn from maps in Pluvier, *Historical Atlas of South-East Asia*, 30, Cribb, *Historical Atlas of Indonesia*, 90; Warren, *The Sulu Zone*, 103.

"maritime prohibitions," Tokugawa leaders also abolished Japanese enclaves overseas, limited the size of oceangoing vessels, and prohibited Japanese from traveling abroad.[21]

Nonetheless there were important differences in the Tokugawa approach to foreign trade. Unlike their counterparts in Mataram, *bakufu* leaders did not initially reduce foreign trade; instead, they chose to rely on domestic partners to help redirect commerce with China through Korea and the Ryukyu Kingdom, and at Nagasaki, to trade with Chinese merchants and just the VOC instead of several European partners. It was not until the 1680s that Tokugawa leaders, concerned about the realm's dwindling silver reserves resulting from increased trade with China, issued edicts to reduce foreign trade on a large scale. When those proved ineffective, they changed tack, first establishing more institutions to supervise trade. Tokugawa leaders subsequently implemented their own brand of "localization" by expanding domestic production of raw silk as well as ginseng and sugar, two other prominent imports. In turn, they developed substitute exports for silver: abalone, sea cucumbers, kelp, and shark fins, which Chinese used as medicines and in many regional cuisines. Overall, Japan's reaction against globalization was swift vis-à-vis outside religious influences but more protracted in its readjustment of foreign trade. Successive Tokugawa leaders showed a willingness to further amend trade practices. In 1763, they ended silver exports through Nagasaki and two decades later created a monopoly over marine products produced throughout Japan. Nagasaki became an entrepôt for marine products, which the *bakufu* used, in a turnabout, to import silver and some gold from China.

Tokugawa leaders could shape Japanese trade in these ways because a vital China market exuded demand for specialized goods such as marine products. Kenneth Pomeranz illustrates that in household and especially luxury consumption, often viewed as important engines of growth in Western states, China matched and sometimes surpassed Western Europe until around 1800.[22] Japan, like other actors in East and Southeast Asian trade, structured much of its foreign trade to meet Chinese consumer demand.

---

21. Arano, *Kinsei Nihon to higashi Ajia*, 3–5, 29–33.
22. Pomeranz, *The Great Divergence*, 114–65.

Via the China market, Japan also engaged with an often forgotten sector of early modern global trade, the exchange of medicinal products. C. A. Bayly notes that medicinal goods were a key commodity on global markets because "until the late eighteenth century, central physiological and agricultural doctrines of Eurasia and Africa were humoral and had been generated from an ancient dialogue between China, the Islamic World, and Greece. This put a premium on different types of medicinal plants, spices, precious metals, or precious stones."[23] For example, eighteenth-century Americans used agaric, a mushroom imported from Siberia via Hamburg, as a laxative, expectorate, and as a cure for more serious ailments. A guidebook for herbal remedies published in serial form in Pennsylvania the 1760s and 1770s advised that, "For persons afflicted with falling evil [epilepsy], an agaric decoction instead of soap should be used to scrub the head."[24]

Although domestic substitutes became available, Japanese consumers, like their American counterparts, sought exotic, and what they perceived as more efficacious, imported medicines. As a result, Nagasaki became an import hub for a wide array of medicinal goods primarily from China: herbs, roots, animal parts, and even fossils, used to cure everyday and serious ailments. Tokugawa leaders adeptly developed means to supervise the import of medicinal goods and to earn a slice of the considerable profits that could be gained from their sale on the domestic market.

Looking at the late eighteenth century overall, we see that Tokugawa leaders moved proactively, shaping Nagasaki into a viable entrepôt that allowed manageable and yet profitable trade with the China market. The significance of the Tokugawa approach becomes clear when we compare it with the policies pursued by the English East India Company in the same period. Because China demanded silver over all other goods, the Company was also frustrated by the loss of silver. With Britons developing a taste for tea, the Company searched for silver substitutes, first failing to sell British woolens on the Chinese market. From the 1760s, it therefore began a decades-long quest to create an

---

23. Bayly, "'Archaic' and 'Modern' Globalization in the Eurasian and African Arena," 53.
24. Weaver, *Sauer's Herbal Cures*, 35.

entrepôt, to collect East and Southeast Asian goods such as marine products, which would serve as substitutes for silver in trade with China. The Company developed a truly effective entrepôt only with the establishment of Singapore in 1819.

With an awareness of these larger eighteenth-century contexts—the continued power of China on the global market and the Japanese trade system developed to interact with it—we can move to consider the decisions of Japanese leaders in the critical decades after 1800. Assuming that Western nations possessed superior economic power, the ideology of seclusion has been used to tidily explain the seeming Japanese stubbornness to interact with powerful Western nations who are assumed to be bringing trade goods produced from their industrializing economies and by implication, a new and viable framework of direct trade between the West and East Asia.

Certainly Britain, leading the way for other Western European nations and the United States, was building upon the industrial foundations that had emerged within its borders in the late eighteenth century. Particularly by exploiting recent inventions such as steam driven engines, Britain and other Western nations were increasing their manufacturing capabilities and by implication their economic power vis-à-vis East Asian states. Yet as Bayly points out, "it was only after about 1840, in fact, that the patchy, but now relentless shift toward industrialization began to 'kick in' at a global level."[25] In East Asian trade, this is illustrated in the fact that for its technological prowess, Britain at last gained an upper hand on the China market and solved its silver dilemma not by exploiting its own manufactures, but by using Indian opium, especially after 1820.[26]

Intra-Asian trade clearly remained viable, and part of the reason for this, as Takeshi Hamashita demonstrates, was the continued vitality of the China-centered tribute system. The system provided a broad structure that allowed people, goods, money, and information to move throughout early modern East and Southeast Asia and did not simply disappear when Westerners arrived in more powerful ships in the mid-nineteenth century. Because of the sustained power of this network and

---

25. Bayly, *The Birth of the Modern World*, 7.
26. Marks, *The Origins of the Modern World*, 114.

the China market overall, Hamashita notes that in the last decades of the nineteenth century, Westerners and Asians alike were not choosing between either the "old" tribute system and the "new" Western-dominated treaty system, but using aspects of both as commercial circumstances dictated. He shows instead that Western diplomats, often acting in concert with their East Asian counterparts, constructed a new treaty system within East Asia by appropriating facets of the existing tribute system.[27]

These Asian and global contexts help explain the decisions of Japanese leaders in the first decades of the nineteenth century. Beginning in the late 1840s, Britain, France, and the United States used their superior military technology to pressure Japan to later conclude treaties that would create new trading relationships favorable to their interests. Yet the actions of Tokugawa, Satsuma, and Tsushima leaders as well as Western merchants, suggest that despite their clear military advantage, the Western visitors did not initially bring a new and viable system of direct Japanese-Western trade. Instead, all parties initially looked to take advantage of more lucrative, established Japanese-Chinese trade ties.

It was only on the eve of the Meiji Restoration that direct Japanese-Western ties supplanted long viable economic links to the China market. At that time, Japanese leaders moved more aggressively to trade with Western merchants and states. They began to purchase cotton and woolen manufactures and advanced Western technologies, such as weapons, while developing specific products, notably silk and green tea, tailored for growing Western markets. At the same time, Japan's larger embrace of Western ideals, including medical practices, brought a shift away from the use of accepted remedies, based particularly on Chinese medicine, and consequently decreased demand for roots, herbs, and other medicinal products from abroad. As a result by the mid 1870s, although its trade with China was still important, a significant share of Japan's foreign trade was shifting to intercourse with Western states.

The Domestic Parameters of the System of Foreign Relations

Pursuing larger agendas for the entire Japanese realm, the *bakufu* created the broader structure of Japanese foreign relations, which it ad-

---

27. Hamashita, "The Interregional System in East Asia in Modern Times," 117–28.

justed according to domestic and global contexts. Within that structure, the *bakufu* was particularly invested in receiving embassies from neighboring states and in gaining intelligence about events abroad. Through the authority of the Tokugawa house, it also controlled relations with the VOC factory and Chinese merchants at Nagasaki. In the Nagasaki trade, the *bakufu* consistently focused on protecting the populace of Nagasaki, which owed its economic livelihood to foreign trade flowing through the port, and in assuring, for the greater social good, imports of medicinal products. Although revenue garnered from commercial intercourse at Nagasaki was prized by the Tokugawa leaders, it was not the primary and overriding motivation to supporting foreign trade at the port throughout much of the Edo period. One of the goals of this study is to present the importance of these broad agendas, building upon the rich statistical analysis of Edo-period trade offered by Japanese scholars.[28]

By contrast, Satsuma and Tsushima represent a local perspective on Japan's interface with the outside world. Satsuma maintained relations with the Ryukyu Kingdom and Tsushima with Korea based upon relationships developed largely independent of Tokugawa authority. Domain leaders therefore most immediately focused on how their respective foreign ties related to their domains, not the Japanese state overall, a stance evident in their commercial, diplomatic, and defensive postures. Matsumae, a domain located on the southern part of the island of Hokkaido, also presents a local perspective as an additional "portal" in relations with the outside world.[29] The ruling clan of the domain, also known as the Matsumae, monopolized relations with the various Ainu tribes that populated what was then called Ezo, a broad territory encompassing Hokkaido, Sakhalin, and the Kuril Islands. Unlike Satsuma and Tsushima, however, the Matsumae gained their monopoly thanks to the support of leaders of central authorities: first Toyotomi Hideyoshi and later Tokugawa Ieyasu.[30] As it focuses mainly

---

28. For example, Nakamura Tadashi, *Kinsei Nagasaki bōeki-shi no kenkyū*.
29. Tsuruta explores the idea of Matsumae, Ryukyu/Satsuma, Tsushima, and Nagasaki as "gates" of interaction with the outside world in the Edo period in "The Establishment and Characteristics of the 'Tsushima Gate,'" 30–32.
30. Matsumae chōshi henshūshitsu, ed., *Matsumae chōshi, tsūsetsuhen*, vol. 1, 349–55.

on the period after 1800, this study, while not denying the importance of events within Matsumae, does not explore them in depth. Rather it considers how Matsumae's commercial activities intersected with the respective agendas and activities of the *bakufu* and especially Satsuma, and Tsushima, which enjoyed comparatively more influence within the larger structure of Japanese foreign relations, particularly after 1800.[31]

Satsuma and Tsushima, looking to fulfill their local goals and the *bakufu*, seeking to implement agendas pursuant to the overall governance of Japan, together facilitated foreign relations through an interdependent system of trade, diplomacy, and defense. In trade, the domains enjoyed autonomy—for example, in the acquisition of goods, transport, and warehousing. As the *bakufu* controlled the domestic market, where imported goods were sold, the domains had to work within Tokugawa guidelines to achieve profits from trade. A reverse situation existed in diplomacy. *Bakufu* leaders wanted Korean and Ryukyuan embassies to visit Edo, a goal they could not accomplish without the cooperation of Satsuma and Tsushima, which facilitated the visits through their independent relations with Korea and Ryukyu. Although explored in less detail in this study, a similar interdependent relationship existed between Satsuma and Ryukyu. While Satsuma held a dominant position, Ryukyu's independent ties with China, maintained through a tribute relationship, gave the kingdom a fair level of autonomy in relations with Satsuma.

The interdependent nature of foreign trade and diplomacy, combined with Japan's specific interfaces with global contexts, created a system of foreign relations in which agency, the ability to exercise discretionary authority in decisions regarding trade, diplomacy, and defense, moved fluidly between the *bakufu* and the Satsuma and Tsushima domains. This conception of agency emerges partly from a principal/agent ideal, in which a principal authority, by virtue of an institutional position, bestows discretionary power on an agent, which acts

---

31. For excellent and comprehensive examinations of Matsumae-Ainu relations and Matsumae's trade with the Japanese market, see Walker, *The Conquest of Ainu Lands* and Howell, *Capitalism From Within*. For a look at Ainu identity and its place in the early modern Japanese state see Howell, *Geographies of Identity in Nineteenth-Century Japan*, 110–30.

on that authority's behalf. In the Edo-period feudal polity, the Tokugawa regime enjoyed a dominant position over the two domains, and therefore, at certain times, acted as the principal authority in foreign relations, directing domain leaders to execute Tokugawa policy in trade, defense, and diplomacy. Because of the domains' respective independent contacts, Satsuma and Tsushima always held some amount of discretionary authority in the three areas, although the level and ability to exercise that authority rose and fell vis-à-vis the *bakufu* over the course of the Edo period.

Chapter 1 offers an outline of Satsuma's and Tsushima's positions, the domains' interdependent relationships with the *bakufu*, as well as overviews of the larger Edo-period polity and foreign relations in the sixteenth and early seventeenth centuries. Chapter 2 examines primarily the *bakufu*, which after 1640 aggressively implemented measures that together formed a reaction against globalization. In pushing an agenda of limiting some effects of globalization, the *bakufu* bestowed commercial authority on Satsuma and Tsushima by making the domains conduits in the silk-for-silver trade with China. Once gained, Satsuma and Tsushima battled with the *bakufu* to preserve and even enhance their agency, a process through which domain officials developed political and rhetorical strategies that their successors would employ over the next century. Chapter 3 demonstrates that beginning in 1764, the *bakufu*, reasserted its authority in foreign relations and moving to redefine Japan's interface with global contexts, initiated what can be viewed as a period of "guarded engagement." Focusing on commerce over diplomacy, the Tokugawa regime kept Japan connected to the outside world but within the boundaries of a system that allowed trade to thrive without the loss of precious silver. In this new system, the *bakufu* became the primary domestic force in foreign trade, and as a result, Satsuma's and Tsushima's agency, particularly in trade, reached a nadir by 1800.

The period between 1800 and 1868 forms the heart of this book because during these decades, Japan's engagement with global contexts merged with the particular, interdependent aspects of the system of foreign relations to create an environment whereby Satsuma gained commercial agency and Tsushima assumed greater defensive agency. Satsuma and Tsushima leaders were consequently in a position to portray their local concerns as important for the entire Japanese realm. Satsuma, because of commercial goals, and Tsushima, due to defensive concerns, pressured the *bakufu* to make revisions in the overall system of foreign relations. For their part, Tokugawa leaders approached foreign relations with greater deference to the desires of the two domains. Together, the domains and the *bakufu* were integrally involved in a series of events that eventually led to the full adoption of international relations after 1868.

Chapter 4 examines the ways in which, after 1800, the overall growth of the Japanese economy, and subsequent increase in consumer demand, especially for foreign medicinal products, created new opportunities in domestic and foreign trade. Satsuma took particular advantage of this new atmosphere, emerging as a veritable trade competitor with the *bakufu*. In so doing, it temporarily regained commercial agency in the system of foreign relations. By contrast, Tsushima struggled, finding limited options to assuage the loss of valuable trade with China via Korea. As explored in Chapter 5, that contrast became more pronounced as Tsushima directly and Satsuma through its control of Ryukyu undertook much of Japan's ground-level engagement with the Western warships, merchantmen, and whalers that increasingly visited Japanese shores after 1840. Satsuma leaders began to chart a more independent commercial and defensive course, while their counterparts in Tsushima emphasized defense and increasingly appealed for Tokugawa financial assistance to help defend their domain.

Chapter 6 considers how Satsuma and Tokugawa officials negotiated the transition from a focus on established Japanese-Chinese commercial links to more direct trade with Westerners during the first few years after Western merchants were allowed to live and trade at three Japanese ports in 1859. It shows on one hand that Tokugawa leaders, still in many ways working under the structure of guarded engagement, chose a conservative course of protecting established trade links with China in part to assure the welfare of the Nagasaki merchant community. Free from such feudal obligations, Satsuma leaders, on the other hand, operated with greater range, finding effective ways to plug Westerners into their domain's thriving trade network.

Because their domain was less directly involved in the larger trade transition, the Tsushima leadership focused on securing the defense of their island, events chronicled in Chapter 7. Desperate for assistance, they attempted to cede their agency in trade, diplomacy, defense—and indeed their rule over the domain—to the *bakufu*. Despite the Tokugawa refusal of those requests, Tsushima leaders continued to lobby not only the *bakufu* but also the imperial court, which was then gaining domestic political prominence, to take greater control and act on behalf of all of Japan in relations with Korea.

The Conclusion explains how after 1868 Satsuma officials, with little prodding from Meiji leaders, and Tsushima officials, through their continued lobbying efforts, actively assisted in a process that allowed the central government to assume, by 1876, full control over all of Japan's foreign relations. The two domains accepted greater control by the central authority not because of an ideological conversion brought by engagement with Western nations but rather because such a step was in accord with initiatives for reform in the existing system of foreign relations present in both Satsuma and Tsushima before the Meiji Restoration. It also outlines the steps taken by Meiji leaders to expand direct trade ties with Western nations, moving beyond the Japanese-Chinese trade ties that had proved more lucrative only a decade before.

Overall, by focusing on central and local perspectives with an eye on the global background, this book demonstrates that Japanese leaders accepted the new global construct of international relations and expanded foreign trade with Western states not merely by interacting with Western nations or because of a desire to imitate their power. Because embracing the Western modernity inherent in international relations was not in itself the overriding goal, the leaders of Satsuma, Tsushima, and the early Meiji government were not concerned with discerning whether a practice was traditional or modern, East Asian or Western. They were not choosing between the past and the future but deciding, based upon their particular agendas, on a course of action that would serve their immediate interests. Their engagement in an improvised and often ad hoc process consequently made Japan's path to adopting new trading structures and international relations evolutionary and not revolutionary—a process shaped, as it had been during the Edo period, by commercial and defensive concerns emerging from interactions with fluid global contexts.

ONE

Interdependent Partners: The Shogunate, Satsuma, and Tsushima

In the Edo-period polity, the samurai class, amounting to only 6 percent of the total population, ruled the majority commoner class composed primarily of peasants (80 to 85 percent) and a smaller merchant community (5 to 10 percent).[1] Following the victory of his forces at the Battle of Sekigahara in 1600, Tokugawa Ieyasu received the title of shogun or generalissimo from the emperor, who while still possessing preeminent authority, played only a minor political role until the mid-nineteenth century. As the shogun, Ieyasu and his successors became the dominant leaders of the Japanese state or "realm" (*tenka*) as it was commonly known. Ieyasu's house assumed control over, and enjoyed revenue from, a huge swath of productive lands in central Japan, making the Tokugawa the largest landholder in the feudal state. The 250-odd samurai lords or daimyo, who ruled their individual domains throughout the rest of the realm, were required to swear alliance to the Tokugawa and a hierarchy developed among them. Those daimyo descending from Ieyasu's three youngest sons, in charge of Owari, Kii, and Mito, had prestige but limited influence in bakufu politics, while daimyo descending from Ieyasu's retainers before Sekigahara, the "direct" vassal (*fudai*) daimyo, enjoyed greater political clout than the nominal vassals or "outer" (*to-*

---

1. Duus, *Modern Japan*, 8.

zama) daimyo. The Tokugawa later bolstered their regime's position by requiring the lords to participate in a system of alternate residence (*sankin kōtai*), whereby each would spend every other year in Edo, maintain a residence there, and leave his wife and family as hostages. These measures, combined with the considerable cost of traveling in a large retinue to and from the capital, hobbled the lords and prevented them from mounting military challenges to the Tokugawa.[2]

The *bakufu* can be seen as an expansive, governing institution created to maintain Tokugawa rule. Even a strong shogun depended upon a deliberative group of senior councilors to make key decisions and to direct their implementation through descending chains of liege vassals, magistrates, superintendents, and inspectors. The *bakufu* governed in a larger, realm-wide way especially in commerce, public works, defense, and religious practice. The *bakufu* regulated commerce, for example, through its administrative offices in key commercial hubs: Kyoto, Osaka, and Nagasaki. A high-ranking Tokugawa official governed commercial affairs in his city primarily by working with city elders, often the heads of prominent merchant families. These elders administered much of the everyday governance in commoner areas, such as overseeing the patrolling of streets to prevent crime. Because Nagasaki was a center for foreign trade, two magistrates, one based in Edo, the other in Nagasaki, oversaw the city's affairs. (For simplicity, the "Nagasaki magistrate," will be used in the text to represent the entire office.) Osaka was governed both by the "Keeper of Osaka Castle," a post that (like the Nagasaki magistrate) was equal in rank to the senior councilor, and by two subordinate magistrates. These were important posts because the city functioned as central market of the realm to which agricultural and specialized commodities were shipped for redistribution throughout Japan.[3]

In public works, the *bakufu* oversaw the construction of highways, roads, bridges, as well as large projects for water control and improvements to transportation routes on rivers and lakes. Following *bakufu* directives, domains supplied corvée labor and financing for these projects, often located in lands far from the domain. For example, in 1753, the *bakufu* ordered Satsuma to contribute men and resources to support

---

2. Ibid., 21–31.
3. Totman, *Politics in the Tokugawa Bakufu*, 40–42.

construction for water control on the Kiso River in central Japan.[4] Overland arteries allowed for the movement of people (such as the retinues of daimyo traveling to and from Edo), and served as routes to move goods, with some transported via pack horses to commercial centers.[5] In the late seventeenth century, the *bakufu* also fostered the reorganization of routes for coastal commerce, which brought a large proportion of goods to Osaka and Edo. Cargo ships, which hugged the coastlines, carried goods chiefly on three main routes: the first being the Westward Coastal Route running along the coast of the Sea of Japan (East Sea),[6] through the Inland Sea, and connecting to the second, the Osaka-Edo Route. The third, dubbed the Eastward Coastal Route, developed somewhat later and ran from the Sea of Japan northward through the Tsugaru Strait, and down the Pacific Coast to Edo (see Map 4).[7]

Each lord, the head of a ruling house or clan such as the Sō of Tsushima and the Shimazu of Satsuma, governed a domain that functioned as a largely independent fiefdom within the realm-wide structures imposed by the *bakufu*. While each domain was usually composed of a contiguous tract of lands, in some cases a lord possessed small fiefs in a distant region. This was true of the Sō, which held its main lands on the island of Tsushima but also ruled smaller fiefs in Kyushu. Because they had been dominant clans in their domains since the twelfth and thirteenth centuries, respectively, the Shimazu and Sō houses became synonymous with the domains themselves. Throughout the realm, each lord provided all his samurai retainers with annual stipends in rice, with the amount determined based upon the rank of each vassal house within the lord's larger retainer band. Much like the shogun, the lord

---

4. The project proved a huge financial drain on Satsuma's finances. Because the arduous physical demands, close to 80 Satsuma men perished, some from disease and, in desperation, by their own hand, leading the domain official in charge to himself commit ritual suicide to take responsibility. Kagoshima-ken rekishi shiryō sentā Reimeikan, *Reimeikan jōsetsu tenji zuroku*, 52–53.

5. Wigen, *The Making of a Japanese Periphery*, 62 offers a map of cargo shipped by packhorse in central Japan in the mid-eighteenth century.

6. While the term "Sea of Japan" is commonly used in much English-language literature, today the maritime area is also referred to as the "East Sea," particularly by South and North Koreans. Both names appear on the maps in this book, but for consistency, the "Sea of Japan" will be used throughout the text.

7. Totman, *Early Modern Japan*, 155; Jansen, *The Making of Modern Japan*, 136–37, 141.

relied upon a group of councilors, usually chosen from the house of a high-ranking retainer, to govern the domain. The remaining samurai of lower ranks were assigned posts designed to maintain military readiness.

As the realm settled into peace over the course of the seventeenth century, the retainers of each lord began to serve more as administrators, living in the towns (which in larger domains were actually substantial cities) that developed around the lord's castle, and overseeing the affairs of the commoners, usually by working closely with prominent merchants. In Tsushima, most samurai lived in the castle town of Fuchū (called Izuhara today), which in the early Edo period had an average population of around 14,000, making up between 30 and 50 percent of the island's total population. Fuchū emerged as the commercial and administrative center of the domain.[8] Although a large number of Shimazu retainers lived in the castle town of Kagoshima (population around 58,000), Satsuma's especially high proportion of samurai, just over 25 percent of the total population, necessitated that samurai also reside in the countryside. Rural samurai, as they came to be known, lived in segregated villages adjacent to villages of peasants, and fishers in coastal areas. Different from most other domains where the head of a peasant village acted as a liaison to the domain officials, Satsuma's rural samurai closely watched the peasants, fishers, and merchants while also supervising their payment of taxes to the lord.[9] Tsushima had a smaller proportion of rural samurai, and therefore the domain collected taxes through a descending hierarchy of domain officials and elite peasants, similar to practices in most domains in the realm.[10]

As was also the case with other domains, Satsuma and Tsushima maintained an administrative office in their daimyo's residence in Edo. A senior domain official posted in Edo would often act as a liaison for the domain with the *bakufu*, presenting appeals and requests on behalf of his lord, and receiving Tokugawa edicts. Satsuma and Tsushima also kept domain offices in Osaka, the commercial center of the realm, and like most domains in the Kyushu region, in Nagasaki as well.

---

8. Nagasaki henshi henshū iinkai, ed., *Nagasaki kenshi, hanseihen,* 977; Shirota offers details about Fuchū in *Tsushima no shomin-shi*, 54–56.
9. Haraguchi Izumi and Nagayama, et al, *Kagoshima-ken no rekishi*, 190–95.
10. Izuhara chōshi henshū iinkai, ed., *Izuhara chōshi*, 85–87 (hereafter *IC*).

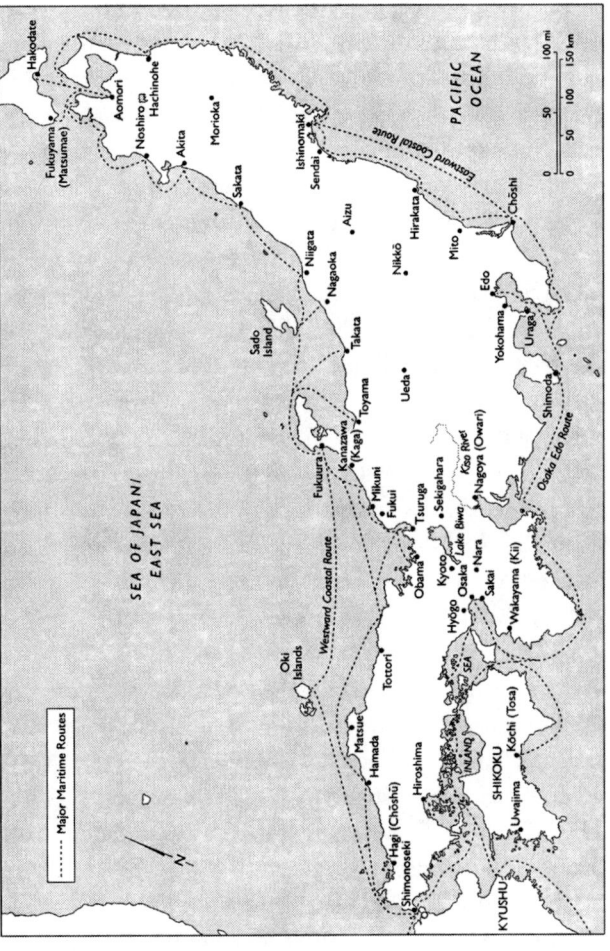

Map 4 Honshu during the Edo period.

Principal cities, castle towns, as well as major maritime coastal routes and ports are given. Other cities and points noted are mentioned in the text. The location of the castle town is given for a domain. Names in parentheses are provided when a domain's name is different from that of its castle town, e.g., Hagi (Chōshū), where Hagi is the castle town and Chōshū the name of the domain. Maritime routes are adapted from maps in Jansen, *The Making of Modern Japan*, 136–37; Shio, *Konbu o hakonda kitamaebune*, 70; Ishii Kenji, *Edo kaiun to bezaisen*, 10–11.

Foreign Relations in the Sixteenth and Early Seventeenth Centuries

In early modern East Asia, Chinese economic and military power, and the Chinese model of a civilized center surrounded by barbarian states, defined how all states in East Asia (and many Southeast Asian states as well) interacted with China and one another. The Ming (1368–1644) and later Qing (1644–1911) regimes in China encouraged surrounding states to dispatch tribute missions that followed established protocols, thereby affirming their status as vassals of the Chinese emperor. When these diplomatic requirements were completed, the envoys, bringing goods from their homelands, were allowed to trade at specified locations. Ming and Qing leaders were generally not concerned if a tribute state maintained a vassal relationship with another state so long as the tribute state continued to dispatch missions to China on a regular basis.

Beginning in the early fifteenth century, the Ashikaga *bakufu* (1336–1573) actively participated in the Chinese tribute system, sending, for example, sulfur, swords, and artistic crafts, which were exchanged for Chinese copper coins, silk, sugar, and medicinal products. As Ashikaga power began to wane, prominent lords gained the privilege of sending tribute missions instead of the *bakufu*, with the Hosokawa and Ōuchi houses trading off in the first decades of the sixteenth century. Ming leaders accepted these missions but were angered when in 1523, rival Hosokawa and Ōuchi missions clashed in the Chinese port of Ningbo, and the Ōuchi subsequently plundered parts of the city.

The events in Ningbo mirrored those perpetrated by the "Japanese pirates" (*wakō*, actually transnational bands of mostly Chinese but also Japanese) that had been harassing Korean shipping and coastal cities since the early fifteenth century. Tsushima, largely because of its position in the middle of sea lanes between the Korean peninsula and western Japan, became a pirate base.

At that time, the Chosŏn Kingdom, established in 1392 by Yi Sŏnggye after he and his supporters had come to dominate the Korean peninsula, was confronted by pirate activity along its southern coastline.[11]

---

11. The Chosŏn Kingdom existed from 1392 to 1910, a period that is also referred to as the Yi or Chosŏn dynasty. In this text, the Chosŏn Kingdom and Korea will be used interchangeably.

The piracy became so pervasive that in 1419 frustrated Chosŏn leaders dispatched a fleet of over 200 ships to Tsushima to attack pirate dens there. Although the force destroyed countless ships and burned several villages, a few years later pirates once again began to launch raids from the island. Searching for a more lasting solution, the Chosŏn court encouraged clans on the island, as well as the Ōuchi based in western Japan, to establish regular ties with it.[12] The court bestowed titles and seals which allowed specific clans to trade with Korea on the understanding that they would endeavor to eliminate piracy and prevent Japanese ships that traded at Korean ports from using forged documents or bogus seals. In 1443, the Chosŏn court granted the Sō clan, the dominant house on Tsushima, the privilege of sponsoring 50 trading ships a year and provided an annual stipend of 200 *koku* of rice. In return, the Sō were expected to verify that Korea-bound Japanese ships were officially sponsored. As an added bonus, the Sō were also able to levy transit duties on cargoes and collect other maritime fees.[13]

In the sixteenth century, the Chosŏn leadership came to see the Sō as indispensable in policing the waters between Japan and Korea. Several times Chosŏn leaders restored ties with the clan despite its participation in pirate attacks against Korea. For example, in 1510, the clan's ships attacked an island off the southern Korean port of Pusan in support of Japanese traders and fishers in the city then rioting in an attempt to gain concessions from Chosŏn officials. Although aware of the Sō's involvement, Chosŏn leaders restored the clan's special privileges just two years later, believing they needed the clan to help suppress potentially more damaging attacks that they feared might be launched from other parts of Japan.[14]

Meanwhile, continued pirate attacks along the Chinese coast—and Japanese connections to these incidents—led the Ming to sever formal ties in the 1550s.[15] The break allowed intermediaries, such as Portu-

---

12. Osa, "Tsushima-tō Sō-shi seikei no seiritsu," 42–53.
13. Elisonas, "The Inseparable Trinity," 239–55.
14. Ibid., 247–49.
15. Tanaka Takeo with Robert Sakai, "Japan's Relations with Overseas Countries," 163–71.

guese ships, to fill the void and bring especially Chinese silk to Japanese ports, where it was exchanged for silver. In the late sixteenth century, lords in Kyushu, eager to gain revenue from trade, developed independent ties with Portuguese and Spanish merchants. Nagasaki, heretofore a minor port, grew in population and importance because of trade with Europeans.

The Jesuit and Franciscan missionaries that accompanied the Iberian merchants helped to spread Christianity throughout Kyushu, where many of the lords involved in trade, including the daimyo who ruled Nagasaki, became converts to the faith and instructed their vassals and peasants to adopt the religion as well. In the late 1580s, Toyotomi Hideyoshi, who had achieved dominance over Japan by building upon the military and institutional successes of his predecessor, Oda Nobunaga, moved to restrict lords from practicing Christianity. As Conrad Totman notes, Hideyoshi, like Nobunaga before him and his Tokugawa successors, was especially concerned that Christianity was creating unauthorized, communal organizations like those developed by "heterodox" Buddhist sects earlier in the sixteenth century. In 1596, angered by rumors that some Spanish had boasted that their missionaries were an advance guard preparing the way for a future invasion, Hideyoshi cracked down more forcefully, executing a handful of priests and converts. His preoccupation with a second (eventually unsuccessful) attempt to invade China via Korea that year (the first invasion in 1592 had also ended in a Japanese defeat) kept him from moving further.[16]

When Tokugawa Ieyasu gained a dominant position over the realm, he pursued much the same course: issuing anti-Christian decrees and sometimes threatening to expel missionaries while continuing to allow trade with Europeans. He also displayed a zeal for foreign trade, allowing Japanese merchants to continue to settle in and trade with Southeast Asian states, thereby obtaining goods from that region and also indirectly, from China. New trade ties with Dutch (and, for a time, English) merchants were established. Although he did not push to develop direct relations with the Ming, Ieyasu encouraged more Chinese merchant ships to bring their silks and other wares directly to Nagasaki,

---

16. Totman, *Early Modern Japan*, 46–47.

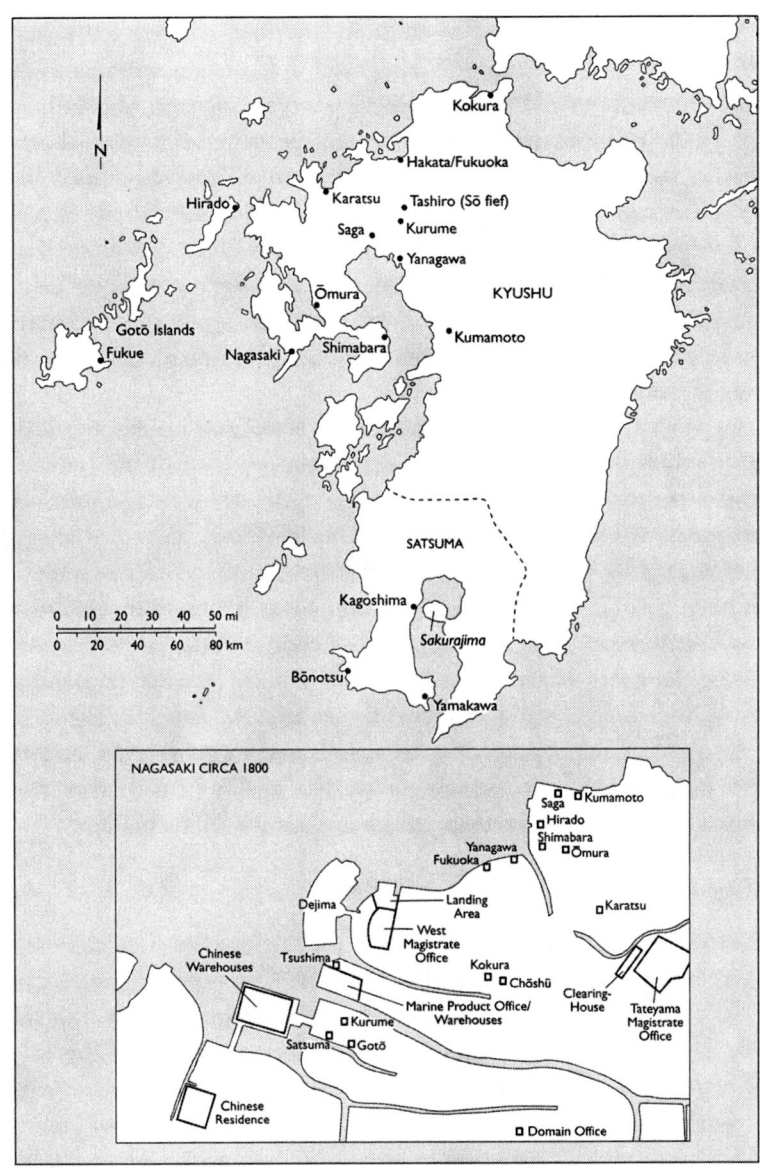

Map 5 Edo-period Kyushu and Nagasaki, circa 1800

Except for Nagasaki, Tashiro, and places in Satsuma, points given are for castle towns of Kyushu domains (Kagoshima being the castle town of Satsuma). Nagasaki map adapted from Earns, *The Development of Bureaucratic Rule in Early Modern Japan*, 115, and several Edo period maps of Nagasaki in Mody, *A Collection of Nagasaki Colour Prints and Paintings*, plates 28–31, 34–37.

and for Chinese merchants to settle in the port, creating trade routes with coastal Chinese cities that prospered well into the nineteenth century.[17] Trade continued to thrive partly because since the sixteenth century, Japanese silver mines had become especially productive, allowing silver to become an export good. Chinese merchants welcomed Japanese silver ingots because of their high silver content. Chinese demand for foreign silver grew because the Ming regime had increasingly begun to collect taxes in silver. In addition, Chinese were using silver instead of paper currency in large market transactions. These trends emerged just as Chinese silver mines were becoming less productive, necessitating increased imports of silver.[18]

As part of the process of establishing Tokugawa hegemony, Ieyasu placed mines throughout Japan under Tokugawa control and moved to create a realm-wide, uniform monetary system. He also commissioned merchants in Osaka and Edo to establish official mints for copper, silver, and gold. Gold coins (counted in *ryō*), subsequently emerged as the basic currency in eastern Japan, and silver (counted in *kan*) in the west. When mines began to supply more copper in the late seventeenth century, Japanese began to use copper coins for smaller transactions. Throughout much of the seventeenth century, the *bakufu* directed that an 84 percent rate of fineness be maintained in gold coins, and that silver ingots contain 80 percent silver. The quality of the silver ingots assured that they would remain in demand on the China market.

Satsuma and Tsushima in the New Tokugawa Foreign Relations Order

After Sekigahara, Shimazu Iehisa, the lord of Satsuma, was anxious to expand his domain's trade with the China market. Nonetheless, because of his new subservient status vis-à-vis the Tokugawa as an "outside" lord, he was not in a position to establish direct ties with the Ming. He therefore gazed south toward Ryukyu, which maintained a tribute tie with the Chinese regime. Iehisa decided to use force to gain control over Ryukyu and by implication, its tribute trade with China. The lord

---

17. Jansen, *China in the Tokugawa World*, 8–10.
18. Innes, "The Door Ajar," vol. I, 26.

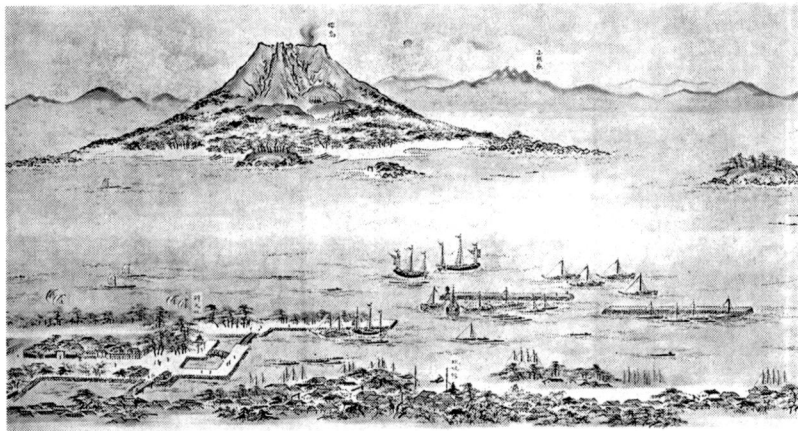

Fig. 1 View of Kagoshima harbor and Sakurajima in the early nineteenth century. The larger vessels, sporting flags from their masts, are Ryukyu ships, probably used to transport an embassy to Kagoshima that would later travel to Edo. The importance of the domain's connection to Ryukyu is also emphasized by the fact that one of the few labeled landmarks is the Ryukyu House, marked with the two flags in the center of the harbor area. *Sappan shōkei hyakuzu–kaihen* [One hundred views of the Satsuma domain—the coastline]. Courtesy of Historiographical Institute, University of Tokyo.

dutifully waited for Tokugawa permission before dispatching a 3,000-man invasion force that subjugated Ryukyu in 1609. Thereafter, the Shimazu assumed direct control between Amami and Ōshima and two other islands in the northern half of the Ryukyu chain. On those islands, they deliberately weakened the established political hierarchy and forced islanders to sever political and religious ties with Shuri, Ryukyu's administrative seat, located near the port of Naha (today both are part of the larger city of Naha) on the island of Okinawa.

The Shimazu allowed the Shō, the Ryukyu royal family, to continue to rule over the rest of the kingdom. The Shimazu received annual tribute from the Shō and directed them, in the fashion of the system of alternate residence, to regularly send members of the Ryukyu royal family to the domain's castle town, Kagoshima, and reside in a guarded compound, the Ryukyu House.[19]

---

19. The residence was originally called the Ryukyu Temporary Residence [*Ryūkyū kariya*] but the name was changed in the late eighteenth century to the Ryukyu House [*Ryūkyū-kan*]. For consistency, I will refer to it as the Ryukyu House throughout.

Historians previously concluded that thereafter the Shō, under the constant surveillance of a Satsuma resident magistrate stationed at Shuri, acted merely as a Shimazu puppet, dutifully following directives from Kagoshima, particularly to expand trade with China.[20] In a stimulating recent monograph, Tomiyama Kazuyuki shows that in fact the Shō enjoyed a fair degree of autonomy, thanks to Ryukyu's place between China and Japan. He demonstrates that in 1611, immediately after returning from Kagoshima where he had sworn fealty to the Shimazu, King Shō Nei (r. 1587–1620) refused to act as an intermediary in the efforts of Satsuma and Tokugawa officials to expand direct Japanese-Chinese trade, in fact warning Ming officials of Tokugawa plans to dispatch an armed fleet to forcibly establish a trading base on Taiwan.[21]

It was only during the subsequent reign of Shō Hō (r. 1621–40) that the court began to take a more conciliatory stance. In another important departure from previous research, Tomiyama explains that the king took this step largely to assure that the Ming would dispatch an investiture mission—during which ceremonies embodying the authority of the Chinese emperor officially enthroned a king—to Ryukyu to sanction his and the Shō family's rule. As Tomiyama explains, Ming officials would only send an investiture mission after receiving documentation from Ryukyu affirming that such a move was fully supported by the king and a majority of the nobility. Facing a faction of court nobles openly opposed to assisting Satsuma, as well as mounting pressure from the Shimazu to expand trade with China, Shō Hō suppressed the anti-Satsuma faction and built a consensus to assist Satsuma. With these moves, he was able to gain enough support within the kingdom to allow the investiture mission to proceed. In so doing, the king codified a "dual tribute" system that allowed Ryukyu to carve out its own autonomous space between Japan and China until the late nineteenth century. Namely, by serving Satsuma and particularly its trade agenda, the kingdom could maintain ties with China that provided vital political legitimacy for Ryukyu within East Asia. To demonstrate this new commitment to Satsuma, Ryukyu officials obtained more silk at Fuzhou,

---

20. Robert Sakai, "The Ryukyu (Liu-Ch'iu) Islands as a Fief of Satsuma," 118–33.
21. Tomiyama, *Ryūkyū ōkoku no gaikō to ōken*, 143–50.

Fig. 2   A Chinese ship, carrying an investiture mission, being escorted into Kumejima. *Hōshi Ryūkyū zukan* [An illustrated scroll of the Ryukyu investiture mission], eighteenth century. Courtesy of Okinawa Prefectural Museum.

Fig. 3   Arrival of investiture mission at Naha harbor. On the shoreline, palanquins stand ready to carry the Chinese envoys through an assembly of welcoming Ryukyuans. *Hōshi Ryūkyū zukan* [An illustrated scroll of the Ryukyu investiture mission], eighteenth century. Courtesy of Okinawa Prefectural Museum.

so much in fact that by the mid-1630s, Ming officials temporarily halted the trade, stating that Ryukyu had surpassed prescribed limits.[22]

The above events demonstrate that the *bakufu*, the Shimazu, and the Shō, although defined by their respective ranks in a clear hierarchy, implemented agendas in trade and diplomacy largely through accommodation of each others' positions and needs. While the Tokugawa dominated the Japanese polity, their vassal, the Shimazu, implemented Tokugawa directives based upon local needs and constraints (a point that will be discussed in more detail below). Moreover, the Shō, always conscious of their place between Japan and China, used a mix of refusal, compromise, flattery, and compliance to protect their agendas and goals in relations with the Shimazu, and indirectly, the *bakufu*.

Satsuma dominated Ryukyu through an intriguing back-and-forth dance, as illustrated by the fact that Ryukyuans would trade with China for Satsuma's benefit but not officially reveal the nature of Satsuma's dominance over the kingdom. Such precautions were taken because the Chinese court might reduce Ryukyu's rank in the tribute system if the former detected overt influence by Satsuma. Such a demotion would permit the kingdom to send envoys to China only once a decade. As long as the Ming (and later the Qing) considered Ryukyu a loyal vassal, it was allowed to dispatch biennial tribute missions, which served as more consistent opportunities for trade than the investiture missions, which also brought Chinese goods to Ryukyu, but only on the ascension of a new king.

Transported to Fuzhou on a Ryukyu ship, a tribute mission would first stay at the Ryukyu House, the kingdom's official residence in the port city. Consistent with practices of the China-centered tribute system, each mission brought official gifts, chiefly local products but also sulfur, copper, and tin. It also carried Japanese silver. Kagoshima merchants initially provided the silver, although by the late seventeenth century the domain supplied an increasing percentage, often by obtaining loans from Osaka merchants.[23] The Ryukyuans presented the sulfur at Fuzhou and then traveled first overland and then via the Grand Canal to Beijing, where the envoys offered the copper and tin. When the required dip-

---

22. Ibid., 64–71.
23. Kagoshima-ken, *Kagoshima kenshi*, vol. 2, 724–28 (hereafter *KK*)

lomatic protocols had been completed, the Ming (and later the Qing) court bestowed valuable presents to confirm the Shō as a vassal. Upon their return to Fuzhou, the Ryukyuans would be allowed to trade with Chinese merchants, exchanging the Japanese silver for silk and other goods.[24] After the mission arrived home, Ryukyu would ship the Chinese goods to Kagoshima. Satsuma ships would eventually take them to Kyoto and Osaka for sale on those markets. Ever ready to find new prospects for trade, Satsuma cleverly developed a practice that allowed them to increase the number of ships dispatched to Fuzhou. They instructed Ryukyu to send a "reception mission" that would escort the envoys' ships on their return voyage. The ships of the reception embassy would also carry silver and other goods, which would be traded at Fuzhou.

In contrast to the Shimazu, the Sō of Tsushima maintained a monopoly on Japanese-Korean commercial intercourse and served as a diplomatic intermediary primarily because Chosŏn leaders dictated it. The Japanese invasions of the Korean peninsula in the 1590s, in which the Sō participated, led the Chosŏn court to terminate the special privileges it had earlier granted the house. When Chosŏn leaders formed diplomatic ties with the newly established Tokugawa regime in 1607, like their predecessors, they believed that their kingdom would be better served by conducting relations with Japan through the Sō. Therefore, the Chosŏn court again made the head of the Sō clan a vassal and bestowed commercial and diplomatic privileges, the most prominent being permission for around 500 Tsushima officials and merchants to reside in a walled complex, the Japan House, just outside Pusan.

In their relations with Korea, Tsushima leaders engaged in diplomacy to facilitate trade, which occurred in private and official categories. The private trade, the area of highest volume, involved Tsushima merchants exchanging goods with officially licensed Korean merchants at a market near the Japan House. Chosŏn officials restricted the overall trade volume by limiting the number and size of ships that Tsushima could dispatch and by sanctioning only a handful of trading days per month. Despite these controls, the domain and its merchants enjoyed handsome profits as the middlemen in the import of Chinese silk and

---

24. Smits, *Visions of Ryukyu*, 36–37.

Korean ginseng, both purchased with high quality Japanese silver ingots. The official trade was part of the Sō's status as vassal of the Chosŏn court. The house dispatched regular diplomatic missions to the Japan House for meetings with Chosŏn officials and received official seals that legitimized the Sō's trade monopoly. Consistent with established East Asian diplomatic practices, the Sō gave and received specific gifts. As part of a small, defined tribute trade within the official trade, the Sō offered Southeast Asian goods obtained at Nagasaki: pepper, sappanwood (used as a red dye), and alum (a sulfate used as an astringent and in the manufacture of dyes). In the remainder of the official trade, the clan presented tin and copper, as well as water buffalo horns (used as military equipment). In return, Chosŏn officials bestowed assorted gifts in kind: small amounts of ginseng, and more importantly, a sizeable amount of cotton.[25]

Because of the Chosŏn court's stance, the *bakufu* awarded the Sō, an "outside" lord like the Shimazu, a monopoly on Japanese trade with Korea. As we shall see, at times the Sō could earn tremendous trade profits, which prompted the *bakufu* to generously estimate the Sō's annual revenue at 100,000 *koku*. Yet trade revenues fluctuated widely and in reality the Sō could count on only around 20,000 *koku* in annual rice production from lands on Tsushima. In the mid-seventeenth century, Tsushima leaders therefore welcomed the decision of the Korean court to reduce exports of cotton and instead annually bestow roughly 8,300 *koku* of rice in the official trade. The domain came to depend upon the Korean rice shipments to supply the Japan House residents, to pay for the cost of envoys on missions traveling between Tsushima and the Japan House, and most importantly, to feed a significant portion of the domain's population. In 1700 it was estimated that of Tsushima's population of 32,000, 18,000 lived on rice and barley grown on the island, 7,000 from rice grown on Sō lands in Kyushu, with the remaining 7,000 dependent upon Korean rice. Tsushima leaders continued to follow the necessary diplomatic protocols

---

25. Tsuruta, "The Establishment and Characteristics of the 'Tsushima Gate,'" 42; For more specific details about the official and private trades, see Tashiro, *Kinsei Nitchō tsūkō bōeki-shi no kenkyū*, 58–71.

Fig. 4 Remains of the *funae* [ship's inlet] in Izuhara harbor, Tsushima. The stone walls formed berths for the Sō trading vessels. Courtesy of Tachibana Atsushi.

not simply out of devotion to the Korean court, but to maintain the vital rice shipments.[26]

In a recent study, James B. Lewis provides a valuable perspective on how Korean officials viewed relations with their Japanese neighbors. He estimates that trade with Japan was significant to the economy of Kyŏngsang province, where the Japan House was located, noting that tax revenues from trade amounted to just over 50 percent of all taxes collected in the province. Nonetheless, he believes that in the end, relations with Tsushima proved a burden because of costs related to the reception of Tsushima envoys—supplies for the Japan House and the gifts presented as part of the official trade, particularly the annual gift of rice—outweighed trade-related revenue. He concludes that Chosŏn leaders maintained ties because they believed that if the people of Tsushima were prohibited from trading, they would turn to piracy, like their ancestors. The Chosŏn court also took seriously the ideal that its

---

26. Tsuruta, *Tsushima kara mita Nitchō kankei*, 56, 65, 79.

kingdom, as a more civilized and advanced state, had an obligation to help the less fortunate denizens of Tsushima.[27]

Lewis stresses that Chosŏn leaders were constantly concerned about affairs at the Japan House. In fact, they often tapped a rising star in the Chosŏn bureaucracy to serve as magistrate of the garrison town and surrounding county of Tongnae in Kyŏngsang province, a post that also included overseeing the Japan House. It was a challenging assignment as the magistrate repeatedly dealt with problems created by Japan House residents: their use of riots as a negotiating tactic, their calls to receive more food and supplies, and their unsanctioned liaisons with Korean prostitutes. Lewis asserts that at times events at the Japan House reverberated beyond the regional level and affected politics at Seoul, the capital. As a result, Chosŏn leaders were usually more occupied with matters at the Japan House and relations with the Sō, than with state-to-state diplomatic ties with the *bakufu*.[28]

As outlined above, Satsuma and Tsushima enjoyed a fair level of agency derived from their contacts with Ryukyu and Korea independent of Tokugawa authority. Yet the two domains were also active members of a polity dominated by the Tokugawa regime. We can therefore understand the extent of the two domains' agency and at the same time the interdependent nature of the larger system of foreign relations by considering the areas where domain leaders dutifully executed some Tokugawa edicts but were lax in others.

The Sō and Shimazu served most prominently as instruments of a Tokugawa state-wide agenda through their roles in the reception of envoys from the Chosŏn Kingdom and Ryukyu. Ronald Toby has demonstrated how the Tokugawa regime used relations with Korea, Ryukyu, and to a lesser degree, the Dutch factory at Nagasaki, to craft a "Japan-centered world" of foreign relations based on Chinese models. He illustrates that the Tokugawa *bakufu*, which had only recently gained military hegemony over the domains of Japan, viewed diplomatic relations with East Asia as an opportunity to bolster the legitimacy of the new regime. As a first step, the *bakufu* leadership created elaborate

---

27. Lewis, *Frontier Contact Between Chosŏn Korea and Tokugawa Japan*, 107–45.
28. Ibid., 146–216.

Fig. 5 The Japan House in Pusan harbor. Korean officials moved the contingent of Tsushima officials and traders, which numbered between 500 to 1,000 men, to this larger compound in Ch'oryang [Sōryō in the Japanese pronunciation] in the late seventeenth century. It remained in use until the late nineteenth century. *Sōryō wakan ezu* [An Illustration of the Japan House in Sōryō]. Courtesy of Tsushima Rekishi Minkoku Shiryōkan.

receptions for periodic Korean embassies that would travel to Edo to celebrate a shogunal succession. Because Chosŏn was an independent kingdom actively participating in the Chinese world order, the reception of its embassies was the cornerstone of the *bakufu*'s "Japan-centered world."

Bakufu leaders viewed the embassies as an opportunity to demonstrate to the Japanese polity that foreign states recognized the Tokugawa house as the legitimate ruler of Japan. They thus went to great lengths to assure their arrival and bore the significant financial cost. The leadership also arranged for the Koreans to travel by sea from Tsushima to Osaka and thereafter slowly proceed overland to Edo, and on several occasions, further north to the mausoleum of Tokugawa Ieyasu at Nikkō, just north of Edo. By having these grand processions (which usually numbered around 350 persons) travel through the most populous areas of the realm, the *bakufu* leadership aimed to publicly demonstrate its sovereignty over all of Japan. The *bakufu* ordered all daimyo to be present for the reception of the envoys at Edo Castle, making it an official state occasion.²⁹

The *bakufu* established a clear hierarchy among the missions: the Korean envoys were treated as distinguished guests, feted at a banquet, and lodged at Tokugawa expense; the Ryukyuans, representing an inferior vassal state, received no banquet reception and were housed in the Shimazu's Edo residence; and the Dutch, representing merely the private entity of the VOC, were even lower on the diplomatic totem pole. The *bakufu* permitted the Dutch to annually travel to Edo, where they presented greetings to the shogun, but did not allow them to engage in the state-to-state diplomatic exchange that was at the heart of the relationship between the *bakufu* and the Chosŏn court.³⁰

Because of the Sō's special relationship with the Chosŏn court, the domain negotiated key details related to the Korean embassies. Tsushima was the first to receive an embassy, and domain officials accompanied the Koreans on the round-trip to and from Edo. The Sō's role in facilitating the reception of embassies and in maintaining overall relations with the Chosŏn Kingdom gave the house a privileged position. This was reaffirmed in 1634, when the shogunate prosecuted the Sō's leading retainer house, the Yanagawa, for forging diplomatic correspondences with Korea several decades earlier. Although it was clear that the Sō were complicit in the forgery, the Tokugawa leadership chose only to punish the Yanagawa, aware that removing the Sō might threaten the stability of relations with Korea. The shogunate severely reprimanded the Sō and established a system where monks from Kyoto, working on a rotating basis in a Tsushima temple, would oversee diplomatic correspondence with the Chosŏn Kingdom.³¹

While this move allowed the *bakufu* to check diplomatic interaction, it did not give the Tokugawa leaders a means to oversee contact between Chosŏn officials and Tsushima merchants and domain represen-

---

29. Toby, *State and Diplomacy in Early Modern Japan*, 53–109.
30. Ibid., 186–92.
31. Arano, *Kinsei Nihon to higashi Ajia*, 191–210.

tatives at the Japan House. In their duties, the monks focused on references to the *bakufu* in diplomatic correspondence but were generally less concerned with trade or matters involving the Japan House. On an everyday basis, therefore, the Sō continued to enjoy a high level of autonomy in their commercial and diplomatic intercourse with Korea.[32]

Satsuma leaders eagerly assisted in the reception of embassies from Ryukyu to enhance the standing of the Shimazu vis-à-vis other daimyo. They actively supported Tokugawa directives, which instructed the envoys to dress in Ryukyuan and later Ming-style garb to accentuate their "foreignness." After arriving in Kagoshima, Shimazu ships would lead the embassy on its maritime journey to Osaka. Thereafter, Shimazu retainers served as escorts for the 100-man Ryukyu troupe during its overland trip to Edo along the same route as the Korean embassies. Like their Tokugawa counterparts, the Shimazu relished the opportunity to gain prestige from the embassies, particularly to display themselves as the only daimyo that dominated a "foreign" state.[33]

Numbering no more than ten men, the Dutch missions to Edo lacked the size and splendor of the Korean and Ryukyuan embassies. *Bakufu* leaders saw themselves as extending to the Dutch the privilege of visiting Edo and having an audience with the shogun during which an exchange of gifts would take place. The Dutch merchants viewed the missions as merely a diplomatic protocol necessary to maintain commercial ties.[34]

Satsuma and Tsushima also used their foreign contacts to gather intelligence for the *bakufu*, especially about events in China. Because of the kingdom's annual tribute missions to Beijing, Chosŏn officials were well informed about affairs in China and would convey information deemed appropriate for Japanese consumption to the Tongnae magistrate who would in turn pass it on to Tsushima officials. Those same officials would produce reports for the *bakufu* describing that information as well as rumors reported by Tsushima merchants at the Japan

---

32. Lewis, *Frontier Contact Between Chosŏn Korea and Tokugawa Japan*, 218.

33. Miyagi, *Ryūkyū shisha no Edo nobori*, 11–29.

34. Dutch accounts of the journeys to Edo as well as a daily record of events at Dejima can be found in Blussé and Remmelink, ed., *The Deshima Diaries: Marginalia, 1700–1740.*

House.[35] For their part, Satsuma officials could easily obtain intelligence about China through Ryukyu's regular embassies to Beijing, and they also would forward that information to Edo.[36] The two domains also served the *bakufu* by facilitating the repatriation of foreign and Japanese castaways. The *bakufu* and all domains would send Korean castaways to the Tsushima domain office in Nagasaki. Tsushima officials would then arrange for the castaways to be sent to the Japan House for repatriation. Satsuma received Japanese castaways from Ryukyu and assisted in the repatriation of Ryukyuans who were shipwrecked on Japanese shores. The *bakufu* decreed that all Chinese and castaways of any other nationalities were to be sent to Nagasaki for repatriation.[37] At least through the eighteenth century, Satsuma appears to have dutifully sent to Nagasaki Chinese castaways stranded on the coasts of the domain.[38]

Despite their cooperation in the above areas, the Shimazu and Sō, because of their domain's distance from Edo and the agency derived from their exclusive foreign contacts, enjoyed a fair level of flexibility in executing *bakufu* edicts, particularly in the arrival of foreign ships and trade. For example, in 1616, the *bakufu* decreed that all Chinese merchant vessels, which had traditionally called at ports throughout Kyushu, were thereafter to trade exclusively at Nagasaki.[39] The Shimazu largely ignored the edict as Chinese ships still regularly visited inlets and harbors on the Satsuma coast. Until the early eighteenth century, in fact, the domain permitted Chinese communities to exist in the village of Bōnotsu, a key port on the Satsuma peninsula, as well as other harbors along the southern Kyushu coastline.[40] The domain

---

35. Tsuruta, "The Establishment and Characteristics of the 'Tsushima Gate,'" 30–33; Toby, *State and Diplomacy in Early Modern Japan*, 145–46.

36. Toby, *State and Diplomacy in Early Modern Japan*, 143–44; Maehira, "Ryūkyū no kaigai jōhō to higashi Ajia," 95–112.

37. Arano, *Kinsei Nihon to higashi Ajia*, 132–45.

38. For example, in 1756, Satsuma sent 46 and in 1765, 57 Chinese merchants whose ships had wrecked on the Satsuma coast to Nagasaki for repatriation. Tanabe and Obara, *Nagasaki jitsuroku taisei, seihen*, vol. 16, 288, 394.

39. Tōkyō Teikoku Daigaku bungaku-bu, shiryōhensan-gakari ed., *Dai Nihon shiryō*, vol. 12.25, 232–33.

40. Mori, "Minami Kyūshū ni okeru Tōjin-machi ni kansuru oboegaki," 127–38.

also employed Chinese interpreters who assisted in trading activities and helped glean intelligence from Chinese ships that might unexpectedly call along the Satsuma coast.[41] Derek Wolff explains that the Shimazu encouraged the Chinese presence in order to increase commercial activity in coastal ports and by implication gain a greater hand in supervising coastal trade. He suggests that such a strategy was necessary because in the early seventeenth century, the Shimazu acted merely as one participant in a crowded field of merchants competing to gain profits from maritime trade.[42] Whatever the limits on Shimazu coastal authority, it is clear that the *bakufu* had at best only minimal influence over commerce along the southern Kyushu coastline. For their part, the Sō also had the ability to circumvent Tokugawa edicts concerning trade with Korea, as will be explained in more detail in the next chapter.

Following the death of his father Ieyasu in 1616, Shogun Hidetada began what was to be an often brutal but ultimately successful repression of Christianity. *Bakufu* officials, working in conjunction with the lords, executed missionaries and groups of their most devoted Japanese followers. They also established methods to detect Christians and force them to apostatize. As a result, many converts who had originally adopted Christianity based upon the directive of their lord—and not because of individual choice—renounced the faith, often through a written oath. By the late 1630s, Christianity had been reduced from close to 300,000 followers at its peak in 1615 to only small pockets of hidden Christians in isolated parts of Kyushu.[43]

To aid the anti-Christian campaign, Tsushima officials pledged to work with their Korean counterparts to stop Christians or Christian texts from entering the realm. Satsuma sent a special envoy to Ryukyu to inform the kingdom's leaders that the *bakufu* sought to track down Christians who might have escaped to the kingdom and to prevent Christian missionaries from the Spanish Philippines from preaching their faith on Ryukyu's southern islands. Officials in Shuri, apparently

---

41. Tokunaga, "Satsuma-han tōtsūji ni tsuite," 52–53.
42. Wolff, "Notes from the Periphery," 158–59.
43. An overview of the suppression of Christianity can be found in Higashibaba, *Christianity in Early Modern Japan*, 126–64.

sharing the zeal to limit Christianity and perhaps seeing an another opportunity to please their Shimazu overlords, in turn instructed officials to be on the lookout for hidden Christians and to increase coastal surveillance in the southern islands. During the Edo period, Satsuma relayed more than 20 Tokugawa directives to maintain vigilance against Christianity.[44]

By moving forcibly against Christianity and by issuing maritime prohibitions in the 1630s, which most notably ended the Japanese presence in Southeast Asia, the *bakufu* initiated its reaction against globalization. Subsequent Tokugawa leaders continued that reaction in what would become a long-term process of finding effective means of engagement, particularly in foreign trade, a story to which we now turn.

---

44. Machira, "Kinsei Nihon no kyōkai ryōiki," 14–15.

TWO

The Reaction against Globalization

In the seventh month of 1639, *bakufu* leaders continued to react against globalization by severing ties with Portuguese merchants, prohibiting their ships from calling thereafter at Nagasaki or any Japanese port. A few weeks later, they instructed all daimyo about protocol for treating future European visitors and enforcing the ban on Christianity. In turn, they allowed the VOC to establish an outpost on Dejima, the man-made island in Nagasaki harbor formerly occupied by the Portuguese. With these measures, *bakufu* leaders sought to eliminate what they perceived as the perils of unchecked intercourse—unwanted Christian missionaries and Portuguese influence—while maintaining the positive elements: the inflow of valued silk and medicinal products. Into the early eighteenth century, successive Tokugawa leaders engaged in what would develop into a trial-and-error process to find effective methods of commercial engagement with the outside world, especially the China market.

The Tokugawa regime tried several strategies, first placing more trade in the domestic hands of the Satsuma and Tsushima domains. Although this proved effective initially, by the late seventeenth century the *bakufu* faced new challenges, such as dwindling domestic silver reserves and increasing numbers of Chinese merchant ships calling at Nagasaki. Searching for a means to conduct trade without being drained of silver, *bakufu* leaders created institutions to regulate trade and promoted the development of new export products. In addition, in the early eighteenth century, Shogun Yoshimune expanded domestic production of silk, sugar, and ginseng, goods imported in high volumes since 1640.

The *bakufu*'s efforts to readjust trade, which were implemented as the regime continued to pursue the diplomatic agenda of the "Japan-centered world," necessarily involved the Satsuma and Tsushima domains. The Tokugawa measures, along with later manipulations of currency, created dynamics whereby the agency of Satsuma and Tsushima increased and waned. Through that process, Satsuma and Tsushima leaders staked out places and roles for their domains in the overall system of foreign relations.

Bakufu leaders sought to maintain a steady flow of silk, most of which came in the form of yarn, to feed strong domestic demand and no doubt to support the cottage silk weaving industry, then steadily growing, especially in the Nishijin district of Kyoto.[1] Soon after the order to expel the Portuguese was issued, the Nagasaki magistrate directed Shimazu Mitsuhisa, the lord of Satsuma, to explore importing more Chinese silk, rapeseed, and woven silk products through Ryukyu to offset the expected loss of those goods previously imported on Portuguese bottoms.[2] In the same month, the *bakufu* instructed Sō Yoshinari, the lord of Tsushima, to investigate the market for Chinese silk and pharmacopoeia at the Korean port of Pusan with an eye on increasing the flow of these imports through Korea.[3] The *bakufu* could take this step because the China market continued to readily accept the high-quality silver ingots used as currency especially in western Japan.

Satsuma's dominance of Ryukyu positioned the domain to become a larger conduit in trade with the China market. As noted earlier, Shō Hō had helped to steer the Ryukyu court in the 1630s to adopt a more cooperative stance in relations with Satsuma. The king was therefore ready to assist when in 1639, the Shimazu sent word that the *bakufu* was anxious to have the ban repealed and to expand the inflow of silk through Ryukyu. Seeing an opportunity to ingratiate himself to not only the Shimazu but also to their Tokugawa overlords, Shō Hō directed his

---

1. Innes, "The Door Ajar," vol. II, 491.
2. Kagoshima-ken rekishi shiryō sentā Reimeikan, ed., *Kagoshima-ken shiryō, kyūki zatsuroku kōhen* 6, *furoku* 1, 42–43.
3. Taigai kankeishi sōgō nenpyō henshū iinkai, ed., *Taigai kankeishi sōgō nenpyō*, 627.

subordinates to appeal to Ming officials for a repeal of the ban, and he personally offered prayers asking for divine intervention to help reopen the trade.[4]

While these efforts helped to restart trade, the fall of the Ming in 1644 and the ensuing battles surrounding the Ming-Qing transition led to much debate within the Ryukyu leadership about whether to hold out for a possible Ming revival or to form ties with the newly established Qing regime. The Shō eventually established a tribute relationship with the new Qing regime in 1652 and received a Qing investiture mission in 1663. Nevertheless, Ryukyu's tribute trade subsequently stalled due to maritime unrest in the East China Sea. The Zheng clan, which gained prominence under the leadership of Zheng Chenggong (known to Westerners as the pirate Coxinga), dominated maritime routes along the southern Chinese coast from a base on Taiwan, as illustrated by the clan's seizure of a tribute vessel and its cargo in 1670. By 1683, however, the Qing had asserted definitive control over southern China and its surrounding seas through their successful suppression of the Revolt of the Three Feudatories and by defeating the remnants of Zheng's forces on Taiwan. Aiming to boost trade in this now more peaceful environment, Satsuma officials issued a new tax structure that allowed the kingdom to pay tribute taxes not only in rice but also in silk and other Chinese goods. They hoped that this would encourage Ryukyuans to obtain more and better quality Chinese goods at Fuzhou. This measure, followed as it was by the Qing decision in 1684 to repeal maritime prohibitions imposed on much of the southern Chinese coast since 1661, increased the flow of silk and other Chinese imports through Ryukyu.[5]

Following the 1639 directive, Tsushima also began to import more silk via its ties with Korea. Merchants accompanying the Chosŏn court's annual tribute mission to Beijing would bring Japanese silver to exchange for Chinese silk and medicinal products at markets specifically established to deal in products brought by tribute missions.[6] Tashiro concludes that in the 1660s, Tsushima was enjoying tidy

---

4. Tomiyama, *Ryūkyū ōkoku no gaikō to ōken*, 64–71.
5. Uehara, *Sakoku to han bōeki*, 85–88.
6. Hamashita, *Chōkō shisutemu to kindai Ajia*, 96–98.

profits from the import of silk, although records of the period are spotty.[7]

Restricting Silver

Meanwhile, at Nagasaki, Dutch and especially Chinese bottoms continued to bring silk, medicinal products, and sugar from China, along with a range of luxury goods from Southeast Asia such as deerskins, animal horns, and aromatic woods.[8] To supervise trade, the *bakufu* permitted, in return of a fee, a guild of yarn merchants from the commercial centers of Sakai, Osaka, and Kyoto in central Japan to monopolize the sale of silk brought to Nagasaki by Chinese and Dutch traders. In 1655, the *bakufu* abolished the monopoly of the yarn merchants, and allowed foreign merchants to trade freely on the Nagasaki market. The laissez-faire Tokugawa stance led to an unexpected rise in prices for imports and allowed more silver to flow out of the realm.

Concerned that Japan was losing too much silver, *bakufu* officials established a system in 1671 whereby officials in Nagasaki would set prices for imports, a step that apparently constricted silver exports to some degree. Moreover, trade at Nagasaki remained manageable because of the Qing maritime prohibitions. Fewer ships from the Chinese mainland arrived at Nagasaki, although Siamese ships, often with Chinese crews, helped to maintain the flow of trade.[9]

The inadequacy of the system was revealed in 1684 when the Qing lifted the maritime bans. Once again, ships from the Chinese mainland could sail to Nagasaki. The following year, the number of Chinese merchant vessels calling at Nagasaki jumped to 85, compared to 24 the previous year. Meanwhile, trade through Tsushima began to boom, with the domain enjoying annual profits averaging between 2,000 to 4,000 *kan*, primarily from the silk-for-silver trade.[10] Even a profit of

---

7. Tashiro, "Tsushima Han's Korean Trade, 1684–1710," 97–99.
8. Nagazumi, *Kinsei shoki no gaikō*, 173–77.
9. Uehara, *Sakoku to han bōeki*, 91–93; Iwao, "Japanese Foreign Trade in the 16th and 17th Centuries," 13.
10. Tsuruta notes that scholars have disputed the level of Tsushima's annual average profits during the halcyon days of the private trade with Korea between 1684 and 1711. Tashiro estimates annual profits at just over 6,000 *kan* while Nakamura Tadashi countered that profits in 1695, a particularly fruitful year, reached just over 3,600 *kan*. Tsu-

2,000 *kan* was substantial, equating to roughly 80,000 *koku* of rice, more than the annual income of most daimyo.[11] *Bakufu* leaders quickly realized that if unchecked, the China market would essentially bleed the Japanese realm of its silver reserves.

In response, the *bakufu* moved to establish specific limits on foreign trade, both at Nagasaki and through Satsuma and Tsushima, thereby initiating a new era of trade policy centered on restricting silver exports. As a first step, *bakufu* leaders set firm ceilings for the Nagasaki market in 1685: a 6,000 *kan* limit on trade with Chinese merchants and 3,000 *kan* on trade with the Dutch. In an effort to enforce the new edicts, Tokugawa officials turned away 12 of the 85 Chinese merchant ships that arrived at Nagasaki that year. The *bakufu* made similar moves relating to domain trade, ordering Tsushima to limit its annual sales of imports on the domestic market to 1,080 *kan* and Satsuma to just over 800 *kan* for Ryukyu tribute missions and 400 *kan* for the welcoming missions.

In the decade after 1685, the *bakufu* achieved limited success at Nagasaki in enforcing the quotas placed upon trade with the Dutch, managing to reduce trade in 1685 and 1686 only to see it surge again in 1688. Although this was cause for concern, Tokugawa officials were more alarmed by the increase in Chinese ships: 194 called at Nagasaki in 1688, of which 77 were refused entry. Instead of returning home, many frustrated Chinese captains traded directly with Nagasaki merchants, thereby effectively mitigating the 1685 ceilings and continuing the outflow of silver.[12] *Bakufu* leaders were also stymied in their efforts to limit the outflow of silver through Tsushima. Tashiro Kazui estimates that silver exports continued to expand, reaching their peak in 1694.[13]

The flow of silver through Ryukyu apparently remained steady, although the *bakufu* did impose some restrictions on that trade as well. In 1684, the shogunate instructed Satsuma to limit Ryukyu's imports of woolen goods to only what could be consumed within the kingdom.

---

ruta therefore suggests that trade profits should be estimated between 2,000 to 4,000 *kan* annually during the boom period. Tsuruta, "The Establishment and Characteristics of the 'Tsushima Gate,'" 43–44.

11. Tsuruta, *Tsushima kara mita Nitchō kankei*, 83.
12. Yamawaki, *Nagasaki no Tōjin bōeki*, 58, 71–72.
13. Tashiro, "Tsushima-han's Korean Trade, 1684–1710," 91.

In 1688, the shogunate allowed the domain the privilege of selling Chinese goods imported through Ryukyu not at Nagasaki but through an officially sanctioned wholesaler in Kyoto.[14] Uehara Kenzen notes that Satsuma and Tokugawa leaders saw the new arrangement as mutually beneficial: Satsuma could gain a sanctioned presence on the Kyoto market, where silk was in high demand, and the *bakufu* could count on the domain to help limit illicit trade, through which silver flowed out of the realm. Satsuma officials thereafter actively enforced Tokugawa anti-smuggling edicts, particularly by assuring that Chinese goods brought through Ryukyu were sold only through the Kyoto wholesaler. Satsuma officials calculated that a show of fealty would protect the domain's trading rights. They also sought to ensure that the silver provided to Ryukyu would translate into more revenue for the domain treasury.[15]

Despite the success in obtaining Satsuma's cooperation, *bakufu* leaders faced difficulties in regulating silver outflows and subsequently moved to substitute other exports in demand on the China market. In 1695, they began to promote copper, which already had been exported in greater volume during the previous decade.[16] Chinese merchants readily accepted Japanese copper, because it was high in quality and offered at a price competitive with that of the Chinese market. In addition, Qing government mints, which annually used 40,000 piculs (approximately 2,740 tons) of copper to produce coins for domestic currency, were clamoring for copper because of poor production from Chinese mines. For both Qing and Tokugawa leaders, copper therefore met political and economic needs. Over the next four decades, Qing mints depended upon Japanese copper to produce coins for domestic use. (The mints moved away from using Japanese copper only in 1738, when mines in Yunnan province came to supply their needs.) While volume declined during over the course of the eighteenth century, Dutch and Chinese ships continued to export copper, making it one of the two primary Japanese exports through the mid-nineteenth century.[17]

---

14. *KK*, vol. 2, 726–27.
15. Uehara, *Sakoku to han bōeki*, 97–102.
16. Nagazumi, ed., *Tōsen yushutsunyūhin sūryō ichiran*, 254–56.
17. Hall, "Notes on the Early Ch'ing [Qing]Copper Trade with Japan," 453–61.

Select marine products also emerged as key Japanese exports, which Chinese ships were carrying home as early as 1681.[18] In 1698, Nagasaki officials polled Chinese merchants about their product preferences, offering tea, abalone, and sea cucumbers as sample exports. The Chinese traders expressed more interest in the abalone and sea cucumbers, goods already widely consumed in China. Although a variety of marine products were exported, the main goods came to be organized into two categories: dried abalone, shark fins, and sea cucumbers (collectively known as *tawaramono*; literally, "goods in rice straw bales"); and dried kelp and an assortment of other marine products (called *shoshiki kaisanbutsu*; "miscellaneous marine products").[19]

Until the mid eighteenth century, Satsuma and Tsushima continued to export silver but like the bakufu, the domains were increasingly diversifying their export portfolios with various silver substitutes. Because the Chosŏn Kindgom used copper to mint coins, Tsushima exported large amounts of the metal through the Japan House after 1684.[20] For its part, Satsuma sent copper, tin, and marine products to Ryukyu to test their viability in the kingdom's tribute trade.[21]

As an additional facet of the effort to limit silver exports, the *bakufu* established new institutions to supervise trade with the Chinese and the Dutch. In 1689, the *bakufu* constructed the Chinese Residence, a compound for Chinese merchants on the shores of Nagasaki harbor. While similar to the existing Dutch compound on Dejima, the Chinese Residence was far larger, consisting of a walled compound of residential barracks, offices, and warehouses occupying roughly seven acres and surrounded by a palisade and moat. At peak times, it housed close to 5,000 Chinese merchants and sailors, although the average was usually around 2,000 men. As was the case with the Dutch on Dejima, the *bakufu* prohibited the Chinese from leaving the compound, except to unload goods from their ships or to conduct sanctioned trade with Japanese merchants. Apart from *bakufu* officials, the only visitors to the

---

18. Nagazumi, *Tōsen yushutsunyūhin sūryō ichiran*, 254.
19. Wakamatsu, "Nagasaki tawaramono o meguru shokubunka no rekishiteki tenkai," 140.
20. Tashiro, "Tsushima-han no Chōsen yushutsu dō chōtatsu ni tsuite," 148–49
21. *KK*, vol. 2, 731–39.

all-male residence were courtesans from the nearby Maruyama pleasure quarters.[22]

In 1698, the *bakufu* took an additional step to regulate trade at Nagasaki by creating the clearing-house, an office that oversaw the copper, silk, and marine product trades, as well as the flow of imports onto the Nagasaki market. Until its abolition in 1867, the new office functioned as the primary regulatory trade organ in Nagasaki. Over subsequent decades, the clearing-house came to more tightly administer the supply of marine products and export copper to Chinese and Dutch merchants, as well as the reception and processing of imported goods. As one of its key functions, the clearing-house controlled sales of imports to Nagasaki merchants, either through a bid system or based upon special arrangements. Its officials handled special imports ordered by the shogun and worked closely with the *bakufu*-sanctioned merchants and the copper and silver mints in matters relating to the export of silver and copper. Finally, clearing-house officials oversaw Tsushima's special purchases of Southeast Asian water buffalo horns, alum, sappanwood, and pepper imported on Chinese and Dutch bottoms. Because they were required in the Sō's tribute trade with Chosŏn, the *bakufu* permitted Tsushima representatives to purchase, at a reduced rate, the highest quality goods available.

The Nagasaki clearing-house allowed *bakufu* officials to regulate the outflow of silver and limit smuggling. Nagasaki officials were aware that merchant guilds were using established contacts with Chinese merchants to continue using silver to purchase imports in contradiction to *bakufu* edicts. By placing all *bakufu* institutions and merchant guilds under the clearing-house's unified regulatory umbrella, the shogunate thus established a means to stifle unsanctioned trade at Nagasaki.[23] As the sole middleman in transactions between Chinese and Dutch merchants and the Nagasaki merchant community, the clearing-house also earned profits that subsidized its operating costs, supported the Nagasaki populace, and provided revenue for Tokugawa coffers. It added a 20-percent markup on the Dutch and Chinese imports sold on the

---

22. Jansen, *China in the Tokugawa World*, 29–30.
23. Yamawaki, *Nagasaki no Tōjin bōeki*, 89.

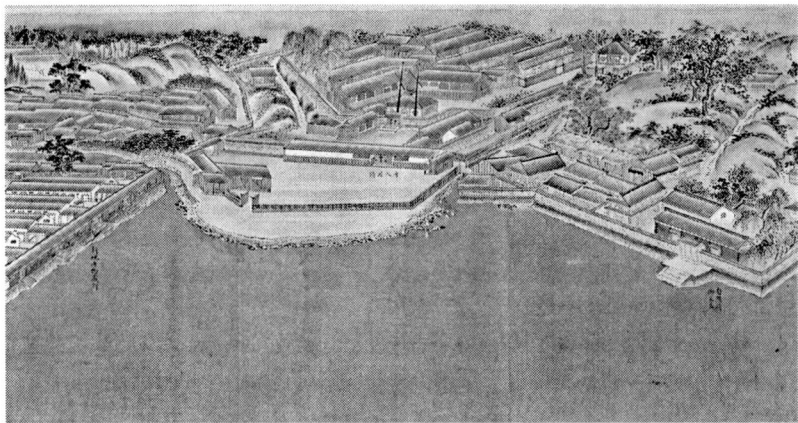

Fig. 6 The Chinese Residence in Nagasaki harbor. *Roshia shisetsu Rezanofu raikō emaki* [Picture Scroll of Russian Envoy Rezanov's Visit to Nagasaki]. Courtesy of Historiographical Institute, University of Tokyo.

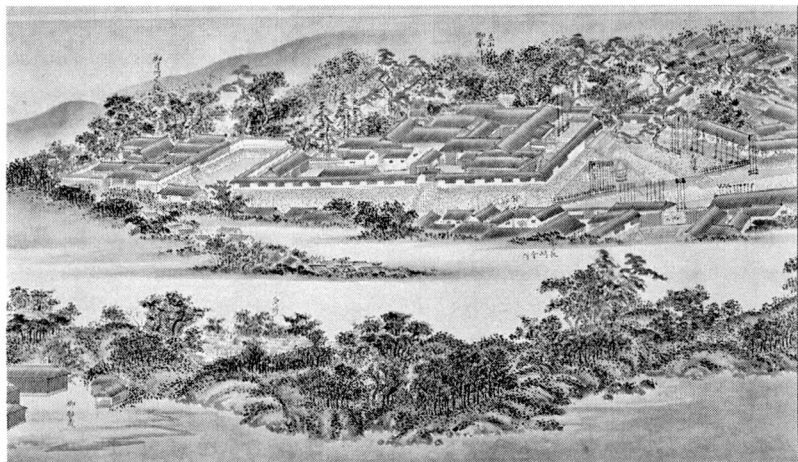

Fig. 7 The clearing-house, in the foreground, and Tateyama magistrate office, the walled complex in the background, in Nagasaki in the early nineteenth century. *Roshia shisetsu Rezanofu raikō emaki* [Picture Scroll of Russian Envoy Rezanov's Visit to Nagasaki]. Courtesy of Historiographical Institute, University of Tokyo.

Nagasaki market. The clearing-house also garnered income through tariffs, royalties from various barter arrangements, and assorted levies. With these profits, the clearing-house would first pay its expenses, chiefly personnel costs, and earmark some funds for advance payments for future trade. It allocated larger portions of its revenue for the districts of Nagasaki and the *bakufu*'s Osaka treasury. For example, the clearing-house garnered roughly 161,000 *ryō* in profits in 1714. Of that amount, it bestowed 70,000 *ryō* to the districts of Nagasaki, allocated 15,000 *ryō* for advance payments of imports, and sent the remaining 76,000 *ryō* to the Osaka treasury.[24] The value of the trade is illustrated by the fact that in 1747, the lord of the wealthy Kaga domain (present-day Ishikawa and Toyama prefectures) spent just over 171,000 *ryō* on expenditures within his domain and in Edo (such as maintaining his residences in the city).[25]

All the while, *bakufu* leaders remained aware of the role that foreign trade played in maintaining stability in certain sectors of Japanese society. For one, the clearing-house continued a decades-old practice of providing funds to the Nagasaki merchant community, which owed its livelihood to foreign trade. In 1663, the *bakufu* had established a system whereby each district within the city would receive an allotment of the profits obtained from a specific Chinese merchant ship, money that was used first to pay the salaries of local officials, with the remainder divided among the district's residents. The districts also received shares of tariffs collected by the clearing-house, rent from the Chinese residence, and various levies. This practice upheld the implied feudal contract between the *bakufu* and its subjects, the residents of Nagasaki. As lord of a city under its direct rule, the *bakufu* was obligated to support the well-being of the denizens of Nagasaki, who because they lived exclusively as merchants, were dependent upon the flow of foreign trade.[26]

The *bakufu* affirmed this social contract when shortages of export grade copper and a reduction in trade volume combined to create an overall economic downturn in Nagasaki in 1711. The reduction affected particularly laborers and petty merchants who owed their livelihoods to the flow of trade. Because of the economic slowdown, these lower strata workers were increasingly unable to purchase rice and other

---

24. Arano, *Kinsei Nihon to higashi Ajia*, 99; Innes, "The Door Ajar," vol. I, 343; Yamawaki, *Nagasaki no Tōjin bōeki*, 281.
25. Tōkyō-to Edo Tōkyō hakubutsukan, *Sankin kōtai: kyodai toshi Edo no naritachi*, 101.
26. Nagazumi, "From Company to Individual Company Servants," 153; Innes, "The Door Ajar," vol. I, 343.

foodstuffs. Many faced famine and in their weakened physical state contracted contagious diseases. In 1713 and 1714, epidemics swept through the city, killing an estimated 5,000 people, mostly from the lower economic strata. Clearing-house officials and the Nagasaki magistrate attempted to assuage the economic hardships by selling imports to Nagasaki merchants at discounted prices and by bestowing a special, temporary grant to each household. While trade levels appear to have stabilized the following year (as illustrated by the clearing-house revenues listed above), the events of 1713 and 1714 demonstrate that *bakufu* officials had to take into account the well-being of the Nagasaki population. Therefore, as they calculated the profits available from foreign trade, *bakufu* leaders had to also consider societal consequences, in this case how trade policies would affect the denizens of Nagasaki.[27]

The Domains and Tokugawa Currency Manipulations

By 1695, *bakufu* leaders had developed an overall trade policy that banned gold exports outright, limited silver exports, but encouraged the export of copper. At the same time, the question of currency was becoming a major domestic issue for the *bakufu* as its reserves of silver were dwindling. As a means of fiscal relief, Shogun Tsunayoshi decided to debase currency in 1695, cutting the percentage of gold in coins to 57 percent and creating a new Genroku silver ingot (so-called for the imperial reign name, 1688–1703) that had only 64 percent silver. This step was part of a larger plan of fiscal renewal, which also included attempts to increase mining production. By some estimates, the debasements allowed the *bakufu* to garner roughly 5 million *ryō* in profits, funds that provided an important boost to the Tokugawa treasury.[28]

Tsunayoshi and the *bakufu* leadership decided to debase silver primarily to boost Tokugawa finances and were not specifically seeking to restrict foreign trade. Nonetheless, they soon learned the detrimental effect that debasement had on Tsushima, which used silver ingots to purchase chiefly Chinese silk and Korean ginseng. Tsushima faced immediate resistance from Korean merchants long accustomed to re-

---

27. Arano, *Kinsei Nihon to higashi Ajia*, 98–99.
28. Innes, "The Door Ajar," vol. II, 577–99; Totman, *Early Modern Japan*, 138.

ceiving ingots of 80 percent quality, which held a high reputation behind only the 90 percent pure Mexican dollar, the standard unit of exchange throughout much of seventeenth-century East Asia.[29] The Koreans therefore feared difficulties in using the new ingots to purchase silk from Chinese merchants. After protracted negotiations, Korean merchants eventually accepted the new ingots, but raised their prices by 27 percent to compensate. The domain consequently endured sharp declines in trade profits because of problems associated with the new currency, indicated by the 1,600 *kan* profit in 1700, down from the robust profits of 4,000 *kan* enjoyed just a few years earlier. The debased ingots thus hindered Tsushima's trade in a way that *bakufu* edicts since 1685 had never accomplished.[30]

Concerned with the Tokugawa moves, high-ranking advisers to the Sō started to debate how to stabilize the domain economy amidst declining trade. Two opposing views emerged. On one side, Amenomori Hōshū, a Confucian scholar, advocated that the domain focus on maintaining and hopefully improving commercial ties with Korea. On the other, Suyama Totsuan, also a Confucian scholar, asserted that the domain economy could be revived by improving agricultural production. Suyama identified the island's abundant wildlife as the chief impediment to an expansion of Tsushima's agriculture. For generations, farmers had battled deer and especially wild boar that ate and trampled crops.

In 1700, domain leaders accepted Suyama's plan to reduce the deer and boar populations, mobilizing all able-bodied men over 20 years old. Some were assigned to build a series of stone walls. Others were organized into groups of 600 and provided with dogs to assist in daily hunts for deer and boar. Using guns (the domain received special permission from the *bakufu* to use firearms) and other noise-making devices, the bands drove the animals into walled areas where they could easily be killed. Over the course the decade-long hunt, thousands of deer and boar were killed. The reduction in wildlife succeeded in bringing about a rise in agricultural production as farmers could more easily till their fields.[31]

---

29. Innes, "The Door Ajar," vol. II, 582.
30. *IC*, 783.
31. Ibid., 763–66.

Meanwhile Tsushima leaders continued to push their case to their Tokugawa overlords. Domain officials appealed to Ogiwara Shigehide, the *bakufu* official spearheading the debasement policy, to make dispensations because of the domain's dependence upon trade with Korea. To support to their appeals, domain leaders cleverly exploited the growing popularity of ginseng, which at the time was almost exclusively imported from Korea as a medicine within Japanese society. As the sole purveyor of Korean ginseng, Tsushima used the domain's residence in Edo as a shop to sell the root, especially to daimyo and other high-ranking samurai. The domain leadership also concluded agreements with several merchant houses to sell directly to commoners and low-ranking samurai. Because there were no limits placed upon purchases, speculators acquired large quantities, forcing up prices and creating shortages. In 1690, people awaiting the morning sale began to line up the night before to improve their chances. Verbal and physical scuffles, often resulting in injuries, were common as people waited to purchase ginseng. One summer morning, a lord-less samurai (*rōnin*) queued in front of an Edo merchant house to purchase ginseng. Upon learning that none was available, he drew his short sword and threatened suicide before being restrained. Although it is unclear if the tactic allowed the samurai to obtain any ginseng, it is certain that *bakufu* officials were concerned about the potential for public unrest exemplified by the incident. A month later, they instructed Tsushima to sell ginseng thereafter only through prearranged orders, in hopes of stopping such incidents in the future while ensuring that the sick who required the root would receive it.[32]

Arguing that ginseng was viewed as a vital medicine, Tsushima officials pressed the *bakufu* to provide additional assistance to stabilize ginseng imports specifically, and by implication, domain trade overall. In 1700, they claimed that due to debasement of silver ingots and decreased ginseng production in Korea, the import price of the root had doubled, prompting domain losses. Domain representatives asserted that they would have difficulty continuing to import ginseng at a financial loss, intimating the possibility of a total import shutdown of an important medicinal product. Sensitive to ginseng's societal function,

---

32. Imamura, *Ninjin-shi*, vol. 2, 470–71.

Ogiwara and the *bakufu* leadership granted two concessions to Tsushima. They allowed the domain to annually sell 1,800 *kan* of imports, an increase from the previous 1,080 *kan* limit. In addition, they bestowed a 15,000 *ryō* loan to use as advance payments to purchase ginseng. When the *bakufu* issued a new ingot debased to only 50 percent silver in 1706, Tsushima claimed that the new ingots would lead to additional trade dilemmas. Domain officials therefore pressed the *bakufu* for an additional privilege: to allow the minting of a special ingot of 80 percent fineness specifically for Tsushima's trade. Although it took several years, the *bakufu* granted the request, and in 1711, the domain began to use the special ingot in its trade.[33]

The appeals of Tsushima and the *bakufu*'s response to them represent a new and more defined incarnation of domain agency. Faced with the prospect of declining trade revenues, domain officials presented Tsushima's trade as an activity that benefited not just the domain but the larger Japanese realm. They skillfully played upon the *bakufu*'s concerns—in this case, the Tokugawa desire to maintain the inflow of a product deemed necessary for the greater social good. In making the decision to preserve ginseng imports, *bakufu* officials acted in a manner reminiscent of their predecessors, who directed Satsuma and Tsushima in 1639 to import more Chinese silk thread to protect the weaving industry in Kyoto.

A few years later, Tsushima officials once again successfully promoted the wider value of domain trade. While debasement proved a quick fix for the Tokugawa treasury, many within the *bakufu* leadership advocated a hard currency policy implemented concurrently with increased domestic production of goods imported from abroad. Arai Hakuseki, a key advisor to shoguns Ienobu (r. 1709–12) and Ietsugu (r. 1713–16), was a strong advocate of hard currency and helped engineer a fresh wave of *bakufu* regulations on foreign trade. Arai opposed the export of precious metals, describing gold and silver as "bones of the earth" that could never be restored once removed. He was particularly critical of the importation of silk, sugar, and luxury goods, which he labeled "unnecessary foreign trinkets." He believed that the overall level of foreign trade should be reduced with the remaining trade more tightly

---

33. *IC*, 783–87.

regulated to eliminate bullion outflows. Arai argued that the *bakufu* should encourage domestic production of ginseng, silk, and other imported products, instead of acquiring them through trade.[34]

In 1714, Arai and other *bakufu* leaders moved ahead with plans to further reduce silver outflows beyond the levels imposed in 1685. Instituted the following year, the new edicts—named after the Shōtoku era (1711–15)—restricted the number of Chinese merchant ships allowed to trade annually at Nagasaki to 30 and the Dutch to two ships a year. Moreover, a credential trading system based on Chinese models was adopted. When a Chinese merchant vessel left Nagasaki to return to its home port, *bakufu* officials issued a document that consisted of half of an official seal. Upon the ship's return the following year, the captain presented the credential, which was placed against the other half of the seal held by Nagasaki officials. If it matched, then the whole document served as a ticket to trade. The system allowed the *bakufu* to close a loophole: the ability of Chinese captains, who arrived after the yearly quota had been filled, to trade by arguing that they had not planned to call at Nagasaki but had merely "drifted ashore" because of capricious winds or currents.[35]

Arai and the *bakufu* leadership also set their sights on domain trade, instructing Tsushima officials of their plans to cut in half silver exports flowing through the island domain. Shocked by the scale of the proposed limits, domain officials dispatched Amenomori to Edo to appeal Tsushima's case. In a series of memorials to the *bakufu*, Amenomori stressed that the export of silver did not merely support the Tsushima domain economy, but also contributed to the overall defense of the realm in significant ways. In 1715, Amenomori wrote:

Silver is being exported to Ryukyu and Korea. The lord of Satsuma has a substantial income and rules a large domain. Therefore, if Satsuma were prohibited from exporting silver, the effect on the domain economy would be minimal. What is more, Ryukyu is a vassal state of Satsuma; while Korea is an independent state with which friendly diplomatic relations are maintained. Silver is the most important product in the export trade and is used to import

---

34. Nakai, *Shogunal Politics*, 111–13.
35. Toby, *State and Diplomacy in Early Modern Japan*, 197–202; Arano, *Kinsei Nihon to higashi Ajia*, 103–9.

ginseng. The lord of Tsushima has a limited income and Tsushima is but a small domain. It is therefore difficult for Tsushima to support itself by its own agricultural production. Through its commercial connections, Tsushima defends a border of the realm with a foreign country. This is because the export of silver ingots to Ryukyu and Korea provides a means for collecting information about the outside world.[36]

In another missive, he stressed that "Tsushima plays a role in the overall defense of the realm by gauging the relative importance of information of foreign countries," and thus defined the island as serving a "primary strategic bulwark" for the realm. He argued that "this task contributes to the protection of all of Japan."[37] Amenomori and other domain officials also emphasized that Tsushima's foreign trade was a privilege granted by Tokugawa Ieyasu to offset the domain's low agricultural production, and more significantly, as a reward for the domain's service of maintaining relations with the Chosŏn Kingdom. In effect, the Tsushima leadership asserted that its diplomatic activities were equivalent to the military levies that the *bakufu* placed on the lords of all domains. While other lords manned castles or were assigned specific responsibilities such as the defense of Nagasaki, the Sō's duty was to maintain and regulate relations with Korea. Faced with such determination, Arai and the *bakufu* leadership backed down. They dropped plans to cut silver exports through the domain and allowed Tsushima to continue to use special silver ingots in its trade with Korea.[38]

The ascension of Tokugawa Yoshimune to the office of shogun in the summer of 1716 led to Arai's departure from the *bakufu* power circle and an easing, but not the repeal, of the Shōtoku edicts. Yoshimune and subsequent *bakufu* leaders increased the number of Chinese ships allowed to trade annually at Nagasaki but made no significant changes to the credential system. Tsushima continued to send silver to Korea in exchange for silk, although in decreasing quantities. Moreover, the

---

36. Amenomori Hōshū, "Kōeki ryōgin genshō no gi osaedasararesōrō ni tsuite onegai no suji kikiawase no kiroku" (1714), quoted in Tashiro, *Kinsei Nitchō tsūkō bōekishi no kenkyū*, 337*n*109.

37. Amenomori, "Rinkō shimatsu monogatari," quoted in Tashiro, *Kinsei Nitchō tsūkō bōekishi no kenkyū*, 337*n*110.

38. Yamamoto, *Tsushima-han Edo garō*, 232–38.

bakufu began to provide Tsushima with financial assistance to facilitate trade, proffering a loan of 5,000 *ryō* in 1717 to be used as an advanced payment in trade with Korea. In 1748, Tsushima gained an additional privilege when the Nagasaki magistrate deemed that the domain played a special role in the defense of the realm by "containing Korea" through its commercial and diplomatic contacts. As a result, the magistrate exempted the domain from dispatching men to assist in the defense of Nagasaki. This marked a change from earlier policy, which dictated that all Kyushu domains assist in the defense of the port city. For example, when two Portuguese ships called at Nagasaki in 1647, eight years after the expulsion of the Portuguese from the port, the *bakufu* instructed all daimyo in the Kyushu region, including Tsushima, to dispatch troops against a possible attack. After 1748, however, Fukuoka, Saga, and other Kyushu domains alone shared the duty of defending Nagasaki.[39]

By articulating Tsushima's case within the larger context of Japan's foreign relations, Amenomori defined a language of domain agency that Tsushima officials would utilize over the next 150 years. Particularly significant is how he identified the domain's role in trade as contributing not merely to a greater social well-being for the entire realm, as had been the case with earlier domain appeals for support for the ginseng trade, but as playing a part in the *bakufu*'s larger diplomatic and defensive agendas for the Japanese state. Amenomori forcefully asserted that Tsushima's (and Satsuma's) trade benefited the realm by facilitating the flow of valuable intelligence, for which the domain should be seen as a primary "defensive bulwark" in Japan's larger defensive structure.

Because the debased ingots also caused problems in the kingdom's tribute trade with China, Ryukyu also appealed in 1704 for permission to use 80 percent ingots. Perhaps because Ryukyu was not importing goods like ginseng, deemed vital for its medicinal value, *bakufu* leaders did not respond to the kingdom's request. To fill the silver gap, Satsuma supplied copper, tin, and marine products to Ryukyu to use as substitutes for silver.[40] As Satsuma officials considered requesting special privileges to export silver similar to those granted Tsushima, matters of

---

39. Arano, *Kinsei Nihon to higashi Ajia*, 217–20.
40. Innes, "The Door Ajar," vol. II, 602.

diplomacy—Satsuma's request for Ryukyu to send an embassy to celebrate Ienobu's ascension to shogun—came to the fore. Since 1644, Ryukyu had dispatched six embassies to Edo to commemorate the ascension of a new shogun or to congratulate the Tokugawa for the birth of a shogunal heir. In 1709, *bakufu* leaders, no doubt as part of the growing concern over the Tokugawa fisc, replied that a formal Ryukyu mission was unnecessary, a stance they had also taken five years earlier when Satsuma asked to send an embassy to commemorate the selection of Ienobu as Tsunayoshi's heir.

Satsuma leaders replied that the shogun should receive Ryukyuan embassies because they helped maintain Tokugawa authority. They described Ryukyu as a foreign state that dutifully offered tribute to the Qing, yet also maintained its status as a Tokugawa vassal through the dispatch of embassies to Edo. Satsuma leaders suggested that a break in the arrival of embassies would tarnish Tokugawa authority by showing that a foreign state no longer displayed the proper fealty and respect. The Shimazu further asserted that they needed the embassies to maintain their dominance over Ryukyu. In a 1710 memorial, the daimyo, Shimazu Yoshitaka, noted that when his ancestor Iehisa subjugated Ryukyu in 1609, his rank had been raised. Yet Mitsuhisa, who had succeeded as lord of the domain a few decades later, subsequently had his rank reduced. Yoshitaka complained that as a result of this move, the Ryukyu elite viewed the Shimazu in a diminished light, and by consequence Shimazu authority in the kingdom had been tarnished. There is little doubt that more than their position in Ryukyu, Satsuma leaders were focused on using the embassies to enhance the standing of Yoshitaka vis-à-vis other lords, particularly the highest-ranked daimyo, the Maeda of Kaga. Nonetheless, the dual arguments of maintaining Shimazu and Tokugawa authority proved effective, as *bakufu* leaders relented, permitting Ryukyu to dispatch an embassy and decreeing that Yoshitaka's rank would be increased when the embassy traveled to Edo in 1711. Thereafter, the rank of the Shimazu lord was raised by one level each time a Ryukyu embassy journeyed to Edo.[41]

On the trade front, Satsuma officials once again requested permission in 1712 to use higher quality silver ingots in Ryukyu's tribute trade.

---

41. Kamiya, *Taikun gaikō to higashi Ajia*, 137–43.

Unlike the Sō, the Shimazu requested the use of Genroku ingots of 64 percent purity, probably because the *bakufu* had instituted an additional debasement in 1711, creating ingots of only 20 percent quality. Satsuma officials emphasized that silver exports were important not so much for Satsuma but for the economic and political stability of Ryukyu, because they allowed the kingdom to maintain its tribute ties with the Qing. They argued that of the permitted 800 *kan* of silver that envoys carried to Fuzhou, 350 *kan* was used as gifts to Qing officials with the remainder used to purchase silk and medicinal products which were sold on the Japanese market. Satsuma officials noted that without silver, Ryukyu would have difficulty maintaining its tribute ties with the Qing. They expressed particular concern about the investiture missions, so vital to Shō sovereignty, one of which was scheduled to arrive the following year. The officials stressed that if the tribute tie were cut, Ryukyu would face economic hardship because of the loss of trade. They implied that the powerful Qing court might also become disgruntled and direct its dissatisfaction against the *bakufu*. Here again, Satsuma leaders adeptly pointed to both Ryukyu's economic vulnerability and the significance of the kingdom's tribute ties with China.

They evidently struck the right chord because in 1713, *bakufu* officials permitted Satsuma to supply Genroku ingots of 64 percent purity to Ryukyu, stressing that the privilege was being offered because of the scheduled to expected investiture mission. When Arai Hakuseki reestablished the 80 percent purity standard in 1715, *bakufu* officials allowed Ryukyu to use the reconstituted ingots. The following year, however, they ordered the domain to cut the total amount of silver used annually in Ryukyu's tribute missions from approximately 800 to 600 *kan* and for reception missions from just over 400 to 300 *kan*, ceilings that remained until the early nineteenth century. Overall, while they had succeeded in the debate over the continuation of Ryukyu's embassies and the use of silver in trade, Satsuma leaders did not gain the trade concessions awarded to Tsushima (which was able to increase its trade ceiling by nearly 800 *kan*) but actually lost over 300 *kan* in annual trade revenues.[42]

---

42. Uehara, *Sakoku to han bōeki*, 104–16.

Nonetheless, in its battle over silver exports with the *bakufu*, we find Satsuma leaders, like their Tsushima counterparts, articulating the role of domain trade within the larger foreign relations system of the Japanese realm. While less explicitly than Amenomori, Satsuma officials expressed how their domain's trade contributed to the overall defense by invoking the specter of a break in Ryukyu's ties with the Qing. As it did with Tsushima, the *bakufu* later officially recognized Satsuma's contribution. In 1748, the Nagasaki magistrate characterized Satsuma's defensive role as "containing" Ryukyu, just as it had defined Tsushima as contributing to the overall defense by "containing" Korea. The domain was therefore also exempted from dispatching men for the defense of Nagasaki.[43]

Localization

Yoshimune started the final phase of the reaction against globalization when he initiated what proved to be an extremely successful plan of localization: growing at home the sugar, ginseng, and silk that Japan had been importing. The shogun approached foreign trade seeking to find viable, practical solutions to its challenges, the most intractable of which continued to be silver exports. Emblematic of his energetic style, he personally initiated surveys of flora and fauna that increased overall knowledge of medicinal products and helped set in motion domestic production of ginseng. Following Yoshimune's orders, Tsushima officials in 1718 used their contacts in Pusan to gather information about Chinese and Korean fauna and flora as well as obtain samples of Korean ginseng, which later came to be widely cultivated in Japan. The shogun subsequently ordered that Chinese and Dutch merchants in Nagasaki be queried about their knowledge of medicinal plants, and in 1722, he commenced a comprehensive survey of medicinal plants in Japan extending from Ezo in the north to Nagasaki in the west, which was not completed until 1753.[44]

---

43. Arano, *Kinsei Nihon to higashi Ajia*, 217–20.
44. Tashiro, *Edo jidai Chōsen yakuzai chōsa no kenkyū*, 65–66, 183–218.

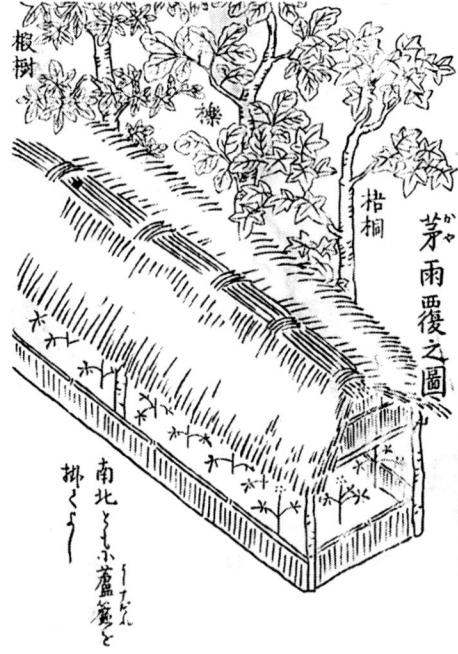

Fig. 8 As domestic ginseng production expanded over the first half of the eighteenth century, manuals were published to aid farmers cultivating the root. From one such manual, this diagram outlines how to build a thatched shelter, facing north and south, to protect ginseng seedlings. After planting, it took several years, and much care, for ginseng roots to mature. This structure, with reed roofs, was used to protect the seedlings against heavy rain. To counteract insects and worms that would eat the young roots, the handbook suggests that tobacco diluted water be spread around the seedlings or that eel bones be burned nearby. Finally the manual recommends that certain trees be planted around the ginseng to enhance growth: the Chinese parasol tree, as well as varieties of oak and fir. *Chōsen ninjin kōsaku ki* [A Chronicle of Ginseng Cultivation]. Courtesy of the General Library, University of Tokyo.

Concomitant with these surveys, scholars began to publish new texts in the fields of botanical studies, agricultural writing, and natural history that offered fresh perspectives on reforming agriculture to help tackle larger social issues. Ellen Nakamura concludes that physicians increasingly studied Chinese botanical treatises with an eye on learning how certain plants could be cultivated to combat famine and related diseases. She notes that in 1756, Takebe Seian, a physician trained in Western medicine, published a study, based upon Ming-period sources, that outlined a botanical approach to fighting famine, a departure from earlier writings on famine that focused on improving governance. Takebe offered practical strategies for samurai rulers and commoners alike to prevent and assuage famine, a constant concern of the era.[45] It is perhaps because of this new intellectual climate that Yoshimune was remembered as promoting domestic ginseng cultivation in order to protect the greater social welfare. Writing in 1790, officials in the area around Nikkō, where much ginseng was produced, concluded that Tokugawa aid, dating back to Yoshimune's time, was necessary to expand domestic production and thereby make ginseng available and affordable.[46]

Yoshimune also played a key role in developing domestic cultivation and production of sugar. In the seventeenth century, large amounts of brown, refined white, and rock sugar were imported into Nagasaki in Chinese and Dutch bottoms. After the Qing gained control of Taiwan in 1683, Chinese ships began to bring Taiwanese sugar to Nagasaki, while the Dutch brought Javanese sugar. The flow of imported sugar continued generally unabated despite import limits imposed by the Shōtoku edicts in 1715.[47] Ever active, the shogun tested a sugar cane crop at his seaside villa and later acquired information about sugar refining from Satsuma officials in Edo. With his encouragement, Owari and Kii in central Honshu, as well as domains in Shikoku and western Honshu, began to cultivate and refine sugar cane, complementing production in Ryukyu and the Amami islands. By mid-century, middling samurai households counted sugar as a necessity along with bean paste (*miso*), sugar, and tea.[48] The success of domestic sugar production became especially clear just after 1800 when observers commented that consumption of domestic sugar had surpassed that of imported varieties.[49]

Although Yoshimune was apparently less personally involved, domestic silk production also increased in central Honshu and other areas. Many of these areas produced not only silk yarn but also developed silk weaving enterprises, emblematic of an expansion of production in rural areas at the expense of urban ones. For example, Kären Wigen notes

---

45. Ellen Nakamura, *Practical Pursuits*, 116–17.
46. Imamura, *Ninjin-shi*, vol. 2, 511–12.
47. Davidson, *The Island of Formosa*, 445; Mazumdar, *Sugar and Society in China*, 99.
48. Vaporis, "Samurai and Merchant in Mid-Tokugawa Japan," 213.
49. Iwao, "Edo jidai no satō bōeki ni tsuite," 17.

that the end of Chinese imports spurred the development of sericulture and silk reeling in the southern Shinano region (present-day Nagano prefecture), industries that expanded in the late eighteenth and nineteenth centuries.[50] The increased domestic production contributed to the decline of the Nishigin district in Kyoto, whose craftsmen had thrived making silkwares with predominately Chinese yarn since the early seventeenth century.[51]

Conclusions

By the 1750s, Tokugawa initiatives, coupled with changing global contexts, made Japanese foreign trade look quite different than it had when the *bakufu* began its reaction against globalization just over a century before. Successive Tokugawa leaders had displayed the ability to move proactively to create new methods of interaction with the China market, first by making Satsuma and Tsushima trade channels. They later showed the same flair in forming the institutional means, particularly through the creation of the Nagasaki clearing-house, to limit silver outflows while continuing foreign trade. It was again evident in Yoshimune's program of localization. To be sure, anti-foreign trade views in the decades around 1700, represented most prominently by Arai Hakuseki, as well as the debasement of currency, contributed to the decline in the total volume of Japanese foreign trade.

Yet as we look at the century overall, we see a Tokugawa regime making decisions based not upon ideology but rather a series of agendas related to the governance of the Japanese realm: the need to assure the flow of goods through Nagasaki, to sustain a "Japan-centered world" in diplomacy, as well as to gain intelligence as part of defending the realm. As the Tokugawa regime pursued these agendas, it had to work with Satsuma and Tsushima at almost every step. Because of the interdependent nature of the larger system of foreign relations, the domains were generally able, when their agency gained in the mid-seventeenth century was threatened, to force the Tokugawa to compromise and make concessions to their positions in trade and diplo-

---

50. Wigen, *The Making of Japanese Periphery*, 97–98.
51. Innes, "The Door Ajar," vol. II, 503.

macy. Moreover, we see how, especially for Satsuma, obtaining profit from trade through Ryukyu involved another set of accommodations and compromises with the kingdom. While the nature of domain-*bakufu* relations would continue to evolve, by the early eighteenth century, Satsuma and Tsushima had successfully articulated and later defended their places within the larger system of foreign relations.

THREE

Guarded Engagement

The year 1764 was a watershed for foreign relations in which Tokugawa leaders decisively moved from reacting to the challenges of the earlier global commercial and cultural waves. Instead, they began to interact with the outside world based on a judiciously selected framework of guarded engagement that would define Tokugawa policy until the mid-nineteenth century. After 1764, *bakufu* leaders established foreign trade practices that effectively ended silver exports while continuing to fulfill the interconnected Tokugawa agendas of supporting the Nagasaki merchant community and maintaining the flow of medicinal products into Japan. Also presenting a guarded diplomatic stance, they reduced the size and scale of diplomatic contacts, seeing the financial cost of receiving embassies as outweighing the political benefits. Finally, Tokugawa leaders, imbued with a new commercial spirit, aggressively engaged in foreign trade and exploited a new global commercial context. Like their contemporaries in coastal regions throughout East and Southeast Asia, the Tokugawa leadership directed that marine products—sea cucumbers, abalone, and kelp—be harvested expressly for the China market, no longer viewing them merely as substitutes for silver and copper.

Guarded engagement also did not bring stasis in domestic trade but was defined by Japanese commercial penetration into Ezo in the north and Ryukyu in the south. These frontiers of the Japanese state became increasingly important sources for products traded and consumed within Japan, as well as for goods exported to China. In Ezo, marine products were harvested and processed for the China market. In the south,

Satsuma increased its commercial dominance over the northern Ryukyu chain, establishing sugar plantations on Amami Ōshima and two other islands. By the end of the eighteenth century, Satsuma sold large amounts of Ryukyu brown sugar on the Osaka market. Japanese commercial interests were clearly moving beyond the economic and geographic boundaries of the seventeenth century.[1]

1764 as a Trade Watershed

On an autumn day in 1764, *bakufu* officials set alight a sizeable cache (450 *kin*, 270 kilograms or 595 pounds) of contraband "Canton ginseng" outside the Chinese Residence in Nagasaki. Responding to Japanese demand, Chinese merchants had introduced this new type of ginseng during the previous two decades. Although it was popular, the medicinal value of this ginseng was questioned by physicians and botanists, as it differed from accepted varieties. By 1763, these experts had convinced *bakufu* officials to ban imports of Canton ginseng. After all, it was not grown in China, the trusted source for medicines. Instead, Amerindians harvested the wild ginseng in North American forests and sold it to Europeans, who shipped the root to Canton.[2]

Although the fire was a small event in itself, the incident points to several larger trends that contributed to the development of guarded engagement. First, there is the institutional trend: the effectiveness of Tokugawa institutions to regulate foreign trade at Nagasaki. In 1698, *bakufu* leaders had created the clearing-house primarily to limit unsanctioned exports of silver. In subsequent decades, the clearing-house, in conjunction with the Nagasaki magistrate, had battled endemic smuggling in and around Nagasaki as part of its regulatory effort. For *bakufu* officials, the fire was therefore a public demonstration to Nagasaki and Chinese merchants of their determination and ability to stop smuggling. At the same time, consistent with the pursuit of upholding the

---

1. Bruce Batten notes that the weakness of the indigenous societies in Hokkaido and Ryukyu vis-à-vis those in Japan made expansion easier along a north-south axis than to the west, where comparatively stronger states existed on the Korean peninsula and in other parts of the Asian mainland. Batten, *To the Ends of Japan*, 49.

2. Nagasaki shiyakusho, ed., *Nagasaki sōsho*, vol. 2, 189.

greater social good, they declared that questionable medicinal goods had been burned to protect Japanese from bogus products.[3]

Second, the fire illustrates how eighteenth-century Japanese foreign trade continued to intersect with global trade channels emerging from proto-globalization. Because of the pull of the China market, Amerindians harvested and processed ginseng, a product they did not consume, for a consumer on the other side of the globe. In 1764, Peter Collinson, an English naturalist, asserted that Chinese demand had prompted a wholesale and destructive harvest of naturally growing ginseng in the forests of what would become Canada. He lamented, "all the mountainous and uncultivated country was ransacked for this valuable root, and imported hither by hogsheads full, and the market in China glutted with this root." Echoing the concerns of Japanese physicians, Collinson also believed that the ginseng "had been artfully concealed and prepared by the Chinese, and sold under secrecy to the great people for true Chinese Ginseng."[4]

The third and most influential trend evident in the fire is the success of Yoshimune's effort to produce at home major imports: ginseng, silk, and sugar. By 1764, Japanese could purchase both domestic and imported ginseng. Because of the increased domestic supply, *bakufu* officials began advocating the use of home-grown ginseng. Just four months before the fire, they had urged the shogun's private physicians to prescribe domestic instead of Korean ginseng.[5]

In foreign trade, the increased domestic production shifted imports away from bulk goods such as sugar and silk. Because of this move and continuing *bakufu* restrictions, fewer but often larger Chinese ships called at Nagasaki: from 22 in 1754 to 15 in 1764. Over the remainder of the century, an average of 11 Chinese merchant ships arrived annually in Nagasaki.[6] As before Chinese merchants still brought a variety of lucrative, specialty goods, such as tortoiseshells, sandalwood, candles,

---

3. Ibid.
4. L.W. Dillwyn, *Hortus Collinsonianus* (Swansea, 1843), 37. Quoted in Appleby, "Ginseng and the Royal Society," 131.
5. Imamura, *Ninjin-shi*, vol. 2, 496–99.
6. Nagazumi, ed., *Tōsen yushutsunyūhin suryō ichiran*, 5; Jansen, *China in the Tokugawa World*, 33–34.

ivory, and Persian leather.⁷ They also imported medicinal roots, herbs, and oils used to treat over 400 ailments. Prominent medicinal imports included: China root, from a plant akin to sarsaparilla, used, for one, to combat venereal disease; Chinese rhubarb, a dried root stock from a Chinese perennial (*rhei rhizome, daiō* in Japanese) used for stomach ailments; and skullcap root, from a plant in the mint family, prescribed as a diuretic to treat edema and depression (Tsushima also imported a Korean variety of skullcap root). These medicinal products, even in small amounts, fetched high prices on the Japanese domestic market, helping to maintain Tokugawa profits although fewer ships were calling.⁸ For their part, VOC ships also imported pharmacopoeia as well as various European manufacturers, such as glasswares, fire pumps and watches, special ordered by the shogun or *bakufu* officials. They also brought printed cotton calicos, which in the late eighteenth century began to be chiefly European, displacing the previous dominance of Indian textiles.⁹

The emergence of guarded engagement is even more prominently illustrated in the end of silver exports through Tsushima and Nagasaki, through which large volumes had flowed since the early seventeenth century. *Bakufu* leaders apparently did not pursue a direct strategy in relation to Tsushima, but their continued debasement policies led to the de facto elimination of silver exports. Hoping to stabilize prices for rice and other goods, Yoshimune ordered the minting in 1736 of new gold and silver coins, the latter of which had only 46 percent purity. With domestic production of silk and ginseng increasing, the *bakufu* no longer needed to support Tsushima's trade in these goods. It therefore ended the domain's access to a special ingot of 80 percent purity. As a result, by some accounts the domain shipped at best an annual

---

7. "Meian chōhōki" [A Record of an Investigation during the Meiwa and An'ei Eras] in Nagasaki kenshi hensan iinkai, ed., *Nagasaki kenshi, shiryōhen*, vol. 4, 476–77. The source provides useful insights on the sales of imported goods on the domestic market. It is believed to have been compiled several decades after the Meiwa and An'ei periods (1764–81) for which it is named. *Nagasaki kenshi, shiryōhen*, vol. 4, 7.

8. Yamawaki, *Nagasaki no Tōjin bōeki*, 236–37; Ren, *Kinsei Nihon to Nitchū bōeki*, 295.

9. Ishida, "Edo jidai no sarasa yunyū," 75–77; Chaiklin, *Cultural Commerce and Dutch Commercial Culture* is a thorough study of the import of European manufactures.

Fig. 9 Goods being offloaded from a Chinese merchant ship in Nagasaki harbor, from a late eighteenth-century illustrated scroll. Numerous Nagasaki officials, wearing the two swords of their samurai status, are shown on board the vessel observing and supervising the transfer of goods to smaller shore-based craft, which transported the goods to the harbor area. Several Chinese, distinguished by their hats, are also aboard one of the official harbor boats in the background. *Nagasaki tōkan kōeki zukan* [Illustrated scroll of trade at the Nagasaki Chinese residence]. Courtesy of Kobe City Museum.

average of 509 *kan* in silver although domain officials later reported that they exported no silver in the decade after 1736. In any case, Tsushima's silver exports were clearly declining, and during the Hōreki period (1751–64), the domain gradually discontinued shipments, switching instead to copper.[10]

Although no specific order was apparently issued, for all intents and purposes *bakufu* officials ended silver exports through Nagasaki in

---

10. Tashiro, *Kinsei Nitchō tsūkō bōekishi no kenkyū*, 323–29. In a request for aid in 1746, Tsushima claimed that it had not been able to export silver after the 1736 devaluation. "Gotaigan kiroku no uchinukigaki," Sō-ke bunko shiryō, kirokurui III 43 ukagaisho, held in the Tsushima Rekishi Minzoku Shiryōkan, Tsushima. I thank Tsuruta Kei for providing me with a transcribed copy of this document and for sharing his conclusions on the issue.

1763 when they moved to instead import silver and gold from abroad (a trade that will be explored below).[11] This move was made possible by the success of domestic production of ginseng, silk, and sugar. In the autumn of the same year, the *bakufu* also reduced the outflow of copper, another export mainstay since the early seventeenth century. Nagasaki officials informed Chinese and Dutch merchants that because copper mines in Akita in northern Honshu were exhausted, their annual export quotas of the metal would be reduced. The *bakufu* later allowed the Dutch to export only 800,000 *kin* of copper, a 300,000 *kin* reduction, and forced the Chinese to cut their quota by 200,000 *kin*.[12] Thereafter the Nagasaki clearing-house still used copper in trade with Dutch and Chinese merchants, but in decreasing volume.

Yet as it reduced the outflow of precious metals, the Tokugawa regime did not turn its back to trade. As economic historian Ryuto Shimada reveals, the *bakufu* pursued a sophisticated policy of manipulating copper prices to assure profits for the clearing-house and the Tokugawa treasury, even with the drop in export volume. He points out that Tokugawa officials directed that mines sell copper for export at prices substantially lower than what mines required simply to recoup production costs. Shimada concludes that mines recovered losses accrued in sales to the *bakufu* by charging higher prices to domestic buyers. In turn, the Nagasaki clearing-house provided copper to Dutch merchants at rates markedly lower than the acquisition price. He believes that the clearing-house made up for this shortfall because it acquired imports at prices far lower than the value of the goods on the Japanese market. The clearing-house could therefore garner substantial profits when it sold imports to Nagasaki merchants. Shimada emphasizes that the *bakufu* implemented this complex price structure in order to assure a steady level of trade through Nagasaki that would safeguard the livelihoods of Tokugawa officials and the people of Nagasaki.[13]

The *bakufu* decision to limit copper exports reverberated overseas, contributing to the expansion of copper mining in Yunnan in southern

---

11. Yamawaki, *Nagasaki no Tōjin bōeki*, 319.
12. Blussé and Remmelink, ed., *The Deshima Diaries, 1740–1800*, 295.
13. Shimada, *The Intra-Asian Trade in Japanese Copper*, 57–59.

Guarded Engagement 79

Fig. 10 Goods from the Chinese ship are brought to the Chinese Warehouse, where they are inspected. *Nagasaki tōkan kōeki zukan* [Illustrated scroll of trade at the Nagasaki Chinese residence]. Courtesy of Kobe City Museum.

Fig. 11 The goods are then placed in the storage facilities. *Nagasaki tōkan kōeki zukan* [Illustrated scroll of trade at the Nagasaki Chinese residence]. Courtesy of Kobe City Museum.

China, where by 1800, roughly 500,000 were involved in the mining industry. Chinese also set up mines in West Borneo and Vietnam. (In the 1760s, the Trinh regime of northern Vietnam, or Dai Viet, earned half of its revenue from levies placed on Chinese mines.) The growth in mining was part of a larger surge in Chinese commercial activity in mainland and insular Southeast Asia. To meet Chinese demand, Southeast Asian states increased production of spices and foodstuffs. Because of this surge in commerce, some historians have dubbed the eighteenth century the "Chinese century" in Southeast Asia.[14]

China asserted such economic influence because Qing territorial expansion and tremendous population growth revitalized the Chinese economy in the eighteenth century. The population increase resulted largely from the introduction of New World crops, especially the sweet potato, maize, and peanuts, which proved easy to grow and nutritious. More Chinese meant that global trade networks focused anew on the China market and huge amounts of South American silver once again flowed into China. Dennis Flynn and Arturo Giráldez assert that after 1700, Spanish American mines increased production to meet Chinese demand, creating a new surge of silver flowing into the Middle Kingdom that tapered off only around 1750.[15]

More Chinese consumers created a greater demand for luxury goods including marine products, which were used in haute cuisine and as medicines. Kelp was sold as an alternative to vegetables and shark fins were used to make a variety of soups. In Sichuan province, sea cucumbers and camel meat were key ingredients in a popular stew. In some Chinese regions, kelp was believed to be a cure for syphilis, while sea cucumbers were known as the "ginseng of the sea."[16] Fishers and merchants in coastal areas throughout the Pacific and Indian Oceans began to harvest and process sea cucumbers, abalone, and shark fins, expressly for export to China. In the early eighteenth century, trepang (from the Malay word *trīpang*), a variety of sea cucumber, began to flow into the VOC-controlled port of Makassar on the island of Sulawesi. In the 1770s, the trade surged with an average of nearly 80,000 pieces shipped annually from the port mainly to Amoy (Xiamen) but also to Batavia (on Java, the main VOC port in Southeast Asia) for transshipment to Canton.[17] Because demand remained steady, fishing grounds around

---

14. Reid, "Chinese Trade and Southeast Asian Economic Expansion in the late 18th and early 19th Centuries," 23–24.
15. Flynn and Giráldez, "Cycles of Silver," 405–8.
16. Yano, *Awabi*, 112–16; Tsurumi, *Namako no me*, 372.
17. Knaap and Sutherland, *Monsoon Traders*, 146–47.

Makassar became less productive. In response, south Sulawesi fishers started to sail regularly to points on the coast of Arnhem Land in northern Australia to harvest and process trepang, a product they did not consume.[18] Another intriguing flow of marine products existed in the overland trade from Burma to western China. Gradually following trade eastward from their original bases in western parts of Asia, Armenian merchant families established a presence in Burma by the eighteenth century. These Armenians, who presumably also did not consume marine products, acquired sea cucumbers and bird's nests and sold them to Chinese merchants.[19]

The English East India Company also sought to gain a share of the growing marine products trade. Beginning in the 1760s, the Company focused its efforts on expanding sales of British produced goods in India and Southeast Asia, as well as in untapped markets in the Qing Empire. Many Company officials hoped that Tibet and northern China would prove "vents" for British woolens and in so doing allow the Company to obtain tea and other Chinese goods without using precious silver. Such trade remained elusive, first because of the limited appeal of British woolens to the Chinese and because Qing leaders allowed trade only at the southern port of Canton. Alexander Dalrymple was apparently the first Company official to conceive of creating an entrepôt, strategically located on Asian trading routes, which would solve the dilemma of the trade with China.[20] Under his initiative and supervision, in 1763 the Company obtained the island of Balambangan just north of Borneo in the Sulu Sea and attempted to draw not only Company vessels and English country traders (merchants engaged in private commerce between India, insular Southeast Asia, and China), but Chinese and other Asian merchant ships to the island. Dalrymple envisioned that Asian traders would bring agar-agar, shark fins, cowries, bird's nets, and pearls, which would attract Chinese junks to Balambangan bearing tea, silks, and porcelain. With such a trade, the Company could obtain Chinese goods, without using bullion, and ship them for

---

18. Macknight, *The Voyage to Marege'*, 1–16.
19. Bayly, "Archaic and Modern Globalization in the Eurasian and African Arena, ca. 1750–1850," 63.
20. Tagliacozzo, "A Necklace of Fins," 27.

sale on the European market. Dalrymple also hoped that Chinese ships would bring Chinese immigrants, with their knowledge of Asian trading networks and the Chinese market, to settle the island and to supervise much of the trade. When the settlement was finally established on the island in 1773, Dalrymple was no longer a Company employee, having been dismissed in a salary dispute. John Herbert, the self-seeking commander of the outpost, never effectively developed the entrepôt model and more importantly clumsily tended relations with the Sultan of Sulu. After a series of incidents, a cousin of the Sultan led a successful attack on the island in 1775, ending the Company presence there.[21]

The Commutation Act of 1784, which dramatically reduced British tariffs on imported Chinese tea, increased consumption of the beverage in Britain and pushed Company officials to continue the quest to establish an island entrepôt. Based on the Balambangan model, they established a more successful trading base on the island of Penang, off the west coast of the Malay Peninsula, in 1786. With its free port status, the island attracted Company ships, country traders, and native Southeast Asian traders from points throughout insular Southeast Asia, carrying pepper, Indian piece goods, opium, and tin. Merchants also brought sizeable volumes of "Straits produce": betel nut, elephant teeth, and a range of marine products, including trepang, shark fins, and mother-of-pearl.[22] Penang's somewhat distant location from active trade routes further south, as well as piracy along the Malay peninsula, were two key factors that helped to limit the amount of trade through the island.[23] Company and British government officials therefore searched for a more optimal entrepôt location, with many advocating what Westerners called Cochin China, the autonomous kingdom of Đàng Trong ruled by the Nguyễn and composed of what is today central and southern Vietnam.[24] In 1806, John Barrow, a second secretary in the British Admiralty who accompanied Lord Macartney on a British

---

21. Fry, *Alexander Dalrymple (1737–1808) and the Expansion of British Trade*, 36–93; Warren, *The Sulu Zone*, 17–37.
22. Tregonning, *The British in Malaya*, 120–26.
23. Tagliacozzo, "A Necklace of Fins," 28–29.
24. For more on Cochin China (alternatively spelled Cochinchina) in the late eighteenth century, see Li, *Nguyễn Cochinchina*.

diplomatic mission to China (the mission, which also visited Đàng Trong, left Britain in 1792 and returned in 1794), suggested

It would still be a desirable object to accomplish an equalization of trade between this country [England] and China, and thereby put a stop to the annual drain of specie required by the latter. An intimate connection with Cochinchina would, in my opinion, go a great way towards effecting this object. This country furnishes many valuable articles suitable for the China market, and would open a new and very considerable vent for many of our manufactures, and its situation in the direct route from England to China is an unexceptionable consideration. [Barrow goes on to detail the pepper, spices, sugar, rice, and various woods that Cochin China supplied to the China market.] To these productions may be added . . . swallow's nests, which are collected in great abundance on the large cluster of islands running parallel with the coast; the *Bichos do Mar*, or sea-snakes, more properly sea-slugs, and usually called *Trepan* in commercial language [sea cucumbers], which with sharks' fins, *Moluscas* [mollusks such as snails and mussels] or sea-blubbers, and other marine products of a gelatinous quality whether animal or vegetable, are at all times in demand by the Chinese.[25]

Barrow's statement and the Company moves affirm the avid British interest in the China market and the protracted search to find effective bases from which to engage with it. He also makes clear that British officials consistently viewed marine products, along with spices, tin, and a range of luxury goods, as viable substitutes for bullion in the China trade. Overall, the activities of the English East India Company, as well as other European and Asian merchants involved with it, demonstrate the key role that marine products played in late eighteenth- and early nineteenth-century Asian maritime commerce.

Given this context, it is not surprising that *bakufu* leaders, like other actors in the Asian maritime trading world, moved to develop marine products to optimize Japan's trade with China. In the third month of 1764, the Nagasaki magistrate dispatched officials to coastal areas throughout the realm to assess the production potential for sea cucumbers and abalone, followed a year later by a similar order concerning shark fins. Based on these investigations, *bakufu* leaders gauged

---

25. John Barrow, *A Voyage to Cochinchina* (London, 1806), 344–49; quoted in Lamb, ed., "British Missions to Cochin China: 1788–1822," 158.

the amount of marine products a coastal area could produce annually and assessed a levy, stipulating that a given domain would annually sell prescribed amounts of marine products at fixed prices, which were established in 1757. The *bakufu* contracted Nagasaki merchants to assure the delivery of the marine products to Nagasaki.[26]

These steps display definitive aspects of the new framework of guarded engagement: trade to obtain specific goods but restricted to prevent a deleterious outflow of silver. Yet guarded engagement did not mean commercial stagnation. In the watershed year of 1764, the *bakufu* began to use marine products to achieve a new goal: importing silver and gold through Nagasaki. In their particular brand of mercantilism, *bakufu* officials aimed to import Chinese gold and silver—and interestingly, Japanese gold exported in previous decades. To acquire bullion, *bakufu* leaders chose not to reform import quotas, namely the 2,750 *kan* annual limit on Chinese ships, established with the Shōtoku edicts; rather, from 1763 to 1803, the *bakufu* developed 57 different types of supplemental trade quotas. Some quotas permitted Chinese captains, with personal connections with clearing-house officials, to trade beyond their ship's established limit. Others allowed Chinese sailors individually to bring goods for trade or accommodated ships delayed by weather or unforeseen circumstances. Whatever their rationale, most quotas were designed to increase bullion imports. Of the 57, 6 were aimed specifically at importing silver, while 29 were used to import gold. In 1769, the clearing-house also began to receive silver from the VOC. Until 1800, an average of 14 percent of exported copper was exchanged for Dutch silver coins.[27]

Nakamura Tadashi estimates that the supplemental trade encompassed just over 31 percent of the overall trade through Nagasaki in the second half of the eighteenth century. He concludes that *bakufu* leaders used the supplemental trade primarily to support the clearing-house and to increase revenue for the *bakufu* treasury. The clearing-house

---

26. "Nagasaki kaisho gosatsu mono" [The Five Ledger Books of the Nagasaki Clearing-house] in Nagasaki kenshi henshū iinkai, ed. *Nagasaki kenshi, shiryōhen*, vol. 4, 41–42; Arai, *Kinsei kaisanbutsu keizaishi no kenkyū*, 21–27, 75.

27. Nakamura Tadashi, *Kinsei Nagasaki bōekishi no kenkyū*, 423–59; Shimada, *The Intra-Asian Trade in Japanese Copper*, 63.

would impose 35 percent levies on imported gold and 7 to 9 percent tariffs on silver, thereby garnering considerable profits before the bullion was sent to *bakufu* treasuries. Thanks to the levies, the clearinghouse obtained the funds necessary to supply the stipends of officials and day laborers employed by the institution. In addition, the *bakufu* continued to receive profits and thereby uphold its larger agenda in foreign trade. Nakamura calculates that in its inaugural year of 1763, 360 *kan* of gold and silver were imported. The figure jumped to 875 *kan* the following year and to 890 *kan* in 1765 and 1766.[28] Because of the supplemental trade and increased marine product exports after 1764, the overall monetary value of all foreign trade at Nagasaki remained at a fairly constant annual level from 1711 until 1840.[29]

The supplemental trade exemplifies the particular commercial strategies that defined the guarded Tokugawa approach. *Bakufu* leaders sought to trade with the outside world but were reluctant to repeal official restrictions that checked the outflow of silver. They consequently developed the supplemental trade to allow them to regulate trade based upon specific circumstances of a given year. With such a system, they enjoyed the flexibility to work with a trusted Chinese captain or to obtain bullion through a special arrangement, all the while maintaining the rigid official quota. *Bakufu* leaders developed a means to interact with the global market, but in a measured—and for their purposes, more beneficial—manner.

In a larger sense, therefore, guarded engagement emerged because Japanese leaders had finally solved the dilemma of foreign trade that had existed since the seventeenth century: how to trade without being bled of silver. The Japanese realm could benefit by importing valued goods, especially medicinal goods, as well as silver and gold in exchange for products tailored for the China market. Japan remained connected with the vital China market but in a more managed and thus less threatening way.

By increasing marine product exports and bullion imports via the supplemental trade, *bakufu* leaders continued to develop what Conrad Totman terms the "managerial shogunate." Under Yoshimune, the *ba-*

---

28. Nakamura Tadashi, *Kinsei Nagasaki bōekishi no kenkyū*, 447.
29. Yamawaki, *Nagasaki no Tōjin bōeki*, 162–65.

kufu had become more proactive, assuming direct control over many facets of the Japanese economy. Yoshimune enacted sumptuary legislation and began to grant charters to merchants allowing them to establish commercial fiefdoms centered on one product. Merchants established chartered trade associations (*kabu nakama*), which held the production and marketing rights of prominent goods such as cotton, tea, salt, and tobacco with little direct Tokugawa interference. In this arrangement, the *bakufu* forbade non-sanctioned groups from infringing upon the activities of the chartered merchant houses. In exchange, members were expected to pay fees to the *bakufu* and police themselves while also maintaining stability in pricing, supply, and quality.[30]

As part of the managerial policy, subsequent *bakufu* officials established clearing-houses throughout the realm. Staffed by Tokugawa officials, they handled not just acquisition and sales, but also the collection, storage, and transport of specified goods. The Nagasaki clearing-house represented the most important such institution in foreign trade. In turn, *bakufu* officials reorganized existing merchant organizations (*za*) that by virtue of a Tokugawa-sanctioned monopoly, dominated and regulated aspects of the market but with more Tokugawa oversight than the chartered trade associations. As an initial step, the *bakufu* reorganized the respective gold and silver merchant organizations established in the early sixteenth century and allowed them to assert greater control over both the precious metal market and coinage. In 1766, the *bakufu* banned private sales of copper and created a new merchant organization in Osaka that handled not merely the minting of copper but all shipments to Nagasaki. With these steps, *bakufu* officials in Nagasaki were assured a steady stream of copper for the export trade.[31] In the same vein, the *bakufu* established a new ginseng merchant organization in Edo in 1764 to regulate sales of not just imports but also the increasing level of domestic ginseng on the Japanese market. Consistent with earlier policy, *bakufu* officials asserted that the new organization was necessary to ensure the availability of a product vital to the realm's social welfare.[32]

---

30. Totman, *Early Modern Japan*, 300–301.
31. Hall, *Tanuma Okitsugu*, 74–75; Hayashi, ed., *Tsūkō ichiran*, vol. 3, 541–53 (hereafter *TI*).
32. *TI*, vol. 4, 541–53.

Tanuma Okitsugu, who rose to prominence within the *bakufu* leadership in 1767, established still more clearing-houses and merchant organizations, many related to aspects of foreign trade, in an effort to increase fees collected by the Tokugawa regime. In the early 1770s, Kudō Heisuke, a physician from the Sendai domain (composed of Miyagi and parts of Iwate and Fukushima prefectures), presented a memorial to the Nagasaki magistrate, ostensibly about strategies to reduce smuggling of imports, but which provided broader suggestions for how the Tokugawa regime could optimize foreign trade for its benefit. Although it is unclear if Tanuma implemented any of the specific points presented in it, Kudō's memorial underscores that in discourse about foreign trade in the late eighteenth century, the role of merchant organizations and imports of medicinal products were widely discussed. Kudō's views are especially noteworthy because he was a physician who developed a thorough understanding of trade at Nagasaki. Moreover, he was not simply an outside critic but an individual who contributed to formation of Tanuma's policies, particularly vis-à-vis Ezo.

Echoing Arai Hakuseki, Kudō asserted that gold and silver are akin to "bones of the earth," and as such, Japan must limit their outflow. Yet he believed that foreign trade is necessary, suggesting that a fixed amount of copper be annually earmarked to allow Japan to obtain medicinal products "vital to the entire realm." He detailed just how important imported medicines had become throughout Japanese society: from the court nobles who used longan (a fruit used as a tonic and sedative in Chinese medicine), to the chaulmoogra oil available throughout the countryside (used to treat syphilis and Hansen's disease), to the oil made from cardamom seeds prescribed daily by physicians apparently for stomach and intestinal ailments. Kudō concluded that because of their widespread use, medicinal products are the most valuable goods exchanged at Nagasaki and as such have come to be smuggled widely. To limit illicit trade, which he believed allowed silver and gold to surreptitiously flow out of the realm, Kudō urged that merchant organizations for medicinal imports be established in Edo and Osaka, which would receive medicinal products imported at Nagasaki. He claimed that the organizations would control smuggling while allowing the *bakufu* to garner some of the profits lost under the existing system whereby imports were sold to Nagasaki merchants, who in turn shipped them to Edo and Osaka via other merchant houses. Kudō also suggested that the organizations would stabilize prices for medicinal products, thereby helping the disadvantaged of the realm who depended upon them.[33]

Given that existing merchant associations were reformed and many new ones established during the decade and a half that Tanuma dominated the Tokugawa leadership, it is clear that he shared Kudō's zeal for merchant organizations, especially as monetary sources for the Tokugawa treasury. For example, during the Tanuma era, the *bakufu* revived the alum clearing-house, established in 1758 to regulate the product's import through Nagasaki and Ryukyu. The shogunate also issued edicts that gave increased power to the cinnabar merchant organization, which monopolized imports of the red pigment, used as a dye. The monopoly is noteworthy because it regulated cinnabar imported through Nagasaki and through Ryukyuan commercial channels dominated by Satsuma. The Tanuma regime left no commercial stone unturned, exemplified by the creation of a merchant organization to regulate trade in Borneo camphor. Like their Chinese counterparts, Japanese medical practitioners most valued the aromatic crystals naturally found in Borneo's *Dryobalanops aromatica* trees, dubbed Borneo camphor. Dutch and especially Chinese ships brought these natural crystals along with a Chinese, artificially made (a thus cruder version), which was created by steaming parts of other camphor tree and shrub varieties. Using the Chinese technique, enterprising Japanese began to produce a domestic brand of artificial Borneo camphor extracted from the native camphor laurel tree (*Cinnamomum camphora*). In 1768, the shogunate established a merchant organization to regulate sales of imported and domestic-made Borneo camphor. *Bakufu* officials suspended it in 1782 because of widespread adulteration of the domestic, artificial variety.[34]

Tanuma's most enduring move concerning foreign trade came in the creation of an expansive Tokugawa monopoly of the marine product trade. In 1785, just a year before the English East India Company established its trading entrepôt on Penang, Tanuma moved to secure a steady supply of marine products to Nagasaki to buoy imports of bul-

---

33. *TI*, vol. 8, 485–504. I thank Nishizawa Mihoko for bringing this reference to my attention.

34. *TI*, vol. 4, 147–48.

lion. He eliminated the role of merchant houses and directed that the *bakufu* would purchase all kelp, sea cucumbers, abalone, and shark fins destined for export. For this purpose, he created clearing-houses that facilitated the collection, sale, and transport of marine products. Regional offices in the western Honshu port of Shimonoseki, Osaka, Edo, and Hakodate thereafter purchased the key marine products from domains and oversaw their transport to Nagasaki. Tanuma based the new collection system on Tokugawa feudal prerogative: domains were instructed to sell, at the 1757 purchase price, an amount of marine products determined by Tokugawa surveys. The order not only brought a more steady flow of marine products to Nagasaki, but affirmed the commercial supremacy of the Nagasaki clearing-house by directing that it would monopolize exports. The Nagasaki clearing-house quickly garnered increased profits from the supplemental trade: from 795 *kan* in 1784 to 1,432 *kan* annually between 1785 and 1788.[35]

The string of *bakufu* moves in the second half of the eighteenth century suggests the important niche that foreign trade goods held on the domestic market. Although the volume of alum, cinnabar, and Borneo camphor imported into Japan was never great, the retail value of these products, even in small amounts, was significant enough to attract the Tokugawa regulative net. Under Tanuma, the shogunate greatly expanded its involvement in domestic sales of imports as part of a broad effort to enhance the Tokugawa fisc. The encompassing monopoly of the marine product trade represented the capstone of this effort. We can also locate a consistency in *bakufu* policies: attention to flow of medicinal products for the greater social welfare as well as to support Nagasaki's clearing-house and merchant community. The new *bakufu* institutions also began to regulate products imported not only through Tokugawa-controlled Nagasaki but through Satsuma-dominated Ryukyu as well.

The Local Impact

At the local level, producers, officials, and merchants adjusted their agendas and activities based upon the new structures of guarded en-

---

35. *TI*, vol. 4, 130; Nagasaki kenshi henshū iinkai, ed., *Nagasaki kenshi, taigai kōshōhen*, 577–80; Nakamura Tadashi, *Kinsei Nagasaki bōekishi no kenkyū*, 447.

gagement. In the north, fishers and merchants in Matsumae and Ezo, like their counterparts throughout Asia, began to harvest more marine products to supply trade with the China market. For Matsumae, the move was part of a larger transformation of the domain economy. During the preceding decades, Matsumae officials had moved away from an economy centered upon mining and supplying specialty goods, such as hawks, to the Japanese market. Instead, domain officials established a fishing industry, based primarily on herring, which was used as fertilizer throughout Japan. Around the same time, domain and Ainu fishers began to harvest more kelp expressly for export to China. In the 1780s, the Nagasaki clearing-house exported 2,000–5,000 *koku* of kelp annually, much of it harvested in the waters around Hakodate. More sea cucumbers and abalone, destined for Nagasaki, were also collected along the coastlines of Ezo. The harvesting of these two goods boomed, for example, with 79,000 *kin* of sea cucumbers taken in 1788, up from 43,000 *kin* in 1744.[36]

Events in the Sendai domain illustrate how other domain leaders scrambled to fulfill their obligations under the marine product levy. After 1785, Sendai leaders continued to rely on officially contracted merchants to purchase abalone and sea cucumbers from producers in the domain and in turn sell those goods to *bakufu* collection centers. Facing Tokugawa demands, domain leaders first sent officials to coastal villages to pressure individual village leaders to increase production. When this proved ineffective, domain officials eliminated the role of merchants and began to purchase abalone and sea cucumbers directly from coastal villages. This move unquestionably made the harvesting and production of marine products acts of tribute for villagers. When explaining the policy change to leaders of coastal villages, domain officials stressed that the *bakufu* had instructed coastal domains throughout the realm to increase the production of marine products. The officials emphasized that they realized the harvest and production of marine products was "different from usual commercial enterprises" because villagers could expect little personal profit given the *bakufu*'s low purchase prices. They urged village leaders nonetheless to endeavor to increase production in order to meet the Tokugawa demands, implying

---

36. Matsumae chōshi henshūshitsu, ed., *Matsumae chōshi, tsūsetsuhen*, 683.

their production allowed the domain's lord to fulfill his feudal obligations to the Tokugawa and thus benefited the domain overall.[37]

For Tsushima, the implementation of guarded engagement brought a string of challenges. During the first half of the eighteenth century, the domain failed to sustain the surge in agricultural production that followed the deer and boar hunts in the first decade of the eighteenth century. In addition, Tsushima saw its trade profits decline further as increased domestic silk and ginseng production eliminated the need to import Chinese silk and Korean ginseng through the domain. To make up for the resulting financial shortfalls, Tsushima officials borrowed heavily from Osaka and Edo merchants. They also lobbied the *bakufu* to provide financial aid, which it granted in 1746 in the form of an annual 10,000 *ryō* stipend. Because the *bakufu* discontinued the grant three years later, domain officials made fresh appeals in 1750. Different from earlier petitions surrounding currency debasement and trade quotas, Tsushima leaders now pushed *bakufu* officials to provide loans and direct grants to assuage the domain's financial difficulties resulting from the decline in trade with Korea. In 1754, Tokugawa officials recognized Tsushima's need and offered a 15,000 *ryō* loan, followed by a 10,000 *ryō* grant the next year. In 1758, they provided an annual installment of 10,000 *ryō* in loans for five years. With these funds, Tsushima leaders were able to stabilize the domain economy, at least for the time being.[38]

In the 1770s, however, the level of trade continued to decline, leading domain leaders to declare that the private trade had for all intents and purposes, "ceased." In 1772, the Nagasaki magistrate sent an official to investigate the domain's trade with Korea and its overall financial situation. His report was bleak: Tsushima bore an annual loss of just under 1,500 *kan* in trade, which dropped the domain's annual income to only around 23,000 *koku*. In addition, many merchant houses now refused to grant loans because of the domain's failure to repay previous ones. Seeing no other recourse, a high-ranking Sō retainer, Sugimura Naoki, began to petition Tokugawa officials for additional

---

37. Wakamatsu, "Sendai hanryō ni okeru Nagasaki tawaramono no seisan shūka," 325–26.
38. Tsuruta, *Tsushima kara mita Nitchō kankei*, 89.

aid. In 1776, Sugimura convinced them to establish a 12,000 *ryō* annual grant, which continued until 1862. Hailed as a savior by the daimyo, Sugimura was allowed to make further reforms, such as reducing domain expenditures by eliminating over 20 bureaucratic posts and by closing domain offices in Iki (an island between Tsushima and Kyushu), Hakata, and Kyoto. Sugimura also conceived plans to import more Korean ginseng but was stymied by the root's lower sale price on the domestic market, a result of increased production in Japan. Moreover, Korean merchants, perhaps because they earned better profits selling to China, were less inclined to sell ginseng to their Tsushima counterparts.[39]

After ascending to power in 1787 after Tanuma's precipitous exit amidst charges of corruption, a new dominant senior councilor of the shogunate, Matsudaira Sadanobu, began to pressure Tsushima to address its debts owed to both the *bakufu* and to merchants in Edo, Osaka, and Nagasaki. The change of power in Edo prompted heated debate within the Tsushima leadership circle, with one faction continuing to support Sugimura, while others asserting that he should be replaced, fearing his ties to the former Tanuma regime might compromise Tsushima's position. In the end, Sugimura was sacked and a new group of officials formulated plans to tackle the domain's debts. In 1790, the domain presented a revised schedule that included regular payments to the *bakufu* and to merchants over the next decade. While it offered a means to reduce the sums owed to the *bakufu*, the plan aimed to merely whittle down the interest owed to merchants, without even tackling the principal. It also did not account for the costs that the domain bore for duties such as trips to Edo in the system of alternate residence. As a result, the proposal was doomed and Tsushima's debts remained substantial, despite Tokugawa aid.[40]

Tsushima officials were more successful in executing Tokugawa directives to increase harvesting of marine products on the island. They began to ship domain-produced abalone and sea cucumbers to the Nagasaki clearing-house, and thanks in part to advance payments of copper allowed by the *bakufu*, they also imported sea cucumbers from

---

39. Nagasaki kenshi henshū iinkai, ed., *Nagasaki kenshi, hanseihen*, 1044–48.
40. Ibid., 1049–53.

Korea. Indeed the Nagasaki clearing-house began to expect Tsushima to annually deliver more sea cucumbers from Korea (13,000 *kin*) than from Tsushima shores (6,500 *kin*). At Nagasaki, Tsushima exchanged the Korean holothurians for water buffalo horns (used in the official and private trades with the Chosŏn Kingdom), and sold the remainder to the clearing-house, which in turn exported them to China.[41]

Around 1800, domain officials saw shipments of domain-produced marine products fall between 17 and 25 percent. The shortfalls arose because Tsushima fishers grew dissatisfied with the financial returns from harvesting marine products and turned instead to more lucrative whaling. Domain officials initially responded by dramatically increasing imports from Korea. Tsushima officials also invited fishers from the Hiroshima and Hirado domains to harvest abalone and sea cucumbers on domain shores. By offering the sojourners a lower purchase price than their domain counterparts, the domain was able to increase production, and in turn enjoy an enhanced profit margin. Tsushima fishers, however, took umbrage at the fact that outsiders were now fishing in previously protected fishing grounds. Amidst these protests, Tsushima was forced to offer higher prices to domain fishers, thereby mitigating any profits gained through transactions with the Hiroshima and Hirado fishers.[42]

Tsushima officials also tried persistently to develop new avenues for trade. They began to obtain more of a Korean variety of skullcap root, which had been long been imported but in small quantities. During the Edo period, Japanese apparently differentiated between Korean and Chinese varieties, although both were harvested from a plant in the mint family. The domain also began to import Korean cowhides. Although many of the hides were shipped to the Japanese domestic market to be used in making armor, the trade in hides, as Tsukada Takashi argues, was actually part of an effort to diversify the domain economy by developing a sandal-making industry on the island. He points out that as early as 1789, Tsushima peasants began to make leather sandals, which were sold in the domain. Sensing an opportunity

---

41. Nagasaki kenshi henshū iinkai, ed., *Nagasaki kenshi, hanseihen*, 1041–42; Ogawa, "Tsushima han no tawaramono seisan to tōsei," 54–58, 66.

42. Ogawa, "Tsushima-han no tawaramono seisan to tōsei," 66–71.

to sell sandals on the Osaka market, the domain leadership made plans to bring a large number of outcasts to Tsushima from domain lands in Kyushu. The domain planned to employ them in the manufacture of sandals using Tsushima produced and imported Korean leather. In the end, opposition from Tsushima peasants who refused to work with the outcasts put an end to this intriguing plan.[43]

If we consider Tsushima's overall situation at the end of the eighteenth century, its agency was clearly diminished. Domain officials were no longer able to convince Tokugawa leaders to revise currency policies and trade practices in ways beneficial to the domain; instead, they received financial help, a trend that would continue in subsequent decades.

Satsuma, with its larger and more diverse economy, felt less economic pain despite the declining returns on its sales of Chinese silk thread and silk damask on the domestic market through its sanctioned wholesaler in Kyoto. Nevertheless, domain leaders sought new trade avenues and succeeded in expanding shipments of camphor to domestic and foreign markets. Although also obtained by steaming chips of camphor laurel tree, in the case of camphor, the crystalline extract was manipulated to have a more solid, gum-like consistency than artificial Borneo camphor crystals. Utilizing the domain's large stands of the tree, Satsuma shipped some camphor to Osaka for domestic distribution. The Dutch also purchased large amounts of Satsuma camphor (packed in tubs) at Nagasaki. Valued especially as a medicinal good, the VOC could readily sell Japanese camphor on European markets and in India, where the company garnered a 20 percent profit. Following the end of silver exports, camphor emerged as an export substitute along with copper and marine products. To exploit the trade, Satsuma established an office that encouraged production and also oversaw the collection of camphor within the domain as well as shipments to Nagasaki. Although its trade volume never rivaled that of other exports, camphor did provide Satsuma with consistent revenue, estimated at 1,000 *ryō* annually. Records are spotty for exports on Chinese ships, but it appears that 1765 was a banner year for the domain, with 160,000 *kin* exported, of which 150,000 came from Sa-

---

43. Tsukuda, "Ajia ni okeru ryō to sen," 256–60.

tsuma. Although exports dropped in later decades, Satsuma continued to ship camphor to Nagasaki until the 1860s.⁴⁴

Satsuma created an even more profitable enterprise by developing sugar cane farming and sugar production on three domain islands in the Amami chain: Ōshima, Tokunoshima, and Kikaijima. The domain established a series of official posts to oversee production, and approximately 1.13 million *kin* (678 metric tons) of Ryukyu brown sugar was sold on the domestic market in 1713. In 1745, the domain ordered the islanders to pay their tribute taxes in brown sugar instead of rice, dramatically reducing their amount of subsistence farming. This policy brought disaster in 1755, when 3,000 residents of Tokunoshima died in a famine that resulted when the sugar cane crop failed. Despite the tragedy, Satsuma leaders aimed to extract greater amounts of sugar. In 1777, the domain instituted measures whereby it would directly purchase all sugar, beyond what was shipped to Kagoshima as tribute, produced on the Amami islands. Domain leaders apparently later deemed the direct purchase arrangement too harsh and eliminated it a decade later. In its place, they allowed island residents to exchange sugar for rice and other necessary foodstuffs at a rate that afforded a reasonably better living standard. Despite their softened stance, Satsuma leaders had established a structure of colonial extraction in Amami. Islanders were forced to forgo most subsistence agriculture and instead focus on farming and refining sugar, from which Satsuma gained profits through sales on the domestic market.⁴⁵

It is useful here to consider global contexts, in this case colonial production of sugar in other parts of the eighteenth-century world. For one, Satsuma's development of sugar plantations in Ryukyu paralleled trends in the Caribbean. On Jamaica and Barbados, for example, British colonial officials created plantations where workers were forced to cultivate, harvest, and process sugar cane. As was the case with the Satsuma and Amami relationship, the British profited not only by selling Caribbean sugar on the British market (where increasing amounts were

---

44. *KK*, vol. 2, 543–53; Yokoyama, "Japan and Ryukyu in the Bakumatsu Period," 51. Miyashita details the subtle differences between camphor and artificial Borneo camphor in *Nagasaki bōeki to Ōsaka*, 13–41.

45. Haraguchi and Nagayama, et al., *Kagoshima-ken no rekishi*, 215–16.

being consumed), but also by shipping in return food and other consumables produced in the British Isles and in their American colonies.[46]

Of course, there are important differences between the British and Japanese cases, such as the fact that Japanese consumed less sugar than their British counterparts. More significantly, Satsuma did not use indentured servants or imported slave labor but instead successfully exploited the resident population. By contrast, British planters initially sought to use native labor but failed, partly because disease ravaged the Amerindian population. As a result, they tried first without success, to employ indentured servants before eventually importing slave labor from Africa.[47] The case can be made that at least in the south, the geographic limits and nature of Japanese colonial enterprises were defined by Satsuma's success in exploiting native labor, which thereby mitigated the need to obtain imported labor, as was the case with the British.

Satsuma leaders also developed ways to tap the resources of Ryukyu, where production of sugar and turmeric (*ukon*, used as a yellow dye) had become important sectors of the kingdom's economy. They ordered the Ryukyu court to focus less energy on importing Chinese silk and instead deliver more sugar to Satsuma. Although the annual level is unclear, Ryukyu ships brought increasing amounts of sugar to Kagoshima that were sold within the domain and by Satsuma agents on the Osaka market.[48]

Ryukyu had increased production under the guidance of a more proactive leadership, which based its policies upon Confucian ideals to a greater extent than in the seventeenth century. Historian Gregory Smits explains how Sai On, a prominent official, instituted policies that allowed the kingdom's leaders to assert more control over the populace, and by implication, their harvests.[49] At the same time, the royal government created measures to profit also from the bounty of the seas. In 1758, Ryukyu officials instituted an internal tribute system whereby the Yaeyama island group (Ishigaki, Iriomote, and Yonaguni) sent sea

---

46. Mintz, *Sweetness and Power*, 52–61. Mintz also outlines the growth of sugar consumption in Britain (108–50).
47. Williams, *Capitalism and Slavery*, 7–9.
48. Fukuse, "Ryukyu-kan ni miru Satsuryū kankei," 49.
49. Smits, *Visions of Ryukyu*, 117–18. For example, Smits explores Sai On's measures to improve the management of Ryukyu's forests (103–8).

cucumbers as tribute to the capital at Shuri on the main island of Okinawa. This measure complemented existing flows of shark skins and fins, also used in the tribute trade with China. As the flow of sea cucumbers from Yaeyama gradually increased, a powerful tsunami devastated the islands in 1771, killing an estimated 10,000 people. Yaeyama and its shipments of sea cucumbers to Okinawa did not recover until the early nineteenth century. Despite the setback, Ryukyu leaders continued to carve out lucrative commercial enterprises apart from the dictates of Satsuma.[50]

Russian Probes

In 1763, for the first time a Japanese merchant ship journeyed to Kunashiri in the Kuril Islands, a trip emblematic of increasing Japanese commercial penetration in Ezo. While kelp, abalone, and sea cucumbers were harvested in areas further north, the commercial herring fishery, which grew in scale over the course of the second half of the eighteenth century, primarily drove this northern economic expansion. Japanese and Ainu fishers harvested increasing amounts of herring for shipment to the Japanese market. As David Howell shows, the fishery emerged from the overlap of two regional economies: a labor economy, which included Ainu and Japanese and encompassed all of Hokkaido, northernmost Honshu, and parts of the Japan Sea coast; and a marketing economy that extended the length of the Japan Sea coast, the Inland Sea region, as well as Osaka and other areas in central Japan.[51] Meanwhile, in 1765, a handful of Russian merchant adventurers moved from the Kamchatka Peninsula into the northern Kuril Islands, an area still largely unknown to the Japanese. The following year, Russians ventured further south to Etorofu, where they explored commercial opportunities and gauged the Japanese presence. In subsequent years, Russians made more frequent contact with Ainu and Matsumae merchants in the Kurils.[52] The Russians' choice to make the long and perilous journey to Kamchatka and the Kurils was motivated by the sizeable financial reward available on the world market for furs. In

---

50. Maehira, "Ryukyu ōkoku ni okeru kaisanbutsu bōeki," 228–30.
51. Howell, *Capitalism From Within*, 14.
52. Matsumae chōshi henshūshitsu, ed., *Matsumae chōshi nenpyō*, 231–37.

Siberia, Russians merchants had established tribute relationships with native peoples as a means to obtain beaver and other valuable pelts, which could be sold in China and Europe. They began to form similar relationships with Kuril Ainu.[53]

Russian merchants in the Pacific and especially officials in the capital of St. Petersburg hoped to extend trade further south. Japanese castaways who ended up in Russia had described their homeland as rich in gold and silver, while Russian envoys in Beijing reported that the Dutch trade at Nagasaki consisted primarily of the exchange of skins for Japanese gold, silver, and porcelains. These rumors led many Russians to speculate that they might be able to sell furs on the Japanese market in exchange for gold and silver.[54]

Such interest helped prompt the court at St. Petersburg to send Adam Laxman as its official envoy to Japan in 1792. Bringing Japanese castaways for repatriation, he called at Nemuro, on the eastern part of Ezo Island (Hokkaido), stating that he wished permission to travel to Edo to appeal his case for an opening of commercial relations. Matsumae officials stalled for time, while back in Edo, Matsudaira Sadanobu considered his options. In the summer of 1793, Matsudaira decreed that Laxman could not deliver the Japanese castaways to Edo and would not be allowed to negotiate for an opening of commercial ties in Matsumae. He declared that negotiations could only take place at Nagasaki and offered a permit that allowed the bearer to enter the port at a future date. Laxman reluctantly departed, although he remained optimistic that the permit would allow a future Russian mission to establish commercial ties with Japan.

In 1804, the Russian government tried again, this time sending Nikolai Rezanov to Nagasaki, bearing the permit that Laxman had received. Officials in St. Petersburg stressed that Rezanov's most pressing task was the establishment of trade with Japan, which Russian leaders believed was now more possible because of the weakness of the Dutch

---

53. Walker, *The Conquest of Ainu Lands*, 162–63.
54. Lensen, *The Russian Push Toward Japan*, 41.

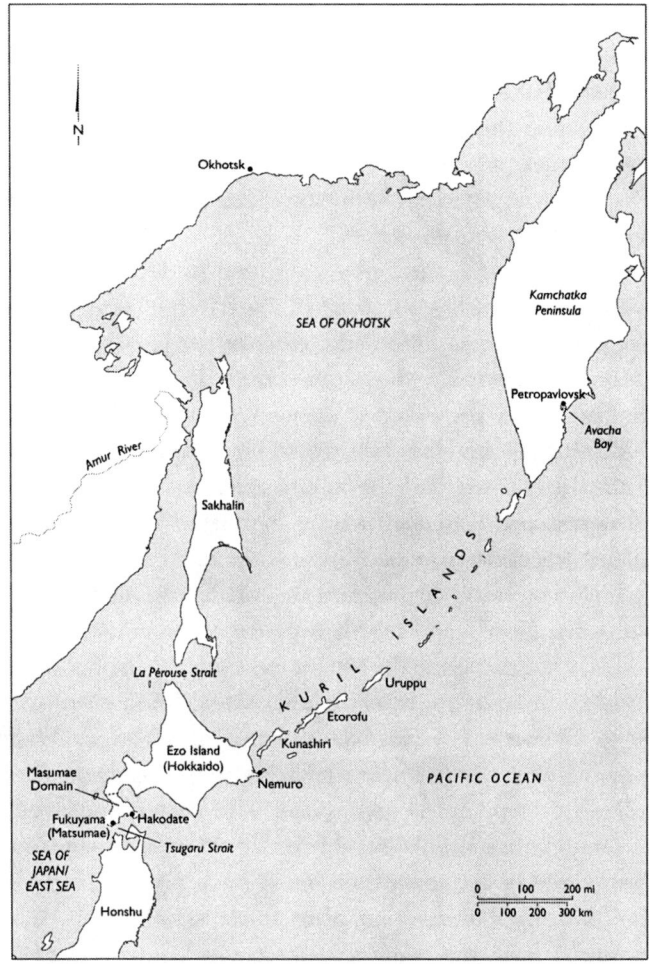

Map 6 Matsumae, Ezo, and Russian outposts in the late Edo period

commercial empire in Southeast and East Asia in the wake of the Napoleonic Wars. He was instructed to explain to the Japanese that Russian ships could bring furs, walrus and elephant tusks, fish, leather goods, and woolen cloth to be exchanged for rice, copper, and silk.[55] Russian officials hoped trade with Japan could bring profit and simultaneously supply colonies in the Pacific by acquiring rice and other

---

55. Rezanov, *Nihon taizai nikki*, 383.

foodstuffs. Some Russians conceived of even more expansive commerce. On the eve of the embassy's departure, a Russian newspaper opined that: "If the embassy will succeed in its intention, we will get from Japan some things much better than from China. Japanese tea, porcelain, lacquer, silk and cotton materials are better than Chinese ones. The Russian American Company [chartered in 1799] can obtain them in exchange for its goods."[56]

Others involved with the embassy aspired to develop a global trading network akin to what the English East India Company was then developing. A few years before the embassy to Japan, Captain Adam Johann von Krusenstern, who commanded the two vessels of Rezanov's embassy, had presented a detailed proposal for establishing a Russian global trade network that would benefit particularly from trade with China. In his proposal, he emphasized that Russian colonies in North America and Kamchatka were hampered by their dependence on overland transport routes. Krusenstern described how food and supplies, including heavy rigging and anchors for the ships that sailed to Kamchatka, the Kurils, and North America, were annually transported across Siberia to the coastal outpost of Okhotsk using upwards of 4,000 horses. In addition, Russian ships would bring North American furs first to Okhotsk. The furs would then be shipped, at considerable cost, to an inland outpost where they were sold to Chinese merchants, a process that took nearly two years. Krusenstern believed that a chain of maritime trade links would reduce the cost of supplying Russian colonies and at the same time boost trade profits for the Russian America Company. He drew up plans for Russian vessels, laden with supplies, to sail from the Baltic directly to the Aleutians and Alaska to provision Russian America Company outposts. The ships could then fill their hulls with furs and sail directly to Canton, where the furs would be exchanged for Chinese wares, which could be sold for handsome profits on the Russian and European markets. Krusenstern concluded that if the ships could not procure a full cargo in Canton, they could stop at Manila, Batavia, and Indian ports to acquire still more goods to sell. Krusenstern contended that if this network could be established, "the Russian American Company could not fail of becoming

---

56. Lensen, *The Russian Push Toward Japan*, 128.

in time of so much importance that the smaller East Indian Companies of Europe would not be able to stand in competition with it."[57]

These plans were hampered by the pitiful state of Russian colonies in Kamchatka and North America, where food and basic supplies were scarce. In 1805, Krusenstern visited Kamchatka and was shocked by the conditions there:

> Nothing is visible here that could at all persuade any one of its being inhabited by civilized people: not only at Awatscha [Avacha] bay, but the three adjoining ones are entirely forlorn and uninhabited; nor is the beautiful harbor of St. Peter and St. Paul [Petropavlovsk] enlivened by a single boat. Instead the shores are strewed with stinking fish, among which a number of half starved dogs are seen wallowing and contending for possession.

After noting his despair at the wreck of a ship in the harbor and the few dilapidated buildings of the harbor area, Krusenstern adds:

> As the greater part of the inhabitants are from Sachalin [Sakhalin], and are absent during the whole day, you may remain here several hours without meeting a single person; and in the pale emaciated countenances of those you do at length perceive, it is not easy to recognize the descendants of the heroic Von Rimnik, and of Trebbia.[58]

Another member of the embassy, Georg Heinrich von Langsdorff, offered similar sentiments about the Russian colony at Sitka in what is today Alaska. Finding many colonists ill with scurvy and malnutrition, he lamented:

> What shocked me the most under these circumstances, and really harassed my feelings, was, that while so large a portion of the people lay in this state of wretchedness, the directors and under-overseers, the clerks and their friends, the officers and their hangers-on, of their own authority sent the Aleutians out to hunt or fish, and fed sumptuously upon . . . [lists various foods] whatever was afforded either by nature or the storehouses.[59]

---

57. Krusenstern, *Voyage Round the World*, xix-xxix.
58. Ibid., vol. 2, 217–18. Krusenstern refers to Alexander Vasilyevich Suvorov, Count of Rymnik, a general who guided a Russian army to victory over French forces in the Battle of Trebbia in 1799.
59. Langsdorff, *Voyages and Travels in Various Parts of the World*, vol. 2, 93.

As historians of Russian America have chronicled, Russia's North American outposts were perpetually hampered by food shortages, which often led officials to purchase supplies from visiting American merchant vessels.[60] Indeed, Langsdorff recorded how during his visit, the Sitka colony was saved from starvation by the arrival of an American ship packed with provisions.[61]

Overall, when considering Russian overtures to Japan, we should underscore first that because of the often desperate state of their colonies, Russians officials looked to expand trade with Japan partly to secure new sources for food and basic supplies. Second, the Russian American Company, which lacked bullion reserves, had to depend upon commodities obtained outside of Russia to possibly develop trade with Japan. Third, Russian officials aimed to develop not simply bilateral trade ties with Japan but to create a larger commercial network that would thrive primarily by exploiting trade with the China market.

The Reforms of Matsudaira Sadanobu

Bakufu leaders in Edo had taken little notice of the Russian outposts in Kamchatka and the Kurils until they received a translation of an alarming letter from a Hungarian-born adventurer, Baron Moritz Aladar von Benyowsky, who briefly visited Japan in 1771. Benyowsky warned of Russian plans to attack Matsumae with a small but powerful naval force. After presenting this fabricated story, Benyowsky departed, never to return. Nonetheless, his letter had a lasting impact. Concerned over a possible Russian incursion, Kudō Heisuke urged the *bakufu* leadership to take a more direct interest in Ezo. Using information gained primarily from interaction with Dutch merchants at Nagasaki, he wrote a treatise in 1773 describing how the Matsumae house was benefiting from a secret trade with Russian merchants in eastern Ezo. As historian Brett Walker notes, Kudō offered little hard evidence to substantiate his claims of Matsumae-Russian trade links, but his opinions, along with those of a scholar of military science, Hayashi Shihei, prompted Tanuma Okitsugu to dispatch a mission in late 1785 to investigate

---

60. Haycox, *Alaska*, 90–91.
61. Langsdorff, *Voyages and Travels in Various Parts of the World*, vol. 2, 88–90.

Matsumae's trade and defenses, to gauge the Russian presence, and to explore potential commercial opportunities for the *bakufu*.[62] The mission increased awareness of Ezo in the Tokugawa leadership circle, knowledge that helped facilitate the implementation of the Tokugawa monopoly over the marine product trade the following year. Around the same time, Matsumoto Hidemochi, an ally of Tanuma, formulated plans to develop Ezo by settling 70,000 outcasts there to tame the northern wilderness.[63] Yet before the plan could be implemented, Tanuma and Matsumoto suddenly fell from power in the autumn of 1786 amidst the aforementioned accusations of corruption.

Tanuma's successor, Matsudaira Sadanobu, profoundly reshaped Japan's foreign relations at the close of the eighteenth century. He is often considered a conservative reactionary, a clear contrast to the progressive Tanuma. John W. Hall concludes that Matsudaira, guided by a Confucian ideal that emphasized agriculture over trade, dismantled Tanuma's proactive commercial programs and thus brought foreign trade in the Edo period to its nadir. According to Hall, Tanuma's energetic mercantilism—a force not unlike that which powered the English economy of the same period—was stifled by Matsudaira. He argues that if Tanuma's effort had been allowed to bloom, this mercantilism could have prompted Japan to move quickly and independently toward industrialization. For Hall, Matsudaira's conservative policies helped lay the foundation for Japan's economic and thus military weakness vis-à-vis Western nations in the mid-nineteenth century.[64]

Hall's stark contrast of the two leaders is problematic. Although Matsudaira brought a conservative slant to *bakufu* policy and foreign trade, he did not dismantle the institutions, established by Tanuma, that allowed the *bakufu* to regulate and profit from trade. As a result, trade through Nagasaki continued to thrive after Matsudaira left office. In addition, Hall downplays the influence of long-term trends, such as economizing in diplomacy, which remained constant across the eighteenth century. Matsudaira made his most lasting impact by reducing the scale of Japan's diplomatic contacts. In so doing, he codified and

---

62. Walker, *The Conquest of Ainu Lands*, 164–65.
63. Ōishi Shinzaburō, *Tanuma Okitsugu no jidai*, 145–46.
64. Hall, *Tanuma Okitsugu*, 57–60, 86.

further defined guarded engagement. As a *bakufu* senior councilor from 1787 to 1793, he moved vigorously, revamping the Tokugawa diplomatic network by reducing the frequency and size of diplomatic missions received by Tokugawa leaders at Edo. In this step, Matsudaira fulfilled an economizing trend building since the 1764 watershed. In that year, Shogun Ieharu (r. 1760–86) received a 472-person mission at Edo castle to celebrate his succession to the office of shogun. Embassies from Chosŏn, as an independent, neighboring kingdom, formed the bedrock of the "Japan-centered world." Yet the 1764 mission proved the last Korean embassy to travel to Edo. Subsequent *bakufu* leaders showed less interest in receiving Korean and Dutch embassies. Thanks to a century and a half of Tokugawa hegemony, they no longer needed those embassies to enhance their regime's sovereignty. Instead, Tokugawa leaders increasingly grew concerned with the financial burdens involved in bringing the Dutch and particularly the larger Korean embassies overland to Edo.

The Tokugawa faced a smaller but significant financial burden in subsidizing Tsushima for its role in bringing Korean embassies to Edo. When currency debasement reshaped trade in the 1710s, Tsushima officials appealed to the *bakufu* to assuage the domain's financial strain associated with the Korean embassies. *Bakufu* leaders agreed and awarded the domain a 50,000-*ryō* loan to help defray diplomatic costs. They also proffered a supplemental loan in 1717 and similar grants in 1718 and 1746. Finally in preparation for the 1764 embassy, Tsushima procured 100,000 *ryō* not in loans but outright grants from the shogunate.[65]

While Tsushima leaders were happy to gain Tokugawa aid, which was, of course, in addition to grants and loans received to make up for losses in trade, prominent domain officials began to openly question the value of receiving embassies in light of ever-decreasing trade revenues. Two years before his death, Amenomori Hōshū again argued Tsushima's position, urging *bakufu* leaders in 1753 to reform the practice of receiving Korean embassies. Conceding that *bakufu* sovereignty was enhanced by arrival of Korean embassies, Amenomori asserted that financial costs related to the missions had become an excessive

---

65. Arano, *Kinsei Nihon to higashi Ajia*, 234–35.

burden for the *bakufu*, Tsushima, and domains along the route of the procession to Edo:

> Counting the time for the arrival and return trip of each mission, an embassy will stay in a domain for 20 to 30 days and there is no limit to the labor expenses incurred during that period. As the official duties are numerous and as they must be diligently executed, these expenses become a major burden. In addition, there are the fees for men and horses related to supporting the embassy's entourage. In the end, the money spent on the arrival of embassies is not of great benefit to the Japanese realm.

When trade with Korea had prospered, he wrote, Tsushima was financially able to assist in the reception of the embassies. In recent years, however, trade had declined and Tsushima had begun to receive loans from the *bakufu* to defray the costs, funds that the domain had difficulty repaying. Amenomori stressed that the most sensible choice for "Japan's future" was to stop receiving embassies, or at least have them not travel all the way to Edo.[66]

Matsudaira, like his predecessors in the *bakufu* leadership, certainly shared the sentiments of Amenomori. In his memoir written after leaving office, he asserted that reform had been necessary because villages along the embassy route had to pay roughly 100 *koku* in combined special taxes. In addition, he concluded that daimyo also bore financial burdens paying for horses, porters, and other costs related to the long Korean procession to Edo. Matsudaira believed this financial commitment a waste of precious resources, especially considering that famines had killed ten of thousands in recent years. He asserted that the reception of missions from the Chosŏn Kingdom was simply a "spectacle" and thus ripe for reform.[67]

Matsudaira moved quickly upon assuming office, instructing Tsushima in 1788 to negotiate with Chosŏn officials to revise protocols for a scheduled Korean embassy to Edo that would congratulate Tokugawa Ienari on his accession to the office of shogun. Chosŏn officials were receptive to reform, as they too sought to slash costs in relations with Tsushima. For Korea, an embassy to Edo also involved the reception

---

66. Amenomori, *Hōshū gaikoku kankei shiryō shokanshū*, 310–11.
67. Matsudaira, *Uge no hitokoto, shugyōroku*, 133–35.

of several small preparatory embassies from Tsushima, occasions during which Chosŏn officials welcomed their "less-civilized" Japanese guests with expensive gifts. Seeking to cut costs even further, Matsudaira ordered Tsushima in 1791 to negotiate a fundamental change in the Tokugawa-Chosŏn diplomatic relationship. Instead of receiving a grand Korean embassy at Edo, Matsudaira proposed that an envoy of the shogun and an ambassador of the Chosŏn court meet in Tsushima, where diplomatic letters would be exchanged. The Korean side at first rejected this proposal, asserting that established diplomatic protocols must be maintained. After protracted negotiations, the Koreans eventually agreed, and in 1811 a Korean embassy traveled to Tsushima to congratulate Ienari (27 years after his succession) through an exchange of official letters with a representative of the shogun. Around the same time, Matsudaira also reduced the scale of diplomatic contacts with the Dutch, directing that their annual missions to Edo should now take place once every five years. Thereafter, each mission consisted of three men instead of four and the Dutch were instructed to halve the amount of gifts presented to the shogun and other officials.[68]

Ryukyuan missions to Edo continued, but the Ryukyu court also faced increasing financial constraints, particularly in acquiring Chinese and locally produced gifts to present at Edo. In 1790, as Ryukyu prepared to send a mission to Edo to congratulate Shogun Ienari on his succession, kingdom officials appealed to Satsuma, stating they were unable to gather the necessary funds to finance the mission. In response, Satsuma provided loans to Ryukyu, and in turn, asked *bakufu* officials for assistance. In 1794, *bakufu* leaders complied, providing Satsuma with a loan of 10,000 *koku* of rice and 20,000 *ryō* in gold to defray Ryukyu's costs. In subsequent decades, the shogunate authorized loans to Satsuma each time a Ryukyuan embassy traveled to Edo. The Ryukyu court was also burdened with outlays related to the dispatch of biennial embassies to Beijing and the periodic reception of investiture missions from the Qing court. Satsuma subsidized some of the costs

---

68. Kasutani, "Naze Chōsen tsūshin-shi wa haishi sareta ka-Chōsen shiryō o chūshin ni," 8–11; IC, 843–57. Nakamura Tadashi, *Kinsei Nagasaki bōekishi no kenkyū*, 498.

associated with the arrival of a Qing investiture mission in 1800, and as before, provided funds for tribute missions to Fuzhou and Beijing.[69]

Satsuma and Tokugawa leaders no doubt declined to reform Ryukyu's diplomatic ties because of the kingdom's dual tribute status. The Shō still required the investiture missions to support their sovereignty and Satsuma did not want the kingdom to sever its tribute ties, which of course brought concomitant trade revenue for the domain. Moreover the Shimazu almost certainly still valued the prestige gained in escorting Ryukyu missions to Edo. As a result, Ryukyu's diplomatic connections, to both China and Edo, remained in place into the mid-nineteenth century.

Matsudaira and Foreign Trade

In regard to trade at Nagasaki, Matsudaira displayed the same energy for reform, focusing on reducing exports and "unnecessary" imports and weaning the city's merchant community from its dependence upon trade. In his memoir, he stressed that his restructuring of trade used the precedent of *bakufu* edicts issued in 1742. While not fully implemented, these edicts directed that commerce with the Dutch and Chinese be halved, chiefly because of declining copper production from Japanese mines. Matsudaira asserted that *bakufu* officials in the 1790s had simply needed to execute these edicts and reduce the number of permitted Dutch and Chinese ships. He had hoped that executing the limits would begin the process of abolishing trade with the Dutch. Matsudaira concluded that the elimination of trade with the VOC would not adversely affect Nagasaki, which he believed was illustrated by the fact that the failure of the annual ship to arrive in 1791 had not caused great financial hardship. If trade with the VOC had been eliminated, he argued, redundant translators and other officials could have been transferred to Edo and Osaka, and if needed, the savings on salaries used to support the Nagasaki populace. Matsudaira stressed that he had pushed the people of Nagasaki to increase agricultural production and to expand craft industries—especially in pottery and fabric making. He as-

---

69. Kamiya, *Taikun gaikō to higashi Ajia* 144–45; Miyagi, *Ryūkyū shisha no Edo nobori*, 192–201.

serted that he had simply sought to help the people wean themselves from their dependency on foreign trade and instead base their livelihood on industry, a step that would "assure the future of Nagasaki."[70]

Yet while he hoped to reduce trade with Chinese merchants, Matsudaira indirectly conceded that it would be difficult to eliminate it completely, particularly because Chinese ships brought books and especially medicines vital to the realm. He concluded that if Chinese ships did not call, Japanese would recklessly travel to "China" and reside there, primarily to obtain medicinal products, as was the case before prohibitions were imposed in the Kanbun era (1661–73). Although he uses a word for China (*Tōdo*), it is likely that Matsudaira was referring broadly to China and Southeast Asia, the latter of which was dotted with Japanese settlements until the early seventeenth century. While Matsudaira believed that the previous edicts had eliminated such practices, he stressed the need to maintain prohibitions on Japanese traveling overseas as the desire for medicinal goods could prompt Japanese to travel especially to China, "a place that people from around the world visit, and we cannot expect the Chinese to impose restrictions." Overall, he grudgingly concluded that trade with China should continue, although he hoped that a focus on industry might one day allow the people of Nagasaki to end their economic dependence on foreign trade.[71]

During his tenure, Matsudaira was never able to eliminate trade with the VOC. Nonetheless, the "feared and hated" councilor, as the Dutch came to call him, implemented a series of measures to reduce the annual limit of VOC ships from two to one.[72] Yet in 1790s, for reasons not related to the *bakufu*, the Dutch became an inconsistent trading partner. Due to the Netherlands' involvement in the French Revolutionary Wars, VOC officials faced challenges in securing their own vessels and indeed no Dutch ship arrived in Nagasaki in 1796. To maintain its factory in Japan, VOC officials turned to hiring ships from other countries, for example, the *Franklin*, an American vessel that sailed from Batavia to Nagasaki in 1799.[73]

---

70. Matsudaira, *Uge no hitokoto, shugyōroku*, 101–3.
71. Ibid., 103.
72. Blussé and Remmelink, ed., *The Deshima Diaries: Marginalia 1740–1800*, 608, 620.
73. Blussé, *Visible Cities*, 62.

Although the number of permitted Chinese ships was also reduced to just ten ships annually after 1790, trade with Chinese merchants remained lucrative for the Nagasaki clearing-house. Through the supplemental trade, which involved primarily Chinese merchants, the clearing-house imported unprecedented amounts of gold and silver in the years following Matsudaira's departure from the *bakufu* leadership. For example, in 1801, the clearing-house recorded 2,742 *kan* in bullion imports via the supplemental trade. This marked the highest figure to date and was just under the official annual quota of 2,750 *kan* placed on Chinese merchant vessels. Clearing-house officials, accustomed to gaining profits from the supplemental trade, no doubt endeavored to see it continue. Overall, we can conclude that Matsudaira achieved mixed results in his effort to reduce the Nagasaki trade. Like his Tokugawa predecessors, he confronted vested interests in Nagasaki, as well as the need to preserve the flow of medicinal products into the realm.[74]

In domain trade, Matsudaira sought to cut back Tsushima's exports of copper to Korea. Using tactics perfected by their predecessors, Tsushima officials adroitly parried the proposal. They asserted that trade with the Chosŏn Kingdom was a right of the domain, affirmed by their Tokugawa overlords since the days of Tokugawa Ieyasu. They also stressed that their domain was already having difficulty maintaining the import level of marine products, hides, and ginseng, products that could be procured only with copper. Domain officials asserted that if less copper became available for trade, the domain risked losing the imports of Korean rice upon which Sō retainers and the Tsushima populace depended. The loss of rice imports, they warned, might cause unrest among the Sō retainer band, and by implication, hurt diplomatic relations with Korea. Once again, such remonstrations proved effective. *Bakufu* leaders continued to allow Tsushima to acquire up to 100,000 *kin* of copper annually for export.[75]

Matsudaira was more successful in imposing limits on Satsuma. In an effort to restrict any possible unsanctioned flow in Chinese goods that might be seeping out of the domain into the domestic market,

---

74. Nakamura Tadashi, *Kinsei Nagasaki bōekishi no kenkyū*, 447; Nagasaki kenshi henshū iinkai, ed., *Nagasaki kenshi, taigai kōshōhen*, 789.

75. Tashiro, "Tsushima-han no Chōsen yushutsu dō chōtatsu ni tsuite," 191.

Matsudaira directed in 1794 that except for silk, any Chinese goods brought to Satsuma must be consumed there. Reaffirming an order issued by the Nagasaki magistrate in 1789, he also directed that Satsuma was permitted to sell only raw silk and silk damask outside the domain, transactions that must continue through the sanctioned Kyoto wholesaler. For Satsuma leaders, this order proved especially distressing. Because of the growth of domestic silk production, the import of Chinese silk had become one of the less profitable sectors of Japanese foreign trade.

As the above discussion illustrates, Tsushima and Satsuma increasingly lost agency vis-à-vis the shogunate in the decades after 1764, particularly because of the elimination of the silk-for-silver trade with China. No longer depending upon the domains to deliver foreign goods, *bakufu* leaders were less receptive to domain appeals to protect their respective rights to sell imports on the domestic market. Although Matsudaira's anti-trade measures certainly contributed to a decrease in domain trade, the Tokugawa regime was also now more directly involved in foreign trade. As a result *bakufu* officials were less inclined to facilitate domain trade because it now presented competition to the Tokugawa dominated trade links. Whereas Tsushima officials in particular were still able to negotiate concessions, by the late eighteenth century Tokugawa leaders had more direct involvement when compared to a century before.

The Presentation of Guarded Engagement

Tokugawa assertiveness was also evident in diplomatic intercourse with Russian envoys. In well-known incidents, *bakufu* leaders rejected the overtures of Laxman in 1793 and Rezanov in 1805. In his dismissal of Laxman, Matsudaira presented a description of the structure of Japanese foreign relations as he explained his regime's refusal to open intercourse with the Russians.

When a ship of a foreign country with which we do not have diplomatic ties [*tsūshin*] comes to Japanese territory [*Nihon no chi*], members of the ship's crew are usually arrested or the ship is driven off with cannon fire. This has been our law since ancient times. Nothing has changed since then. If you bring castaways from our land, you must come to Nagasaki but you are not allowed to dock there. . . . If you come to Nagasaki, the rules dictate that each ship must have an individual permit [*shinpai*] to enter. Also, it is difficult to arbitrarily grant exceptions to established diplomatic [*tsūshin*] and commercial [*tsūshō*] contacts. If you have pressing business in the future, you must go to Nagasaki and your case will be heard there. You must now depart as soon as possible.[76]

In this response, Matsudaira set precedents first by refusing an overture from a European state, and second, by developing strict definitions of Japan's diplomatic and commercial relationships. As Ronald Toby notes, Matsudaira created normative categories that thereafter became part of the larger "language" of Japanese diplomacy.[77] Therefore to Rezanov *bakufu* officials stated that while "we realize that you desire to open intercourse with us but what you request, diplomatic (*tsūshin*) and commercial (*tsūshō*) ties, are not possible because these types of contacts are already firmly established."[78]

The next chapter will discuss how future *bakufu* leaders continued to draw upon Matsudaira's definition as they maintained guarded engagement, sometimes with the shows of force that Matsudaira had boldly proclaimed were part of Japanese policy since ancient times. But for now it is important to consider what caused this resolute stance. Rather than the influence of a shared ideology of seclusion, the contexts of diplomacy and trade that emerged after 1764 provide more viable answers. In diplomacy, Tokugawa leaders had developed a new posture that included economizing in diplomacy. Two years before Laxman's arrival, Matsudaira had moved to reduce diplomatic contacts with the Chosŏn Kingdom and the Dutch factory at Nagasaki. It is reasonable to conclude that the projected financial cost of opening relations with the Russians contributed to the *bakufu*'s refusal to establish ties.

Even more important to consider is the larger Tokugawa trade agenda, especially with the China market, carefully crafted over the previous decades. Tokugawa officials had created a means to obtain desired goods from the China market without losing precious silver. What the Russians could bring to enhance that system was of great interest to *bakufu* officials, indicated by their queries to Rezanov and his officers. According to Langsdorff, Tokugawa officials asked:

---

76. *TI*, vol. 7, 94–95.
77. Toby, *State and Diplomacy in Early Modern Japan*, 240–41.
78. *TI*, vol. 7, 192–93; Lensen, *The Russian Push Toward Japan*, 154–55.

What productions Russia could and would bring to Japan as objects of trade? Whether Russia would furnish sugar, rye, skins, medicines and other articles? How many ships she could and would send annually to Japan? Whether four, five, or even more? Whence the ships would come, whether from Kamchatka or from Europe? How long the ships would be in coming? . . . All these questions were on our side answered only on general terms. The ambassador said that it was impossible to enter into such a variety of matters all at once; that they must be the subject of subsequent conversations.[79]

Tokugawa officials clearly considered possible trade through the lens of established commercial ties. As Chinese and Dutch merchants brought sugar and medicines, they concluded that Russians would also be interested in trading in such commodities.

According to his orders, Rezanov was to appeal to his Japanese counterparts to develop trade ties that would allow Russia to obtain copper, rice, and silk. Yet would trade in such items prove beneficial for Japan? We can conclude that *bakufu* leaders were reluctant to export more copper, given the recent moves to reduce exports in previous decades. Moreover, using copper in trade with Russia might have compromised the carefully balanced price structures for selling copper on the domestic market and to the Nagasaki clearing-house for export.

As rice was grown throughout Japan, the *bakufu* might have conceivably begun to export it. There was also perhaps potential for exporting silk, which would emerge as Japan's most prominent export in the decades after the Meiji Restoration. Yet even if the *bakufu* mobilized to develop rice and silk exports, what could the Russians have brought to exchange? Like the British, the Russians probably would have sought to avoid trading bullion, and instead have offered furs, which as we have noted the Russian American Company sought to sell at Canton. But at that time, sea otter pelts, then the most valuable commodity produced in Russian colonies, were already available on the Japanese market. Since the sixteenth century, Kuril Ainu had trapped sea otters and sold their pelts to Japanese merchants, a trade that continued in the late eighteenth century despite Russian forays into the Kuril chain.[80]

---

79. Langsdorff, *Voyages and Travels in Various Parts of the World*, vol. 1, 237.
80. Walker, *The Conquest of Ainu Lands*, 156–58.

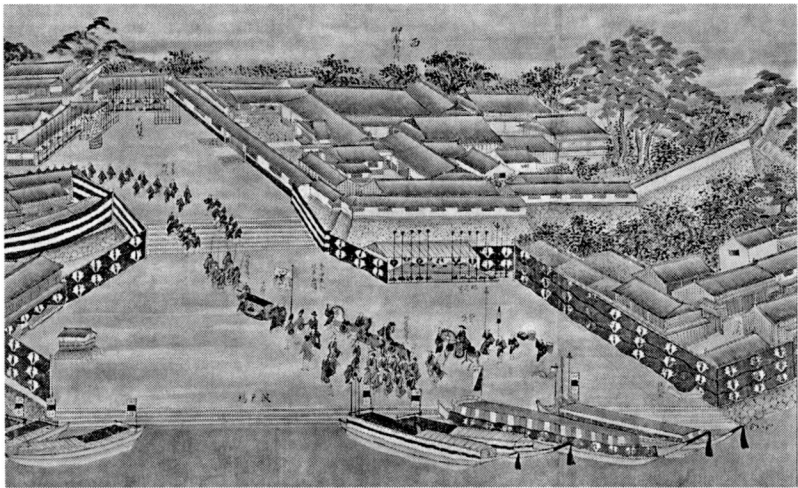

Fig. 12 Russian envoy, Nikolai Rezanov, received at the harbor landing area in Nagasaki, 1805. *Roshia shisetsu Rezanofu raikō emaki* [Picture scroll of Russian envoy Rezanov's visit to Nagasaki]. Courtesy of Historiographical Institute, University of Tokyo.

If the Russians had offered to bring bullion, sugar, or even medicinal products, *bakufu* officials might have been more receptive. As it was, the Russians seem to have lacked an understanding of the larger flows of trade in East Asia. For example, they did not propose trade in marine products, which would have been more geographically viable because of the proximity of their colonies to the rich Ezo fishery. Here, too, it is useful to speculate that the Tokugawa might have welcomed Russian imports of kelp or abalone, using them, like those of Korean marine products, to trade with Chinese merchants at Nagasaki.

Given the above factors, the following statement, offered in the *bakufu*'s official proclamation rejecting Rezanov's overtures, appears to be based upon careful consideration of the pros and cons of trade with Russia: "In the instance of commerce, it may appear that adding things which your country has to those which our country lacks would be of mutual benefit. After detailed deliberation, we have concluded that in exchange for foreign items of little value, we would lose useful Japanese goods. All things considered, such trade would not be in the interest of the realm as a whole."[81]

---

81. *TI*, vol. 7, 193; translation draws on Lensen, *The Russian Push Toward Japan*, 155.

In China, Qing officials offered similar rejections to British requests, which provide a useful comparison to consider the Tokugawa position. In the same year that Laxman visited Ezo, Britain's Lord Macartney traveled to China in hopes of expanding British trade with the Middle Kingdom. In his letter to George III refusing these overtures, the Qianlong emperor made a statement that James Hevia notes has come to stand for "China's traditional culturalism, isolationism, and sense of self-sufficiency nicely and conveniently compacted into one text." The Emperor asserted: "The Celestial Empire, ruling all within the four seas, simply concentrates on carrying out the affairs of Government properly, and does not value rare and precious things. . . . [We] have never valued ingenious articles, nor do we have the slightest need of your Country's manufactures."

Joanna Waley-Cohen argues that in these statements, Qianlong sought not to uphold isolationism but to encourage domestic production and to reaffirm that China could maintain economic self-sufficiency. Namely, she stresses that the emperor moved based upon domestic agendas rather than a particular ideology.[82] Like their counterparts in Japan, Qianlong and his officials considered the manufactures then produced in the British Isles and found little that warranted a broad restructuring of existing trade ties between Britain and China.

In the late eighteenth century, the British, like their Russian counterparts, were still clearly searching for goods to allow them to more deeply penetrate the lucrative markets of East Asia. Yet despite all their enthusiasm to trade in East Asia, Britain and Russia simply did not yet enjoy the commercial prowess to convince Chinese and Japanese leaders to alter their established trading regimes.

Conclusions

In a larger sense, the articulation of guarded engagement demonstrates that Japanese leaders possessed a new understanding of their place in the world. Seeking to enhance Tokugawa sovereignty, seventeenth-century *bakufu* leaders imitated China to create a "Japan-centered

---

82. Hevia, *Cherishing Men From Afar*, 239; Waley-Cohen, "China and Western Technology in the Late Eighteenth Century," 1525–44.

world." Yet in their interactions with Russian envoys, Tokugawa leaders made no such pronouncements. The absence of rhetoric about a "Japan-centered world," coupled with the decision to reduce diplomatic contacts, indicates that a more guarded and commercially centered approach had been adopted.

Because foreign trade was far from stagnant, Tokugawa leaders never seriously considered severing commercial ties with the China market as they reduced diplomatic links. Such a step was not necessary because with guarded engagement, they had in many respects found the key to the China market for which Russia and particularly Britain searched: a means to trade with China without the detrimental outflow of silver. Thanks particularly to Japanese economic penetration further north, the Nagasaki clearing-house could ship many of the same marine products that its European and Asian counterparts also sent to the China market. What is more, the *bakufu* had reshaped Japan into a net importer of silver, a move that would have important implications for Tokugawa initiatives in the early nineteenth century.

FOUR

Domestic Demand and Foreign Trade

As the nineteenth century dawned, Satsuma officials appealed to the *bakufu* to allow the domain greater flexibility in its sales, on the domestic market, of goods imported from China via Ryukyu. They hoped to be able to operate outside the permitted commercial channel of the Kyoto wholesaler. In addition, they sought to sell not just raw silk and silk damask, but also medicinal products imported through Ryukyu. In the eleventh month of 1802, the *bakufu* rejected Satsuma's appeal, leading Uemura Kyūhachirō, a Shimazu retainer, to present the following sharp critique of the Tokugawa stance.[1]

Ryukyu has strictly executed Tokugawa edicts, but in the end, the kingdom has found it extremely difficult to suppress illicit commerce. This is because there is a shortage of medicinal goods throughout Japan caused by the Tokugawa policy of allowing their import only at Nagasaki.

The walls around the Yoshiwara pleasure quarters [located outside of Edo] are intended to contain the flesh trade to a single area of Edo. Yet Yoshiwara alone does not meet the overall demand for prostitutes. Inns in all directions employ women as maidservants but it is common knowledge that they are

---

1. The *bakufu* rejection can be found in Takayanagi and Ishii, ed., *Ofuregaki, Tenpō shūsei*, vol. 2, 846–47.

actually prostitutes. Although the shogunate issues edicts prohibiting inns from engaging in such practices, they are seldom effective.

The *bakufu*'s attempt to restrain trade in Chinese goods to Nagasaki is the same as limiting the flesh trade to Yoshiwara alone. Like the ubiquitous inns employing prostitutes, Ryukyu will continue to serve as an entry point for Chinese imports. In the end, the restrictions on trade will not prove effective. Moreover it shows a lack of compassion to restrict the trade in medicines, which are necessary for human life.[2]

As Ijichi Sueyasu, another Shimazu retainer, noted in an assessment of foreign trade in 1841, Uemura proved prophetic: the *bakufu* efforts to limit trade in medicinal and other imports to Nagasaki were futile. Ryukyu's inability to control smuggling contributed somewhat to this failure, yet as we shall discuss, the biggest factor in weakening Tokugawa efforts was Satsuma's aggressive commercial enterprises.

With his colorful analogy of medicines and prostitution, Uemura anticipated a trend that would define foreign trade after 1800: increased domestic demand for imported medicinal products from China and elsewhere. While it involved many of the same goods as the late eighteenth century, trade in medicinal imports jumped dramatically after 1800, a fact born out in the rise in volume through Nagasaki. In the mid-eighteenth century, that port's pharmacopoeia imports reached around 600,000 *kin* in active years, but in 1804, the volume rose to 1.08 million *kin* and continued to surge, reaching 1.58 million *kin* in 1813 before tapering off to around 750,000 *kin* by 1821.[3]

This demand accompanied a trend then reshaping the domestic economy: proto-industrialization, that is, the production of specialized goods expressly for sale in distant markets. The economic historian Saitō Osamu identifies the 1820s as a turning point during which the engine of growth decidedly shifted from farming to proliferating, proto-industrial production of agricultural and some manufactured commodities.[4] As they produced higher volumes and a greater variety of goods,

---

2. Ijichi Sueyasu, a compiler of historical records of the Satsuma domain, quoted Uemura in a memorial presented in the sixth month of 1841. Kōshaku Shimazu-ke Henshū-sho. *Sappan kaigun-shi*, vol. 1, 176–77.

3. Yamawaki, *Kinsei Nihon no iyaku bunka*, 207–8.

4. Saitō, "Scenes of Japan's Economic Development and the Longue Durée," 16.

rural areas began to assume increased commercial power vis-à-vis established urban centers such as Osaka and Kyoto. In addition, more ships plied coastal routes along the Sea of Japan, transporting products not only from coastal ports but from Ezo and Ryukyu as well.

As the new century dawned, the surge of proto-industrialization not only increased trade but also allowed Japanese consumers to enjoy a wide variety of domestically produced goods. We can see this in the ledgers of the Mitsui merchant house in Osaka, which recorded monthly prices for daily necessities: rice from domains throughout the realm, as well as barley, vegetable oil, cotton, charcoal, and wax produced in, for example, Fukuoka, Fukui, and Satsuma. Moreover, that consumers could choose between domestic and imported varieties of the same good is illustrated in the ledgers for sugar, which listed imported rock, high-quality white, and low-grade "Dejima" (refined Javanese sugar imported by the Dutch) as well as white sugar produced in Shikoku, western Honshu, and brown sugar from Amami.[5] The same was true of the ginseng market, where consumers could choose between grades of domestic ginseng as well as Korean, Chinese, and American varieties (the ban on "Canton ginseng" had been lifted in 1788).[6]

On the long list of medicinal products being imported from China were parts of the forsythia plant, used to treat syphilis, and zinc carbonate (an ingredient in modern calamine lotion), which was then employed as a cure for conjunctivitis. Japanese physicians also sought dinosaur and mammoth fossils, which were thought to alleviate uterine bleeding and vaginal discharge.[7] Via the special order system, the Dutch delivered narwhal tusks, which they cleverly marketed as those of the mythical unicorn. Apothecaries mixed the narwhal tusks (or if available, rhinoceros horns) with ginseng, aloe, musk, bear's gallbladder, and stones from the intestine of cattle to create a medicine

---

5. Mitsui bunko, ed., *Kinsei kōki ni okeru shuyō bukka no dōtai*, 2. Iwao, "Edo jidai no satō bōcki nitsuite," 6–16.

6. *TI*, vol. 4, 145; Mitsui bunko, ed., *Kinsei kōki ni okeru shuyō bukka no dōtai*, 2.

7. Yamawaki, *Kinsei Nihon no iyaku bunka*, 210–11.

Domestic Demand and Foreign Trade

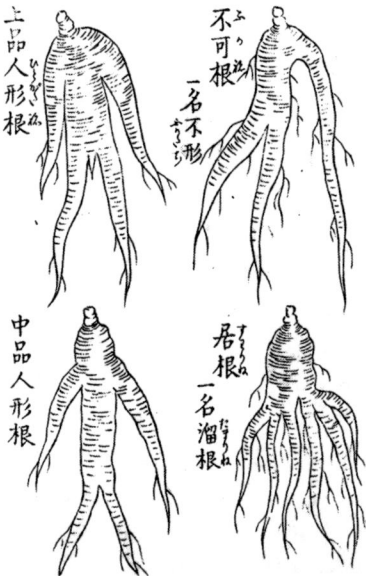

Fig. 13 The above image illustrates one way in which medicinal goods were graded. Although a few types of ginseng grew naturally in Japanese forests, they were viewed as far less efficacious than Korean varieties, which began to be cultivated in the early eighteenth century. Elongated roots over forty centimeters (approximately sixteen inches) and free of small root "hairs" were judged to be of top quality. Other types, such as the one shaped like a human body in the upper left corner, were also valued. Yet as the illustration is intended to show, the "human body root" needed the correct proportions. Thus the root in the lower left corner, which has disproportioned legs and arms, achieved only a middle grade. The roots on the right were even less valuable because of their multiple "legs." The root in the lower right, called colloquially the "sitting root" because with its many legs it would "sit" when placed on the ground, was deemed of particularly low quality. *Chōsen ninjin kōsaku ki* [A Chronicle of Ginseng Cultivation]. Courtesy of the General Library, University of Tokyo.

for treating childhood diseases. The Dutch imported annually about 30 kilograms of narwhal horns after 1800.[8]

Much like other peoples across Eurasia, Japanese had long used wood extracts and other natural products to create pleasing and relaxing aromas, incorporating them, for example, into Buddhist ceremonies.[9] The medicinal use of aroma therapies, while also well es-

---

8. Miyashita, *Nagasaki bōeki to Ōsaka*, 5–12.

9. Donkin, *Dragon's Brain Perfume*, 3–35 outlines the trade in and the use of aromatics throughout Eurasia.

tablished, appears to have increased in the Edo period. By the early nineteenth century, many Japanese valued Borneo camphor as an aroma therapy, both to clear "bad air," and to treat common ailments. Naturally produced Borneo camphor was seen as the most efficacious and therefore desirable, but artificially made (and thus less prized) imported Chinese and domestic varieties were also gaining in popularity. After 1765, imports of Borneo camphor averaged around 140 *kin* annually. Chinese and Dutch ships brought an annual average of over 1,000 *kin* after 1820, however, with the level spiking to just over 1850 *kin* between 1831 and 1835.[10]

Japanese physicians, who increasingly prescribed Borneo camphor, certainly contributed to the increase in demand. In 1836, Takano Chōei, a prominent practitioner of Dutch and Japanese medicinal techniques, recommended that Borneo camphor be used to avoid epidemic diseases and to treat maladies, such as severe headaches, which occurred during times of famine. In a pamphlet that offered methods for avoiding epidemic diseases, Takano provided a detailed description and diagram for making refined Borneo camphor vinegar. He urged readers to use Borneo camphor as part of a strategy to avoid poisonous air. "In an earthen bowl place some Borneo camphor vinegar and heat it over a low heat filling the room with the steam. One should sniff it every now and then."

To treat severe headaches, the physician suggested that as an initial remedy, leeches be placed on the temples to draw blood. If this proved ineffective, he asserted that patients should be induced to sweat, which was presumed to alleviate pain. To bring a sweat, he prescribed a practitioner to "take three *rin* of [Borneo] camphor and five *bu* of saltpeter and make into a fine powder. Add wheat flour to make a starchy ball. This [medicine] may be used twice. If the patient cannot sweat, dissolve three *fun* of powdered borax in four *monme* of strong vinegar, and administer all at once. In most cases, the patient will sweat."[11]

---

10. Miyashita, *Nagasaki bōeki to Ōsaka*, 16–34.

11. Quotations from Ellen Nakamura, *Practical Pursuits*, 203, 211; "Borneo" added to second quotation as per the original Japanese text (Takano Chōei zenshū kankōkai, ed., *Takano Chōei zenshū*, vol. 1, 228–29).

New Domestic Market Dynamics

In the decades after 1800, domains with little prior connections to foreign trade became involved in it. For example, several domains began to produce ginseng not only for the domestic market but also for export to China. In the 1840s, the Matsue domain (on the coast of the Sea of Japan in western Honshu) and the Aizu domain (in north-central Honshu) started to ship export-grade ginseng to the Nagasaki clearing-house, which sold the root to Chinese merchants. Two decades later, the Kumamoto domain, in central Kyushu, also started to send its ginseng to Nagasaki for export.[12]

Other domains moved to take advantage of the abundant opportunities made available by the high domestic demand for imported and domestic medicines. The Toyama domain, which since the early eighteenth century had enjoyed a reputation as a purveyor of efficacious medicines, set up offices to support and regulate shipments of medicinal products to other domains. In the early nineteenth century, Toyama merchants traveled extensively throughout Japan to peddle their goods.[13] The Kumamoto domain established a relationship with the prominent Ishimoto merchant house that allowed it to acquire imported medicinal goods not only from the central Osaka market, but also directly from Nagasaki. The domain benefited by receiving a fee from the Ishimoto in exchange for the monopoly they enjoyed over the Kumamoto market.[14]

As before, officials of the Nagasaki clearing-house profited by selling imports well above their purchase prices, and by continuing to charge special fees and levies to the merchants purchasing imports and re-selling them on the domestic market. Since the councillorship of Tanuma in the late eighteenth century, merchant fees had become an increasingly important source of revenue. When Mizuno Tadakuni came to dominate the *bakufu* leadership in the late 1830s (a period that will be explored in more detail below), he accelerated this trend, increasing fees to the point that by 1841 they came to represent just under a

---

12. Honma, "Aizu-han yōtashi Adachi-ke ni tsuite," 71–80.
13. Sakai Seiichi, *Toyama-ken no rekishi*, 137–42.
14. Yoshinaga, "Kokusan kaisho shihō no seiritsu to tenkai," 26–27.

quarter of all revenues.[15] As many of these fees could be garnered from the flow of goods imported through Nagasaki and onto the domestic market, *bakufu* leaders were increasingly concerned about protecting established Tokugawa privileges in those areas. The same was true on the export side, where the *bakufu* maintained its monopoly on the marine product trade. In order to increase the flow to Nagasaki, the *bakufu* began to offer more cash rewards to areas that produced marine products beyond established annual quotas.[16]

Japan continued to be far from alone in the Asian marine product trade. Sea cucumbers, shark fins, and assorted other marine products were harvested throughout the coastlines of insular Southeast Asia and shipped to China. Writing in 1835, John Phipps concluded that the sea cucumber alone "forms the most important article of commerce between the islands of the Indian archipelago and China, excepting, perhaps, pepper."[17] At Penang, the overall trade volume dropped after 1800, largely because British country traders bypassed the port as they transported increasing amounts of opium from India to China. Yet the value of trade in bird's nests, trepang, and dammar through the island remained steady into the 1820s.[18] Soon after its establishment as a free port in 1819, Singapore emerged as a new center for the marine product trade.[19] In fact, Chinese demand for marine products remained so steady that harvesting began in other parts of the Pacific Ocean. For example, Fijian islanders began to harvest and dry sea cucumbers, selling them to American merchants who in turn transported them to Canton. The trade reached a peak in 1830 when sea cucumbers became Fiji's largest export.[20]

As trading in marine products remained active in Pacific maritime routes, Japanese came to eat more kelp, abalone, and sea cucumbers, placing a new pressure on the Tokugawa regime's carefully constructed

---

15. Totman, *Politics in the Tokugawa Bakufu*, 88.
16. Yano, *Awabi*, 118–19.
17. Phipps, *A Practical Treatise on the China and Eastern Trade*, 321.
18. Cowan, ed., "Early Penang and the Rise of Singapore," 15.
19. Phipps details how Chinese junks transported sea cucumbers, shark fins, and agar-agar from Singapore to Amoy and Canton. Phipps, *A Practical Treatise on the China and Eastern Trade*, 281.
20. Lal and Fortune, *The Pacific Islands*, 210–11.

system of foreign trade. New demand from the domestic market certainly influenced trade in kelp. Even today, kelp (*konbu*) remains a key ingredient in Japanese cuisine. Ōishi Kenichi notes that Japanese in Hokkaido, the Hokuriku region (along the Sea of Japan coast including today's prefectures of Toyama, Ishikawa, and Fukui), Kyushu, and Okinawa prefecture each consume kelp in different ways. In Hokkaido it is used chiefly to make stock (*dashi*), while in Hokuriku grated dried kelp is an ingredient in various dishes. (By contrast, areas on Japan's eastern coast have traditionally consumed far less kelp as evident in the fact that today's Mito prefecture has one of the lowest consumption levels in Japan.) The Kyushu and Okinawa regions consume large amounts of long kelp (*nagakonbu*). In those areas, the kelp is often boiled, the stock discarded, and the remaining tender leaves eaten. Ōishi traces the origin of this particular consumption pattern in Kyushu and Okinawa to the late eighteenth century and concludes that increased trade between Ezo and Ryukyu allowed consumers in Okinawa and Kyushu to develop a taste for long kelp, a variety often harvested in the Kurils. Indeed, Ōishi identifies 1799 as the start of the "long kelp period" defined by Satsuma's expanding commercial network (that we will explore below), which allowed consumers in tropical Ryukyu to develop a taste for a product harvested in the cold northern reaches of Ezo.[21]

Japanese also ate more abalone, purchasing it either raw or marinated in local shops or enjoying it along with rice wine (*sake*) at neighborhood restaurants and drinking establishments. Many also believed the shellfish helped to relieve eye ailments, further increasing demand. For fishers, the consumer preference for raw abalone was a godsend as selling the shellfish raw meant significant savings in the cost and time associated with drying the shellfish for export. Thus fishers increasingly began to sell raw abalone directly to merchants who would in turn sell the abalone to shops and restaurants.[22]

Since the eighth century, Japanese had used sea cucumbers in Shinto religious rituals and presented them as gifts of tribute. Holothurians were also considered medicinal products, believed effective in alleviat-

---

21. Ōishi Kenichi, *Konbu no michi*, 85–89, 91–93.
22. Yano, *Awabi*, 121–23.

ing high fevers.[23] Unlike other marine products, Japanese viewed dried rather than fresh sea cucumbers as a more desirable, high-class food. In other another example of a developing consumer market, more urban eateries began selling cuisine that included dried sea cucumbers, while cookbooks offered recipes for preparing them on skewers.[24] Yet sea cucumbers were used for more than food: courtesans of the pleasure quarters fashioned them as French ticklers to amuse their patrons.[25] For fishers, the task of preparing holothurians, often through a combination of boiling in metal pots, and subsequently drying in the sun, was time consuming. In addition, many coastal villages probably had to bear costs related to the processing, such as obtaining the necessary metal pots and firewood.[26]

For *bakufu* leaders, the new dynamic of consumer demand for kelp, abalone, and sea cucumbers created a challenge to the Nagasaki-centered trade system codified in the 1780s. The *bakufu* based the system of gathering of marine products on feudal prerogative, instructing domains to deliver set quotas of kelp, abalone, and sea cucumbers, for which domains were compensated at a fixed purchase price. In the late eighteenth century before the consumer market had begun to thrive, this system had proved viable. After 1800, however, fishers began to enjoy more market options, such as selling kelp and abalone not only to domain officials for transport to Nagasaki but also directly to merchants. Although such transactions were not sanctioned, merchants usually offered prices higher than the *bakufu*'s official price. A fisher would have been hard pressed to resist selling fresh abalone, on which he did not have to spend money and time drying, at a price significantly higher than that offered for dried abalone by a Tokugawa agent. A similar situation existed with sea cucumbers, which a fisher had spent time, and perhaps his own funds (for example to purchase fuel) to boil and dry.

---

23. Ibid., *Awabi*, 123.
24. Tsurumi, *Namako no me*, 344–35, 376–79.
25. Dalby, *Geisha*, 55.
26. Tsurumi, *Namako no me*, 387–88. Tsurumi also describes how Ainu fishers used boiling and drying to prepare sea cucumbers for sale to Matsumae officials (427).

Domestic Demand and Foreign Trade

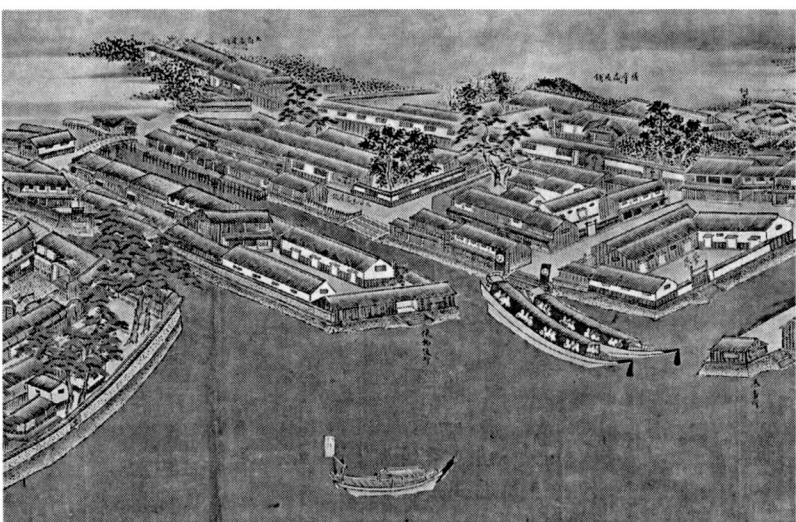

Fig. 14 Dejima and the Marine Product Office and Warehouses in the early nineteenth century. The Tsushima domain office is located in the background, between Dejima (left) and the Marine Product Office (center). *Roshia shisetsu Rezanofu raikō emaki* [Picture Scroll of Russian Envoy Rezanov's Visit to Nagasaki]. Courtesy of Historiographical Institute, University of Tokyo.

Tokugawa officials were certainly aware of the power of the consumer market, as evidenced by the string of *bakufu* memorials in the late eighteenth and early nineteenth centuries ordering especially those in major cities to stop consuming sea cucumbers and abalone. For example in 1812 the Osaka magistrate, citing recent shortages at Nagasaki, ordered a prohibition on consumption of the two goods, stressing their important place in the export trade. *Bakufu* leaders hoped this sumptuary approach would limit domestic consumption and thereby maintain the flow of marine products to Nagasaki and by extension, support commercial links to China.[27]

The Emergence of the Satsuma Entrepôt

Into the newly active domestic market stepped Satsuma, which by taking advantage of both domestic and foreign trade opportunities established itself as a new entrepôt that rivaled the *bakufu*'s Nagasaki-centered trade.

---

27. Yano, *Awabi*, 120–23.

Four factors contributed to this rise: first, a particular series of political events in the 1820s and 1830s; second, a spirit of "commercial opportunism" among Satsuma leaders that took advantage of the multitude of domestic and foreign trade avenues that emerged in the early nineteenth century; third, a disregard for the feudal obligations that guided the *bakufu* in its pursuit of foreign trade; and fourth, an ability to exploit the concern of Tokugawa leaders over the stability of Ryukyu to gain valuable trade concessions. Taken together, these factors demonstrate that Satsuma leaders enjoyed flexibility in creating a broad commercial network to benefit the domain. This flexibility not only allowed the domain to garner more income from trade but also indirectly to undermine *bakufu* power and thereby challenge Tokugawa authority, especially in the regulation of foreign trade.

A political crisis resulting from massive domain debts was the first trigger whereby Satsuma became more involved in domestic and foreign trade. The demands of the system of alternate residence and other administrative expenses led the Shimazu to borrow heavily from Osaka and Edo merchants, pushing domain debt to around 40,000 *kan* in 1750. In 1801, the figure reached 72,600 *kan*. Due to lavish spending by successive daimyo and the continued burden of trips to Edo, the level of debt reached an enormous 320,000 *kan* in 1827, making the Shimazu lord the poorest daimyo in the realm. Satsuma leaders were thus spurred to action, fearing a possible political crisis within the domain.[28]

Assigned the unenviable task of solving Satsuma's financial woes was Zusho Shōzaemon, a domain official with considerable commercial acumen who used a mixture of deceit and bribes to rescue the domain from its financial quagmire in the late 1820s and 1830s. In one of his more famous actions, Zusho brashly informed domain creditors in Osaka and Edo in 1836 that Satsuma had devised a new payment plan whereby the principal, but not the interest, would be repaid at 0.5 percent a year over the next 250 years. The aggrieved merchants appealed to the *bakufu* but received no redress. Zusho apparently had deftly bribed key *bakufu* officials to keep them from taking action against

---

28. Haraguchi Torao, *Bakumatsu no Satsuma*, 187.

domain leaders. Although the merchants were clearly the injured party, they had little recourse against the ruling samurai class.[29]

Zusho also reorganized Satsuma's financial house by creating domain monopolies of the established agricultural mainstays of the domain: rapeseed, sugar, and rice. He imposed quality control through regimented practices in harvesting and processing of these products. As quality improved, the reputation and consequently the sale price of two especially lucrative products—Satsuma rice and Amami sugar—rose on the Osaka market. As part of this effort, Zusho reinstated the system whereby the domain purchased at a low, fixed rate—about one-third of the price that could be fetched on the Osaka market—all sugar produced in Amami and the other northern Ryukyu islands under Satsuma control.

Zusho also deepened the economic dependency of Amami and these other sugar-producing islands. To eliminate any remaining ability of the islanders to produce food themselves, he ordered that all remaining rice paddies be drained and converted to sugar cane fields. Men from 15 to 60 and women 13 to 50 were assigned a field to work. Satsuma prohibited islanders from using money and from trading among themselves. The domain obliged them to buy food and other necessities from Satsuma at inflated prices. Although the overall production of sugar did not measurably expand (just over 4,000 metric tons were shipped to Osaka annually), with these measures Satsuma was still able to raise its profits from sugar sales by increasing quality and lowering purchase prices.[30]

To ensure that as much sugar as possible reached the market, Zusho also took steps to stifle low-level smuggling within the domain, which often took the form of a captain and crew of a domain transport ship or individual crew members independently selling sugar liberated from the ship's hold. Domain officials were under orders to execute or banish anyone caught smuggling sugar. Accounts from sailors working the routes between the Amami islands, Satsuma's ports, and Osaka attest to the rigor of domain officials. Ships from the domain ports of Bō-

---

29. Haraguchi and Nagayama, et al., *Kagoshima-ken no rekishi*, 214.

30. Haraguchi and Nagayama, et al., *Kagoshima-ken no rekishi*, 215–16; Yoshinaga, "Kokusan kaisho shihō no seiritsu to tenkai," 24–25.

notsu and Yamakawa, which carried cotton, textiles, tea, kelp, and foodstuffs to be sold on Amami and the other northern Ryukyu islands, were inspected as they loaded sugar for the return voyage. Upon arrival at Satsuma, other officials examined both cargo and crew and, if they discovered smuggling, banished the captain and the crew for several years. As there are reports of crews dumping smuggled sugar in the face of an inspection, Satsuma officials appears to have asserted a high level of control.[31]

Despite Satsuma's successes in regulating trade, Ryukyu officials again found a way to carve out a modicum of autonomy and obtain profits for the kingdom. In 1804, Satsuma had reaffirmed restrictions that allowed Ryukyu to produce sugar only for consumption within the kingdom, with any remaining production taxed by the domain. Satsuma officials saw this as a means to increase tax revenue and to limit competition on the Osaka market for sugar produced in the Amami islands. Nonetheless, the Ryukyuan government circumvented this scheme because it now had a handful of ships that Satsuma had reluctantly permitted it to use beginning in the late eighteenth century.[32] These ships transported sugar produced in the kingdom to Satsuma ports well ahead of the domain ships arriving from Amami. As a result, the Ryukyuan sugar often reached Osaka first and sold for higher prices than the later-arriving Amami sugar. Because of the vital place of sugar in the Ryukyu economy, Satsuma officials were reluctant to place more strict controls on the kingdom's production and sales. In 1831, they therefore allowed Ryukyu to send a sizeable amount of sugar to Satsuma in place of the rice previously received as tribute.[33]

Meanwhile, to further expand Satsuma's commercial net, Zusho looked to exploit the increased trade in and around Kyushu and especially of thriving networks along the Japan Sea coast. In the first decades of the nineteenth century, the Toyama and Kaga domains had encouraged the building of ships that could ply the routes from Ezo to the Inland Sea, establishing trade links that domain leaders hoped would allow their domains to break their dependence on the Osaka

---

31. Iwakura, ed., *Sasshū Yamakawa baisen kikigaki*, 18–20.
32. Tomiyama, *Ryūkyū ōkoku no gaikō to ōken*, 219–23.
33. Tomiyama and Takara, *Ryūkyū Okinawa to kaijō no michi*, 98–99.

market.³⁴ Namely, they aimed to sell more domain goods directly to other domains, and in return obtain products from those domains at prices lower than those at Osaka. Robert Flershem details how ships from the Kaga domain achieved particular success transporting a wide array of goods between ports throughout the Japan and Inland Seas. For example, in the 1860s, ships of a Kaga merchant house transported tea, tobacco, and oranges to Ezo, where they obtained kelp and herring, which they in turn sold at a port in Tottori (present-day Tottori prefecture in western Honshu). The house's ships also purchased potatoes and paper in Shimonoseki and sugar in Osaka, which were sold at Niigata and other ports along the Sea of Japan. Flershem concludes that trade on the Westward Coastal Route, along the Sea of Japan coast and through the Inland Sea, handily surpassed that flowing on the Eastward Coastal Route through the Tsugaru Strait and down the Pacific Coast to Edo.³⁵

To obtain a share of this trade, Zusho enlisted the help of the large merchant houses of Satsuma involved in smuggling throughout Japan. In essence, he allowed domestic merchant groups to become "legitimate" smugglers for the domain. The most prominent of these groups, the Hamazaki family, became a key agent in Satsuma's commercial expansion. Evidence for the Hamazaki's activities is slight because many of the family's records are not extant. Nonetheless, surviving documents and interviews with men involved suggest that the Hamazaki created a maritime network of smuggled rice, rapeseed oil, vegetable wax, and sugar provided to markets in Kyushu, western Honshu, Edo, Osaka, and Nagasaki. In other words, they were involved in the same commercial enterprises as Satsuma.³⁶

To extend his domain's commercial reach further north, Zusho brokered a deal granting the Hamazaki a freer hand in coastal trade in return for a portion of the profits. The Hamazaki assumed responsibility for shipbuilding and transport, and stationed their agents throughout the domain and in other key Japanese ports to facilitate the expansion

---

34. Takase, *Kaga-han ryūtsūshi no kenkyū*, 704.
35. Robert Flershem, "Some Aspects of Japan Sea Shipping and Trade in the Tokugawa Period," 185–86, 211–12.
36. Miyazato Gennojō and Sawada Nobuto, eds., *Kaijō-ō Hamazaki Taiheiji den*, 27.

of trade: to Ryukyu, Niigata, and Sado Island on the Sea of Japan coast, and to the port of Hakodate in Matsumae. For their part, Satsuma officials often allowed the Hamazaki to use domain ships, provided seed money, and helped defray transportation costs. With the domain's blessing, by the 1830s the Hamazaki had built a commercial enterprise that complemented Satsuma's existing commercial network: Satsuma and Hamazaki vessels transported Ryukyu sugar to Osaka, and sugar and sweet potatoes to Niigata and Matsumae, from which they returned with kelp, sea cucumbers, and abalone.[37]

Commercial opportunism was particularly evident in Satsuma's burgeoning involvement in the marine product export trade. Unlike the *bakufu*, the domain was not bound by the feudal obligations, notably the Tokugawa's commitment to maintain the flow of marine products through Nagasaki to support the clearing-house and the city's merchant community. Instead, Satsuma could circumvent the *bakufu* monopoly and illicitly obtain marine products from a number of sources. For one, domain agents purchased marine products at peripheral ports around the Tokugawa collection centers of Osaka and Shimonoseki. Satsuma officials also permitted medicine merchants from the Toyama domain to sell their goods in Satsuma for a fee paid in marine products. In addition, Satsuma merchant ships developed their own wide network: for example, traveling to the port city of Niigata and other nearby ports to procure marine products in exchange for sugar and sweet potatoes.[38]

In exchange for these marine products, Satsuma obtained valuable imports in illicit trade with Chinese ships that the domain leaders now allowed to blossom at Bōnotsu and other ports along the domain coastline. Satsuma also shipped kelp to Ryukyu, where much of it was consumed. Ryukyu tribute missions to the Qing would also take kelp, along with sea cucumbers, abalone, and shark fins to Fuzhou, where they would be exchanged for medicinal products and other goods. Satsuma would then obtain those medicinal products and other Chinese imports from Ryukyu and sell them at Nagasaki, Osaka, and other commercial centers on the Japanese domestic market. There is strong evidence that Satsuma was not alone in such smuggling. For example, a Kaga mer-

---

37. Ibid., pp. 29–37.
38. Uchara, *Sakoku to han bōeki*, 273–79.

chant, Zeniya Gohei, is reported to have traded furs and kelp obtained in Ezo for foreign goods in encounters with Chinese and possibly Western merchants in exchanges along the coast of the Sea of Japan.[39]

Nonetheless, Satsuma leaders achieved particular success in their smuggling and legitimate trade endeavors. In the 1820s, the domain was able to expand its purview to sell goods imported via Ryukyu on the domestic market. Previously, the *bakufu* had allowed Satsuma to sell only select Chinese imports—silk and silk damask—on the domestic market, and then only through the Kyoto wholesaler, established in the late seventeenth century. Because of the success of domestic silk production, Satsuma enjoyed only scant profits from the sale of these goods. As noted earlier, Satsuma requested permission in 1801 to sell selected Chinese medicinal products on the domestic market. The following year, *bakufu* officials, seeking to protect the Tokugawa share of the lucrative medicinal import trade, flatly refused and later reaffirmed that silk and silk damask were the only permitted imports.[40]

Undeterred, Satsuma officials continued to appeal regularly for concessions in order to "aid Ryukyu." In 1810, *bakufu* leaders relented and provided a small concession, allowing Satsuma to sell at Nagasaki, for a three-year period, woolens, lead, fishing line, and five types of Chinese paper. Following a devastating famine in Ryukyu in 1816, Tokugawa officials allowed an additional eight imports, again for a trial, three-year period. Although the majority of these goods were of Chinese origin, they came to be known collectively as "Ryukyu products," a term that continued to be used to describe the imports Satsuma sold at Nagasaki. These items proved a failure on the domestic market, providing the domain a measly annual profit of 3.4 *kan*.[41]

Satsuma's fortunes soon changed because of a sad turn of events in Ryukyu. Successive typhoons and droughts continued to bring poor harvests and in turn more famine to Ryukyu, events that prompted Satsuma to renew its appeals to Edo. The domain argued that because of these natural calamities, an expansion of sales of Chinese imports at

---

39. Flershem, "Some Aspects of Japan Sea Shipping and Trade in the Tokugawa Period," 219.

40. *TI*, vol. 8, 481.

41. Nakamura Tadashi, "Nagasaki kaisho Tenpō kaikaku-ki no shomondai," 68–69.

Nagasaki was necessary to assuage the kingdom's economic woes. In 1825, *bakufu* officials finally relented by permitting Satsuma to sell a total of sixteen items including tortoise shells, ginkgo wood, and—in a major concession—several valuable medicinal goods: borax, Chinese rhubarb, aloes, Chinese-produced skullcap root, as well as Chinese, artificially-made Borneo camphor (less valuable than natural Borneo camphor). In total, the *bakufu* allowed Satsuma to sell 1,720 *kan* in goods annually, well up from the earlier limit of just over 900 *kan*, in effect since 1716. Yet while they granted these concessions, *bakufu* officials instructed Satsuma not to interfere in the export of marine products and the import of several particularly lucrative medicinal products, which they considered fundamental to the stability of trade through the Nagasaki clearing-house.[42]

As discussed earlier, Satsuma officials had diligently executed Tokugawa anti-smuggling edicts during the late seventeenth century in order to protect domain privileges to sell goods on the domestic market granted by the *bakufu*. In the 1820s, however, Satsuma leaders had quite different ideas of what was expedient for the domain and quickly overstepped the bounds of the Tokugawa dispensation. Using the new-found privileges, the domain first began to sell, beyond the prescribed 1,720 *kan* annual limit, Chinese goods imported "legitimately" through the officially sanctioned Ryukyu channel. Then, domain agents would bring to Nagasaki Chinese imports, procured with marine products, in clandestine exchanges with Chinese merchants along the Satsuma coast. In these endeavors, Satsuma took advantage of a general laxity of *bakufu* administration in the port and apparently bribed *bakufu* officials in Nagasaki to facilitate specific transactions.[43] Overall, guided by commercial opportunism, Satsuma leaders used a variety of initiatives, which when enhanced by *bakufu* concessions, allowed them to greatly expand the domain's trading network in the 1820s and 1830s.

---

42. Nakamura Tadashi, "Nagasaki kaisho Tenpō kaikaku-ki no shomondai," 68–69; *KK*, vol. 2, 747–50.

43. Uehara, *Sakoku to han bōeki*, 223–224; Yanai, ed., *Tsūkō ichiran zokushū*, vol. 1, 153–56 (hereafter *TIZ*).

Reasserting Tokugawa Authority at Nagasaki

Satsuma agents were not the only ones bribing Nagasaki officials. In the early 1820s, Chinese merchants seem to have also paid their share of under-the-table gifts, which allowed them to move freely throughout the city and trade directly with Japanese merchants, no longer restricted to the Chinese Residence. The permissive stance of Tokugawa officials toward the Chinese may have been due to the fact that the Dutch remained an inconsistent commercial partner, making trade with Chinese merchants, which by contrast remained steady, all the more important. From 1800 to 1807, the Dutch factory in Nagasaki (which came to be controlled by the Dutch government following the demise of the VOC at the end of 1799) was sustained largely by chartered American ships (but also two from other Western European nations), which carried Dutch officials and goods between Batavia and Dejima. Because of continued warfare in Europe and the British takeover of Java from 1811 to 1816, the subsequent decade also proved challenging and in several years, no ship called at Nagasaki.[44] When the Dutch presence in Southeast Asia and thus at Nagasaki was stabilized after 1816, regular trade was restored.[45]

When they eventually learned of the lax atmosphere at Nagasaki, *bakufu* leaders in Edo were clearly concerned, especially because Chinese merchants were no longer trading through the clearing-house. The Nagasaki office gained revenue from controlling transactions for imports and exports, revenue that it first used to pay personnel and maintenance costs, with additional revenue sent to the Tokugawa treasury. Following orders from Edo, in 1827, the Nagasaki magistrate instructed Kuroda Naritaka, the lord of the Fukuoka domain, to take action. Fulfilling his duty to defend the port, Kuroda stationed guards at the entrances of the Chinese Residence to keep Chinese merchants from rambling throughout the city. Yet putting the genie back in the

---

44. Blussé, *Visible Cities*, 92. In 1808, 1810–12, and 1815–16, no Dutch or chartered ships arrived in Nagasaki. Iwao and Ōmori, ed., *Oranda fūsetsugaki shūsei*, vol. 1, 86–87.

45. In most of the fifteen years after 1817, two Dutch vessels called annually at Nagasaki, although from 1833 to 1840 only one ship arrived. Iwao and Ōmori, ed., *Oranda fūsetsugaki shūsei*, vol. 1, 86–87. For a nice account of a Dutch ship calling at Nagasaki in the nineteenth century, see Paul, "De Coningh on Deshima," 347–64.

bottle proved difficult. After several years of unrestricted trade, Chinese merchants were infuriated by the new restrictions and showed their displeasure during a three-day riot in the streets of Nagasaki. Kuroda's men were eventually able to restore order, but only after incarcerating a large number of Chinese.[46] Although Kuroda reinstated Tokugawa oversight at the Nagasaki port, the clearing-house did not immediately enjoy the benefits. Indeed, by 1830, trade declined to the point that the clearing-house was operating in the red. In response, Edo was forced to provide over 15,000 *ryō* in subsidies.[47] To make matter worse, in the summer of 1834, two scheduled Chinese merchant ships arrived late with their holds nearly empty.[48] The level of trade through Nagasaki was spiraling downward.

After investigating the situation, frustrated *bakufu* officials quickly pointed the proverbial finger at Satsuma. In the third month of 1835, senior councilor Ōkubo Tadazane forwarded a report to financial magistrate Hijikata Katsumasa, detailing rumors of Satsuma's smuggling activities. Ōkubo concluded that Chinese ships destined for Nagasaki called first at Satsuma before sailing to Nagasaki, if at all. As evidence, he cited reports of Chinese ships traveling directly to harbors on the Satsuma coast to trade. The senior councilor asserted that Satsuma was mixing contraband Chinese merchandise with legal imports (namely those imported through Ryukyu) and selling them on the Nagasaki market. Ōkubo also presented reports that Satsuma representatives were bribing clearing-house officials to allow them to sell contraband Chinese goods, namely goods outside of the sixteen items permitted in 1825. He also mentioned reports that Satsuma obtained Ezo-produced marine products in the area from roughly Takata to Sakata along the Sea of Japan coast and then traded them to Chinese merchants. *Bakufu* leaders gained concrete proof of Satsuma's activities when a Satsuma ship carrying Chinese medicines wrecked in that area in 1836.[49]

---

46. *TIZ*, vol. 1, 153–56.
47. Nakamura Tadashi, "Nagasaki kaisho Tenpō kaikaku-ki no shomondai," 45.
48. *TIZ*, vol. 1, 162–64.
49. Yamawaki, *Nukeni*, 102; Niigata shishi hensan kinseishi bukai, ed., *Niigata shishi, shiryōhen* 2, *kinsei* 1, 216.

Domestic Demand and Foreign Trade 135

Fig. 15 Marine cargo ships in harbor, late nineteenth century. This type of vessel operated throughout Japan's coastline and especially along the Sea of Japan coast from the eighteenth century into the early Meiji period. Courtesy of Nagasaki University Library.

Ōkubo also claimed that Satsuma had extended its network even to Korea. He quoted rumors that the Shimazu dispatched merchant ships to Chosŏn ports and periodically received Korean traders as part of a clandestine trade in Japanese swords and weapons. We do not know if Ōkubo verified this activity, but historians have uncovered strong circumstantial evidence to support his claims. Since the early Edo period, Satsuma officials had provided stipends for Korean-language translators in the domain, no doubt to facilitate trade.[50] Ōkubo asserted that through this illicit trade with the Chosŏn Kingdom, Satsuma was not merely overstepping its legitimate trade parameters, but also adversely affecting the Sō of Tsushima: "In recent years, Tsushima's trade with Korea has declined with fewer goods being exchanged. In fact, there are rumors that the diplomatic relationship with Korea (*tsūshin*) is being affected by the slowdown in trade. Because Tsushima is a domain that obtains most of its revenue from trade, the financial situation of the Sō has been dismal in recent years . . . indeed, it seems that Satsuma's

---

50. Tokunaga, "Satsuma-han no Chōsen tsūji ni tsuite," 18–33.

profit from trade with Korea is higher than that of Tsushima."[51] As will be explored below, Tsushima leaders, more than possible competition from Satsuma, were largely to blame for their domain's economic woes. Nonetheless, by bringing in Tsushima, Ōkubo fueled the perception that Satsuma had created a broad network that was inflicting harm throughout the Kyushu region.

Most galling to Ōkubo and the other *bakufu* officials was a sense that Satsuma was making a mockery of *bakufu*'s trade concessions intended to provide economic assistance for Ryukyu. In the seventh month of 1836, Hijikata and Nagasaki magistrate Kuze Hiromasa complained bitterly that Satsuma had been allowed to sell more products at Nagasaki to "aid Ryukyu," not to fill the Shimazu coffers.[52] Moreover, Hijikata and Kuze contended that the clan's illicit trade was harming not just the Nagasaki clearing-house but Tokugawa administration over the realm (*kokusei*). The following year, Kuze called for a complete ban on the sale of "Ryukyu products" in Nagasaki in order to reprimand the Shimazu.[53]

As Nagasaki officials pushed to punish Satsuma, representatives of the Nagasaki merchant community noted the general slowdown in trade through the port in recent years. In an 1837 memorial to the Nagasaki magistrate, they concluded that

> Several times in the Bunka period [1804–18], no Dutch merchant ship arrived. As a result, trade with Chinese merchants became the only source of profits. In addition, since the Kyōwa [1801–4] and Bunka periods, domestic production of sugar has expanded, leading to a decrease in the price for imported Chinese sugar, which has also reduced profits for merchants here. Since 1818, there has been a marked decline in the number of Chinese ships arriving in this port. From 1818 to 1836, 36 ships [of the 180 permitted for that period based on the 10 ship per year limit] did not arrive. Considering that each ship could trade 490 *kan* in goods, the loss at Nagasaki totaled 10,764 *kan* for the 19-year period.[54]

---

51. *TIZ*, vol. 1, 164.
52. Ibid., 185.
53. Ibid., 185–86.
54. From the memo of a clearing-house official, Fukuda Yasuemon, "Kaisho ginsō no gi ni tsuki fūsho motte moshiagesōrō shomen no hikae," quoted in Nakamura Tadashi, *Kinsei Nagasaki bōekishi no kenkyū*, 498–99.

Nagasaki merchants were feeling the pinch not only of the dearth of Dutch ships but also from new challenges created by expanded domestic production of sugar—much of it, of course, from Satsuma.

Amidst the stream of complaints emanating from both *bakufu* officials and Nagasaki merchants, Mizuno Tadakuni, who had recently gained prominence within the *bakufu* leadership, took action against Satsuma in late 1837. The senior councilor decreed that two years hence the sale of Ryukyu products in Nagasaki was to cease for a ten-year period. Additionally, he directed that until the order was executed, the clearing-house should assume control over Satsuma's commercial activities in Nagasaki such as the warehousing of goods, the management of day laborers, and security. Mizuno stressed that he was not imposing new regulations but merely restoring earlier limits, in this case those decreed by Matsudaira Sadanobu.[55] Interestingly, Mizuno seemed unaware that Matsudaira had asserted that his reform effort was an attempt to properly enforce edicts issued in the 1740s.

Only months after the prohibition had been issued, Satsuma leaders asked for its repeal. Handa Keitōji, the head of the domain residence in Edo, submitted a document detailing the economic challenges that Ryukyu would face because of the reduction in trade. He argued that the kingdom's economy was already in a poor state having again been devastated by droughts and famines. In addition, he noted that since the 1790s, Ryukyu had been forced to pay the expenses for the dispatch of four embassies to Edo and during the same period had also spent substantial amounts to receive two investiture missions from China. Moreover, Handa pointed out that as Tokugawa Ieyoshi had ascended to the rank of shogun the previous year, Ryukyu was also preparing to send a congratulatory embassy to Edo. By citing the economic difficulties related to the dispatch of embassies, Handa intimated that without trade revenues, Ryukyu might also be too weak economically to send embassies to the Qing as well as to Edo. As his predecessors had done in their appeals over a century before, Handa hoped the threat of tarnished Tokugawa prestige would prompt *bakufu* leaders to grant concessions.[56]

---

55. *TIZ*, vol. 1, 185–86; Nakamura Tadashi, "Nagasaki kaisho Tenpō kaikaku-ki no shomondai," 71.

56. Uehara, *Sakoku to han bōeki*, 250–51.

As historian Uehara Kenzen explains, the petitions put Tokugawa leaders in a quandary: should they choose a path of mercy and help an economically weak Ryukyu or remain firm in order to protect Tokugawa authority, which might be damaged if the edict were not executed? After internal debate, the *bakufu* leadership crafted a compromise. They upheld the ban but earmarked 5,000 *ryō* annually for a three-year period specifically to aid Ryukyu. Uehara concludes that the payments allowed *bakufu* leaders maintain the edict but avoid being perceived as abandoning Ryukyu.[57] Although not as explicitly stated, *bakufu* leaders also no doubt took into account Ryukyu's system of dual tribute, particularly the vital role of Qing investiture in the maintenance of Shō authority and the overall economic well-being of the kingdom. Nonetheless, over the next few years, the *bakufu* leadership offered no further concessions and used the ban to boost trade flowing through the Nagasaki clearing-house. In late 1840, Mizuno directed that a cache of medicinal products, imported via Ryukyu in the lag between the issuing of the ban and its execution, be sold through the clearing-house, aiming to increase the clearing-house's revenues at the expense of Satsuma.[58]

In others areas, Mizuno acted with vigor and initiative particularly in implementing measures beyond Nagasaki to rein in Satsuma and restore Tokugawa commercial authority, especially amidst reports of illicit Satsuma trade along the Japan Sea coast. In the ninth month of 1841, the *bakufu* received a document reporting that since 1835, approximately six Satsuma ships a year had arrived in the port of Niigata. In the spring, Satsuma vessels would bring sweet potatoes, and in the summer, sugar, to be traded for medicines and cinnabar. Satsuma was also reportedly peddling Chinese goods at Niigata: Chinese medicinal products and textiles, rugs, coral, as well as porcelain and pottery.[59]

At Mizuno's prompting, in the first month of 1843, Shogun Ieyoshi ordered that the Niigata port and the nearby Niigatahama village, part of the Nagaoka domain (now part of Niigata prefecture), be placed

---

57. Ibid., 251–53.
58. Ibid., 253.
59. Niigata shishi hensan kinseishi bukai, ed., *Niigata shishi shiryō-hen* 2 *kinsei* 1, 216–17.

under the direct rule of the shogunate.[60] This was part of a larger effort to bring valuable lands under direct Tokugawa administration; for example, Mizuno attempted such a move with lands held by Tokugawa liege vassals and daimyo around Osaka and Edo. Due to resistance from landholders as well as peasants and merchants, however, the plan was repealed in the autumn of 1843.[61] Nonetheless, the Niigata designation remained in effect and the port continued to be an important center for trade along the coast of the Sea of Japan, contributing to its designation as a treaty port in the commercial treaties Japan would sign with Western nations in the 1850s.

Looking at the 1820s and 1830s overall, Tokugawa authority slipped due to lax administration at Nagasaki and the growing Satsuma network of domestic and foreign trade. As *bakufu* leaders assessed the problem, they discerned Satsuma's activities to be a system-wide virus affecting Tsushima and even more widely undercutting Tokugawa authority and revenues. Consequently, they directed their responses to points throughout the realm: increased oversight of Chinese merchants at Nagasaki, placing Niigata under direct *bakufu* rule, and the stifling of Satsuma's sale of products imported through Ryukyu.

The latter two points represented new ground for the *bakufu*, which had instituted limits on the sales of imports since the 1680s but had never imposed a complete prohibition on a domain's sales of imports on the domestic market. Now, however, using the new dynamics of proto-industrialization and increased domestic consumer demand to its advantage, Satsuma had forged its own course, making itself the center of a new commercial network that rivaled Nagasaki. Against an unprecedented threat—the newly vibrant commercial rival of Satsuma—*bakufu* leaders acted in an unprecedented way.

Tsushima: "We Are a Small Island Domain with Little Agricultural Production"

Satsuma was not the only Kyushu region domain striving to develop ways to gain revenue from the sale of domain-produced goods, par-

---

60. Ibid., 228–29.
61. Bolitho, "The Tempō Crisis," 153–54, 163.

ticularly on larger urban markets. In 1805, Saga established a domain-administered clearing-house for Imari porcelain, a Saga product prized on the Osaka and Edo markets. The Fukuoka domain developed a similar clearing-house for Hakata silk goods, which included luxury silks and lower-quality weaves tailored for a wider market. During the eighteenth century, Hakata producers had begun to use Japanese instead of imported Chinese silk, allowing them to create a more diversified portfolio of products beyond their previous focus on high-end wares.[62]

By contrast, Tsushima leaders failed to move aggressively to take advantage of opportunities created by proto-industrialization and the thriving domestic consumer market. Agricultural production, particularly on Tsushima itself, continued to stagnate. Although some rice was grown on the island, barley was more widely cultivated, with an annual production of 6,000–7,000 *koku*. Without a significant surplus, the domain could not ship agricultural goods to the Osaka market, as, for example, Satsuma did with rice and rapeseed oil. Tsushima therefore created a clearing-house only for wax produced in domain lands in Kyushu and did so in 1852, decades after other Kyushu domains had established their clearing-houses. In addition, Tsushima failed to develop a domain-produced specialty, other than wax, that could be marketed at Osaka or Edo.[63]

To be sure, Tsushima leaders faced obstacles. Because the mountainous terrain of Tsushima itself hampered production, a good portion of the domain's overall agricultural output came from Sō lands in Kyushu. Domain leaders no doubt also had to bear additional maritime transport costs because of Tsushima's distance from key commercial centers. Yet despite these drawbacks, domain leaders lacked initiative. They did not move aggressively to expand either agricultural or proto-industrial production or to market domain goods at domestic commercial centers.

Trade with the Chosŏn Kingdom continued within the established frameworks of official and private trade. In the official trade, Tsushima, as before, shipped copper, alum, pepper, sappanwood, and water buf-

---

62. Yoshinaga, "Kokusan kaisho shihō no seiritsu to tenkai," 12–14.
63. Yoshinaga, "Kokusan kaisho shihō no seiritsu to tenkai," 28; Tsuruta, "Tenpō-ki no Tsushima-han zaisei to Nitchō bōeki," 68–70.

falo horns to Korea, receiving in exchange Korean rice. The domain still imported sea cucumbers from Chosŏn, which it used to obtain the pepper, alum, and sappanwood on the Nagasaki market, which were in turn shipped to Korea as part of the official trade.

In the private trade, Tsushima exchanged copper for Korean skullcap root and cowhides, importing from 11,000 to 25,000 hides annually with a peak of 35,000 in 1854. Given that beef was not generally consumed in Japan, cattle were rare, so Korean hides fulfilled a specific market demand for leather and as such proved especially profitable for the domain. By contrast, Tsushima achieved disappointing profits from sales of Korean skullcap root, particularly in comparison to the late eighteenth century. This was because Japanese consumers refused to pay high prices for the Korean variety of the root, now viewing it as less efficacious than the Chinese variety. The domain also achieved declining profits in the import of Korean sea cucumbers, continuing that trade simply to acquire holothurians, which in turn could be used to obtain, at Nagasaki, pepper, alum, and sappanwood for the domain's official trade with the Chosŏn Kingdom.

Yet thanks to the thriving domestic market of the early nineteenth century, Tsushima officials were able to find two new imports: cattle hooves and horns. Osaka craftsmen fashioned them into "Flat Korean Ivory" and "Korean tortoiseshell" hair accessories, imitations of the combs and hairclips made from tortoise shells imported by Chinese and Dutch merchants. The new lower-priced hair accessories proved popular in urban areas.[64]

Tsushima's combined annual profits from the official and private trades totaled roughly 1,060 *kan* in early 1840s, a figure that was probably representative of trade income throughout much of the first half of the nineteenth century. Although this revenue was significant, it was disappointingly small when compared to the 2,000–4,000 *kan* sums earned annually in the late seventeenth century.[65]

---

64. Tashiro, "Kinsei koki Nitchō kankei bōekishi kenkyū joron," 79–83; Tashiro, "Bakumatsu-ki Nitchō shibōeki to Wakan bōeki shōnin," 174–82.

65. Tashiro, "Tsushima Han's Korean Trade, 1684–1710," 92–93; Tsuruta, "Tenpō-ki no Tsushima-han zaisei to Nitchō bōeki," 71–73.

Hoping to expand trade, Tsushima officials campaigned (in a manner similar to Satsuma officials and their effort to sell a wider variety of Chinese imports on the domestic market) throughout the first decades of the nineteenth century to convince the *bakufu* to provide concessions in copper exports. They focused on copper under the premise that an expansion of trade with Korea was possible only if the domain were allowed to acquire more copper at prices below market cost. In a string of petitions, Tsushima officials bemoaned their domain's limited agricultural production and the financial hardship caused by the lack of trade with Korea. The phrase, "we are a small island domain with little agricultural production" became a fixture in these and later domain petitions, as common as seasonal greetings in today's Japanese written correspondence. Domain leaders also employed the familiar rhetoric stressing that their diplomatic contacts with the Chosŏn Kingdom contributed to the defense of the realm. They argued that *bakufu* assistance was therefore required to stabilize not only the domain but by implication, the realm overall.

In 1814, the *bakufu* relented and allowed Tsushima special privileges in the acquisition of copper. Although it continued to cap the domain's copper procurement at 100,000 *kin* annually, the *bakufu* now allowed Tsushima to obtain copper directly from the Osaka copper merchant organization, albeit at market prices. In a further concession, however, Tsushima would be allowed to delay paying for the copper for two years, until the domain would presumably have garnered enough profits from sales of Korean imports on the domestic market. Nonetheless, Tsushima officials still bemoaned their position, claiming that the high cost of purchasing copper on the domestic market crippled their ability to continue the vital official trade with Korea. In an effort to force the *bakufu*'s hand, domain officials stressed that Tsushima would have difficulty maintaining diplomatic ties with the Chosŏn Kingdom if it could not easily obtain copper for the official trade. In 1825, the *bakufu* relented on this point as well, allowing the domain to purchase copper at below market price.[66]

Tsushima also benefited from the fact that Tokugawa officials began to see the domain's trade with Korea as a new avenue for importing

---

66. Tashiro, "Tsushima-han no Chōsen yushutsu dō chōtatsu ni tsuite," 194–98.

silver from China, as had been done through the Nagasaki clearing-house since the 1760s. The move was prompted by the aforementioned slowdown in trade at Nagasaki during the late 1820s. The *bakufu* annually allocated 1 million *kin* in copper for trade with Chinese merchants, but because fewer ships were calling at Nagasaki, the clearing-house was confronted with surpluses of up to 300,000 *kin* of copper per year. To help reduce these surpluses, in 1827, *bakufu* officials began to sell 50,000 *kin* annually to Tsushima, copper that the domain used to acquire silver in the way that the Nagasaki clearing-house used copper and marine products to obtain bullion in the supplemental trade. With this copper, Tsushima presumably garnered fees from the transaction and delivered roughly 100 *kan* of silver annually to the *bakufu*, funds no doubt deposited in the *bakufu* treasury.[67]

This was not the only copper scheme involving Tsushima. Based upon an agreement with Korea in 1836, Tsushima began to export an additional 3,000 *kin* of copper in place of the water buffalo horns delivered annually as part of the official trade. True to form, Tsushima officials tried to use this shift in trade as a means to gain still more aid from the *bakufu*. They claimed that while they were currently shipping 3,000 *kin*, the Koreans sought still more copper, a request that the domain was obligated to fulfill. Domain officials consequently asked permission to purchase an additional 11,000 *kin* per year. Tashiro concludes that the Tsushima leadership was unquestionably exaggerating its case and that Chosŏn officials had made no such request. Nonetheless, the domain appeals reached sympathetic ears within the *bakufu*. Ōkubo Tadazane, the senior councilor who had vigorously advocated the ban on Satsuma's sales in order to protect the Sō, acted on Tsushima's behalf. In 1838, he directed that Tsushima be given permission to obtain an additional 11,000 *kin* of copper for a five-year period. Following appeals by Tsushima, the *bakufu* permitted the domain to continue the practice between 1841 and 1844. Although the *bakufu* abolished the supplemental shipments from 1845 to 1847, it allowed Tsushima to continue to receive the extra copper from 1849 to 1852 and again from

---

67. Ibid., 196–200.

1854 to 1866.⁶⁸ More often than not, Tsushima leaders found that a constant stream of exaggerated appeals brought results.

Obtaining concessions in copper purchases and exports was just one part of Tsushima's sustained effort to acquire financial aid. Indeed, it is not an exaggeration to say that domain officials made subsidies and grants a focal point of their policy. The *bakufu* often granted the domain's requests, usually after a barrage of petitions. For example, in the 1810s, Tsushima gained several grants, the first 90,000 *ryō* in gold plus another 30,000 *ryō* as a loan, in the preparation for the arrival of a Korean embassy to the island in 1811. The *bakufu* also granted an annual stipend of 2,500 *ryō*, for 20 years, to reduce the economic pain inflicted by the slowdown in trade, an award in addition to the 12,000 *ryō* that the domain had received annually since 1776. In addition, it bestowed 10,000 *koku* of rice to offset the reduction in imported rice that resulted from poor harvests in Korea. To cap it off, as reward for the success of the 1811 embassy, the domain was awarded lands in Kyushu in 1818 valued at 20,000 *koku*. Domain leaders used this new windfall not to feed the people of the domain but to repay debts to Osaka merchants.⁶⁹

As a form of indirect aid to Tsushima, the *bakufu* also permitted the Sō to be lax in the biennial ritual of alternate residence. Between 1810 and 1842, the daimyo and his entourage traveled to Edo only five times. In the same period, daimyo from major domains would have made up to fifteen trips. The alternate-residence requirement was a tremendous financial drain on all lords; for the Sō, the round trip to Edo cost approximately 1,315 *kan*.⁷⁰

Yet despite all of the Tokugawa aid and concessions, Tsushima's trade remained largely stagnant in the first decades of the nineteenth century. Except for hides, hooves, and horns, the domain never found a niche on the domestic market. In particular, the domain could not exploit the active market in imported medicines because medicinal goods from Korea such as skullcap root were less valued than their

---

68. Ibid., 200–202.
69. Yamamoto, *Tsushima-han Edo garō*, 156–57; Arano, *Kinsei Nihon to higashi Ajia*, 234–35.
70. Tsuruta, "Tenpō-ki no Tsushima-han zaisei to Nitchō bōeki," 61.

Chinese counterparts. As a result, domain finances remained in a dismal state. In 1835, the domain was saddled with a staggering 8,530 *kan* (133, 281 *ryō*) in debt to Osaka and Edo merchants.[71] Now, though, Tsushima officials were in no position to simply reschedule the debts as Zusho was then doing in Satsuma. As a result, they turned to the *bakufu* for help.

Why did *bakufu* leaders provide so much assistance to a feckless and commercially inept Tsushima leadership, especially since past Tokugawa leaders had usually refused to aid debt-plagued domains?[72] For one, *bakufu* leaders no doubt realized that while trade was at an all time low, Tsushima nonetheless needed to maintain the official trade because it provided a considerable portion of domain revenue. More importantly, the domain population was also dependent upon Korean rice, a fact that Tsushima leaders did not let their Tokugawa overlords forget. Tsushima leaders consistently intimated that if the diplomatic relationship with Korea were severed, Tsushima would have faced an economic catastrophe, and by consequence, possible political unrest. Although a financial drain, *bakufu* leaders therefore probably surmised that the financial aid was a smaller price to pay than the potential challenges resulting from a weak Tsushima and the loss of diplomatic ties with Korea.

Maintaining the Outward Face of Guarded Engagement

In his rejection of Russian overtures, Matsudaira Sadanobu, the *bakufu* senior councilor in the 1780s and 1790s, developed a historical narrative of Japan's foreign relations, asserting that the *bakufu* had created a division of diplomatic and commercial contacts in the seventeenth century. *Bakufu* leaders continued to uphold this definition of foreign relations, as illustrated by the Tokugawa rejection of a Dutch appeal in 1844 for revisions of established practices in trade and diplomacy.

In an effort to ease *bakufu* restrictions on trade in Nagasaki but still maintain the privileged status of the Netherlands as the only European state allowed to trade with Japan, Dutch officials composed a special let-

---

71. Nagasaki kenshi henshū iinkai, ed., *Nagasaki kenshi, hanseihen*, 1109.
72. Bolitho, "The Tempō Crisis," 139.

ter from King William II addressed to the shogun. They hoped to underscore the importance of the letter by also providing details about the warship that would bear it and described how the man-of-war would offer a cannon salute when entering Nagasaki harbor.[73] In the letter itself, William emphasized the long history of relations between Japan and the Netherlands. The Dutch king further noted that the Qing regime had been weakened by its recent defeat in the Opium War (1839–42). He warned, "Such disasters now threaten the Japanese Empire. A mere mischance might precipitate a conflict. The number of all sorts of vessels sailing the Japanese seas will be greater than ever before, and how easily might a quarrel occur between the crews of those vessels and the inhabitants of Your Majesty's Dominion." The king continued, "It is our friendly advice, [to] ameliorate the laws against the foreigners, lest happy Japan be destroyed by war. We give Your Majesty this advice with honest intentions, free from political self-interest."[74]

Tokugawa senior councilors, including Abe Masahiro, who had recently assumed the post, coolly rejected the Dutch appeal. Restating the position formulated by Matsudaira, they asserted that in order to maintain peace in the surrounding oceans, Japan had since "ancient times" limited its diplomatic contact to Korea and Ryukyu and commercial engagement to the Dutch and China. The *bakufu* leaders therefore concluded that while commercial ties could continue in their present form, changes, such as the opening of formal diplomatic ties with the Netherlands, were not possible.[75]

It is tempting to view William's letter as representing the knock of modernity—a warning that Abe and the other *bakufu* leaders, with ideologically tuned ears, chose not to hear. Many historians see the Tokugawa rejection as part of a pattern of obstinacy in the face of rising British, and especially American, power that would be fully revealed when Perry arrived in 1853.[76] Offering another explanation, the diplo-

---

73. Ishin shiryō hensan jimukyoku, ed. *Dai Nihon ishin shiryō*, vol. 1.1, 112–19 (Hereafter *DNIS*); Nagazumi, "Tsūshō no kuni kara tsūshin no kuni e," 44–46.

74. Greene, "Correspondence between William II of Holland and the Shogun of Japan," 110–14. Greene provides the original text as well as English translations of the Tokugawa response.

75. *TIZ*, vol. 2, 526–28.

76. For example Tsuzuki, *The Pursuit of Power in Modern Japan*, 38–39.

matic historian Mitani Hiroshi suggests that power struggles within the *bakufu* leadership led to the refusal, concluding that Abe avoided radical reforms in favor of gradual consensus building.[77]

Although Mitani cites significant internal political dynamics, he overlooks the commercial context of the early nineteenth century. As Western ships appeared, hoping to convince a supposedly stagnant Japan to embrace foreign trade, *bakufu* leaders such as Ōkubo Tadazane and Mizuno Tadakuni were actually taking aggressive steps, especially against Satsuma, to reconstitute Tokugawa dominance in foreign commerce. Acting within the parameters of guarded engagement, they moved to ensure that the Tokugawa regime would benefit from domestic and foreign trade, which thrived anew thanks to proto-industrialization and increased consumer demand. It would have been a drastic step for Abe and his counterparts in the *bakufu* to have restructured the system at Nagasaki to provide concessions for the Dutch, given that previous leaders had just restored the commercial role of the Nagasaki clearinghouse. In addition, they had moved aggressively to regulate, for Tokugawa benefit, the thriving commerce along the Sea of Japan coast.

Moreover, as was the case with the Russians four decades earlier, the Dutch did not offer a convincing case for the benefits to Japan of expanded trade. Following the conclusion of the Napoleonic Wars in 1815, a steady trade with the Netherlands had been restored. Yet for the *bakufu*, trade with Chinese merchants remained far more lucrative and still provided a route to import of silver and some gold. Taken together, these circumstances suggest that Tokugawa leaders, informed by the context of foreign trade at that time, acted to maintain a system that most clearly benefited their regime.

Conclusions

In the first half of the nineteenth century, Britain was emerging as an increasingly dominant commercial force in East Asia, thanks to an opium trade that allowed it, for the first time, to obtain large amounts of silver in trade with China. Military victories against Qing forces in the Opium War built upon that commercial success and allowed Britain

---

77. Mitani, *Escape from Impasse*, 54–56.

to gain trade and territorial concessions, such as Hong Kong, which solidified its new powerful position in East Asia. Yet increasing British influence did not mean that the China market lost vitality across the board. For one, the huge population of the Qing Empire continued to demand specialty goods, including marine products produced in Southeast Asia, Micronesia, and Japan.

Thus, while Western power was gradually emerging, Japan's foreign trade and its overall system of foreign relations continued to be dominated by its connections with China. As we have seen, Japanese consumers still valued Chinese medicines and Southeast Asian medicinal goods imported via the China market. Indeed, the dominance of the China market is illustrated in the case of Tsushima, which saw its profits from imports of Korean skullcap root drop as Japanese consumers chose instead the Chinese variety, imported through Nagasaki and Ryukyu. Although skullcap root was only one import item, its trade patterns nonetheless illustrate the dilemma faced by Tsushima leaders: although trade with Korea was a fairly steady source of revenue, it would never compare to the revenue stream that the domain previously enjoyed when it has acted as a middleman in the silk-for-silver trade with China. Without a link to the China market, Tsushima could not expect to increase its trade revenues and was forced to continue its appeals for Tokugawa aid. In the same vein, the most promising means for Ryukyu to regain economic stability following the damage of successive typhoons and droughts was to expand its role as a conduit in trade between China and Japan.

The trade battle between the *bakufu* and Satsuma also occurred within the larger context of intercourse with the China market. A domestic market with increased consumer demand for marine products and foreign medicines brought new pulls and opportunities for foreign trade. In this environment, Satsuma created a trade network that threatened the carefully crafted Tokugawa trade system centered on Nagasaki. In building its commercial web, Satsuma exploited Ryukyu's need to remain connected to the China-centered tribute network. In so doing, Satsuma began to reclaim some agency in the system of foreign relations, although the shogunate extinguished the domain's drive, at least temporarily, by imposing severe limits on Satsuma's trade and by strengthening Tokugawa authority in the important Sea of Japan port of Niigata.

Yet it was not simply competition from Satsuma or a desire to restore Tokugawa authority that prompted Mizuno and the Tokugawa leadership to act so forcefully. Since the emergence of guarded engagement in the 1760s, the *bakufu* had increasingly come to rely upon commercial fees, assessed on domestic and foreign commerce, as a revenue source. A century earlier, *bakufu* officials had regulated foreign trade primarily to protect Nagasaki and to limit deleterious outflows of silver. Generally speaking, *bakufu* leaders viewed the profits gained as useful in providing funds to maintain the clearing-house with any excess funds being a bonus to be added to Tokugawa coffers. These factors continued to shape Tokugawa policy in the 1840s, but protecting the profits gained from commercial fees had become a more pressing concern, reflected in the expansive and unprecedented actions of Mizuno. Like Satsuma, the *bakufu* had become more invested in foreign and domestic trade.

FIVE

Local Japan Encounters the West

The arrival of Western ships—increasingly powered by steam engines and armed with superior weapons—profoundly affected Japan and East Asia in the mid-nineteenth century. Representing the vanguard of emerging Western power, the captains of merchantmen, whalers, and warships made aggressive appeals to establish commercial and diplomatic ties.

Because of the perceived Tokugawa monopoly on Japanese foreign relations, historians have traditionally portrayed *bakufu* officials as both formulating polices for, and overseeing engagement with, these Western visitors. What is more, the ideologically driven *bakufu* policy is often seen as embodied in the Shell and Repel Order, in effect from 1825 to 1842, which directed that coastal domains repel, with cannon fire, all foreign vessels approaching the Japanese coastline. With the focus on the *bakufu*, the experience of the coastal domains and the Ryukyu Kingdom, which constituted the front lines of engagement with Western visitors, is often overlooked. Indeed, while *bakufu* leaders promulgated and later repealed the Shell and Repel Order in the wake of the British victory in the Opium War in 1842, coastal domains had the responsibility of implementing it and on many occasions, actually chose not to do so.

During the seventeen years the order was in force, only two coastal domains executed it at all, and at that inconsistently. In 1837, Satsuma fired upon the private American ship *Morrison*, and Matsumae shelled unidentified vessels off Ezo in 1831 and 1834. Yet Matsumae batteries did not shell other foreign ships spotted off Ezo in 1832 and 1834.[1] Moreover, Ryukyu officials provisioned the *Morrison* and allowed its crew to stroll around the city of Naha and its environs before continuing on to Japan.[2] Although records of these incidents are spotty, they indicate that domains (and Ryukyu) were not merely instruments of Tokugawa policy but executed the Shell and Repel Order on an ad hoc basis. This absence of a unified response demonstrates that local issues and concerns shaped much Japanese engagement with increasing Western power.

The foreign ships that approached the Japanese coastline in the mid-nineteenth century often called at Matsumae, Tsushima, Satsuma, and Ryukyu because of their geographic positions along prominent sea lanes, especially those connecting to China, which most vessels visited before sailing to Japan. Western knowledge of Japan was certainly limited, but some vessels chose to stop at the above areas based on scraps of information indicating that the three domains and Ryukyu were important nodes for foreign trade. For example, in his account of the *Morrison*'s mission, a member of the crew, C. W. King, stated that his ship visited Satsuma because he and his crew believed the domain was ruled by "one of the most powerful and least dependent of the feudal princes." King was convinced that the prince's "authority extends over all the islands southward as far as Taiwan," and therefore concluded that "the possession of, and commerce with these groups, are supposed to give a maritime cast to the government and people of this principality. Here, too, the Chinese junks are said to come, to smuggle the remainder of their cargoes after leaving Nagasaki."[3] Satsuma officials chose to obey the Shell and Repel Order and fire on the *Morrison*. Yet as we shall see in this chapter, the incident was not representative of subsequent domain policy, which came to be defined more by accommodation than confrontation with Western visitors.

---

1. Taigai kankeishi sōgō nenpyō henshū iinkai, ed., *Taigai kankeishi sōgō nenpyō*, 866–80.
2. King, *Notes of the Voyage of the Morrison from Canton to Japan*, 87–111.
3. Ibid., 138–39.

Western Visits to Ryukyu and the Satsuma Response

Since the late eighteenth century, Western ships had periodically landed at islands throughout the Ryukyu chain. The Westerners and Ryukyuans usually had peaceful exchanges, although violence occurred in 1824 when a British whaler visited Takarajima, a small island in the Tokara island chain. When the whaler's crew killed one cow and stole two others, a gun battle broke out between the British and the locals. During the skirmish, a Shimazu retainer killed one of the crew, whose body was preserved in salt as evidence.[4]

In the 1840s, the number of vessels calling at the island kingdom increased dramatically. During that decade, an average of four Western vessels visited Ryukyu annually, whereas only seven ships had called throughout the 1830s.[5] The visit of the French ship *Alcmène* in the early spring of 1844 marks the beginning of a wave of Western pressure on Ryukyu. With Satsuma being distant and its governance indirect, Ryukyu officials made the initial decisions about how to deal with Western visitors.

When Western ships arrived, Ryukyu officials were kind and accommodating, offering fuel, water, and food, usually refusing payment in return. The islanders were evasive, however, when asked about trading, and declined to negotiate. When the captain of the *Alcmène* requested the establishment of trade ties, officials voiced what came to be the prescribed response to any Western inquiry. First, they lamented that their kingdom was poor, with its overseas trade comprised mainly of tribute trade with China and limited intercourse with Japan. Given its dependent status, they insisted that the kingdom was therefore not in a position to expand overseas trade. Finding the Ryukyuans unwilling to establish any agreement, the *Alcmène* departed but left behind a missionary, Theodore Augustin Forcade, and his Chinese interpreter to promulgate Christianity as well as to study the local culture and language. The officers of the French vessel warned that Forcade would prepare the ground for a large force that would soon arrive and press for an agreement. Over the next decade, the captains of French, British,

---

4. *TI*, vol. 6, 467–68.
5. Akamine, *Daikōkai jidai no Ryūkyū*, 78–82.

and American ships who visited the kingdom requested the establishment of diplomatic and commercial contacts, protocols for repatriating castaways, and aid for ships in distress. Subsequent French missions also repeatedly asked for permission to dispatch additional Christian missionaries to the kingdom.[6]

When Western vessels came into port, Ryukyu officials would submit reports about the encounters to the royal government at Shuri. If a tribute mission to China were scheduled, the Ryukyu court would provide details about the Western visits to the mission's chief envoy. The envoy would in turn brief Chinese officials when the mission stopped at Fuzhou en route to Beijing. In the 1840s and 1850s, Ryukyu remained a loyal Qing vassal, dutifully sending tribute missions despite turmoil within China resulting from Western military actions and the Taiping Rebellion. On its return trip from Beijing in 1853, a Ryukyu mission had to seek refuge for several months in northern Fujian province to avoid Taiping troops.[7] As more Westerners appeared on Ryukyu's coastline with some remaining for extended periods, Ryukyu envoys also repeatedly called on Chinese officials to assist the Shō, the Qing's loyal vassal. They asked for Chinese officials to request Western diplomats in Beijing to instruct the captains of their nation's vessels to stop calling at Ryukyu. On at least one occasion, Ryukyu officials also acted independently, in 1843 presenting a formal complaint to British diplomats in Fuzhou over the visit of a British vessel to several islands in southern Ryukyu.[8]

Ryukyu officials would also provide reports to the Satsuma resident magistrate, the head of the handful of Shimazu retainers stationed near Naha. The magistrate, who did not himself interact with Western visitors, relied almost exclusively on information from Ryukyu officials to prepare the reports he forwarded to Satsuma authorities in Kagoshima. Upon receiving those reports, the Satsuma leadership would decide on a course of action and determine what information to send to the

---

6. "Zairyū futsujin shokan ni taisuru tsūsho wakai daini," 1844/04/14, "Ryūkyū gaikoku kankei monjo" (hereafter *RGKM*). Dates are given according to the Japanese calendar in the form of year/month/date.
7. Maehira, "Higashi Ajia no kaigai jōhō to Ryūkyū rūto," 145–46.
8. *KK*, vol. 2, 789–90.

bakufu, often embellishing or withholding certain items if deemed beneficial to the domain. Domain leaders might also delay a report to Edo or to the Nagasaki magistrate, blaming the lapse in communication on rough weather or a tardy messenger ship.[9]

News of Westerners calling at Ryukyu ports exacerbated existing factional divisions within the Satsuma leadership. The domain is often described in this period as politically split between a "younger" radical faction led by the heir apparent Shimazu Nariakira, and a conservative one headed by his father, the daimyo Narioki and his chief adviser Zusho Shōzaemon. Viewed from the perspective of the Meiji Restoration, the younger faction appears more dynamic and receptive to institutional change and Western ideas. (Ōkubo Toshimichi and Saigō Takamori, two heroes of the Restoration who later implemented the expansive reforms of the early Meiji period, are seen as emerging from this radical faction.)[10]

Whether "conservative" or "radical," the two factions shared the spirit of commercial opportunism. Because of mutual suspicion, they were generally not aware (or chose not to be) of their common ground. However, under Western pressure, the leaders of both factions explored using Satsuma and Ryukyu-produced goods in new commercial schemes centered on the Japanese domestic market. They also generally sought to take advantage of established trade links with China, in preference to developing direct commercial ties with Western states. Importantly, while Western pressure shaped the commercial opportunism within the domain, Satsuma's enterprises were not imitations of Western-style trade or directly influenced by Western commercial principles.

In 1843, Godai Hidetaka, a domain Confucian scholar, wrote a secret memorial describing how Satsuma might respond to Western requests concerning Ryukyu. In it, he outlined policies that in various forms would eventually be adopted by all factions within the domain. Godai stressed that because Satsuma could not hope to repel a Western military attack on Ryukyu, negotiation was a better option. Ryukyu should first refuse to open trade on the grounds that it is small and

---

9. Robert Sakai, "Shimazu Nariakira and National Leadership in Satsuma," 214–15.
10. Iwata, *Ōkubo Toshimichi*, 35–36.

Fig. 16 Yamakawa, a stop for ships sailing between Kagoshima and Ryukyu, as pictured in an early nineteenth-century illustrated scroll. Three Ryukyu vessels, again marked by flags flying from their rigging, lay anchored in the harbor near numerous cargo ships. *Sappan shōkei hyakuzu: kaihen* [One hundred views of the Satsuma domain: the coastline]. Courtesy of Historiographical Institute, University of Tokyo.

poor. If Westerners continued to push, Godai argued that Ryukyu should assert that as a tribute state of China, requests for trade and diplomatic intercourse should be directed to Beijing. While Godai believed that this strategy was worth trying, he realized that in the wake of China's defeat in the Opium War, Western nations were inclined to ignore edicts from the Chinese government. Therefore, he offered a third option: to present a more accurate account of the kingdom's situation. Namely, that Ryukyu sends embassies to China, but it also dispatches them to Japan, from which it receives protection. If a Western nation wants to engage in trade, it must negotiate with the *bakufu*. It appears that Godai expected a Western nation would continue to force the issue and so presented a fourth and final option: open limited trade at selected ports in Ryukyu. Godai's first two options express a desire to maintain the established system of trade and diplomacy by using stall tactics to keep a Western probe at bay. If that failed, he suggested passing the buck to China or the *bakufu*. The final alternative was opening trade at Ryukyu—but not at Satsuma.[11]

The daimyo Narioki and his adviser Zusho appear to have considered Godai's proposals as they responded to the arrival of the *Alcmène* in the early spring of 1844. A few months after the ship's arrival, Narioki ordered 150 armed retainers to travel to Ryukyu, although not with alacrity. The group left Kagoshima on the 25th day of the sixth

---

11. Kuroda, "Kōka-ki no Ryūkyū gaikō jiken to Satsuma-han," 121–22.

month, but for unknown reasons, it remained in the port of Yamakawa until the 20th day of the eighth month.[12] The force arrived in Ryukyu early in the ninth month and took positions on the main island of Okinawa until being recalled to Satsuma six months later. Although the dispatch of troops was reported to the *bakufu*, their withdrawal was not.[13]

The agenda of the Narioki/Zusho faction explains why the troops were tardily dispatched and then removed so quickly. In his memoirs, Shimazu retainer Ebihara Sōnojo asserts that Zusho realized that the Westerners were as strong as "sumo wrestlers," while by comparison Satsuma had the strength of a "three- or four-year-old boy."[14] Zusho was convinced that the dispatch of a large force to Ryukyu would be futile. If hostilities broke out, the outgunned Satsuma men would lose badly. The more prudent option was to take a course like that advocated by Godai: instruct Ryukyu officials to engage in evasive negotiations and to make concessions incrementally, in response to escalations in French pressure.

This stance was tested by a new wave of Western visitors to Ryukyu that began two years later. On the fifth day of the fourth month of 1846, a British ship arrived at Naha and dropped off another missionary, Bernard Jean Bettelheim, along with his family and a Chinese translator.[15] Two days later, the French warship *Sabine*, with a crew of 300, arrived at Naha, requesting the opening of commercial and diplomatic ties, as well as permission to promulgate Christianity.[16] During subsequent meetings, Ryukyu officials refused the French proposals, asserting that the kingdom could not freely establish new trade ties because of its existing tribute tie with China. In addition, they urged French officers to stop sending Christian missionaries, declaring that the kingdom's Confucian traditions made Ryukyuans reluctant to em-

---

12. "Ryūkyū-koku ni shugo hakken no heiin oyobi buki no kazu," *RGKM*, 1844/06/23.

13. *KK*, vol. 2, 789.

14. Quoted in Uehara, "Bakumatsu Satsuma-han no tai Okinawa seisaku," 10.

15. *DNIS*, vol. 1.1, 300–308.

16. Ryukyu officials and the Satsuma resident magistrate recorded details of the *Sabine*'s visit (*DNIS*, vol. 1.1, 314–57).

brace Christianity.[17] They also subsequently stated that because of recent famines, the kingdom's economy had deteriorated, making increases in foreign trade impossible. In the following weeks, the *Sabine* moved to a harbor just south of Naha and began putting men ashore. On the thirteenth day of the fifth month, two more French warships appeared, raising the French force to 1,500 men. During their sojourn, the crew of the small French flotilla charted the coast, rode hired horses throughout the island, and freely associated with the people of Ryukyu. Finding the Ryukyuans unwilling to negotiate, French ships departed early in the eighth month of 1846.[18]

When Abe Masahiro, the *bakufu* senior councilor, received word of the French arrival, he requested more information from Satsuma. At Edo, Zusho, representing the Satsuma daimyo, briefed Abe and discussed options for dealing with the French. Consistent with Godai's memorial, Zusho suggested that Ryukyu might buy time by directing the French to make their appeals directly to the Qing court, a stance Abe supported. Zusho also stressed that Ryukyu representatives should urge that trade be opened in China, at Fuzhou, instead of their kingdom. When questioned about the number of men sent to defend Ryukyu, Zusho stated that 700–800 men had been dispatched the previous year, when in fact the number was only 150. Evidently, Zusho felt it necessary to assure Abe that Satsuma was strongly protecting Ryukyu, although he was actually pursuing the opposite course.[19] This decision demonstrates the strategic independence inherent in Satsuma's position as Zusho decided what information would be offered to *bakufu* leaders.

Always looking for commercial opportunities, Zusho developed plans to establish an office within the Ryukyu royal government to expand intercourse with the China market. Pursuant to this goal, he informed the Ryukyuans in the tenth month of 1846 that Satsuma would provide 10,000 to 20,000 *ryō* in seed money to commence trade at a Ryukyu port. Zusho envisioned importing goods not from France, but using French traders to bring products from China, especially those

---

17. "Ryūkyū futenkō ni kan torai no jijitsu o gushinsu," *RGKM*, 1844/08/16; *DNIS*, vol. 1.1, 394–400.

18. *DNIS*, vol. 1.1, 485–97.

19. *KK*, vol. 2, 795–96.

that the *bakufu* had recently prohibited Satsuma from selling at Nagasaki. The royal government, however, strongly opposed the measure, fearing it would bring more Westerners to the kingdom. Royal officials argued that if trade were to take place, it should be limited to indigenous Ryukyu products. Frustrated, Zusho instructed his men to explore other options that would allow Satsuma to better profit from trade with China via Ryukyu.[20]

Then, in the summer of 1846, the *bakufu* leadership abruptly chose to reverse course, permitting Satsuma to resume selling Chinese goods imported via Ryukyu at Nagasaki. The shogunate decreed that eleven of the sixteen products originally banned in 1839 could be sold for a five-year period to an overall limit of 1,200 *kan*. Although this was down from the earlier 1,720 *kan* limit allowed in the 1820s, Satsuma nonetheless regained legitimate access to the Japanese domestic market, and now could sell a total of sixteen goods.

Although they granted this concession, *bakufu* leaders nonetheless sought to protect Tokugawa trade revenues. They instructed Satsuma to search for substitute goods for three imports that the Nagasaki clearing-house found particularly profitable: licorice, China root, and the Chinese variety of skullcap root. Via Satsuma, Ryukyu officials declared that they could find no legitimate substitute goods for these medicinal products. The Ryukyu officials also stressed that because the three medicinal imports were especially lucrative, they brought profits that were used to finance tribute missions to the Qing. After further negotiation, Tokugawa officials caved on this point as well and in the end, Satsuma could sell all of the sixteen goods for which the *bakufu* had granted permission in 1825.[21]

These concessions, according to Uehara, were related to the arrival of the French earlier that year as well as the exit of Mizuno and the rise of Abe within the *bakufu* leadership. Abe found it painfully clear that a French or British military force had the power to seize parts of Ryukyu. He and the *bakufu* leadership could no longer dismiss Satsuma's appeals merely as cynical attempts to expand domain trade at the *bakufu*'s expense. Ryukyu might become more vulnerable to a Western attack if

---

20. Uehara, "Bakumatsu Satsuma-han no tai Okinawa seisaku," 11–12.
21. *KK*, vol. 2, 750–51.

trade and thus the kingdom's economy continued to stagnate. This concern, coupled with the fact that the *bakufu* was in no position to unilaterally defend Ryukyu, tipped the scales in Satsuma's favor.[22]

Over the next three years, Satsuma enjoyed an average annual profit of just over 5,600 *ryō* from sales of Chinese imports at Nagasaki. In addition, the domain continued to profit from shipping kelp and other marine products to Ryukyu for consumption there and for export to China.[23] In 1849, the *bakufu* granted the domain an additional five-year extension to sell the sixteen selected Chinese imports at Nagasaki, to once again "aid Ryukyu." Yet *bakufu* officials instructed that the domain must take measures to assure benefits for the Nagasaki clearing-house. Satsuma was to sell the imports through the clearing-house and pay the requisite fees, while also refraining from exporting to China via Ryukyu sea cucumbers, abalone, and other marine products, which were vital to the Nagasaki trade. Moreover, the domain was to be vigilant in preventing smuggling and must keep the level of its trade within the permitted 1,200 *kan*.[24]

Divisions within Satsuma

Satsuma gained these trade concessions partly through the lobbying efforts of Nariakira, the Shimazu heir apparent, who at that time was developing strong personal ties with the *bakufu* senior councilor, Abe Masahiro.[25] Along with personal rapport, the men found in one another an ally for their respective political agendas. Although Abe was concerned about the defense of Ryukyu, he had little say in the implementation of his edicts. He could not control the Satsuma retainers being dispatched to Ryukyu and had no independent method of gathering information about events in the kingdom. He therefore tried to influ-

---

22. Uehara, *Sakoku to han bōeki*, 255–56.
23. Ibid., 270.
24. "Kagoshima Ryūkyū-kan kikiyaku sashidashi oyakata todoke," 1849/11/24, "Dai Nihon ishin shiryō kōhon" (hereafter *DNISK*), KA 015-0756. Organized by chronological subject headings, the *DNISK* manuscript collection is composed of copies of original documents from 1846 to 1874. Each reference to the *DNISK* provides the name of document, the date (given by year, month, day according to the Japanese calendar), and the microfilm reel number.
25. *KK*, vol. 2, 751.

ence Satsuma's response through his personal relationship with Nariakira. Conversely, Nariakira, who was born and raised in Edo, had a weak power base in his familial Satsuma domain and therefore used his connections with Abe and other prominent lords to help push his agendas for Satsuma and Ryukyu.

In the summer of 1846, Abe and Nariakira began to work together to formulate a strategy for the defense of the Ryukyu kingdom. According to their eventual plan, which echoed the options outlined by Godai, Ryukyu officials would divert future French requests by using delaying tactics and by stating that as a tribute state of China, Ryukyu conducted diplomacy through the Qing court. If this ploy failed, limited trade with Westerners could be opened at a port in Ryukyu as a last resort. To assure that the plan would be implemented, Abe arranged for Shogun Ieyoshi to formally invest the younger Shimazu, Nariakira, rather than his father Narioki, with the responsibility for the defense of Ryukyu. Abe subsequently instructed Nariakira to mount a forceful defense that would "leave no regrets" and protect the "Japanese state" (*kokutai*).[26] That Tokugawa leaders were protective of trade at Nagasaki is again illustrated by the fact that two magistrates attending the meeting forcefully objected to the plan, not because it gave too much authority to Nariakira, but because the expansion of trade at Ryukyu might dampen the flow of goods through Nagasaki. To assuage their concerns, Nariakira agreed to endeavor to limit the scale of new trade at Ryukyu.[27]

Thereafter, Nariakira proceeded as ordered to Kagoshima, arriving there late in the sixth month, just about a month after his final meeting with Abe. He became personally involved in strengthening Satsuma's defenses, particularly coastal batteries, interpreting his instructions to defend Ryukyu as also involving a strengthening of the domain's defenses. Nariakira's sudden intrusion helped divide the domain between his supporters and those of his father Narioki and Zusho. Because of the bitter rivalry, Nariakira and Zusho, who formulated most trade policies for his lord, kept their respective plans for trade in Ryukyu se-

---

26. Although *kokutai* had many different connotations in nineteenth-century (and subsequent) discourse, the context of this document suggests that Abe was using it to represent the "Japanese realm" (*DNIS*, vol. 1.2, 30–38).

27. Kōshaku Shimazu-ke henshūjo, ed., *Sappan kaigunshi*, vol. 1, 418–19.

cret, and the opposing factions therefore seem to have been unaware of the common tenets of their overall plans. In actuality, both shared the essential goal of strengthening the domain and were open to the possibility of allowing some trade at Ryukyu ports if Western pressure became too intense. Although Nariakira implemented measurable improvements in domain defenses, Zusho and Narioki, who wanted to limit Nariakira's involvement in domain affairs, resented his presence. Early in 1847, Narioki left Edo and returned to Kagoshima, thereafter regaining influence within the domain. The return of his father, coupled with the fact that Nariakira's role as defensive coordinator was probably deemed less vital because of the French departure from Ryukyu in the late summer of 1846, placed the younger Shimazu in an untenable political situation. Frustrated, Nariakira returned to Edo.

Soon after arriving in Edo, a bitter Nariakira began to scheme against Zusho and Narioki, for whom he apparently held little filial affection. He hoped to push Zusho from power and then force his father to retire as daimyo, opening the way for his succession. In this endeavor, he used personal connections with powerful lords, such as Date Munenari of Uwajima and especially his great-uncle, Kuroda Narihiro of Fukuoka. Abe also supported Nariakira and could have simply ordered Narioki to step down. Yet the senior councilor was circumspect, wanting to avoid the perception that the *bakufu* was intruding too aggressively in domain affairs. After detailed consultation with Kuroda, in the eighth month of 1848, Nariakira leaked details of the covert scheme, proposed by Zusho in 1846, to use Satsuma funds to expand Ryukyu's trade with China through the port of Fuzhou, a plan that had not been submitted to the *bakufu* for approval. Abe soon learned of the scheme, and during a meeting in Edo in the twelfth month, he confronted a shocked Zusho. Fearing that Narioki would now face a Tokugawa reprimand, Zusho, the loyal retainer, committed suicide at the domain residence in Edo, taking responsibility for the tarnish brought to his lord's reputation. In this cutthroat intra-domain rivalry, Nariakira had adeptly used Abe's support to great success.[28]

---

28. Haraguchi Torao, *Bakumatsu no Satsuma*, 164–65.

With Zusho gone, Narioki and Nariakira jockeyed for the next two-and-a-half years over when the elder Shimazu would retire. Although Narioki eventually agreed to step down in the wake of the smuggling allegations, he hoped to enhance the power of Nariakira's half brother, Hisamitsu, whom he promoted to higher posts in the domain leadership. Hisamitsu's mother, Yura, gained the ear of Narioki and urged him to suppress the Nariakira faction. In late 1849, Narioki learned of a plot by supporters of Nariakira to murder Yura and Hisamitsu. Furious, he ordered the arrest of about 40 of the Nariakira faction, instructing that the three ring leaders commit suicide, their samurai status be eliminated, and their bodies crucified. The others implicated were either forced to commit suicide or exiled to remote islands.

Narioki's move seemed to have quashed, at least temporarily, the factional competition. Yet in the end, Nariakira gained the upper hand by adeptly using the support of other powerful lords, most notably Date and Kuroda. With their backing, Abe was able to place enough pressure upon Narioki to force him to retire as daimyo, paving the way for Nariakira's succession, in the second month of 1851.[29]

Nariakira in Control

Local histories of today's Kagoshima prefecture paint Nariakira's ascension as a fortuitous, progressive event for the domain, as he is viewed as possessing a clear understanding of how the Opium War had changed power dynamics within East Asia. The accounts portray Nariakira as using that knowledge to develop foresighted political, commercial, and military polices that strengthened not only Satsuma but the Japanese state as well.[30] Historian Robert Sakai casts Nariakira as a cosmopolitan progressive, fighting against the backward, feudal policies of the Zusho/Narioki faction. "The strong-willed daimyo Narioki and the equally determined Zusho continued to regard Ryukyu as a closed preserve for the *han*, to be controlled without interference from the *bakufu*," writes Sakai. "Nariakira, in contrast, foresaw the danger to the larger political entity, the nation, of which Satsuma was but a minor part."[31] Holding

---

29. Haraguchi Torao, *Kagoshima-ken no rekishi*, 199–201.
30. Shōko Shūseikan, *Shimazu-ke omoshiro rekishikan 2*, 17–18.
31. Robert Sakai, "Shimazu Nariakira and National Leadership in Satsuma," 232.

a larger "national" vision, Nariakira is cast as a more positive force than the provincial and closed-minded Narioki and Zusho.

Yet were Zusho and Narioki the calculating, parochial operators that Sakai describes? Concerning the token dispatch of armed men to Ryukyu, Zusho appears to have acted soberly and taken the only realistic course. If he had sent a large armed contingent to Ryukyu and confronted the French, support from the *bakufu* and other domains would have been slow in coming, if it came at all. Indeed the reluctance of Tokugawa officials to become involved in the events in Ryukyu became clear when in 1854 American envoys requested *bakufu* assistance in establishing commercial ties with the kingdom. *Bakufu* officials flatly refused, asserting that Ryukyu is "a very distant country, and the opening of its harbor cannot be discussed by us."[32] Given this stance, Zusho appears to have chosen a more prudent approach by exploring how to use trade to fiscally strengthen and thus protect Ryukyu and Satsuma.

When we examine Nariakira's stances during the visits of Commodore Matthew Perry to Ryukyu and Japan in 1853 and 1854, the contrast between Nariakira and Zusho/Narioki appears less stark than assumed. In fact, Nariakira's position concerning concessions to Perry and other Westerners was initially not as "progressive" as portrayed.

Perry's arrival near Edo in the summer of 1853 has long been seen as a historical watershed, particularly because it led to the signing of the Kanagawa Treaty (U.S.-Japan Treaty of Friendship) the following year. Less is written about Perry's visits to Ryukyu and how the kingdom's leaders made a series of accommodations to American demands. The American squadron first stopped in the Ryukyuan port of Naha in the early summer of 1853 en route to Japan, where Perry would deliver a letter from President Millard Fillmore. He then sailed, again via Ryukyu, to Hong Kong, where he wintered and awaited the Tokugawa reply. During the second stop at Naha, he tried, unsuccessfully, to negotiate a diplomatic agreement; however, he did establish a coaling station (with a capacity of 500 tons) on Okinawa to provision his and future American vessels. En route back to Japan in early 1854, Perry again briefly dropped anchor at Naha. He made a final visit to Naha in the summer of 1854, as he sailed homeward after achieving his main ob-

---

32. Pineau, ed., *The Personal Journal of Commodore Matthew C. Perry*, 170–72.

jective of opening ties with Japan by concluding the Kanagawa Treaty with the *bakufu*. Because of his success in Japan, Perry was less interested in maintaining an American presence on Okinawa and thus ordered that the coal be removed from the coaling station (although he requested that the building be maintained for possible future American use). Hoping to develop trade ties beneficial to the United States, he pressured Ryukyu officials to sign a treaty.[33]

Based upon his advice to *bakufu* leaders that they take a firm stand in their negotiations with Perry, it would be reasonable to conclude that Nariakira would have pushed Ryukyu officials to deny Perry's appeals. In the memorial he submitted to the *bakufu* following Perry's 1853 visit to a port near Edo, Nariakira implied that the shogunate might want to use military means to expel Westerners. He asserted that the *bakufu* should play for time in negotiating with the United States because "it is certain that, by the time three years have passed, all the provinces [domains] will have completed their preparations. When we have completed our military preparations, I believe there will be ample means to obtain victory if the *bakufu* orders expulsion, for Japan's military spirit has always been heroic." [34]

Yet perhaps because he realized, like Zusho, that a military confrontation at Ryukyu would be futile, Nariakira allowed Ryukyu to pursue a course of greater engagement with the United States, and later other Western nations. With Nariakira's tacit approval, Ryukyu officials concluded an agreement with Perry in the summer of 1854. Drawing on the precedent of the Kanagawa Treaty, the "Compact Between the United States and the Kingdom of Lew Chew [Ryukyu]" allowed American ships to obtain wood and water at any port. The pact also allowed ad hoc, free exchanges of goods between Americans and Ryukyuans at Naha, stating that "whatever either party may wish to buy shall be exchanged at reasonable prices." In turn, it obliged Ryukyu authorities

---

33. The creation and later removal of the coaling station are described in Hawks, *Narrative of the Expedition of an American Squadron to the China Seas and Japan*, vol. 1, 276–80, 495.

34. "Shimazu Nariakira to *Bakufu*, 2 September 1853," in Beasley, ed. and trans., *Select Documents on Japanese Foreign Policy, 1853-1868*, 112–14.

Fig. 17 Shimazu Nariakira (1809–58). Courtesy of Shōko Shūseikan, Kagoshima.

to help American castaways and vessels in distress, and gave Americans visiting the kingdom the "liberty to ramble where they please, without hindrance, or having officials sent to follow them, or to spy what they do."[35] The compact marked the first occasion on which the Ryukyu Kingdom formally submitted to the demands of a Western state.

Although nothing in the agreement allowed for the opening of permanent trade ties, Nariakira no doubt recognized that more extensive commercial relations with Westerners could be based on it. Over the next few years, he instructed Ryukyu officials to offer future Western visitors similar terms. In his subsequent moves, he displayed a hearty commercial opportunism and a reluctance to use any type of military force against Western visitors. When French ships again arrived at Ryukyu in the tenth month of 1855, its officials, acting on instructions

---

35. Hawks, *Narrative of the Expedition of an American Squadron to the China Seas and Japan*, vol. 1, 495–96.

from Nariakira, negotiated a treaty that allowed a French mission to be established on the main island of Okinawa, and for the French, like the Americans, to have the freedom to travel throughout the island.[36]

Nariakira's willingness to deal with Westerners went so far as to actually contravene *bakufu* orders. In the sixth month of 1857, the shogunate instructed Satsuma to strengthen Ryukyu's defenses because the Dutch planned to send an envoy to negotiate a commercial treaty similar to that signed with the French.[37] Instead, Nariakira directed Ryukyu officials to negotiate an agreement that would lay the groundwork for trade with the Netherlands. He stressed the need for secrecy: from China, to protect Ryukyu's tribute trade with the Qing; and from the *bakufu*, as trade between the Netherlands and Ryukyu would threaten Tokugawa trade with the Dutch at Nagasaki.[38]

Nariakira did not stop there. He has often been credited with proactively imitating Western economic practices when he ordered the construction of the Shūseikan, a factory in the Kagoshima harbor that employed 1,200 men in the manufacture of cannon, rifles, glassware, porcelain, and agricultural implements. Less well known are his plans to develop at Ryukyu new trade links with Western merchants and the China market that would not only bring financial rewards but enhance Satsuma's military power. To this aim, Nariakira sent Ichiki Shirō to Ryukyu in the first month of 1858 to procure 1,000 modern rifles and a steam-powered warship from the French. He instructed Ichiki also to acquire a commercial steamship to allow Satsuma to profit from the transport of goods throughout markets within Japan. All the while, Ichiki was to keep his actions discreet to avoid both *bakufu* and Chinese officials from learning of the plans. So pressing were these tasks, Nariakira stated, that if the French mission on Ryukyu failed to cooperate, Ichiki was to order a Ryukyu official to travel to Fuzhou to obtain the ships and guns from English, French, or Dutch merchants at that port.

---

36. "Ryūkyū-Furansu washin kōeki yakujō" (Japanese text), "Ryūfutsu washin jōyaku" (French text), 1855/10/15, *DNISK*, AN 043-0006.
37. "Rōjū tashi," 1857/06/28, *DNISK*, AN 076-0372.
38. "Shinno Suraga, Shimazu Higo mōshitashi," 1857/07/28, *DNISK*, AN 078-0803.

Nariakira also had grand commercial plans for increasing trade with China by establishing a base on Taiwan and by expanding the Ryukyu House at Fuzhou. The breadth of the Satsuma daimyo's aims are revealed in a document dated the first month of 1858, in which he declared: "Although Nagasaki has been the main port of foreign trade for the realm, hereafter we will work to gradually have foreigners come to Ryukyu to trade. At Unten [a port on Okinawa island] and Amami Ōshima, we will establish trading posts that foreigners will chose to visit over Nagasaki."[39]

Ichiki quickly began to implement these proposals. In the seventh month of 1858, he and Ryukyu officials signed a pact with French envoys whereby Ryukyu would purchase a French warship and small arms, an agreement envisioned by both sides as the start of a regular trading relationship.[40] Thus, just after the American envoy Townsend Harris and *bakufu* officials concluded the U.S.-Japan Treaty of Amity and Commerce (in the sixth month of 1858) that set the date for the opening of three Japanese ports to Western-style free trade in the summer of 1859, Nariakira was poised to immediately turn Ryukyu into a trading hub in a bid to integrate the Western powers into Satsuma's commercial network, and by doing so, increase Satsuma's control over trade around Kyushu and Ryukyu.

Ichiki and the Ryukyu officials who negotiated the agreement were unaware, however, of the sudden death of Nariakira just a few weeks before, an event that precipitated a policy reversal within the domain. Nariakira's brother, Shimazu Hisamitsu, assumed control as regent for his under-age son Tadayoshi and ordered the cancellation of the agreement. He arrested some of the Ryukyu officials involved, and would have done the same to Ichiki, had he not gone into hiding.[41]

During the period from 1840 to 1859, Nariakira was not simply imitating Western models nor as some have argued, building upon a tradition of Dutch studies in the domain.[42] Like Zusho and his father before him, the Satsuma lord drew upon the commercial opportunism

---

39. "Shimazu Nariakira shokan," 1858/01/20, *DNISK*, AN 092-0901.
40. "Ryūkyū kanri jōkisen chōbun yakujōsho," 1858/07/26, *DNISK*, AN 110-0747.
41. Kerr, *Okinawa*, 346.
42. Beasley, *The Meiji Restoration*, 120–21.

within Satsuma as he sought to develop new trading opportunities. In addition, Nariakira flexed the agency of his domain as he guided Satsuma on an independent course. Although Nariakira welcomed the assistance of Abe, a *bakufu* senior councilor, in his effort to gain control of the domain, he concealed from the *bakufu* his subsequent plans to expand foreign trade at Ryukyu. Nariakira, who appears to have been even more cunning and deliberate than Zusho, offering rhetoric of working with the *bakufu* while simultaneously pursuing independent programs to enrich and strengthen Satsuma.

Finally, like others before him, Nariakira remained focused on trade with China. The Satsuma lord made expansive plans to develop Ryukyu's trade with China in a way that would complement new intercourse with Westerners.

Tsushima and Western Visitors

As was the case with commercial policies in the early nineteenth century, the domain of Tsushima provides a useful contrast to Satsuma in mid-century. In the 1840s, Western vessels began to appear in great numbers off Tsushima, and domain officials there also had to deal with Westerners who came ashore without permission, requesting trade. Unlike Satsuma, the domain requested greater *bakufu* guidance in dealing with the Westerners, and as before, it also appealed for increased financial aid, this time to help bolster domain defenses. Although Tsushima leaders had become adept at gaining aid from the shogunate, the domain did not receive financial support specifically for coastal defense until the 1840s.

Beginning in 1846, Tsushima officials came to increasingly cite foreign pressure as a rationale for receiving additional financial aid. Their memorials indicate a genuine concern over the defense of the island mixed with an opportunistic desire to use the specter of a Western military attack to extract concessions from the *bakufu*. Tsushima leaders began to define their domain as contributing to the realm's defense not as a source of foreign intelligence but as a key border province that should be fortified to help the overall defense of the Japanese realm.

In the twelfth month of 1846, high-ranking domain officials Sasu Iori and Yoshikawa Saemon presented a long memorial to Abe Masahiro requesting that additional revenue-producing lands be granted to their lord, Sō Yoshiyori, to help defray costs related to coastal defense. The two men noted the recent arrival of Commodore James Biddle of the U.S. Navy at Uraga (near Edo) and how lords of other coastal domains were also dealing with Western visitors. They made particular note of Shimazu Narioki, who shouldered costs related to the recent visits by French warships at Ryukyu but enjoyed a far better financial position to bolster coastal defenses because of Satsuma's size and wealth. Sasu and Yoshikawa also continued to stress Tsushima's important role in relations with Korea and their domain's economic difficulties, which resulted from the dearth of trade with Korea.

In their appeal, they also offered a new interpretation of Tsushima's role in the defense of the Japanese realm. As Amenomori Hōshū had over a century before, they used "bulwark" to describe Tsushima's role, but went beyond Amenomori's assertion that the domain, via its trade with Korea, served primarily as a gatherer of intelligence. Instead, Sasu and Yoshikawa stressed that the island of Tsushima itself, located as it was in the straits between Japan and Korea, functioned as a "bulwark against foreign states," a physical barrier to protect the larger Japanese realm. They argued that the *bakufu* should take special note of Tsushima's role in the larger defense of the realm and therefore help their "small and weak domain," which faced particular challenges in coastal defense because it was surrounded on all sides by the ocean.[43] In the end, the *bakufu* denied Sasu's and Yoshikawa's request for a grant of lands.

Yet seemingly on cue, the number of Western ships arriving off the Tsushima coastline soon increased. In the eighth month of 1847, lookouts at Tsutsu, a village on the southern coast, reported offshore cannon fire to their superiors at Fuchū, the administrative seat of the domain.[44] The following month, domain officials at the Japan House in Pusan reported that two French ships had been spotted off the Korean coast, a report that Fuchū forwarded to Edo.[45] On the seventh day of

---

43. "Fuchū Tsushima-han gansho" 1846/12/18, *DNISK*, KO 0007-0326.
44. "Izuhara hanshu Sō Yoshiyori kerai todoke," 1847/09/23, *DNISK*, KO 014-0151.
45. "Izuhara hanshu Sō Yoshiyori todoke rōjū ate," 1847/09/22, *DNISK*, KO 014-0151.

the third month of 1848, the sound of cannon fire was once again reported, and two days later, a Sō retainer in Tsutsu sent word that a ship had possibly drifted ashore in heavy fog. A week later, villagers reported hearing two more cannon shots and the domain leadership dispatched armed retainers to Tsutsu and nearby coastal villages. The domain subsequently reported to the *bakufu* that during just two days in the third month, ten foreign ships had been spotted offshore.[46]

Although the vessels had not been hostile, the Tsushima leadership was worried that their increasing numbers foretold a future incursion. Domain leaders once again petitioned the *bakufu* for substantial financial support in the seventh month of 1848. As usual, Tsushima officials lamented the domain's dependency upon Korean rice and complained that its coffers were bare because of the slowdown in the once-prosperous trade with Korea. The Tsushima leadership now had additional ammunition, however: with the increase in foreign ships, the domain's unique defensive needs—particularly its position far from other parts of Japan—made more aid necessary. In addition, domain leaders stressed that because Tsushima was surrounded on all sides by water, the cost of fortifying its coastline would prove more onerous than for other domains. *Bakufu* officials evidently found the appeal persuasive, granting a loan of 10,000 *ryō* to be awarded in 5,000 *ryō* installments over the next two years.[47]

Tsushima leaders, already concerned by the growing wave of foreign sightings, became all the more anxious following a face-to-face encounter with Westerners. In the second month of 1849, fifteen foreign ships were spotted off Kuwa village, on the southeast coast not far from Fuchū. One of the ships sent a launch ashore. Using gestures, domain officials learned that they were Americans, probably from a whaling vessel. The meeting was amicable and small items were exchanged. When domain officials asked the Americans to depart, they willingly did so.[48] Although it had been curiosity that prompted the small group of Americans to come ashore, a worried Yoshiyori dispatched some of

---

46. "Izuhara hanshu Sō Yoshiyori todoke rōjū ate," 1848/03/16, *DNISK*, KA 002-0348.
47. "Sō-ke kiroku," 1848/08/12, *DNISK*, KA 005-0508.
48. "Izuhara-han kiroku," 1849/02/27, *DNISK*, KA 010-0234.

his retainers to coastal villages to bolster defenses.[49] Two months later, another American whaler dispatched a landing party to the eastern coast of the island. The Americans spent the night at a coastal village before returning to their ship.[50] In light of the difficulties in communicating with the Americans, the domain also requested permission from the *bakufu* to send several of its Korean-language interpreters, who facilitated trade contacts at the Japan House, to Nagasaki to learn "Dutch writing" to be better prepared to communicate with the crews of Western ships.[51]

Tsushima officials continued to send to Edo and to the Nagasaki magistrate regular reports describing the sighting of foreign ships, which were reaching astonishing levels. For example, in a twelve-day span during the fourth month of 1849, a total of 33 foreign ships were spotted along the domain's western coast. In the next month, Tsushima stated that another 32 foreign ships passed along its western coastline in a five-day period.[52] Perhaps domain lookouts were counting the same ships two or three times as they sailed up and down the coast. Indeed, domain officials at the Japan House in Pusan may have made the same miscalculation, reporting that 54 foreign ships had passed near the Korean coast in recent months.[53] Although these numbers are hard to believe, they can be verified independently by a document from the Hirado domain stating that a ship from the Iki domain brought word of 30 foreign vessels having passed near Tsushima in the past month.[54]

Late in the spring of 1849, domain officials requested additional funds for defense, this time asking that the stipend of 10,000 *ryō* granted the previous year be renewed for two more years. In their request, domain officials asserted that Western pressure on their domain had become relentless, stating that during the previous few months, a stag-

---

49. "Izuhara-han kiroku," 1849/02/21, *DNISK*, KA 010-0234. The document also lists awards of cotton and rice presented to each group (*kumi*) for their duties.
50. "Izuhara-han chō kiroku," 1849/04/18, *DNISK*, KA 011-0853.
51. "Izuhara-han chō kiroku," 1849/04 [intercalary]/02, *DNISK*, KA 011-0853.
52. "Izuhara hanchō kiroku," 1849/04/09, *DNISK*, KA 010-0234; "Izuhara hanchō kiroku," 1849/04 [intercalary]/01, *DNISK*, KA 010-0234.
53. "Izuhara hanchō kiroku," 1849/04 [intercalary]/05, *DNISK*, KA 010-1081.
54. "Hirado shiryō nenpyō," 1849/02/26, *DNISK*, KA 010-0234.

gering 180 ships had been sighted in the waters around Tsushima.⁵⁵ This number is difficult to believe and strongly suggests that domain officials were being creative in their tallies. *Bakufu* leaders were no doubt skeptical of Tsushima's claims and denied the request for extended aid. Two years later, however, the *bakufu* did relent and granted the domain extensions to pay the loans it had received over the past decades.⁵⁶

All the while, Western visitors continue to approach the waters around Tsushima. In the second month of 1850, the domain reported to Edo and the Nagasaki magistrate that during a recent two-week span, twelve ships had been spotted off the coast of the domain. In turn, the domain claimed that in a ten-day span in the second month, fifteen more ships had appeared, with four more sighted off the Korean coast. In early 1851, the domain also reported additional ships off its coastline.

True to form, domain officials once again petitioned the *bakufu* for aid to assuage costs related to defense. This time, Yoshiyori took a new tack, claiming that the increased Western pressure on the Chosŏn Kingdom would force the Koreans to focus more financial resources and manpower on defense. Because fewer Koreans would be engaged in agriculture, he argued, Korea's agricultural production, which had already dropped in recent years, would decline further. According to Yoshiyori, this drop would in turn jeopardize Korean rice shipments to Tsushima, and he therefore appealed for 7,000 *koku* of rice from the shogunate, a request *bakufu* leaders denied.⁵⁷

In looking at Tsushima during the period between 1846 and 1853, we must consider the incredible numbers of ships that domain officials reported to the *bakufu*. It seems clear that Tsushima leaders exaggerated the numbers, but it is difficult to gauge to what degree. Nonetheless, the numbers do provide valuable insight on the mindset of Tsushima leaders. We can speculate that in an effort to receive *bakufu* support, Tsushima officials sought to present a worst-case scenario for the domain amidst the growing Western presence in East Asian waters.

---

55. "Izuhara-han kiroku," 1849/04 intercalary/09, *DNISK*, KA 010-1081.
56. "Izuhara-han kiroku," 1851/11/24, "Izuhara-han mainikki," 1851/04/26, *DNISK*, KA 029-1134.
57. "Izuhara-han kiroku," 1853/06/03, *DNISK*, KA 039-0627.

Table 1: Foreign Ships Reported Near or Landing in Tsushima and Korea, 1847–59

Year	Month	Details
1847	2nd	1 ship passes along Korean coast
	8th	sound of cannon fire
	9th	2 French warships along Korean coast
1848	3rd	sound of cannon fire; unknown number of ships approach coast in heavy fog; 10 ships spotted off west coast
1849	1st	12 ships spotted off western and eastern coasts
	2nd	15 ships pass along western coast; crew of American vessel land on eastern coast
	4th	33 ships spotted along western coast in twelve-day period; crew of American vessel spends night at village on eastern coast
	4th*	32 ships spotted along western coast during five-day period; 54 ships pass along the Korean coastline in past three months
	5th	4 ships pass along eastern coast
1850	1st–3rd	35 ships spotted off western coast; 4 ships pass along Korean coast
1851	2nd–3rd	3 ships spotted off western coast; 5 ships spotted of eastern coast
1852	12th	1 ship passes along western coast; American whaler delivers Japanese castaways to Japan House
1853	2nd	7 ships pass along western coast
	3rd	9 ships pass along western coast
1854	2nd	7 ships spotted off eastern coast
	4th	2 ships spotted off eastern coast
1855	1st–4th	10 ships spotted off eastern coast
	6th	1 ship spotted off eastern coast
	8th	3 British warships call at Pusan; 1 French warship calls at Pusan
1856	2nd	1 ship spotted off eastern coast
	3rd	1 ship (nationality unspecified) calls at Pusan; 4 ships spotted off southwest coast
	5th	3 ships spotted off southwest coast
	6th	crew of foreign vessel (nationality unspecified) briefly visits coastal village; 5 ships spotted off eastern and western coasts
	8th	3 ships (nationality unspecified) call at Pusan
1859	4th–5th	HMS *Actaeon* arrives, crew makes extended stay at several villages
	5th	HMS *Actaeon* calls at Pusan
	10th–11th	HMS *Actaeon* and unspecified British warship call at Pusan
	11th	HMS *Actaeon* and unspecified British warship call

NOTE: Details refer to Tsushima unless Korea is indicated. Asterisk (*) denotes intercalary month.
SOURCES: Number of vessels between 1847 and 1853 compiled from *DNISK*. Numbers between 1853 and 1859 compiled from *DNISK*; Hino, *Bakumatsu ni okeru Tsushima to Ei-Ro*, 3–26; Nagasaki kenshi henshū iinkai, ed., *Nagasaki kenshi, hanseihen*, 1116–17.

Although often verging on the melodramatic, the presentation of Tsushima as a "small and weak" domain unable to sufficiently prepare against a Western incursion was essentially valid. Tsushima officials apparently felt that they had to continually press their case in order to receive attention from the *bakufu*. This effort is abundantly clear in a memorial that Sō Yoshiyori presented in the ninth month of 1853. Like Shimazu Nariakira of Satsuma, Yoshiyori offered his views on how the *bakufu* should respond to the points presented in President Fillmore's letter, which was delivered by Commodore Perry. In his memorial, Yoshiyori offers the perspective of the lord of a frontline domain that had played an integral role in Japanese foreign relations throughout the Edo period. He also speaks from the perspective of a leader who felt issues of coastal defense more keenly because of the arrival of numerous Western ships to his domain over the previous seven years. Yoshiyori, who had ruled Tsushima as daimyo since 1843, echoed themes presented by other daimyo, stressing the need to increase studies of Western gunnery and to use negotiation to buy time to improve the overall defensive posture of the realm. Yet he also urged the *bakufu* to take note of Western pressure on *his* domain. To make his point, Yoshiyori attached an additional statement that detailed how "small and weak" Tsushima was bearing an inordinate brunt of Western pressure. Echoing some of the same grievances presented in earlier appeals, he complained,

> As I stated many times before, the Tsushima domain is a bulwark against foreign states. Yet, our domain is an isolated island separated from the rest of the realm. As we are surrounded on four sides by the ocean, we have a coastline that is over one hundred *ri* [approximately 244 miles]. We cannot defend all of that area alone. Additionally, we must consider how the recent unrest in China [the Taiping Rebellion] will affect defense. The domain is also in a troubled state because there is little hope of restoring trade with Korea to past levels.[58]

Yoshiyori stressed that the defense of the realm was something for which he and his retainers would fight to the death. Like his predecessors, he also lamented the lack of trade with Korea and how more than half of the domain's rice is imported from Korea.[59] His main point was

---

58. "Tsushima Fuchū hanshu Sō Yoshiyori jōsho," 1853/09/04, *DNISK*, KA 052-0942.

59. Ibid., 1853/09/01, *DNISK*, KA 052-0942.

clear: in this time of crisis, when coastal defense was a pressing issue, Tsushima, an important region in the defense of the realm, required extra funds to allow it to repulse a possible foreign attack. Yoshiyori was pleading not to be forgotten.

The memorial illustrates clearly how Tsushima leaders had shifted their position, describing the island as a "bulwark against foreign states," an area that was fundamental in the realm's coastal defense. In other words, Tsushima was continuing to articulate how it functioned as a geographic boundary that needed to be fortified against potential enemies. By the 1850s, the domain leadership had definitely moved away from viewing the domain as performing the role of information collector for the *bakufu*, and more consistently touted itself as a region strategically important in the larger realm.

The arrival at Tsushima of the British warship HMS *Actaeon* in the fourth month of 1859 marked the beginning of a new phase of Western intrusion and caused consternation among domain leaders. Thereafter, Westerner visitors became bolder, many of them viewing Tsushima as a site for a commercial or naval base. During their three-week stay, members of the *Actaeon*'s crew visited several coastal villages and even climbed Mt. Shiratake, the highest peak on the island. After departing Tsushima, the *Actaeon* sailed to Pusan, charting the harbor and sending representatives to the Japan House. When word of this episode reached Fuchū, ten men were dispatched to the Japan House to bolster defenses there. A distressed Yoshiyori thanked the gods of Mt. Shiratake for delivering the domain from the foreign interlopers.[60]

Yoshiyori and his officials were troubled not only by the brashness of the *Actaeon*'s crew but also by the timing of the visit. The commercial treaties that the *bakufu* had signed with the United States, Britain, Holland, and Russia in 1858 stipulated for the opening of Nagasaki, Yokohama, and Hakodate to Western-style free trade in the sixth month of 1859. Soon after the British warship departed, Tsushima official Kaitsu Zenkurō was dispatched to Nagasaki and then to Edo to report details of the *Actaeon*'s visit and to request that the *bakufu* pro-

---

60. Hino, *Bakumatsu ni okeru Tsushima to Ei-Ro*, 4–14. In the autumn of 1859, the *Actaeon* called again at Pusan and Tsushima, remaining for approximately a week in both places, respectively.

hibit all Western ships from calling at Tsushima. The *bakufu* replied that according to the newly established treaties, ships from treaty nations were allowed to stop at Tsushima, but only if they lacked necessary supplies or had suffered damage at sea. These visits were to be as short as possible and no trade was to occur. If a ship ignored requests to leave, Tsushima officials were to record the names and nationality of the ship and its captain and forward that information to Nagasaki. The Nagasaki magistrate would in turn request the consul of that nation to order the ship to depart. Kaitsu also described several specific scenarios of ships arriving and requesting trade, aid, or other concessions, and received policy directives for each.[61]

These directives must have frustrated Tsushima officials. After all, domain leaders had been dealing with Western pressure for over a decade, and through their appeals had been urging their *bakufu* superiors to consider more seriously what they viewed as the domain's perilous situation. The new directives, which essentially allowed *bakufu* officials to pass responsibility to Western diplomats, probably added to the growing consternation of Tsushima leaders. As the next chapter will discuss, Tsushima leaders eagerly sought more Tokugawa guidance and assistance as foreign pressure on the island domain continued in the early 1860s.

Conclusions

When the *bakufu* opened the ports of Hakodate, Nagasaki, and Yokohama to Western-style free trade in the summer of 1859, it took a major step in connecting Japan's overseas trade to Western nations. The path to this event, involving negotiations with Western diplomats and internal political machinations, has been described in many previous studies. However, this chapter has illustrated that the domains of Satsuma and Tsushima were simultaneously moving toward greater engagement with Westerners but through trajectories that only partially intersected, and often preceded, the realm-wide process that developed with the opening of the ports. In the 1840s and 1850s, each domain dealt largely

---

61. Ibid., 15–18.

independently with the arriving Westerners, boosting their respective agency within the larger, realm-wide system of foreign relations.

The ever-increasing Western pressure meant that leaders within the two domains contested policies of engagement. Factions within the Satsuma leadership clashed over how to engage Western visitors, a debate that exacerbated long-held political and personal rivalries. In Tsushima, similar divisions lay dormant; but as the next chapter shows, they emerged with tragic force in the early 1860s.

Local agendas ultimately guided the two domains to divergent policy choices. Imbued with commercial opportunism, Satsuma leaders aggressively explored ways to expand trade through Ryukyu and thus accelerate engagement with Westerners on terms not defined by Tokugawa directives. The more apprehensive and anxious Tsushima leaders, while understanding that they could not avoid engaging Westerners, took the opposite tack, urging the *bakufu* to assume a greater role, particularly by providing financial support for domain defenses. In short, Tsushima leaders were far less comfortable with their domain's increased agency in defense and were wary of the more independent course taken by Satsuma. Finally, despite the seemingly constant arrival of Western vessels, many armed with superior weaponry, Satsuma and Tokugawa officials alike remained deeply interested in trade with the China market.

As for the *bakufu*, Abe and other Tokugawa leaders continued to approach foreign trade through their long-held policy of guarded engagement, especially as it involved established trade links with the China market, most notably the imports of medicinal and select luxury goods in exchange for marine products at the Nagasaki entrepôt. Although they granted concessions to Satsuma, *bakufu* leaders worked to maintain Tokugawa privileges in the still-viable trade with China.

SIX

The Transition in Foreign Trade

The handful of Western merchants who arrived in Nagasaki upon its opening to Western-style free trade on 1 July 1859 were confronted with the fact that Tokugawa officials and Chinese merchants firmly controlled the more valuable trade sectors. British diplomats, who represented the largest group of Western merchants in the port, repeatedly complained to *bakufu* officials about the regulations imposed on trade. Late in 1859, Rutherford Alcock, the British consul, wrote to *bakufu* ministers describing "treaty violations." He stated that *bakufu* officials were unjustly prohibiting trade in marine products and collecting them exclusively for sale to Chinese merchants per long-established arrangements. Alcock wrote: "[A]s they are not specified in the Treaty as *contraband* or prohibited, Article XIV gives us the right to export them, or any other things as merchandise, which may be for sale. Now Government interference alone prevents Erico [sea cucumbers] and Awabee [abalone] being sold to Europeans, while they are actually sold to Chinese."[1] In the spring of 1860, another British diplomat complained that the power of the "Chinese guild" was also hurting British efforts to compete in the copper trade in Nagasaki.[2]

---

1. Foreign Office, "Japan: Rutherford Alcock to Japanese Ministers, 14 December 1859," *British Foreign and State Papers*, 46: 4, 48 Encl. 1.
2. "George Morrison to Nagasaki Magistrate, 17 March, 1860," quoted in Paske-Smith, *Western Barbarians in Japan and Formosa in Tokugawa Days*, 200.

The frustration of British diplomats illustrates how initially after the opening of Nagasaki, Westerners sought to enter profitable Japanese-Chinese trading channels. Although the Western merchants had grand plans for developing direct commercial ties between their home markets and Japan, in reality established Japanese–East Asian trade links remained dominant until viable Japanese-Western connections formed later in the decade. During his visit to Nagasaki in the autumn of 1860, British botanist Robert Fortune described such a situation: "The harbor is now gay with the ships of all nations, and a brisk trade has sprung up between Japan and China—a trade which the quiet old Dutchmen never seemed to have dreamed of." Fortune noted that "large quantities of sea weed, salt fish, and sundry other articles are exported to China; while the Chinese import medicine of various kinds, Sapan wood [sic], and many other kinds of dyes." While listing tea, vegetable wax, and copper as key exports to Europe through the port, he concluded, "At present there is little demand for our English manufactures, but that may spring up in time."[3]

Fortune was correct, as demand for British woolen and cotton goods did increase by the mid-1860s.[4] We also know that tea and silk (both raw silk and silkworms) emerged as key exports in the mid-1860s and remained mainstays in Meiji-era trade.[5] Yet in 1859, it was not a given that these import and export flows would thrive. All parties were unclear what trade sectors and products might prove most profitable. This is illustrated in the case of silk, which developed as a key export primarily because an outbreak of silkworm disease devastated the silk industries of France and Italy, thereby creating a huge but sudden European demand for Japanese silk beginning in early 1862.[6]

It is important, therefore, to see the 1860s as a period of transition from established channels and practices of intra-Asian trade to a focus on more direct commercial ties with Westerners. This chapter explores that transition by comparing the cases of Satsuma and the *bakufu*, ex-

---

3. Fortune, *Yedo and Peking*, 23.
4. Ishii Takashi, *Bakumatsu bōekishi no kenkyū*, 130–72. Ishii provides a breakdown of imports at each of the treaty ports.
5. Sugiyama, *Japan's Industrialization in the World Economy*, 77–110, 140–69.
6. Meron, *French Policy in Japan During the Closing Years of the Tokugawa Regime*, 54–55.

plaining first the factors that led the leaders of Satsuma to more actively embrace commerce with Western merchants than their counterparts in the shogunate, who chose to remain centered on established and still-viable intra-Asian and domestic networks. Second, it describes how Satsuma leaders effectively tapped into domestic trade emerging from the continued surge of proto-industrialization, as well as two other trends that shaped the larger transition in trade: the desires of numerous domains to sell domain-produced goods overseas and to acquire products from foreign markets.

Tokugawa Trade Initiatives

In the 1850s, *bakufu* leaders implemented a series of measures designed to maintain Tokugawa control over the lucrative trade with Chinese merchants and to increase Tokugawa dominance over the domestic market. In the tenth month of 1852, the *bakufu* called for increased vigilance against smuggling and unauthorized sales of Chinese goods, particularly in Kyushu, Shikoku, and western Honshu. It also ordered the Nagasaki magistrate to patrol more aggressively islands around the Nagasaki harbor and to check fishing and merchant vessels for contraband.[7] The arrival of Commodore Perry in 1853 and the subsequent treaties with the United States and other Western powers forced *bakufu* leaders to reassess the manner and methods by which they controlled trade at Nagasaki and regulated commercial activity throughout the realm. In 1855, Abe Masahiro formulated plans for goods produced both in Tokugawa lands and in domains to be shipped directly to Edo, allowing the *bakufu* to earn profits from the subsequent redistribution of the products throughout the realm. Although dissent within the *bakufu* leadership scuttled that plan, two years later *bakufu* leaders developed a new proposal to establish Tokugawa clearing-houses in Edo, Osaka, Hyōgo, Shimonoseki, and Niigata to handle the sales of Ezo products. The *bakufu* hoped that these offices could help obtain profits on maritime commerce then being garnered by Kaga, Satsuma, and other coastal domains.[8]

---

7. "Rōjū tashi," 1852/10, "Tsūkō ichiran zokushū" 16, 1852/10, *DNISK*, KA 035-0565.

8. "Hakodate bugyō negai-rōjū" 1857/4, *DNISK*, AN 074-0123.

In 1857, *bakufu* officials began to implement some of these proposals when they secured an agreement with Dutch diplomats that transformed many aspects of foreign trade at Nagasaki. Negotiated by several Nagasaki officials with little guidance from Edo, the Dutch Supplementary Treaty of 1857 (an addition to a treaty concluded between the *bakufu* and the Netherlands) made one grand concession by allowing the Dutch to trade not only at Nagasaki but also at Hakodate. It also stipulated that, "the number of merchant ships is unlimited. There is no limitation of the trade to a certain sum of money" and that "not only the appointed purveyors, but all merchants may come to Dejima to treat concerning the buying and selling of goods."[9] With the two latter measures alone, *bakufu* officials gave up the Tokugawa prerogatives, held since the seventeenth century, of restricting the movements of foreign and Japanese merchants within Nagasaki and the right to impose a monetary limit on the amount of foreign goods that could be sold on the domestic market.

Several additional aspects of the treaty, as well as subsequent actions of bakufu leaders, indicate that the Tokugawa regime had formulated clear plans to control and profit from Japanese-Chinese and Japanese-Dutch trade. To preserve Tokugawa profits from established trade with Chinese merchants, the treaty prohibited Dutch merchants from exporting copper. In addition, *bakufu* officials sought to ensure that the Nagasaki clearing-house would continue to have a steady supply of marine products for use in trade with Chinese merchants. They therefore upheld edicts stipulating that all marine products be sold— at fixed prices—to regional clearing-houses and exported through the Nagasaki clearing-house. Hoping to develop new opportunities for trade, Dutch diplomats petitioned for permission to purchase marine products directly from Nagasaki merchants. The Nagasaki magistrate flatly refused, stating that they were items of tribute and could not be freely traded. On the same grounds, the magistrate also opposed later proposals to allow direct sales of marine products to Western merchants in Hakodate. These moves indicate a consistent Tokugawa policy of supporting trade for the benefit of the Nagasaki merchant community

---

9. Beasley, "The Dutch Supplementary Treaty," *Select Documents on Japanese Foreign Policy*, 150–51.

and Tokugawa bureaucrats shaping trade policy to preserve their official posts.[10]

Tokugawa officials also hoped to channel domain proto-industrial production into a Tokugawa regulatory net that would allow the *bakufu* to profit in two ways from domestic trade. First, they issued edicts that aimed to have select goods shipped directly to Edo, where *bakufu*-sanctioned merchants would sell them exclusively. Second, they also established means whereby existing institutions, most prominently the Nagasaki clearing-house, would supervise the sale of domestic products to foreign merchants. This plan was evident in the Dutch Supplementary Treaty, which required that Dutch merchants purchase rice, barley, wheat, soybeans, and certain silk goods exclusively from the Nagasaki clearing-house. *Bakufu* leaders also apparently believed that they could use Tokugawa edicts to manipulate foreign trade if it began to move in a direction not to their liking. In late 1860, *bakufu* decrees banned the export of barley and rice flour, and later, raw silk, wax, and lamp oil, although Satsuma and other groups were able to find ways to circumvent these and later orders, especially in the silk trade.[11]

In the first few years after Nagasaki, Hakodate, and Yokohama were opened to Western-style free trade, it appeared that the *bakufu* had chosen wisely in maintaining its grip over certain trade sectors as, for example, the export of marine products remained strong. Historian Arai Eiji estimates that valued in Mexican dollars, marine products represented roughly 39 percent of all Japanese exports, with silk occupying only about 23 percent and tea less than 1 percent in 1859.[12] By 1862, the situation had changed dramatically when silk jumped to over 62 percent and tea to 12 percent with marine products falling to 10 percent of total exports through the three open ports.[13] A com-

---

10. Arai, *Kinsei kaisanbutsu bōekishi no kenkyū*, 399; Nagasaki kenshi henshū iinkai, ed., *Nagasaki kenshi, taigai kōshōhen*, 878.

11. "Takashima-han nikki," 1860/11/03, *DNISK*, MA 017-0033; "Zoku Tokugawa jikki," 1860/03[intercalary]/19, *DNISK*, MA 007-0666; "Rōjū Wakisaka Yasuori shokan," 1860/04/16, *DNISK*, MA 008-0889.

12. Because of their high silver content of around 90 percent, Mexican dollars continued to serve as a global currency and were therefore often used to value foreign trade (and also in contracts between Westerners and Japanese) in the 1850s and 1860s.

13. Arai, *Kinsei kaisanbutsu bōekishi no kenkyū*, 584–85.

parable state of affairs existed in Nagasaki where marine products represented just under 40 percent of all exports by value with silk garnering only 8 percent and tea less than 1 percent in 1859. By 1862, tea had jumped to the lead, occupying roughly 22 percent, silk around 15 percent, and marine products just over 16 percent. While silk came to be exported chiefly through Yokohama, tea was often the top export through Nagasaki in the 1860s. Despite the growth of silk and tea exports, marine products continued to be an important export with kelp alone occupying second place in overall export value at Nagasaki in 1865 and 1866.[14]

As was the case in the 1830s, however, the *bakufu* decision to maintain a fixed purchase price encouraged producers and merchants to trade outside of the Tokugawa monopoly. Enterprising Japanese merchants began to acquire marine products directly from production areas, selling them to British merchants for export. Officials in Hakodate also appear to have been less than strict about enforcing *bakufu* edicts by allowing large amounts of marine products to be sold to British merchants. As a result, in 1860 British ships exported 22,560 *kin* of abalone and 86,371 *kin* of sea cucumbers directly to China from Hakodate.[15] Western merchants also circumvented restrictions on copper by exporting assorted copperwares, bronze, and brass goods. Because the overall level of copper exported outside of Tokugawa channels reached approximately 100,000 *kin* in 1859, the *bakufu* issued orders prohibiting direct sales of copperwares to foreign merchants in an effort to preserve the copper supply for trade with Chinese merchants.[16]

Moreover, *bakufu* officials were not prepared for the dearth of Chinese merchant ships calling at Nagasaki. In 1859, three Chinese merchant ships sold their goods at Nagasaki but were unable to make the return voyage because of unrest at their home ports resulting from the Taiping Rebellion and Anglo-French military incursions. After remaining anchored in Nagasaki for several months, the merchants resold at a

---

14. Ibid., 472–80.
15. Nagasaki kenshi henshū iinkai, ed., *Nagasaki kenshi, taigai kōshōhen*, 884.
16. Nagasaki kenshi henshū iinkai, ed., *Nagasaki kenshi, taigai kōshōhen*, 887; "Rōjū shokan," 1860/03[intercalary] 26, *DNISK*, MA 008-0026; "Rōjū tashi," 1860/10/17, *DNISK*, MA 015-0774.

loss the cargos acquired a few months earlier. Although records are incomplete, they suggest that these were the last Chinese merchant ships to call at Nagasaki and trade with the clearing-house. Some ship captains probably chose not to make the voyage to Nagasaki because of unrest along the China coast. In addition, Western merchant ships, which were increasingly dominating shipping between Nagasaki and Chinese ports, were carrying much of the cargo previously transported on Chinese bottoms. Finally, Chinese merchants formed a new guild in 1861 in an effort to secure a greater share of direct Japanese-Chinese trade at Nagasaki, but many Chinese merchants found more gainful opportunities working as agents for Western firms than in trading with the clearing-house.[17]

As Tokugawa officials waited for Chinese merchant ships to resume trade, marine products and copper began to accumulate, and in 1863, the *bakufu* was forced to sell them at a loss on the Nagasaki market. In subsequent years, there are only two records of the clearing-house selling copper, and that was to Western merchants in 1866 and 1867. All told, the Tokugawa control of copper exports and its marine product monopoly, both cultivated and jealously protected for a century, withered and died. Although copper and marine products were still exported from Nagasaki, the *bakufu* was never able to effectively regulate those exports to its advantage because Japanese and Western merchants exploited weaknesses in Tokugawa regulations. Eventually, the shogunate was forced to abandon its marine product monopoly in the eighth month of 1865. The clearing-house remained in existence until 1867, but without the ability to extract revenue from foreign trade, it ceased to be an institution of any consequence.[18]

As the volume and value of silk and silkworms exported to Europe increased, *bakufu* officials developed plans to allow the Tokugawa regime to benefit from this burgeoning sector of direct Japanese-Western trade. Léon Roches, the French consul, was partly responsible for this

---

17. Nakamura Tetsuo and a team of researchers from Kobe Gakuin University have recently examined and cataloged an archive of records of overseas Chinese merchants who traded in Nagasaki and other Japanese ports from the 1860s until the 1930s. Nakamura Tetsuo, "Relationship of Overseas Chinese in Japan to Modern China," 23–30.

18. Nagasaki kenshi henshū iinkai, *Nagasaki kenshi, taigai kōshōhen*, 889–92.

new strategy, as he had been pushing for increased silk exports to France to help build strong bilateral ties since he assumed office in 1864. Following requests from Roches, *bakufu* officials eased some restrictions on silk sales and exports in the autumn of 1865, and developed new schemes to control transport, domestic sales, and exports of silk and silkworms. In the second month of 1866, the *bakufu* established regional clearing-houses through which raw silk and silkworms were to be directed. Merchants were to ship their silk to specific clearing-houses, pay a fee, and receive an official seal that permitted the silk to be sold on the domestic market and exported. To encourage the growth of the system, the *bakufu* split the fees with the lords of participating domains. The Ueda domain in central Honshu actively participated in the system, setting up levy stations in its administrative seat and in the countryside. The end result, like other Tokugawa commercial plans in the 1860s, was decidedly mixed. Leaders of most domains proved less cooperative than those from Ueda, no doubt seeing more benefit in trading directly with other domains or with Western merchants. Moreover, except for the select merchant houses through which goods were to be directed, most merchants saw little personal benefit in assisting the *bakufu*'s efforts. Indicative of its growing political weakness, *bakufu* leaders were unable to use fiat to force domains and merchants to abandon established commercial relationships in favor of the new Tokugawa framework.[19]

The *bakufu*'s failures highlight some of the reasons for the decline of the Tokugawa regime in the years preceding the Meiji Restoration. In the 1850s and 1860s, the shogunate based its trade policy on tried and tested commercial products and relationships, lucrative since the mid-eighteenth century. If Chinese ships had continued to call regularly as they had for centuries, the *bakufu* might have sustained profits from foreign trade through Nagasaki. When the ships failed to arrive, the shogunate proved unable to capitalize on the shifting commercial focus that was part of the larger transition to Western-centered trade. As the example of the silk trade shows, Tokugawa leaders, while aware of the

---

19. Nishikawa, "Keiō-ki no *bakufu* bōeki seisaku to Yokohama," 34–36; Medzini, *French Policy in Japan During the Closing Years of the Tokugawa Regime*, 108–18.

increasing potential of direct Japanese-Western trade, did not develop the means to harness and profit from it.

Satsuma's Domestic and Foreign Trade Ventures

To many historians, the historical significance of Satsuma's trade network in the 1860s is found in the trade revenue that allowed the domain to obtain modern arms and create an effective military force—one that joined with the Chōshū domain to overthrow the *bakufu* in the Meiji Restoration.[20] While this view certainly has merit, it discounts the motives underlying Satsuma's commercial activities as well as how Satsuma helped accomplish the larger transition from intra-Asian to Western-centered trade. Unlike previous decades, Satsuma's commercial and diplomatic enterprises in the 1860s intersected increasingly with broader Japan-wide politico-economic trends: the growth of intra-domain trade fueled by proto-industrialization, the terrorist movement to expel all foreigners from Japanese soil, and the related political firestorm associated with the 1863 imperial order to expel all foreigners from the realm.

When Nariakira died in 1858, his half-brother Hisamitsu assumed control over the domain as regent for Tadayoshi, the young daimyo. Hisamitsu displayed a conservative streak when he abruptly halted efforts to expand trade through Ryukyu in 1858. In subsequent years, the Satsuma leadership did not aggressively encourage new ties with Western merchants in the kingdom. All the while, Ryukyu continued to participate in the Chinese diplomatic order. In the summer of 1860, a Ryukyu embassy arrived in Fuzhou but because Taiping forces blocked the route to Beijing, the Ryukyuans postponed their departure for several months. In the spring of 1861, Beijing sent word that it was impossible for the embassy to make the trip north and should return home immediately. Anxious to fulfill the duties of vassalage, the Ryukyu envoys steadfastly remained at the Ryukyu House and repeatedly asked for permission to travel to Beijing. Chinese officials denied each request and the regretful embassy eventually returned to Ryukyu. Although the missions could not travel to Beijing, they still brought goods

---

20. Craig, *Chōshū in the Meiji Restoration*, 70.

to trade at Fuzhou, such as the 26,000 *kin* of shark fins that were used to obtain Chinese products for shipment to Kagoshima.²¹

Hisamitsu proved an energetic leader who became deeply involved in the Kyoto political scene. Bringing a large armed contingent to Kyoto in 1862, he forced the *bakufu* leadership to accept his plan for the shogun to visit Kyoto in hopes of stabilizing the political situation in the imperial capital. Hisamitsu also worked hard to unify the fractured political framework by building an alliance between the imperial court and *bakufu*. Meanwhile, under his leadership, Satsuma's domestic and foreign trade enterprises continued to display commercial opportunism. Just as ties with Westerners were being severed in Ryukyu, Satsuma officials were establishing new domestic contacts, most prominently with Chōshū. In the spring of 1858, a Satsuma merchant Nimure Sahei traveled to Shimonoseki in Chōshū with samples of indigo, an increasingly important Satsuma product, in the hope of developing a large-scale exchange of it for Chōshū's salt and cotton. At first, Chōshū's leaders, although accepting that the trade would stimulate the domain's agricultural production, left the matter in the hands of Shimonoseki-based merchant Shiraishi Shōichirō, who apparently had had commercial relations with Satsuma for some time. By contrast, Satsuma's leaders acted more aggressively: they set up a trading office in Shimonoseki in the summer of 1859 and soon afterwards sent two merchant ships to Chōshū laden with indigo, sulfur, and Ryukyu textiles, which were traded mostly for whalebone (used for fertilizer), cotton, and salt. By late spring of 1860, Chōshū's leaders, recognizing the potential value of the trade, sent domain merchant Nakano Hanzaemon, accompanied by a samurai official, to Satsuma to negotiate an agreement designed to expand interdomain trade. Following Nakano's success, Satsuma began to import large quantities of rice in exchange for brown sugar, and over the next few years, sought increasing amounts of whalebone and salt, even sending its ships directly to the salt-producing areas on the Chōshū coast. In return, Chōshū increased its purchases of brown sugar, some of it

---

21. Maehira, "Higashi Ajia no kaigai jōhō to Ryūkyū rūto," 150; Maehira "Ryūkyū ōkoku ni okeru kaisanbutsu bōeki," 228.

resold in other domains.[22] Under Hisamitsu, Satsuma also moved ahead with the acquisition of steamships, another plan championed by Nariakira. In late 1860, the domain purchased the British steamship *England* with the assistance of the Nagasaki magistrate.[23]

As this intra-domain trade thrived, the expulsion movement emerged as a major political force upon the assassination of Ii Naosuke, the grand chamberlain of the *bakufu*, in 1860. The samurai who killed Ii were angry that he and other *bakufu* leaders had not consulted the Emperor Kōmei (r. 1847–66), whom they viewed as the just ruler of Japan, before signing the commercial treaties with Western nations. To remove this tarnish upon imperial power, radical samurai, most daimyo, and many in the *bakufu* leadership began to advocate the expulsion of all foreigners from Japanese soil. Bands of samurai who styled themselves as "men of high purpose" (*shishi*) looked to accomplish expulsion by assassinating the Western interlopers and *bakufu* leaders, whom they blamed for allowing the barbarians to remain. Chōshū became a center of the movement and actively schemed to assume political control in Kyoto. Tapping into this wide pool of support, Emperor Kōmei issued an imperial order specifying that all foreigners be forcibly expelled on the tenth day of the fifth month of 1863. Not wishing to be labeled as soft on expulsion and to contradict an imperial edict, *bakufu* leaders officially supported the order, although many hoped to use negotiation, rather than military force, to achieve expulsion. Tokugawa leaders were placed in a difficult position by the order. The shogun officially used the title of "barbarian-subduing generalissimo" (*seii taishōgun*), a moniker originally developed to reward victorious generals in battles with Emishi foes in northern Honshu in the Heian period (794–1185). The title, and the *bakufu*'s position as the central authority, forced Tokugawa leaders to appear as the great protector of the realm and—at least outwardly—pursue expulsion. Knowing full well that *bakufu* leaders needed to appear tough against Westerners, Chōshū and other anti-*bakufu* factions opportunistically used expulsion, in the words of W. G. Beasley, as a "stick to beat the

---

22. Tanaka Akira, *Bakumatsu ishinshi no kenkyū*, 101–57; Tanaka Akira, "Bakumatsu Satchō bōeki no kenkyū," 69.3, 54–84, 69.4, 29–51; Flershem and Flershem, "Nakano Family Documents, Satsuma-Chōshū, 1856–66," 1–15.

23. Sugiyama, *Meiji ishin to Igirisu shōnin*, 84–85.

bakufu."²⁴ Although they earnestly hoped to expel Westerners from Japan, these groups also schemed that assaults on Westerners would prompt a Western nation to attack the *bakufu* and weaken it politically, thus providing an opportunity to move against the Tokugawa regime.²⁵

Many Satsuma samurai joined the terrorist movement to expel foreigners. Shimazu retainers were among the band that assassinated Ii, and several others participated in the 1861 murder of Henry Heusken, a Dutchman employed by the American legation in Edo.²⁶ Indeed, Hisamitsu became personally involved in one of the more prominent attacks on foreigners. In the eighth month of 1862, samurai accompanying Hisamitsu's procession attacked and killed a British merchant, C. L. Richardson, at the village of Namamugi near Yokohama. The Satsuma retainers believed that Richardson's failure to dismount in the presence of Hisamitsu's procession was an insult that left them no choice but to act. Coming on the heels of a string of attacks on Westerners, British diplomats insisted that Satsuma punish the men involved and later demanded that the *bakufu* pay a huge indemnity. Over the coming months, British representatives threatened to use military action against Satsuma if they did not receive redress. Hisamitsu and the Satsuma leadership remained defiant, informing *bakufu* leaders that they would respond in kind to any British ships that came to Kagoshima to press their case.²⁷

Despite this tough stance, Hisamitsu, like his half-brother Nariakira, continued to pursue trade with Western merchants. Just one month after the Namamugi incident, Hisamitsu appealed to the *bakufu* on behalf of Tadayoshi (for whom Hisamitsu served as regent) to allow Western merchant ships to freely stop at Ryukyu to trade.

Shō Tei, the Ryukyu king, plays a major role in the import of Chinese goods into Japan. Over time, the practice developed where Satsuma brought Chinese goods imported via Ryukyu to Nagasaki for sale. Recently in Yokohama and the other treaty ports, townsmen and peasants have been allowed to freely

---

24. Beasley, *Select Documents on Japanese Foreign Policy*, 16.
25. Totman, *The Collapse of the Tokugawa Bakufu*, 33–39; Beasley, *The Meiji Restoration*, 191–94.
26. Hesselink, "The Assassination of Henry Heuksen," 344–46.
27. Beasley, *Select Documents on Japanese Foreign Policy*, 223–24.

engage in commerce with Westerners. In earlier times, the people of Ryukyu freely engaged in foreign trade and we request they be allowed to once again. In recent years, the trade in Chinese goods at Nagasaki has declined. Meanwhile, ships sailing to and from Yokohama are stopping at Ryukyu hoping to trade. It is natural that foreigners should call at Ryukyu as it beckons as a source of trade. Clearly we cannot stop these visits. In order to protect the prestige of the realm, we therefore request that the practices of earlier times be revived and that foreign ships be permitted to freely call at Ryukyu.[28]

The following month, several *bakufu* senior councilors rejected the appeal stating, "You present as justification the need to help Ryukyu. Yet if you are granted the rights to trade freely that you request, it is likely that Chinese ships will call instead at Satsuma." They stressed that Satsuma had already been granted a dispensation in being allowed to bring Ryukyu products "without limit" to Nagasaki. Satsuma would be granted no further exemption—it had to sell its imports through the Nagasaki clearing-house.[29]

The request is intriguing for a number of reasons. First, it shows how Hisamitsu was playing both sides by simultaneously preparing to fight and trade with Westerners. Second, the rhetoric employed in the document is noteworthy: over three years after the opening of the ports, Satsuma leaders talked not of imitating the new wave of Western-style free trade but instead of restoring Ryukyu to an amorphous past during which unrestricted intercourse prospered. Hisamitsu located this more favorable time before the Tokugawa regulations imposed in the late eighteenth century—and, apparently without irony, during a period of largely free intercourse in the fifteenth and sixteenth centuries before Satsuma's invasion of the kingdom in 1609.[30] Moreover, he gave no indication that he believed that an expansion of trade at Ryukyu would alleviate pressure on Japanese port cities, which at the time were experiencing Western military encroachment because of the expulsion order and the spate of attacks on Westerners. Third, it is puzzling that

---

28. "Sasshū-han gansho,"1862/9/18, *DNISK*, BU 055-0854. Katsu Yasuyoshi (more commonly known as Kaishū) provides the full text of Hisamitsu's request in *Kaikoku kigen*, vol. 3, 2432.

29. Katsu, *Kaikoku kigen*, vol. 3, 2433–35.

30. Ibid., 2432.

Hisamitsu felt compelled to request permission from Edo to expand trade at Ryukyu. After all, Nariakira had only vaguely, if at all, related his plans to Tokugawa leaders. Moreover, Hisamitsu must have known that *bakufu* leaders, occupied with issues arising from Western military and diplomatic pressure on their regime, would have been reluctant to become involved in events at Ryukyu. Given this situation and the references made to the trade in Chinese goods, Hisamitsu sought with his proposal a means to pressure the *bakufu* to relax its control over the sale of Chinese imports at Nagasaki. In other words, this appeal was simply a repackaging of Satsuma's continuing effort to expand its commercial network in what domain leaders still viewed as the lucrative market in Chinese imports.

Hisamitsu was certainly correct in his assertion that Western nations were interested in commerce with Ryukyu. In the tenth month of 1862, Gustave Duchesne de Bellecourt, the French minister in Edo, sent a warship to Ryukyu to learn more about the status of the French treaty signed with the kingdom in 1855. Although Satsuma had scuttled the commercial agreements with the French soon after Narikaira's death, Bellecourt felt that the treaty still afforded the French privileges in Ryukyu. He feared that in the wake of the Namamugi incident, Satsuma leaders would completely repudiate the treaty and close Ryukyu to all Western con-tact and expel the French missionaries still in the kingdom. Following a brief visit to Naha, the French warship returned to Yokohama, reporting that Ryukyu officials would still abide by the treaty. The kingdom would allow French missionaries to preach on its soil and for French ships to receive water and supplies at one Ryukyu port.

Wishing also to secure commercial privileges for his nation, Jan Donker Curtius, the Dutch consul in Nagasaki, began to investigate the status of the Ryukyu-Netherlands Treaty, also signed in 1855. He arranged for a Dutch warship to visit Ryukyu. It carried Dutch representatives who had been ordered to exchange documents that would allow the Dutch government to formally ratify the treaty, paving the way for the establishment of commercial ties. By coincidence, the Dutch ship arrived only a week before the French, and with the assistance of French missionaries, exchanged articles that formally ratified a treaty.

Fig. 18 Shimazu Hisamitsu (1817–87)

As was the case in the 1850s, Satsuma leaders did not oppose these moves, which set the stage for greater commercial intercourse with Western merchants at Ryukyu.[31]

Meanwhile, Satsuma officials continued to pressure the *bakufu* on another front: to allow Satsuma to mint special Ryukyu coins, a move that ever consistent domain officials claimed would, of course, "aid Ryukyu." Since 1855, *bakufu* leaders had rejected such proposals but in 1861, a new group of *bakufu* leaders accepted, apparently once again feeling it necessary to provide an economic boost to Ryukyu. In the sixth month of 1862, Satsuma began to mint 1 million *ryō* in Ryukyu coins (*Ryūkyū tsūhō*) over a three-year period. A large mint in Kagoshima produced the currency used especially to finance the military build-up before the confrontation with Britain in the wake of the Namamugi incident. Within a few years, the Ryukyu coins were being used as currency throughout Ryukyu and Satsuma.[32]

---

31. Yokohama, "Nihon kaikoku to Ryūkyū," 403–6; Medzini, *French Policy in Japan During the Closing Years of the Tokugawa Regime*, 196.

32. *KK*, vol. 3, 12–24.

A few months later in the fourth month of 1863, Satsuma officials again played the defense card, citing the specter of British aggression in appeals for financial support. Reminiscent of the rhetoric used in the campaign to repeal restrictions on domain sales of imported goods at Nagasaki in the 1840s, Satsuma officials asserted that the grave nature of the current foreign threat warranted Tokugawa financial assistance.

> Recently, British warships have come to Yokohama and are frequently threatening to sail to Satsuma. If this should happen, we will respond accordingly. Yet as we have stressed in the past, the Satsuma domain has many remote islands and an extensive coastline. Although we have appropriated funds for defense, we cannot say that our coastline has been solidly fortified. If the entire realm becomes involved in a battle with Western nations, we are not sufficiently prepared. Now with the expulsion order, we are required to earmark additional funds for defense. Also, with the reduction of alternate residence duties, families of daimyo and their retainers stationed in Edo are moving back to the domain. Because we are distant from Edo, moving costs are high. Although it is necessary to spend more on defense, we have other expenses and obligations that make these appropriations difficult. We therefore request a loan of 70,000 *ryō* to help defray costs.[33]

Despite the litany of woes, *bakufu* leaders did not grant financial aid to Satsuma. Indeed, they may have taken offense at the suggestion that the reduction of alternate residence duties was causing financial difficulties. After all, the Tokugawa leadership had recently freed lords from that centuries-old obligation in order to allow them to spend more on defense.[34]

Reviving practices used successfully since the early eighteenth century, Satsuma later appealed for funds to support Ryukyu's diplomatic contacts with the Qing. In the second month of 1865, Satsuma requested a *bakufu* loan of 30,000 *ryō* to help offset costs associated with the Qing investiture mission that was scheduled to arrive in Ryukyu the following year.

> For the ascension of its king, Ryukyu receives an embassy of several hundred persons from China. It is difficult to describe in words the scale of expenses associated with this embassy. The size and cost of receiving this embassy far

---

33. "Bunkyū ki hikki," 1863/4/08, *DNISK*, BU 091-0409.
34. Beasley, *The Meiji Restoration*, 182.

exceeds that of the missions that the kingdom dispatches to Edo. Because Ryukyu is poor and cannot pay for this visit, the Shimazu must subsidize the mission. Due to recent financial troubles, however, our coffers are bare. We therefore request a loan to help defray costs in much the same way the *bakufu* has extended aid for Ryukyu embassies to Edo.[35]

Though it is unclear if the *bakufu* extended the loan, the incident shows that Satsuma leaders were willing to try numerous means to gain more revenue. What proved to be the final Qing investiture mission to Ryukyu arrived, as scheduled the following year.

Hisamitsu's policy of standing for expulsion while continuing commercial engagement is further illustrated in Satsuma's continued acquisition of steamships from British merchants even as tensions with Britain's diplomats continued to mount. Following the Namamugi incident, the domain bought a British steamship in late 1862. In the same year, Shimazu retainer Godai Tomoatsu—whose father had presented the memorial that became in the blueprint for the domain's Ryukyu policy in the 1840s—traveled to Shanghai as part of an official *bakufu* mission to investigate trade. While there, Godai arranged for the purchase of an additional steamship that was delivered in the second month of 1863 by Thomas Glover, a prominent British merchant in Nagasaki.[36]

Meanwhile, British diplomats continued to push their case against Satsuma. British warships arrived in Kagoshima in the seventh month of 1863 and Edward St. John Neale, the acting British consul, tried for three days to negotiate a settlement. When these efforts failed, the British fleet engaged Satsuma ships in the harbor, including several vessels that had been purchased from British merchants in Shanghai and Nagasaki only months before. The British flotilla bombarded Kagoshima for several hours, destroying much of the city, including the Shūseikan factory and the recently constructed mint. (Both were quickly rebuilt in the following months.) Because some of the British ships received heavy damage, the group withdrew and returned to Yokohama two days later.[37] The British departure allowed Satsuma to claim victory

---

35. "Kagoshima-han Wakita Shirō shokan," 1865/02/19, *DNISK*, KE 005-0115.
36. Sugiyama, *Meiji ishin to Igirisu shōnin*, 84–85.
37. Beasley, *The Meiji Restoration*, 200.

in the showdown against the Western enemy. Indeed, the court later officially praised Tadayoshi for executing the expulsion order.[38]

Although many in Satsuma believed that the domain had won the confrontation with the British, Hisamitsu and the domain leadership did not, and dispatched envoys to Yokohama to negotiate a peace agreement, evidently seeing more benefit in trading with the British than in fighting them.[39] Two months later in the ninth month, Satsuma envoys presented Neale with the indemnity for Richardson's murder: funds worth 100,000 Mexican dollars, borrowed entirely from the *bakufu*, which may have granted it based in part upon Satsuma's earlier request for a loan of 70,000 *ryō*.[40] Satsuma leaders also promised to punish the samurai involved in the attack on Richardson. According to British diplomats, the Satsuma representatives accepted the "irresistible superiority" of British power, conveyed their lord's wish to establish friendly relations, and expressed their desire to purchase British warships. Thereafter, Satsuma established deeper commercial relationships with British merchants in Nagasaki, and Harry Parkes, the British minister who succeeded Alcock, made a brief visit to Kagoshima in 1866.[41]

Without question, Hisamitsu adopted a course of increased interaction with the British because he realized that his domain could not hope to defeat militarily Britain or any other Western power. Yet given his earlier actions, we should not see British military strength as causing Hisamitsu and the Satsuma leadership to reverse themselves, from supporting expulsion to embracing engagement with Western states. In the wake of the clash with Britain, it is reasonable to view Hisamitsu and other domain leaders as choosing to abandon the policy of playing it both ways—trading with the Westerners while pushing for their expulsion—in favor of active engagement with Western merchants and diplomats. In other words, defeat at the hands of the British tipped the scales within the domain leadership toward rapprochement, a step made possible by Satsuma's decades-long policies of commercial opportunism.

---

38. Taigai kankeishi sōgō nenpyō henshū iinkai, ed., *Taigai kankeishi sōgō nenpyō*, 940.
39. Ibid., 941.
40. *KK*, vol. 3, 25.
41. Fox, *Britain and Japan, 1858-1883*, 116, 185–86.

As Satsuma developed a stronger bilateral tie with Britain, events surrounding the expulsion order forced the domain to shuffle its domestic trade connections. On the tenth day of the fifth month of 1863, the appointed date for the expulsion of foreigners, Chōshū batteries began to shell ships passing through the narrow straits near Shimonoseki. These attacks continued for several months, and in the second month of 1864, Chōshū guns shelled a Satsuma-sponsored merchant vessel sailing to Nagasaki to sell its cargo of cotton to Western merchants. Satsuma leaders were understandably angered by the attack, first because several crew members were killed, and second because they anticipated garnering part of the sizeable profit from the transaction, made more lucrative because of a dramatic rise in world cotton prices due to the Civil War in the United States.[42] The incident increased tension between the two domains, which reached a climax in the spring and early summer of 1864, when Chōshū brought an armed force to Kyoto in hopes of gaining greater political influence there. In a fierce battle outside one of the gates, Satsuma and Aizu men repelled a Chōshū force that attempted to storm the imperial palace. The court later condemned Chōshū as an "enemy of the court" and *bakufu* leaders organized a punitive expedition against the domain in which Satsuma samurai participated.

Because of these disputes, Satsuma banned trade with Chōshū and instead established commercial links with the domains of Hiroshima and Morioka in northern Honshu (parts of modern-day Iwate and Aomori prefectures). Satsuma exported rapeseed oil, raw wax, and tin to Hiroshima in exchange for rice, copper, and salt. To Morioka, it shipped silk and cotton goods, sugar, tobacco, and medicines in exchange for beans, kelp, copper, and saltpeter. Thus, Satsuma adapted its trade to changing political circumstances and profited from acting as a middleman by trading in a range of goods produced inside and outside the domain. Related to the expansion in trade, the domain also began to produce counterfeit currency. Satsuma made counterfeit copies of the *Tenpō tsūhō*, a *bakufu*-minted coin used as currency throughout the realm. The Satsuma coins circulated widely and were used in trade with

---

42. Haraguchi Izumi, "The Influence of the Civil War in the U.S. on the Meiji Restoration in Japan," 130–31.

Hiroshima and to purchase rice on the Kyoto and Osaka markets. By 1865, Mitsui, one of the larger merchant houses in Japan, freely exchanged them.[43]

The political firestorm surrounding expulsion also allowed Satsuma once again to accrue profits via smuggling. In the spring of 1864, the *bakufu* temporarily closed trade through Yokohama. Subsequently facing a glut, silk merchants looked for ways to move their products. Satsuma quickly stepped in, buying perhaps as much as 20,000 *ryō* worth of silk from producers and merchants and then transporting it to the domain residence in Edo. Domain officials would then illicitly sell the silk to Western merchants at points on the coast just south of Yokohama. Foreigners reported that the records of these transactions bore the Shimazu seal. Although this trade quickly dried up after the *bakufu* reopened Yokohama in the ninth month of 1864, Satsuma had found yet another means to capitalize on the expulsion order.[44]

Following the rapprochement with Britain in late 1863, Satsuma began to buy ships in earnest, acquiring twelve steamships and two schooners over the next four years. Since the opening of the ports, Nagasaki had become an emporium for steam and sailing ships: 106 ships were sold in the port between 1860 and 1867. As a result, Nagasaki also grew into a focal point of domain commercial activities: a market to sell domain products and goods obtained from other domains as well as to acquire ships and Western weaponry. For example, Satsuma sold sugar and rapeseed oil at Osaka and purchased camphor from Tosa in Shikoku, high-grade silk thread and tea from the Yanagawa domain in Kyushu, and wax and dried seaweed from the Uwajima domain on Shikoku. These products were then shipped to Nagasaki and used as part of the payment to acquire a Western-built vessel. Satsuma also exchanged Western goods obtained at Nagasaki for rice from Hiroshima.[45]

Beginning in the mid 1860s, Satsuma officials approached numerous Western merchants in an attempt to open new markets for Ryukyu and domain products, and to obtain Western armaments and steamships,

---

43. Tanaka Akira, *Bakumatsu ishinshi no kenkyū*, 130-131; KK, vol. 3, 12–24.
44. Nishikawa, "Keio-ki no *bakufu* bōeki seisaku to Yokohama," 36–38.
45. Tanaka Akira, *Bakumatsu ishinshi no kenkyū*, 130-131; KK, vol. 3, 67–72.

which they planned to use as both merchantmen and warships. The parallel efforts made by American and British merchants at Yokohama and Nagasaki attest to their comprehension both of the range of Satsuma's commercial network and its maritime agency in Japanese waters. In 1864, Thomas Glover, acting as an agent for the large China-based trading house of Jardine, Matheson & Company, began to buy cotton goods from Satsuma for export abroad. The following year, he arranged for the company to provide Satsuma with a large loan to finance what he called the "Ōshima scheme." Named for Amami Ōshima, the scheme aimed to increase the production of raw silk, sugar, tea, and rice, which Glover would arrange to sell to Chinese and Western merchants at Shanghai in return for an agent's commission.[46] Although the scheme never got off the ground, Glover maintained his ties to domain officials. He competed for Satsuma's trade with Eugene Van Reed, an American merchant working in the Yokohama office of Augustine Heard & Company, an American trading firm based in Canton. Van Reed believed that trade with Satsuma would not only prove profitable, but also offer Western diplomats an "opening wedge" that would undermine the authority of the Tokugawa regime, which he and many Western merchants perceived as trying to stifle foreign trade. Although nothing came of his diplomatic plan, Van Reed aggressively pursued trade with Satsuma. In a letter to Augustine Heard written in 1863, Van Reed described an agreement he had made with the Shimazu lord whereby he was "to build men of war, supply him with the most approved weapons of warfare, regulate his shipments of produce to foreign countries, and generally superintend his foreign trade."[47] Van Reed maintained close ties with Satsuma officials, and he and his associates at Heard worked hard to promote trade with the domain.[48] For example, Van Reed and Heard men tried to persuade Satsuma officials to buy an American steamship and rifles, less for the profit to be made and

---

46. Sugiyama, "Thomas B. Glover," 115–38.

47. Van Reed to Heard, private, 20 September 1863, Heard Family Collection, Baker Library Historical Collections, Harvard Business School. For a biographical sketch of Van Reed, see Notehelfer, ed., *Japan through American Eyes*, 97–98.

48. Notehelfer, "Looking for the Lost," 183–85. I thank Fred Notehelfer for allowing me to read an earlier version of this essay.

more to lay the foundation for a long-term commercial relationship. Late in 1864, Van Reed explained to Heard:

About Satsuma! In Kanagawa [Yokohama] I think I have the good will of his [the lord's] highest officers residing the Palace of Yedo [Edo], but you are aware that it is with difficulty that they see you at all, the government [*bakufu*] being so jealous. *I do not forget* your wishes in respect to his connection, or any other Prince; there is money to be made out of them, but it will require a little patience.[49]

Kerry Smith speculates that S. J. Gower, a British merchant who was the agent of Jardine, Matheson & Co. at Yokohama, also negotiated with Satsuma in 1863–64 under the assumption that he was offered an exclusive commercial relationship.[50] Satsuma officials, who appear to have been exploring the possibilities of trade with any number of Western merchants in the treaty ports, probably intimated to each that the domain was seeking to make an exclusive arrangement. They understood the potential benefits from expanding the domain's commercial network to include the Western merchants based at the treaty ports.

In the fall of 1867, Heard appeared to have made a breakthrough: a written agreement with Satsuma that included more detailed commercial plans than those outlined earlier by Van Reed. Satsuma agreed to build warehouses to be used by both the domain and the firm at Hyōgo, in central Japan, which was scheduled to become a treaty port on 1 January 1868. The agreement stated:

The Prince of Satsuma will send to the agent of Augustine Heard and Company the various products of his territory suitable for foreign consumption such as tea, silk, camphor, wax, etc.—to be sold by them at Hyōgo, or to be sent abroad. And Augustine Heard and Company will also bring foreign goods suitable for the Japanese market—such as manufactured cotton and woolen goods and other articles which may come into demand—to be sold through the Prince of Satsuma's agents.[51]

---

49. Van Reed to Heard, private, 10 November 1864, Heard Family Collection, HM-58.

50. Smith, "Selling the *Fire Dart* and Other Adventures in Business," 22. I thank Kerry Smith for allowing me to read the paper.

51. "Agreement with Prince Satsuma, Hiogo [Hyōgo]," 29 October 1867, Heard Family Collection II: case 30.

The agreement stipulated that Heard would act as the domain's agent in acquiring "vessels, munitions of war, steamers, or any other articles" it sought abroad, and would supervise the sale of any goods which "can be sold to better advantage in China or in foreign markets." In an acknowledgment of the range of Satsuma's political as well as commercial influence along the Japanese coastline, Heard stipulated that the company's steamships should travel between ports on the Inland Sea under Satsuma's flag, which would enable them "to trade between ports unopened to commerce under the foreign treaties." In return, Satsuma would receive one-quarter of the net profits from the trade.

While negotiating with Heard, Satsuma leaders also moved to create a domain-run, domestic, joint-stock company based near Hyōgo to take advantage of the trade opportunities that sprouted throughout Japan and to complement their links with Westerners. In the summer of 1867, they decided on the commission they would charge other domains that sold goods to the company for export abroad, and agreed to extend to their ships carrying the company's goods the protection of sailing under the Shimazu flag. Domain leaders were confident they could provide protection to vessels sailing in Japanese waters, stating that a ship from another domain, sailing under the auspices of Satsuma's joint-stock company, would be safe even from pirates or foreign vessels. "Although it has not been a problem, ships might occasionally encounter pirates or a foreign vessel might impede shipping. In that case, Satsuma ships would provide effective protection." [52] Just months before the Meiji Restoration, Satsuma leaders were on the cusp of taking their domain's commercial network to a new, more expansive level.

Godai Tomoatsu and Commercial Opportunism in Europe

The energy behind Satsuma's effort is further evident in how domain officials moved aggressively to develop direct trade links with the European market. Godai Tomoatsu, who took the lead in this effort, is often portrayed as an innovator. William Hoover suggests that Godai tried to develop new commercial ties for the domain after learning firsthand about the military and economic power of the West. Hoover highlights a memorial that Godai presented to the domain's lord in

---

52. Ōtsuki Fumihiko shuki", 1867/06, *DNISK*, KE 133-0384.

1864 outlining a plan to increase profits by exporting rice, raw silk, and Ezo kelp directly to Shanghai. He claims that the memorial "made clear that Godai's experience and observations while a student at Nagasaki, his travels to Shanghai, and his contact with the British in the Satsuma-British skirmish had been instrumental in opening his eyes to the accomplishments of Western nations. His awareness of the outside world made him deeply sensitive to the dangers facing Japan and helped motivate him to formulate a program for constructive action."[53] In sum, not until Godai had personally experienced the West had he recognized the commercial opportunities available to the domain. While Godai took the domain in new directions, his actions suggest that his plans derived from Satsuma's existing commercial network as much as from his encounter with the West; the domain had, for example, exported rice and kelp to domestic and foreign markets for 30 years. Indeed, Godai seems to have pursued enterprises that complemented those spearheaded by other domain officials in Yokohama and Nagasaki. If anything, Godai was simply continuing the policy of combining enterprises in domestic and foreign trade.

In the spring of 1865, Godai and two other domain officials, in pursuit of the goal of extending the domain's commercial network to Europe by tying it directly to the Western states, toured Britain, Belgium, Prussia, and France, visiting factories and buying armaments and industrial equipment, notably a cotton-spinning machine that later formed the kernel of a plant in Kagoshima. In Brussels, the group met Charles Comte de Montblanc, a Belgian of French birth who had had commercial dealings with the *bakufu* and was aware of the commercial opportunities in Satsuma. In the fall of 1865, Godai and Montblanc signed a provisional contract to set up a mining company in Satsuma and factories to produce steel, weapons, textiles (including silk), and tea, and to open three ports in Ryukyu. Montblanc also agreed to act as the domain's agent in France to facilitate the display of domain products at the Paris Exposition in 1867.[54]

In the ninth month of 1865, during a mission to France, Shibata Takenaka, a senior *bakufu* official, learned of Satsuma's contract with

---

53. Hoover, "Godai Tomoatsu (1836-85)," 78–79.
54. Kōshaku Shimazu-ke henshūjo, ed., *Sappan kaigunshi* vol. 2, 958–62.

Montblanc. Shibata was surprised to discover that Satsuma officials were working throughout Europe and angered when Montblanc visited him in Paris to tell him of his plans for Satsuma's display at the exposition. Shibata, who wished Satsuma to include its products in a unified Japanese exhibit that highlighted Tokugawa authority, was heartened to learn early in 1866 that the exposition's organizers had rejected Satsuma's proposal for a separate exhibit. But Montblanc was reported to be proposing a separate Ryukyu exhibit in which Satsuma could present itself on the world stage as outside the Tokugawa orbit. Shibata soon headed home to Japan in the hope of finding a way to limit Satsuma's bid to demonstrate its autonomy.[55]

In the spring of 1866, Godai returned to Satsuma. His arrival coincided with a rapprochement between Satsuma and Chōshū that was codified in the first month of 1866 when the two domains signed a secret pact to work for the overthrow of the Tokugawa regime. The treaty came as the two domains began to restore the commercial ties suspended after Chōshū's attack on the Satsuma vessel in early 1864. Following Chōshū's failed coup in Kyoto and the *bakufu*-led military expedition against the domain in late 1864 and early 1865, the Chōshū leadership moved away from advocating and executing expulsion and began to aggressively explore new trade opportunities. Takasugi Shinsaku and Kido Takayoshi, two domain leaders, pushed to restart the trade with Satsuma at Shimonoseki. Different from a few years earlier, the Chōshū leadership became more actively involved in the specifics of the trade, assigning officials to directly control it. In the same month as the treaty was signed, two Satsuma merchant ships arrived in Shimonoseki carrying brown sugar, rapeseed oil, tobacco, and wax. Thereafter, trade between the two domains bloomed again, this time under the closer supervision of officials from both domains. In addition, Satsuma began to ship sugar directly to Chōshū, instead of via Osaka.[56]

Fresh from Europe, Godai sought to find ways to further expand the Satsuma-Chōshū trade. In the tenth month of 1866, he traveled to Shimonoseki and met with Chōshū officials. Kido expressed his sup-

---

55. "Gaikoku bugyō Shibata Takenaka jōshinsho," 1866/02/09, *DNISK*, KE 047-0772; Ericson, "The *Bakufu* Looks Abroad," 401–4.
56. Tanaka, *Bakumatsu ishin-ki no kenkyū*, 136–37.

port for Godai's proposal that Chōshū join the joint-stock firm that he had recently established with Montblanc. Godai later met with a representative of the Ōmura domain in Kyushu and discussed ways in which Chōshū could cooperate with Satsuma to profit from trade at Nagasaki.[57]

Montblanc outmaneuvered the Tokugawa when the exposition's organizers agreed to the separate Ryukyu exhibit. In the eleventh month of 1866, Satsuma sent a delegation to Paris, aboard an English ship, headed by a domain senior councilor, Iwashita Masahira. In two separate shipments, it also sent 400 boxes of products including white and brown sugar, millet brandy, and printed calicos from Ryukyu, as well as Satsuma-made lacquer and pottery. Soon after his arrival in Paris in early 1867, Iwashita, with Montblanc's help, arranged to display the goods in a separate exhibit under the patronage of the Shimazu lord given the title, "His Highness Matsudaira Shuri no Daibu, Minamoto Shigehisa, Ruler of Ryukyu," one that acknowledged no dependence on the Tokugawa.[58]

When the *bakufu* delegation, headed by Tokugawa Akitake, the shogun's younger brother, reached Paris just before the exposition's official opening on 1 April, it tried to persuade the organizers to incorporate the Ryukyu exhibit into a unified Japanese exhibit. Failing in that, it met with Montblanc and Iwashita in an attempt to persuade them to drop the reference to Ryukyu and to use the title, "Matsudaira Shuri no Daibu." Iwashita refused, instead deciding to display not only the Ryukyu goods but also the Satsuma goods under an even bolder title— "The Government of the Viceroy of Satsuma of Japan" (Nihon Satsuma taishu seifu)—and striking medals that bore the Shimazu family crest surrounded by Chinese characters that read: "The Kingdoms of Satsuma and Ryukyu," which he presented to dignitaries, including Napoleon III. Faced with Satsuma's intransigence, the *bakufu* exhibited its goods under the name "The Government of the Great Prince of Japan" (Nihon taikun seifu). The *bakufu* officials had no doubt, however, that the separate exhibits revealed the Tokugawa regime's impotence to the world. The

---

57. "Godai Tomoatsu den," 1866/10/15–17, *DNISK*, KE 096-0993; Tanaka Akira, *Bakumatsu ishin-ki no kenkyū*, 138.

58. *KK*, vol. 3, 227–29.

French press, aware of the tension within the Japanese delegation, described the *bakufu* as merely one political entity within a federal Japanese state.[59] By asserting the domain's agency at a world event, Satsuma's leaders did more than embarrass the Tokugawa. Although Satsuma had been steadily asserting its claims in recent decades, the use of a separate title represented a bid for autonomy, a challenge to the Tokugawa claim to status as Japan's central authority.

Conclusions

Historians have viewed Satsuma's claim to autonomy presented in Paris as historically significant in setting the stage for the political and military tumult of the Meiji Restoration in which Satsuma's forces, in alliance with Chōshū and other domains, toppled the Tokugawa regime. In other words, Satsuma's actions, both in Japan and abroad, are best understood as prongs of a defining, domain-wide drive to gain wider political power.[60]

Many Satsuma leaders pursued that goal, but the domain's commercial endeavors reveal that was not the sole focus. Satsuma officials were not simply anti-Tokugawa stalwarts focused on toppling the *bakufu*, nor should they be seen as more "enlightened" than their *bakufu* counterparts for moving more quickly to commercial engagement with Western merchants. Hisamitsu and other high-ranking officials adopted policies based primarily on specific domain agendas, although Japan-wide movements, notably expulsion, also shaped their decisions. Importantly, as they pushed to expand engagement with Westerners, Satsuma leaders maintained established trade links with China through Ryukyu to allow the domain to benefit from sales of Chinese products at Nagasaki. Hisamitsu and his officials were also keen to protect the commercial benefits that Satsuma enjoyed from Ryukyu's tribute trade with China. Overall, Satsuma leaders, like their Tokugawa counterparts, took actions based upon existing contexts of intra-Asian trade. The decisions of domain leaders demonstrate that this was a transition involving jumps and starts: there was no clear watershed in which the

---

59. Ibid., 229–30.
60. Beasley, *The Meiji Restoration*, 247.

domain abandoned its established foreign trade ties to focus exclusively on trade with Western nations.

Satsuma and Tokugawa leaders grappled with the same challenge: would the new commercial opportunities presented by Westerners prove profitable and thus warrant the risks inherent in adopting a new economic relationship? As discussed above, Western merchants did not arrive in 1859 with viable plans for direct Japanese-Western trade but instead jockeyed to enter established networks of Japanese-Chinese trade. By 1863, silk worms and raw silk had emerged as key exports in direct Japan-European trade—but would the boom last? Indeed, the question must have been difficult as established products, particularly marine products, continued to prove lucrative in trade with China.

Compared to the shogunate, then, why did Satsuma more quickly embrace, and thus enjoy, greater benefits from engagement with Western merchants? Satsuma leaders achieved more for some of the same reasons that explain their earlier successes: without the feudal and bureaucratic constraints that defined Tokugawa policy, they could operate far more freely. Domain leaders did not have, for example, merchant and bureaucratic constituencies like those in Nagasaki that defined Tokugawa actions. They could therefore more easily develop new ties with Western merchants both in Japan and later in Europe. This flexibility, combined with the continued presence of commercial opportunism within the domain, allowed Satsuma to succeed in many of its commercial endeavors and drive the transition to broader commercial engagement with Western nations.

Moreover, Satsuma, unlike the *bakufu*, was not bound by the commitment to act in the overall defense of the realm, even in areas such as Ryukyu, which the Tokugawa realistically had no ability to defend. As the expulsion movement raised concerns of a Western attack, Tokugawa leaders felt compelled to prevent Ryukyu's economy from weakening further and thus granted Satsuma concessions, such as the minting of Ryukyu coins. As was the case in earlier decades, Tokugawa leaders were caught in bind: the need to support Ryukyu, but also the awareness that such actions would allow Satsuma to increase its trade profits. They granted concessions no doubt believing that while Satsuma would benefit, expediency required that Ryukyu be given the opportunity to use trade to maintain economic stability.

Bureaucratic and feudal commitments prompted *bakufu* leaders to continue to pursue a time-tested formula: earn foreign trade profits by protecting established contacts with Chinese merchants. At the same time, they sought to refashion established institutions and systems to meet the new circumstances created by the opening of the ports and the growth of domestic trade. In the years immediately after the ports were opened in 1859, *bakufu* leaders attempted to increase profits and maintain Tokugawa dominance over the domestic market by establishing institutions through which to funnel trade and commercial activity, maintain strict controls over the flow of prominent consumer goods, and continue to monopolize the export of copper and marine products. In sum, *bakufu* leaders expected that established practices in domestic and foreign trade would remain viable. As the central power, they had more to gain from preserving established commercial systems and as such attempted to use them well into the 1860s. Although they were also willing to explore trade with Westerners, they understandably sought to maintain existing commercial advantages. Tokugawa leaders, therefore, took a more conservative stance. They remained committed longer to established channels of East Asian trade, in a sense hedging their bets that China-centered trade would continue to thrive despite the growing Western influence.

SEVEN

Defending the Domain and the Realm

In early 1860, the Tsushima leadership was engrossed in defensive preparations, convinced it was only a matter of time before more Western ships would arrive at domain shores. Sō Yoshiyori and his advisors believed that the nature of Western visits, which had been constant since the late 1840s, had changed the previous year when the warship HMS *Actaeon* had put men ashore at both Tsushima and Pusan. They concluded that with the opening of Nagasaki, Yokohama, and Hakodate to Western-style free trade, more Westerners would seek to establish a base of operations on Tsushima or even at Pusan.

At the same time, Tsushima leaders assured Chosŏn and *bakufu* officials of its commitment to the existing diplomatic system. Tsushima asked the *bakufu* for permission to inform Chosŏn of the commercial treaties signed with Western powers and the subsequent opening of several ports to trade. After receiving approval, Tsushima sent word that Westerners were now trading in the realm but stressed that the domain remained committed to its relationship with the Chosŏn Kingdom and the prohibition on Christianity. Tsushima officials also pledged to bring Korean envoys to Tsushima in the near future. *Bakufu* officials were less enthusiastic, instructing Tsushima to postpone, until 1866, a proposed Korean embassy to commemorate Iemochi's 1858 ascension to shogun.[1]

---

1. Tsuruta, "Man'en gannen, Tsushima-han ni yoru Chōsen e no shikoku tsūshō kokuchi ikken," 79–92; Taigai kankeishi sōgō nenpyō henshū iinkai, ed., *Taigai kankeishi sōgō nenpyō*, 927.

Confronted by Tokugawa indifference and concerned about future Western incursions, Tsushima leaders turned to what many within the domain believed would be a permanent solution to their defensive and economic woes: for the *bakufu* to assume direct control of the domain. For decades, domain leaders had considered this option, but it was not officially presented to the *bakufu* until Sasu Iori, the domain's chief councilor in Edo, did so in late 1859. Sasu proposed that in light of the present threat from Western nations, the *bakufu* should transfer the Sō to a domain in central Honshu. The *bakufu* would assume direct control over the domain, and with the Sō acting as advisors, administer trade and diplomacy with Korea. Sasu began preliminary negotiations with *bakufu* officials, but his effort stalled in the wake of the assassination of Ii Naosuke, the *bakufu* regent, in early 1860.[2]

As it turned out, the Tsushima leadership was correct in seeing the *Actaeon* as a harbinger of a new wave of Western pressure. Western diplomats, and especially the captains of the Western vessels that subsequently visited the island, did consider it as a possible commercial and military base primarily because of its position in the straits between Kyushu and the Korean peninsula. For example, in the summer of 1861, Rutherford Alcock, the British consul, wrote that the island possessed "fertile soil, [a] small but industrious population, a fine climate and numerous land-locked and excellent harbors, situated right in the fairway to China, and shutting, as it were by a turnpike gate, egress from the Japanese Sea, and all ingress consequently to the Chinese waters from that side."[3]

Russian naval officers certainly shared Alcock's view and saw Tsushima, with harbors superior to those in Sakhalin, as a potential base for Russian military and commercial operations in the North Pacific. Their interest, along with that of Russian diplomats, increased when they learned of the *Actaeon*'s visit to the island.[4] It is unclear, however,

---

2. *IC*, 914–15. Because of the extraordinary challenges facing the Tokugawa regime, Ii had been given the seldom used position of regent (*tairō*) that placed him in authority over all senior councilors in the *bakufu*.

3. Foreign Office, "Japan: Rutherford Alcock to Lord Russell, 2 August, 1861," *British Foreign and State Papers*, 46 (36).

4. Lensen, *The Russian Push Toward Japan*, 447–48.

Fig. 19 Aerial view of Asō Bay, Tsushima. Courtesy of Nii Takao.

if the Russian naval command or an arm of the czarist government ordered the corvette *Posadnik*, under the command of Captain Birilev, to sail to Tsushima in early 1861. When his ship arrived in Asō Bay, the large inlet in the center of the island, on the third day of the second month, Birilev told domain officials that his ship had sustained damage in a storm and requested to remain anchored until repairs could be completed. Yet days turned into weeks and the *Posadnik* remained, supplied on several occasions by other Russian warships, which later departed. Continuing to ignore requests to leave, the crew of the *Posadnik* built several buildings on shore and appeared intent on staying.[5]

Domain officials immediately sent word of the Russian presence to Sasu in Edo. Seeing this as the expected Western attempt to seize the domain and fearing that British ships would soon arrive as well, Sasu and other high-ranking officials met at Edo and decided to again appeal for a transfer of the Sō. Making some revisions and citing the Tokugawa takeover of the Matsumae domain in 1854 as a precedent, Sasu proposed that the Sō and their high-ranking retainers be transferred to a 100,000

---

5. Shim, "Bakumatsu-ki no bakufu no Chōsen seisaku to kikō no henka," 104; Hino, *Bakumatsu ni okeru Tsushima to Ei-Ro*, 32–33.

koku domain in Kyushu and that the entire island be placed under direct *bakufu* control. He also suggested that lords of Kyushu domains alternate in dispatching troops to protect the island, in the same way that lords from other parts of the realm defended areas around the treaty ports of Nagasaki, Yokohama, and Hakodate. As before, he urged the *bakufu* to assume control of relations with Korea with the Sō acting as advisors. He argued that once the island was under Tokugawa control, the shogunate could then lease the sixteen villages around Asō Bay to the Russians and also be in a position to defend against a British takeover.[6] It is striking that Sasu viewed the British as a more significant threat even while Russian ships lay anchored in his domain. Sasu's concern seemed to be confirmed when HMS *Raven* and two other British warships sailed into Asō Bay late in the fourth month, but the vessels remained only a few days.[7]

On Tsushima, tensions continued to mount. In the fourth month of 1861, an incident occurred at Ōfunakoshi, a narrow passage that was the only route through which a vessel could enter Asō Bay from Tsushima's eastern shore. Although it had been roped off, a Russian launch forcibly entered the channel. Angry peasants and several samurai on the shore threw rocks and sticks at the Russian sailors, who responded with gunfire, killing one samurai and a peasant. The skirmish probably developed spontaneously, although one historian concludes that the Tsushima officials planned the attack in order to aid the transfer request.[8] Regardless of who initiated the hostilities, the episode, and another clash in the same area a few weeks later, raised tensions. Although Tsushima officials began military preparations, it is clear that they hoped to avoid hostilities, either via the transfer of the Sō, or as a last resort, by fleeing the island. After the clashes with the Russians, Yoshiyori assured his retainers that he would personally fight to protect the domain. Nonetheless, domain officials formulated a secret plan for the daimyo and his immediate family to flee to Kyushu should full scale hostilities break out.[9]

---

6. *IC*, 914–15.
7. Hino, *Bakumatsu ni okeru Tsushima to Ei-Ro*, 99–101.
8. Hyŏn, "Bunkyū gannen Tsushima-han no ihō undō ni tsuite," 69–86.
9. Hino, *Bakumatsu ni okeru Tsushima to Ei-Ro*, 103–5.

Defending the Domain and the Realm 211

Fig. 20   Imozaki, Asō Bay, Tsushima. In 1861, the Russians established their outpost on the small peninsula behind the lighthouse. Courtesy of Tachibana Atsushi.

Rumors of the Russian ships and the skirmishes at Ōfunakoshi soon reached other parts of the realm. After learning of the Russian presence daimyo Mōri Takachika of Chōshū and his retainer Kido Takayoshi visited the Sō residence in Edo and offered to dispatch men to Tsushima to bolster defenses. The Chōshū leaders took a special interest in Tsushima because of a family connection: Jihōin, a daughter of the previous Chōshū daimyo, had married the previous Tsushima daimyo, Sō Yoshiaya, (r. 1838–42). Although Yoshiaya was no longer daimyo, Jihōin still held a position of influence within the domain leadership. The Tsushima leadership refused the offer, perhaps fearing that a band of Chōshū samurai might further inflame an already tense situation.[10]

Meanwhile, two high-ranking *bakufu* officials, foreign magistrate Oguri Tadamasa and inspector Mizoguchi Katsuyuki, arrived in Fuchū on the seventh day of the fifth month.[11] Oguri, the more senior official, had traveled to the United States the previous year as part of the first Japanese embassy to a Western nation. As one of the shogunate's veteran diplomats, he appeared well suited to broker an agreement for a Russian withdrawal. Oguri visited the *Posadnik* but could not persuade Birilev to depart. The captain steadfastly demanded a meeting with

---

10. *IC*, 906–7; Shibahara, *Kaikoku*, 170–71.
11. "Oguri Tadamasa todokesho," 1861/05/07, *DNISK*, BU 010-0597.

Yoshiyori, the daimyo, whom he believed would lease areas around Asō Bay for a Russian base. During a meeting between Oguri, Yoshiyori, and Birilev a few days later, Yoshiyori declined the Russian's request. Although the domain leadership was not opposed to leasing certain areas of the island (Sasu had included that option in the transfer request), Yoshiyori probably refused in order to maintain pressure on the *bakufu*. He would only agree if the *bakufu* took control over the domain and transferred the Sō. All told, Oguri's visit did not markedly alter the standoff, and he left the island on the 20th day of the fifth month.[12]

As was the case with Satsuma, the expulsion movement also influenced the situation on Tsushima. Also in the fifth month of 1861, a band of Mito samurai attacked the British legation in Edo, resulting in 21 casualties. Before the role of the Mito samurai was confirmed, rumors abounded in Edo and Yokohama that Yoshiyori had ordered the attack in retaliation for the incident at Ōfunakoshi.[13] Tsushima became a topic in meetings between *bakufu* officials and Rutherford Alcock, the British consul. Facing increased domestic pressure to execute expulsion, *bakufu* leaders hoped to improve relations with Britain to provide room to maneuver. Senior councilor and chief coordinator of foreign affairs Andō Nobumasa believed that if the British would agree to a delay in the opening of more Japanese ports, the expulsion movement might lose some momentum. *Bakufu* leaders could also present themselves as having the strength to resist Western demands, bolstering the regime's domestic position.[14] Furthermore, Andō realized that the British might help to defuse the situation on Tsushima. In meetings with Alcock and Rear-Admiral Sir James Hope of the British Navy early in the seventh month, he assured the two men that the *bakufu* would punish all involved in the attack on the legation and provide an indemnity for those injured. In return, he asked Hope for his assistance in securing the departure of the Russians from Tsushima.[15]

---

12. Hino, *Bakumatsu ni okeru Tsushima to Ei-Ro*, 141–66.

13. In his diary entries for 11 and 12 July 1861, Francis Hall, an American merchant in Yokohama, noted such rumors. Notehelfer, ed., *Japan Through American Eyes*, 355–56.

14. "Kuze Hirochika and Andō Nobumasa to Rutherford Alcock, 30 May 1861," in Beasley, *Select Documents on Japanese Foreign Policy*, 208–11.

15. Fox, *Britain and Japan, 1858–1883*, 219–32.

Table 2: Russian and British Vessels at Tsushima, 1861

Date	Details
2/3	Russian warship *Posadnik* anchors in Asō Bay
2/29	Russian warship *Najezdnik* supplies *Posadnik* and departs
3/19	Russian warships supply *Posadnik*, depart
4/12–14	British warship anchors at Fuchū, cruises nearby coast
4/21–24	Russian warship anchors at Asō Bay
4/22–27	HMS *Raven* and two British warships visit Asō Bay
5/8–22	Two Russian warships supply *Posadnik*
7/22–24	HMS *Ringdove* and HMS *Encounter* visit Fuchū and Asō Bay
7/26	Russian warship *Oprichnik* arrives at Asō Bay
8/15	*Posadnik* departs Asō Bay
8/23	Russian warship *Abrek* arrives at Asō Bay
8/25	*Abrek* and *Oprichnik* depart

SOURCES: Compiled from *DNISK*; Hino, *Bakumatsu ni okeru Tsushima to Ei-Ro*, 31–274; and Taigai kankeishi sōgō nenpyō henshū iinkai, ed, *Taigai kankeishi sōgō nenpyō*, 932–33.

Hope agreed, and with great speed brought HMS *Ringdove* and another warship to Tsushima, arriving on the 22nd day of the seventh month. He met with domain officials and urged the still intransigent Birilev to leave. The British pressure, and a few days later the arrival of another Russian ship, the *Oprichnik*, which delivered orders to depart Tsushima issued by the Russian naval command and the Russian consul in Hakodate, Iosif Antonovich Goshkevich, finally changed Birilev's mind. Although he delayed for a few more weeks, Birilev eventually ordered the *Posadnik* out of Asō Bay on the fifteenth day of the eighth month. Goshkevich, who opposed the move against Tsushima, had won out in a policy battle he had been waging with high-ranking officers in the Russian navy. While Birilev and other naval officers felt that by taking Tsushima, Russia could improve her strategic position in East Asia, Goshkevich believed that Russia's interests would be better served by developing friendly relations with the *bakufu*. Yet Goshkevich had a difficult time securing the departure of all Russian vessels, dispatching one more ship, the *Abrek*, to make sure the *Oprichnik* would also leave Tsushima. On the 25th day of the eighth month, all the Russian ships had departed, ending a difficult six months for Tsushima.[16]

---

16. Lensen, *The Russian Push Toward Japan*, 450–51; Hino, *Bakumatsu ni okeru Tsushima to Ei-Ro*, 242–75.

As the *bakufu* was helping to engineer the departure of the Russians, Tsushima officials continued to press for the transfer of the Sō. The domain submitted the request in the sixth month and officially presented it to Andō on the 20th day of the seventh month of 1861. The same day, Andō ordered the new magistrate for foreign affairs, Nonoyama Kanehiro (Oguri had resigned upon returning to Edo), to Tsushima to investigate the Russian presence, the domain's transfer request, and the possibility of opening the island to Western-style free trade. By the time Nonoyama reached Tsushima early in the tenth month, the Russians had departed, leaving on his agenda the transfer request and the foreign trade question.[17]

Nonoyama's group made an extensive, two-month investigation of Tsushima's harbors, defenses, and economy. In his report, the *bakufu* official offered few positive assessments. He criticized the domain's peasants as lazy, particularly because he believed they were not working to open new lands, especially hillside terraces, for agricultural production. In addition, Nonoyama stressed that the peasants were content to use outdated farm tools and had little interest in improving their yields by adopting better implements and more advanced agricultural methods used in other domains. As a result, he bemoaned that the domain imported from Osaka goods which he believed should have been produced on the island: salt, tea, soybean paste (*miso*), paper, and wax.

Moreover, Nonoyama lamented that the inhabitants of coastal villages had only small, leaky boats, which while serviceable for coastal fishing, did not allow deep sea fishing or whaling. As a result, the domain depended upon nearly 150 boats from Hiroshima and Chōshū to harvest fish and whales in its waters. Yet while Tsushima ships were not exploiting these resources, the sojourning vessels apparently did hire hundreds of Tsushima men on a seasonal basis and annually paid around 1,750 *ryō* in various fees, which no doubt provided an important revenue source to the strapped domain government.

As for trade with Korea, Nonoyama affirmed the dearth in commerce stated by domain officials for decades. He described only minimal commerce in cow hides and hooves, and concluded that imports of medicinal products from Korea had further declined because of the

---

17. Hino, *Bakumatsu ni okeru Tsushima to Ei-Ro*, 277–87.

opening of Nagasaki, Yokohama, and Hakodate. Moreover, he believed that the overall weakness of the Chosŏn Kingdom's economy, coupled with the troubles in China related to the Taiping Rebellion, indicated that prospects for future trade were not good.[18]

For Nonoyama, the poor state of Tsushima's economy and the dearth of trade with Korea were key factors in his recommendation, in the second month of 1862, that the *bakufu* deny the Sō transfer request and not establish a treaty port on Tsushima. He emphasized that given Tsushima's remote location and the lack of trade with Korea, the island had little chance of becoming a viable commercial entrepôt. He suggested that Tsushima leaders therefore should focus not on trade, but on improving the agricultural production of the island. In addition, he underscored the potential financial and diplomatic challenges that the *bakufu* would face if it were to assume control over the domain. With the Tokugawa in control, would Chosŏn leaders eliminate the annual shipments of rice, upon which the Tsushima populace depended? If so, how would the *bakufu* deal with that shortfall, and in addition, revise the long-established protocols for sending ships and envoys to the Japan House? While he affirmed that Asō Bay was a suitable harbor for large merchant vessels and warships, he noted the significant financial outlays that would be required to strengthen Tsushima's defenses, particularly because the Sō possessed few Western-style cannon and rifles. In addition, the *bakufu* must also consider the costs associated with administrating a treaty port on the island. All told, he made a convincing case, which led the *bakufu* leadership in the fifth month of 1862 to formally reject both the Sō's transfer request and the possibility of opening a treaty port on Tsushima.[19]

The decision of *bakufu* leaders to refuse to take direct control over a part of Japanese territory ripe for foreign takeover, especially at the prompting of its lord, is, at first glance, puzzling. Such a step could have demonstrated that the Tokugawa regime could act as a definitive defender of the realm, thereby displaying Tokugawa vigor in an increasingly competitive East Asian geopolitical scene.

---

18. Hino provides the full text of Nonoyama's memorial, with annotations, in *Bakumatsu ni okeru Tsushima to Ei-Ro*, 315–29.

19. Ibid., 330–35.

In the end, however, *bakufu* leaders concluded that such an enhancement of the Tokugawa position would come at too great a financial cost. In their rejection, they intimated that given Nonoyama's conclusions about the languid state of Tsushima's trade with Korea, the *bakufu* could not hope to use revenue from Korean-Japanese trade to finance the administration of Tsushima and the strengthening of the island's defenses. In addition, based upon Nonoyama's report, they were clearly aware that a Tokugawa takeover of Tsushima and the establishment of a treaty port on the island would have entailed reforming long-established ties with the Chosŏn Kingdom, a process that would have required additional Tokugawa resources. *Bakufu* officials would also have been forced to commit time and energy to relations with Korea at a time when they were already engrossed in vital negotiations with Western diplomats, as well as trying to control the growing movement to expel foreigners from the realm. All told, Tokugawa leaders, much as they had done concerning trade at Nagasaki, made a conservative—but for them, prudent—decision in denying the transfer request and the plan to open Tsushima to foreign trade.[20]

For Sasu, the Tsushima chief councilor, the rejection was a devastating political blow. He believed the transfer would stabilize the domain and protect it against future Western incursions. This placed him at odds with many domain samurai, who had opposed the request, asserting that it equated to the Sō abandoning their ancestral land. These same samurai also resented Sasu because of a long dispute over the selection of an heir for Yoshiyori. Since the 1840s, two consorts of Yoshiyori had competed to have their sons become the heir. In the subsequent years, a son of each consort was eventually chosen, but each died while still quite young. When the son of Yoshiyori's commoner consort Midori died in 1859, many in the domain opposed Sasu

---

20. A few months after *bakufu* leaders in Edo rejected the possibility of opening a treaty port on Tsushima, Tokugawa envoys in London, who had not communicated with Edo, agreed in principle to such a plan, apparently upon the urging of Rutherford Alcock. Despite the actions of their envoys, *bakufu* leaders subsequently kept plans to open trade at Tsushima off the negotiating table, although the American consul, Robert Pryun, again proposed Tsushima as a treaty port in the eighth month of 1862. "Rutherford Alcock's Confidential Memorandum of 14 February 1862," "London Protocol, 6 June 1862" in Beasley, *Select Documents on Japanese Foreign Policy*, 213, 217.

and the domain leadership's choice of her surviving son as heir. They accused Sasu of unjustly favoring Midori's line and instead supported Yoshinojō, the daimyo's son by his samurai wife. Opposition to Sasu reached a boiling point in the tenth month of 1860 when an armed force of several hundred men descended upon Fuchū. The band freed seven men earlier imprisoned by Sasu, among them Higuchi Kennosuke, Tada Shōzō, and Katsui Gohachirō. Under this armed pressure, Yoshiyori relented and removed Midori's son, replacing him with Yoshinojō. Sasu remained in power, but his position was severely weakened.[21]

These factional disputes were put aside when the *Posadnik* arrived, but resurfaced when the Russians departed and the transfer request was rejected. In the seventh month of 1862, Higuchi and a group of samurai traveled to Edo ostensibly to bolster defenses at the domain residence and to prepare for the succession of Yoshinojō. In truth, the band of 42 men—which included Katsui, Tada, Ōura Norinosuke, and a young retainer, Ōshima Tomonojō—looked to depose Sasu from his leadership position. Stopping first at the graves of the famous 47 lordless samurai (*rōnin*) for inspiration, the band proceeded to the domain residence on the 24th day of the eighth month of 1862. Following a heated verbal confrontation, they murdered Sasu. The band rationalized the act on the grounds that Sasu had corruptly adjudicated the succession dispute, disregarded samurai ethics, and shamed Sō ancestors by urging the daimyo to abandon the territory that the clan had ruled for six centuries.[22]

Following the coup, Higuchi, Tada, Ōshima, and others in the group reorganized the domain leadership, giving Yoshinojō more influence. Through Sō familial ties, the new leaders also began to cultivate a closer relationship with the ruling family of Chōshū, the Mōri. They hoped that Chōshū, which they viewed as a rising star on the domestic political scene, would become a powerful advocate for the domain in Kyoto and Edo. Having faced the near constant arrival of Western ships since the 1840s, and most recently, the extended Russian visit, the new leadership circle also supported policies then championed by Chōshū: the

---

21. *IC*, 906–10.
22. Ibid., 918–19.

plan to expel foreigners from the realm and simultaneously increase the role of the imperial court in political affairs.

Jihōin, the daughter of the previous Chōshū daimyo and widow of Yoshiyori's father, was influential in bringing leaders of the two domains together, leading to an alliance formed in the ninth month of 1862. Tsushima leaders pledged to support Chōshū's efforts to advance expulsion, and in return, Kido Takayoshi personally agreed to lobby the *bakufu* to speed the official succession of Yoshinojō. Kido worked with Tsushima retainers in Edo and Kyoto to push through the retirement of Yoshiyori in the twelfth month and the subsequent succession of Yoshinojō, who took the name Yoshiakira, becoming the 34th and final lord of the Tsushima domain.[23]

Ōshima Tomonojō and the Campaign for Bakufu *Aid*

Soon after the coup, Ōshima Tomonojō emerged as the domain's point man in this new relationship with Chōshū. He also came to be deeply involved in a new Tsushima effort to secure Tokugawa financial aid. While honestly concerned about the additional defense that his domain would have to muster, Ōshima also probably saw the expulsion order as an opportunity to gain increased financial support. Ōshima pushed Tsushima's case by actively soliciting advice and assistance from several powerful individuals with influence at the imperial court and in the *bakufu* leadership. As a first step, he approached Kido. The Chōshū samurai, who became Ōshima's life-long friend, proved receptive and helped him gain access to powerful men in both Edo and Kyoto. Kido was deeply troubled by the Russian incursion the previous year, and believed that it was only a matter of time before a Western nation would move against Tsushima or Korea, and then against Chōshū and all of Japan. In order to protect the realm, Kido therefore advocated improving the defenses of Tsushima and even proposed a Japanese invasion of Korea to forestall a Western military incursion on the peninsula.[24] Because they were so intent to execute expulsion, Kido and others in the Chōshū leadership were also seriously concerned that the

---

23. Ibid., 919–20.
24. Kim, *The Last Phase of the East Asian World Order*, 93; Kido, *The Diary of Kido Takayoshi*, vol. 1, 348–49.

execution of the expulsion order would bring Western military retaliation. Perhaps because of recent French military incursions in China, Kido had an idée fixe about France: that it would move first against Korea before seizing Tsushima to use as a base of operations to attack Kyushu and Honshu. Kido therefore sought to strengthen Tsushima to make it a buffer that would protect Chōshū and the rest of the realm.[25]

In the twelfth month of 1862, Kido arranged for Ōshima to present an appeal to the court through Chōshū intermediaries. In his memorial, Ōshima explained that Tsushima's already challenging defensive position had become even more precarious because of the impending expulsion order. He lamented Tsushima's reliance on commerce with Korea and criticized the diplomatic system that left the domain dependent on Korean rice. He also asserted that Tsushima's strategic position would make it a military target when the order was executed. If Tsushima were to fall into the hands of a foreign power, Ōshima argued, it would tarnish imperial authority and increase the possibility of full-scale Western invasion. He therefore urged the court to view Tsushima's defense as a pressing issue for the entire realm.[26]

On the basis of the memorial, in the first month of 1863, the court issued an edict recognizing Tsushima's strategic position. "Soon foreigners will be expelled. As a remote island in the distant sea, the Tsushima domain is a key territory in the defense of the realm."[27] Here, at last, was definitive recognition of what Tsushima leaders had pushed for since the 1840s—the affirmation from a central authority that the domain was a physical border bulwark, vital to the overall defense of the Japanese realm.

While satisfied with the imperial edict, Ōshima was well aware that the court, which had no independent treasury, could not provide the funds necessary to improve Tsushima's defenses. He therefore used the edict to support further appeals to the *bakufu*, which had the financial resources to grant aid. In the first month of 1863, Ōshima and several domain officials accompanied their daimyo as he presented appeals

---

25. Kido and Tsumaki, *Kido Takayoshi monjo*, vol. 2, 283; Suematsu, *Bōchō kaitenshi*, vol. 4, 204–14.
26. Kimura, "Bunkyū sannen Tsushima-han enjo yōkyū undō ni tsuite," 708–10.
27. Nagasaki kenshi henshū iinkai, ed., *Nagasaki kenshi, hanseihen*, 1131.

for aid to Mizuno Tadakiyo and Itakura Katsukiyo, two *bakufu* senior councilors.[28] Kido continued to offer his support, introducing Ōshima to Yamada Hōkoku, a Confucian scholar and mentor of Itakura, in the same month. For several years, Yamada had advocated a Japanese invasion of the Chosŏn Kingdom and Qing territories that would exploit the now weakened Qing regime, which had been unable to stop a brief Anglo-French occupation of Beijing in 1860 and to quash the long-running Taiping Rebellion. In 1861, he had urged Itakura to present memorials to the *bakufu* leadership suggesting that the shogunate dispatch a three-pronged force, composed of Chōshū and Satsuma troops and *bakufu* warships, to conquer China, Korea, and Taiwan. Yamada concluded that it would be possible to capture the hearts and minds of the Chinese and Korean people by governing in a righteous manner that would restore the customs and order of the golden age of the Tang Dynasty (581–907).[29]

When Ōshima and Kido asked for assistance, Yamada must have seen a new opportunity to push his agenda. He therefore arranged for Itakura to meet once again with Sō Yoshiakira to discuss the domain's situation. In the fourth month of 1863, Ōshima again conferred with Itakura, and in an indication of Yamada's influence, discussed not only aid for Tsushima, but an invasion of the Chosŏn Kingdom. Itakura subsequently ordered an investigation of the situation in Korea to assess the chances of a Western power gaining a foothold on the peninsula and how this might present a threat to the Japanese realm.[30]

All the while, Ōshima continued to solicit backing from other influential figures. Capping off a busy month, Ōshima, Kido, and Yamada met with Katsu Kaishū, then head of the *bakufu* naval training facility at Hyōgo. Katsu had been troubled by the events on Tsushima in 1861 and supported strengthening the domain's defenses. In diary entries during the weeks following the above mentioned meeting, Katsu recorded several visits by Ōshima and noted his belief that a solution

---

28. "Tsushima Fuchū-han mainikki" 1863/1/25, "Izuhara Fuchū-han mainikki," 1863/1/27, *DNISK*, BU 076-0380.
29. Tabohashi, *Kindai Nissen kankei no kenkyū*, vol. 1, 299–300; Kim, *The Last Phase of the East Asian World Order*, 83–88.
30. Kimura, "Bunkyū sannen Tsushima-han enjo yōkyū undō ni tsuite," 716.

for Tsushima's defensive concerns should be found.[31] During these meetings, Katsu and Ōshima discussed a possible expedition to Korea. Katsu's actual support for an invasion has been debated by historians, but he did become another key supporter of Ōshima's campaign to obtain additional aid for Tsushima.[32]

Having secured support at several levels, Ōshima formally submitted his memorial to the *bakufu* in the fifth month of 1863. Emphasizing many of the same points presented earlier to the imperial court, he criticized Tsushima's dependence on a "failed" diplomatic and commercial relationship with Korea. He stressed that Tsushima lacked the ability to feed and provision the number of men required to ward off an attack that might arise when the expulsion order was executed. In addition, he implored *bakufu* leaders to consider the strategic importance of Tsushima in the realm's overall defense, especially in light of recent rumors of Western plans to invade Korea and then perhaps move against Japan.

The most prudent next step, Ōshima contended, was to send an expedition to Chosŏn to assess the situation and, if possible, conquer the kingdom before a Western power could use it as a base to attack the Japanese islands. He asserted that Japanese forces could quickly gain the support of the Korean people by presenting themselves as virtuous liberators. If the Koreans did not obey, Ōshima concluded that it would be necessary to use Japanese military power to subdue them.[33]

Confident that the Tokugawa regime would send a force against Korea, Ōshima also urged *bakufu* leaders to consider Tsushima's position after the invasion had begun. Because a military move against Korea would bring a temporary end to all trade as well as Korean rice shipments to the island, he cautioned that Tsushima would no doubt soon be gripped by famine. To help the domain regain its economic footing, it would therefore be necessary for the *bakufu* first to provide food aid

---

31. Katsu, *Kaishū zenshū*, vol. 9, 17–21.

32. Kimura believes that Katsu was an advocate of an invasion, while Matsuura Rei concludes that he advocated only diplomacy. Kimura, "Bunkyū sannen Tsushima-han enjo yōkyū undō ni tsuite," 731; Matsuura, "Bakumatsu-ki no tai Chōsen-ron: dōmeiron to seikanron," 49.

33. Kimura, "Bunkyū sannen Tsushima-han enjo yōkyū undō ni tsuite," 720.

to assuage the famine and then to grant Tsushima a major share of the restored trade with the soon-to-be-subjugated Korea. Ever fearful of a Western attack, he also requested that *bakufu* officials loan warships to the domain to allow it to protect itself against Western military incursions, which perhaps might come in retaliation for the Japanese invasion. Probably at Kido's urging, he also pushed Tokugawa officials to prepare a coastal defense plan in coordination with Chōshū and other Kyushu domains. Ōshima concluded the memorial with his primary request: an annual grant of 30,000 *koku*, a far larger sum than previous Tsushima officials had requested, to cover the domain's expenditures for defense and provide relief for its strained economy.[34]

Within a few months, Ōshima's initial plan to gain financial aid had morphed into a broad scheme to invade Korea and revise the existing system of trade and diplomacy. Kido (a representative of the powerful Chōshū domain), Yamada (a prominent scholar), Itakura (a *bakufu* leader), and Katsu (an expert of naval defense and man of influence in the realm) had all attached their agendas to the request. Because the plan expanded so quickly, it is important to consider whether Ōshima added these points merely to help his cause or if he wholeheartedly supported plans to invade Korea and revise Japanese-Korean relations.

On one level, Ōshima appears to have acted in a manner consistent with that taken by Shimazu Hisamitsu of Satsuma. Although swayed by political trends, Ōshima always looked for ways to use those trends for the benefit of his domain. His primary goal was to gain financial assistance to strengthen Tsushima's defenses. In order to achieve this, he skillfully co-opted the agendas of powerful figures, and like Hisamitsu, used the expulsion order as a tool to pressure the *bakufu*. It is difficult to determine if Ōshima originally advocated invading the Chosŏn Kingdom or if he added it upon the urging of Kido and Yamada. Whatever the case, Ōshima continued to promote of a Japanese invasion of Korea in subsequent years.

After a fortnight of internal consultation, *bakufu* officials granted all of Tsushima's requests except for the loan of warships.[35] *Bakufu* leaders

---

34. Ibid., 718–20.
35. Ibid., 721–22.

thus signaled their willingness to provide assistance that would assuage Tsushima's defensive concerns. By granting the aid request, Tokugawa leaders, really for the first time, supported the contention trumpeted by Tsushima leaders for two decades that the island domain was a strategically important territory that required Tokugawa financial assistance to bolster its defenses.

Although not accepting outright Ōshima's proposal to invade Korea, the *bakufu* leadership took steps to better discern the defensive situation in Tsushima and the veracity of the rumors of Western plans to invade the Chosŏn Kingdom. In the sixth month of 1863, the *bakufu* leadership ordered Katsu to sail to Tsushima to investigate the situation there and, if possible, also travel to Korea to gauge the likelihood of a Western invasion of the peninsula. Tsushima leaders had high expectations for Katsu's visit, believing that it could be a step to a new, more beneficial commercial and diplomatic relationship with Korea.

In the end, Katsu never made the journey. Soon after they issued the memorial, *bakufu* officials ordered Katsu to transport Shogun Iemochi to Osaka to speed his trip to Kyoto. After that mission was completed, *bakufu* officials dispatched the naval expert on additional business to Nagasaki. Thus occupied, Katsu was never able to undertake an expedition that was certainly high on his personal agenda.[36]

Although disappointed that Katsu's visit never became a reality, the Tsushima leadership still anticipated receiving the grant of 30,000 *koku*. The expected infusion of funds (and perhaps Nonoyama's biting assessments as well) probably prompted domain leaders to finally create domain monopolies and clearing-houses that would allow Tsushima to gain profits from the sale of domain products on the wider Japanese domestic market. The domain sold monopoly rights to merchants and allowed them to sell shares of those monopolies. Additionally, as Satsuma and other Kyushu domains had been doing for decades, Tsushima provided money to encourage the production of specialized products and established a clearing-house to supervise the sale of those goods outside the domain. In addition, the domain set up an office in Osaka that expedited the sale of local products, as well as Korean imports such as cowhides, on the domestic market. These steps did

---

36. Kimura, "Bakumatsu no Nitchō kankei to seikanron," 29.

allow the domain to increase its profit margin on sales of Korean imports as well as domain goods on the Osaka market. Yet the profits did not measurably reduce the domain's considerable debts to Osaka and Edo merchants.[37]

Meanwhile, Tsushima's leadership circle, now dominated by men who advocated the expulsion of foreigners and reverence for the emperor, moved to build a loyal cadre of supporters that would help them maintain power. To this aim, in the second month of 1864, they opened the Nisshinkan, a school that became the stronghold of those advocating the expulsion of foreigners from the realm. Under the direction of Ōura Norinosuke, one of leaders in the movement that overthrew Sasu, the Nisshinkan educated 200 students in martial arts, Confucian teachings, history, and calligraphy.[38]

Just as the expulsion advocates seemed to be settling into a position of strength, the capricious political winds changed direction at Edo in 1864, a shift that influenced events in Tsushima. As part of a wave of conservatism within the *bakufu*, new men such as Takemoto Masaaki and Abe Masatō were promoted to leadership positions, forcing out those who supported aid for Tsushima and moves against Korea. This new leadership did not favor expulsion and wanted to move more aggressively against challenges to Tokugawa rule emerging from the court and powerful daimyo, such as the Mōri of Chōshū. Suspicious of his cooperation with Kido and other men from Chōshū, they forced Itakura from the leadership in the fourth month of 1864.[39] The new *bakufu* leaders were also concerned about Katsu and his "strange collection of lord-less samurai and loyalists." They soon forced him to resign his position as head of the naval training center.[40]

Around the same time, Chōshū, Tsushima's other benefactor, also dramatically fell from its position of political prominence in the realm. In the seventh month, Satsuma and Aizu forces repelled a Chōshū move to seize control of the imperial place in Kyoto, leading the *bakufu* to call for an expedition to punish the domain. In addition in the eighth

---

37. *IC*, 923–24; Yoshinaga, "Kokusan kaisho shihō no seiritsu to tenkai," 7.
38. *IC*, 941–42.
39. Totman, *The Collapse of the Tokugawa Bakufu*, 124–25.
40. Jansen, *Sakamoto Ryōma and the Meiji Restoration*, 182.

month, American, British, French, and Dutch warships bombarded batteries at Shimonoseki, the key Chōshū port city that guarded the straits between Honshu and Kyushu. Fearing for his life, Kido went underground. Within a few months, Ōshima's allies had lost their leadership posts. To make matters worse, the new *bakufu* leaders believed that Tsushima's aid request and the plans to move against Korea were part of Chōshū's attempt to seize political control. As they readied a military expedition to punish Chōshū, the *bakufu* leadership cited the coming campaign as the reason for revoking the 30,000 *koku* in aid, which was set to begin in 1865. With one stroke, Tsushima leaders had lost their long hoped for economic lifeline.

Now without his benefactors, an undaunted Ōshima set about presenting anew the domain's case to the *bakufu* leadership. He eventually found one *bakufu* official, inspector Mukōyama Kōson, who would listen. In the tenth month of 1864, Ōshima submitted a lengthy petition to Mukōyama in which he offered his opinions on the situation in Korea and Tsushima's relationship with the kingdom. Ōshima again cited defense and the domain's dependence on a faltering trading system with the Chosŏn Kingdom as Tsushima's two most pressing problems. Yet, different from before, he focused less on receiving financial aid and more on articulating how an invasion of Korea, and a concomitant redefinition of Japanese-Korean commercial and diplomatic relations, would solve larger, realm-wide defensive concerns and simultaneously help Tsushima as well.

Ōshima divided his request into a preface and seven sections. In the preface, he emphasized three themes to guide the invasion: justice, mercy, and benefit. He then described how an invasion would allow beneficial reform of the existing diplomatic and commercial relationship with the Chosŏn Kingdom. Instead of the established system that permitted only single men to reside at the Japan House in Pusan, Ōshima wanted to allow Japanese merchants and their families to live and trade freely in several Korean ports, as was the case in the sixteenth century. He also stressed the importance of capturing the hearts of the people of Korea. As Yamada had declared several years before, Ōshima contended that the Korean people, repressed by unjust leaders, would welcome virtuous Japanese rule.

In the third and fourth sections, Ōshima stated how trade could be improved by establishing a more open commercial relationship with the Chosŏn Kingdom to bring benefit to both Korea and Japan. This would involve removing prohibitions on trade, particularly the ban on arms sales, and by dispatching Japanese technicians to Korea to improve efficiency in mining and other areas of production. In the fifth section, Ōshima stressed the need to display Japanese military power and heroism in the invasion. Again echoing Yamada, Ōshima explained that Japanese forces should first display superior Japanese justice and moral strength. Because the "backward" Koreans might not welcome such virtue, he suggested that overwhelming Japanese military strength might be necessary to force them to accept Japanese goodness. In his sixth section, Ōshima advocated the opening of a trade route with China. He envisioned Korea serving as an intermediary for increased trade with the Qing, a role that he asserted would bring benefit to an economically weak Chosŏn Kingdom. He believed that by expanding trade with Korea and China, income could be created to help build a strong Japanese navy, his seventh and final proposal.[41]

Ōshima's memorial demonstrates a continued faith in intra-Asian trade that mirrors the stances taken by Satsuma and Tokugawa officials in the early 1860s. Shuttling between Edo and Osaka and meeting constantly with prominent political figures, Ōshima was certainly aware of the growing trade with Western merchants conducted at the treaty ports. Yet instead of advocating new commercial ties with Western merchants, he focused on how to expand trade with Korea and especially the China market. Anxious about potential military threats to Tsushima, Ōshima may have also believed that a return to the sixteenth-century trade system, in which Japanese merchants freely lived and traded in Chosŏn's port cities, would offer a means to enhance the defense of Tsushima—and by implication, that of Japan.

It is also useful to consider why Ōshima remained an ardent advocate of an invasion of Korea. If he had proposed an invasion to gain Itakura's support, a key invasion advocate, Ōshima could have quickly abandoned that strategy when Itakura was removed from the *bakufu*

---

41. The complete document can be found in Tanaka Akira, ed. *Kaikoku, Nihon kindai shisō taikei* vol. 1, 108–17.

leadership. Because he still trumpeted the benefits of an invasion after Itakura's exit, we can conclude that Ōshima had embraced the belief that Koreans would welcome a Japanese invasion of their kingdom.

Finally, and most importantly, while Ōshima was certainly still hoping to gain Tokugawa financial aid for Tsushima, he was now more focused on implementing a fundamental revision of established methods of Japanese-Korean relations that would consolidate power and authority for those relations in the hands of the shogunate.

Apparently in response to Ōshima's memorial, the *bakufu* soon ordered the magistrate for foreign affairs to travel to Tsushima to investigate the situation there.[42] Amidst growing tensions surrounding the first *bakufu* expedition to chastise Chōshū, however, the mission was cancelled. As *bakufu* leaders subsequently faced increasing internal discord, policy moves concerning Korea were not initiated for several years.

Bitter Factional Rivalry

Ōshima was fortunate to be assigned the post of Tsushima's representative in Osaka from 1863 to 1866. If he had been on Tsushima during those years, he would have been drawn into the bitter factional rivalries that resulted in hundreds of deaths. In a discussion of the 1860s, a local history of Tsushima concludes, "it is said that the most famous product of the Tsushima domain was factional rivalry. If we look back at the history of the domain, there is a pattern. As soon as one figure gained power and established his position, another group emerged to oppose him."[43] As was the case with Satsuma, Tsushima's initiatives in foreign relations were colored by factional rifts that intersected with the movement to expel foreigners from Japan. Although some of clashes emerged from ideological differences, the battles were just as often driven by bitter personal feuds and political machinations.

Two years after the coup that brought the Tada, Higuchi, Ōura, and Ōshima faction to power, a rival group emerged to challenge the faction's rule. The leader was Katsui Gohachirō, earlier imprisoned by

---

42. Taigai kankeishi sōgō nenpyō henshū iinkai, ed., *Taigai kankeishi sōgō nenpyō*, 944.
43. Shin Tsushima tōshi henshū iinkai, ed., *Shin Tsushima tōshi*, 436.

Sasu, and a member of the group that had executed the coup at Edo in 1862. Katsui, the uncle of the daimyo, Yoshiakira, had opposed the treaty with Chōshū and the domain leadership's focus on expulsion, instead favoring strengthening ties with the *bakufu*. He was particularly concerned that the relationship with Chōshū, a rogue domain after its defeat in Kyoto, might also jeopardize the annual grant of 30,000 *koku* from the shogunate. Indeed, his fears came to pass in late 1864 when the *bakufu* leadership revoked the grant slated for the following year. Katsui believed that with the new, more conservative *bakufu* leadership that had assumed control in early 1864, Chōshū's position within the realm was weakening. He concluded that it was therefore foolish for Tsushima to align itself with a falling star. Katsui was correct in his assessment. By late 1864, the combined weight of defeats at Kyoto and Shimonoseki plus the scheduled *bakufu* military expedition against the domain severely weakened Chōshū's position. Indeed, Chōshū envoys visited Tsushima, appealing for military assistance and for Tsushima to prepare for the possible arrival of the Chōshū daimyo, who reportedly planned to flee to the island and perhaps even to Korea if his retainers were unable to repulse the expedition.[44]

While acting on behalf of his domain, Katsui also clearly harbored great personal resentment of Ōura. Frustrated with the course of events in the domain, in the fourth month of 1864 he led a group of men to the domain office in Kyoto. Reminiscent of events in Edo two years earlier, Katsui confronted the chief official there, Ōura's son Sakubei. After a heated exchange, Katsui mortally wounded Sakubei and then fled to Tashiro, a Sō fief in Kyushu. Intent upon taking control of the domain, he raised a force of men and clandestinely sailed to Fuchū. Katsui and his men stealthily entered the daimyo's residence and seized control, placing Yoshiakira under house arrest. He accused Ōura Norinosuke of transferring authority in domain affairs to Chōshū and professed that his faction would restore just rule.[45]

Ōura and his faction were furious over the murder of Sakubei and the subsequent coup. Nonetheless, they were woefully disorganized and failed to mount any kind of organized opposition, despite their martial

---

44. Nagasaki kenshi henshū iinkai, ed., *Nagasaki kenshi, hanseihen*, 1136–39.
45. Ibid., 1139–42.

training at the Nisshinkan. Beginning in the tenth month, Katsui consolidated his rule, closing the Nisshinkan and jailing Norinosuke and other leaders of the rival faction. Over the next few months, Katsui's men killed many of Ōura's supporters and forced dozens to commit ritual suicide. All told, close to 100 people died as a result of this factional strife, including many young children and wives of samurai in Ōura's faction. The Ōura family was struck particularly hard: in addition to Sakubei, Norinosuke died in prison as result of a hunger strike, his seventeen-year-old grandson was executed, and another grandson, only eleven years old, committed suicide.[46]

By early 1865, Katsui had settled into a position of power, installing himself as chief councilor, a position he used to manipulate Yoshiakira. Yet true to form, another faction rose to oppose his Katsui's rule. The latest figure was Hirata Ōe, a high-ranking official serving at the domain office in Kyoto. Hirata appears to have supported in principle the expulsion movement and therefore the Ōura faction, but withdrew his backing when he gauged that expulsion was no longer practical, given Chōshū's weakness and the rise of more conservative leaders in the *bakufu*. Thus, Hirata initially supported Katsui, a close friend, believing that he could steer the domain away from the expulsion agenda. Hirata quickly withdrew his backing, however, when he learned of the violence associated with the coup. Recruiting the assistance of Tada Shōzō, a close supporter of Ōura, he began a campaign to enlist the aid of Chōshū, which still upheld its alliance signed with Tsushima but no longer advocated an aggressive policy of expulsion. Hirata also met with representatives of the Satsuma, Fukuoka, Hirado, and Ōmura domains, and with Sanjō Sanetomi, a court noble then in exile in Kyushu. In these meetings, he extolled the virtues of restoring imperial rule and requested assistance in returning order to his domain. Hirata quickly gained the support of the leaders of Fukuoka and Hirado, who dispatched envoys to Tsushima to appeal for an end to the violence and to smooth the way for Hirata's return. Katsui responded that Hirata's campaign was not warranted and that it threatened to further sour relations with the *bakufu*.[47]

---

46. Ibid.
47. *IC*, 928–32.

A few months later, an envoy of Sanjō, accompanied by a group of Chōshū samurai, arrived at Fuchū and urged Katsui to ease his repressive rule and allow Hirata to return. Under this pressure, Katsui relented and Hirata arrived with his men a few weeks later. Thanks to Hirata's presence, Yoshiakira was able to act more freely and gave his blessing to plans to remove Katsui from power. Sensing that the tide had turned, Katsui and several key supporters fled but were apprehended and executed. With the assistance of Higuchi Kennosuke, Hirata assumed control, continuing to depend upon envoys from Satsuma, Fukuoka, and Chōshū to reinforce his position. When these envoys eventually withdrew, Hirata stood alone, and some of Katsui's remaining supporters moved against him. In the eleventh month of 1865, he was attacked and killed. Higuchi, another member of the group that had killed Sasu in 1862, assumed control, only to be murdered in the third month of 1867. Although less violent than in previous years, Tsushima nonetheless remained mired in factional discord when the Chōshū-Satsuma alliance seized power in Kyoto in early 1868.[48]

The drama of Tsushima in the 1860s demonstrates that domain leaders were driven by factional and personal motivations as they strove to gain support from a greater power in the realm: either the court, Chōshū, or the *bakufu*. Following the 1862 coup, Ōura's group took control, advocating expulsion and closer ties with a powerful Chōshū. His faction was probably the most devoted to purging foreigners from the realm. With the failure of expulsion and Chōshū's fall from prominence, Katsui stepped in, moving away from the alliance with Chōshū and instead stressing the need to stay in favor with the leaders of a newly vigorous *bakufu*. Finally, Hirata came to power, championing emperor-centered rule and gaining the support of both Chōshū and Satsuma, at that time increasingly working together, an arrangement that would lead to the signing of a secret alliance in the first month of 1866. The factional battles clearly moved in conjunction with shifts in the larger, realm-wide political landscape; nonetheless, personal grudges and feuds played prominent roles in perpetuating the violence on the island.

Also of note is the involvement of Sanjō, as well as officials from Chōshū and several Kyushu domains. Following the formation of their

---

48. Nagasaki kenshi henshū iinkai, ed., *Nagasaki kenshi, hanseihen*, 1148–49, 1165–66.

alliance in 1862, Chōshū leaders consistently maintained an interest in Tsushima's affairs. Kido actively supported Ōshima's campaign for *bakufu* aid and subsequent Chōshū leaders assisted Hirata, even sending men to help him dislodge Katsui. Satsuma, Fukuoka, and Hirado leaders appear to have been concerned that Katsui's rule, achieved through vicious violence, was leading Tsushima into chaos. In addition, as the leaders of these domains gradually positioned themselves in opposition to the Tokugawa regime, they were troubled by Katsui's pro-*bakufu* stance. In this fluid political scene, Kyushu leaders acted to stabilize a strategic part of their region and install in Tsushima leaders who would support their positions. It is unclear if Kyushu leaders acted in conjunction, but there appears to have been a shared concern that chaos in Tsushima was detrimental to the Kyushu region overall. The Kyushu leaders moved quickly to eliminate that threat, apparently without consulting the *bakufu*.

Ōshima and Tokugawa Initiatives

As factional strife continued on Tsushima, foreign incursions into the Chosŏn Kingdom came to influence *bakufu* policy toward its neighbor, and by implication, toward Tsushima as well. In the summer of 1866, the American merchant ship *General Sherman* sailed up the Taedong River to P'yŏngyang without receiving permission from Chosŏn officials. En route, the vessel grounded on a sandbar and later, an armed clash between the crew and a Korean contingent ensued. Angered by what he saw as the *General Sherman*'s audacious moves, the provincial governor ordered the vessel burned and its crew of 24 men killed. Although Qing officials learned of the incident from Chosŏn envoys visiting Beijing, American diplomats in China did not, and were reported to be planning an armed mission to Korea to ascertain the fate of the vessel.[49]

In the early autumn of 1866, French Rear-Admiral Pierre-Gustave Roze brought a seven-ship flotilla to Kanghwa Island near Seoul to chastise Korea for the murder of several French missionaries two years earlier. He sent an armed landing party ashore and in response, Chosŏn leaders assembled a force of 20,000 men. Greatly outnumbered, Roze

---

49. Kim, *The Last Phase of the East Asian World Order*, 52.

withdrew, allowing the Chosŏn court to report a great victory over the Western barbarians to the Qing.[50]

Tokugawa Yoshinobu, who became shogun in late 1866, received word of these clashes, along with rumors that the United States, France, and perhaps Britain would soon mount a punitive expedition against Korea. One of the more effective Tokugawa leaders of the period, Yoshinobu initiated a broad plan of civil and military reform to revive the Tokugawa regime after the failure of the second expedition to chastise Chōshū. The shogun believed that a diplomatic initiative vis-à-vis Korea could provide another means to restore Tokugawa prestige and power. In the second month of 1867, he selected Hirayama Yoshitada, a magistrate for foreign affairs, to lead a delegation of several warships and two battalions of troops to Pusan and perhaps even to Seoul to mediate Korea's conflicts with the United States and France. In the sixth month, Tsushima informed Chosŏn officials of the *bakufu*'s plan. The officials asserted that their kingdom did not require such mediation and rejected this and subsequent overtures.

Yoshinobu appears to have viewed the mission as a means to build stronger ties with Western nations. He informed Robert Van Valkenburg, the American minister in Japan, that the *bakufu* was distressed by the "outrages" committed by Koreans against American citizens and asserted that "should Korea, by Japanese influence, abandon its mistaken ways and sue for peace, it is hoped that the United States would bury its grudges and establish friendly relations with Korea." As Key-Hiuk Kim notes, this proposal represented the first instance of the *bakufu* identifying with a Western power rather than its Asian neighbors. After years of taking only a moderate and inconsistent interest in Korea and related defensive issues, Yoshinobu signaled a new era of Tokugawa commitment.[51]

As was the case with other planned Japanese missions to Korea, a political turn at Edo soon threatened it. When Yoshinobu surrendered political and administrative power to the court in the tenth month of 1867, it appeared that Hirayama's trip would be cancelled. This set the

---

50. Kim, *The Last Phase of the East Asian World Order*, 45–51; Tabohashi, *Kindai Nissen kankei no kenkyū*, vol. 1, 52–75.

51. Kim, *The Last Phase of the East Asian World Order*, 102–3, 108.

stage for Ōshima Tomonojō, who earlier had returned to Tsushima to take several high-ranking positions in the domain leadership after a stint working at the domain office in Osaka. In 1867, Ōshima was selected to return to Osaka and again became involved in diplomatic initiatives concerning Korea. Believing that Yoshinobu's initiative might be a first step to bring definitive reform in the system of trade and diplomacy with the Chosŏn Kingdom, Ōshima presented a memorial to the court, which had officially assumed control over the *bakufu*'s diplomatic responsibilities. He stressed that since Tsushima had already notified Chosŏn officials, the mission should not be cancelled merely because of domestic political events. On the same day, Yoshinobu also asked the court to be allowed to proceed. The court granted permission and the following month, Hirayama and his party left Edo for Osaka to begin final preparations. The very day on which he was scheduled to meet with Yoshinobu to finalize details of the mission, Satsuma and Chōshū troops clashed with *bakufu* forces near Kyoto in what came to be known as the battle of Toba-Fushimi, the start of the Boshin War. As Japan plunged into civil war, the mission to Korea was forgotten.[52]

Conclusions

The local perspective of Tsushima provides a ground-level view on how and why the system of Japanese foreign relations was on the verge of change in the 1860s. Following the steady stream of Western visits since 1847, Tsushima leaders viewed the six-month Russian occupation of a small part of their island as the final straw. The intense Western interest in Tsushima and (as Ōshima and other domain leaders concluded) in Korea as well, could not be ignored. They believed that because Tsushima, hampered by its weak economy, could not hope to stave off a future Western incursion, fundamental revisions in the established system of relations with the Chosŏn Kingdom were necessary. First, Sasu and later Ōshima concluded that the domain needed to abrogate its long-held privileges in intercourse with the Chosŏn Kingdom in favor of a greater role by the central authority, the Tokugawa shogunate. The importance of these proposals to the domain overall

---

52. Ibid., 104–5.

can be seen in how the proposals became entwined in the bitter factional battles that plagued the domain. As shown by events in the domain during the 1860s, local needs and circumstances rather than pressure from above pushed Tsushima, well before the Meiji Restoration, to advocate change in established methods and systems of intercourse with Korea.

CONCLUSION

The End of Domain Agency and the Adoption of International Relations

Following a palace coup in the first weeks of 1868, a group of young samurai from Satsuma and Chōshū proclaimed Emperor Meiji (r. 1867–1912) the definitive ruler of Japan, a position that emperors had held in name only since the fourteenth century. A few months later, the emperor issued a five-article Charter Oath decreeing how his nation would thereafter be governed. The Oath's fourth article was especially bold, declaring: "We shall break through the shackles of former evil practice and base our actions on the principles of international law." Kido Takayoshi of Chōshū, a man of growing influence in the new government, inserted this article pursuant of his goal to expand Japan's diplomatic and commercial contacts with the outside world.[1] Ishii Ryōsuke speculates that Kido intended "former evil practice" to connote the foreign relations policies of the toppled *bakufu*.[2] With this statement, Kido articulated the desire of many in the new leadership to move toward adopting international relations, namely to conduct diplomacy with all nations based upon Western principles, and at the same time, increase trade and intercourse with Western nations and the world. Moreover, he asserted that the emperor and his government would firmly control

---

1. Inaba, *Meiji kenpō seiritsu-shi*, 9–15.
2. Ishii Ryōsuke, *Japanese Legislation in the Meiji Era*, 143–44.

all foreign relations of the Japanese state, a strong statement at a time when samurai leaders, the nobility, and the lords had not yet resolved how power would be apportioned in the new regime.[3] Indeed, the Satsuma and Chōshū men heading the new Meiji government (as historians have come to call it) had to solidify their position before they could move to implement the pronouncements of the Oath. Several northern domains, supporters of the ousted Tokugawa regime, openly opposed the new government, which established its capital in Tokyo, the new name for Edo after 1868. Over the next two years, Satsuma and Chōshū forces and the northern domains fought a protracted civil war that ended only when the last Tokugawa stalwarts were defeated in Hokkaido in early 1870. Because of the unsettled internal situation, Meiji government moves to revise ties with neighboring states were initially limited in scope.

When the Meiji government did begin to take steps to adopt international relations, leaders in Satsuma and Tsushima, whose domains enjoyed privileges in the established system, did not resist. The lack of opposition is noteworthy, particularly considering events in neighboring Korea, where adopting tenets of international relations was a more protracted process partly because it involved a still valued tribute tie with China. In the 1860s, Chosŏn leaders rejected diplomatic overtures to establish Western-style free trade and successfully fought off attempts by Westerners to use force to open to trade. They also rebuked appeals to adopt diplomatic tenets of international relations offered by officials at the Zongli Yamen, a Qing office established in 1861 to conduct diplomacy based on Western principles. Under increasing Western military pressure, the Chosŏn court envisioned safety and protection in the ideal of the tribute system.[4] As long as they dutifully dispatched missions to Beijing, Korean leaders expected to be protected by their powerful Qing lord. In addition, as later moves indicate, they also no doubt felt that the Chosŏn Kingdom's status as Qing vassal afforded particular privileges in a still-lucrative Korean-Chinese trade. As Hamashita Takeshi demonstrates, in negotiations with the Qing in the early 1880s, the Chosŏn leadership adroitly used its tribute tie as a means to gain

---

3. Breen, "The Imperial Oath of April 1868," 426.
4. Wright, "The Adaptability of Ch'ing Diplomacy," 379.

trade concessions.[5] Korean leaders clearly still had something to gain by maintaining established practices of trade and diplomacy.

By contrast, events over previous decades and their domains' particular agendas led Satsuma and Tsushima leaders to advocate expansive and immediate reform. They therefore assisted in the dismantling of established practices, actively helping to implement Meiji government initiatives that revised relations with Korea and Ryukyu, and at the same time, placed those relations firmly in Tokyo's control.

This is apparent in the series of events whereby Satsuma officials willingly ceded their domain's agency in Ryukyu's affairs to the new Meiji regime. When the court ordered all daimyo to return their land and population registers to the emperor in the summer of 1869, the Kagoshima domain was created from the territory of the Satsuma domain, the Amami islands administered by the Shimazu, and the Kingdom of Ryukyu. As a result, Shimazu Tadayoshi, now governor of the Kagoshima domain, was given the right to officially administer Ryukyu. After the Meiji regime abolished domains and established prefectures in the summer of 1871, Ryukyu remained a part of the newly established Kagoshima prefecture, composed of the same territory as the previous domain.

The fact that men from Satsuma, such as Ōkubo Toshimichi and Saigō Takamori, held key positions in the new Meiji government, no doubt helped to accelerate Kagoshima's implementation of Meiji government initiatives concerning Ryukyu. Nonetheless, we find Kagoshima officials, apparently without direct orders from Tokyo, acting with alacrity to eliminate their prefecture's control over Ryukyu. In early 1872, Narahara Kogoro and Ijichi Sadaka traveled from Kagoshima to Okinawa to push leaders in Shuri to reform established financial and political practices between the prefecture and the kingdom to make them more in "tune with the times"; namely, to become in line with reforms implemented in Japan. In an attempt to gain support from their Ryukyu counterparts, the officials declared that 50,000 yen in debts owed by Shuri to the Shimazu would be forgiven in order to provide relief for all classes in the kingdom. In the seventh month, Narahara and Ijichi

---

5. Hamashita, "Tribute and Treaties," 25–45.

returned to Kagoshima bringing word that reforms would be implemented and also the news that a few months earlier, a Ryukyuan merchant ship had wrecked on the coast of Taiwan and that aborigines, who encountered the castaways, had murdered 54 of the crew. Leaders in Kagoshima subsequently appealed to Tokyo for a warship to transport an armed force that would punish the aborigines, but the Meiji leadership did not dispatch such a military mission to Taiwan for another two years.[6]

Later in the seventh month, a Ryukyu embassy, headed by the king's uncle, Prince Ie, arrived in Kagoshima. It then made its way to Tokyo, reaching the capital on the second day of the ninth month. A few days later, the prince participated in ceremonies commemorating the opening of the rail line between Tokyo and Yokohama. On the fourteenth, the Emperor and Empress Meiji received Prince Ie and his entourage, ostensibly to commemorate the Meiji Restoration, but actually to symbolically incorporate the kingdom into the Meiji state. After receiving congratulatory gifts of fine silks, Chinese scrolls, and ten bottles of Ryukyu spirits from the envoys, Emperor Meiji promulgated a decree:

> We, by the grace of Heaven, having succeeded to the Imperial Throne occupied by one line for ten thousand years, possess the four seas and rule as sovereign over the eight islands. Ryukyu is now our southern border, its territory is the same as ours and its language differs not. For generations it has served Satsuma and now you, Shō Tai, have acted with reverential sincerity of heart. We will confer on you a signal honor by raising you to be king of the Ryukyu domain and appointing you a noble. You, Shō Tai, attaching proper weight to the duties of the domain, shall rule over your people, and obey the imperial will while supporting the Imperial House.[7]

In a series of proclamations over the next few days, the emperor decreed that a grant of 30,000 yen be bestowed to assuage the kingdom's debts, and that all treaties concluded between Ryukyu and foreign countries were now under the jurisdiction of the Foreign Ministry of

---

6. Endō and Gotō, *Ryūkyū shobun teikō*, 1–3. For a comprehensive examination of the 1874 Japanese expedition to Taiwan, see Eskildsen, "Of Civilization and Savages."

7. Translation of *Daijōkan nisshi*, 16 October 1872, in *The Japan Weekly Mail*, 16 November 1872.

Fig. 21 "View of Sakarajima from the Harbor." The port battery and the volcanic peak of Sakurajima as seen from Kagoshima Harbor. Uchida Kuichi, who later snapped iconic photos of the Emperor Meiji, took this photo when he accompanied the emperor on his progress through western Japan in 1872. The ship in the foreground is believed to have transported several Ryukyu officials who greeted the emperor in Kagoshima in the sixth month of 1872. This vessel or one like it probably transported Prince Ie and his entourage to Kagoshima the following month. Courtesy of Nagasaki University Library.

the Meiji government. He also showed his "generosity" by giving Shō Tai a residence in Tokyo, a not-so-subtle hint that the king was to reside thereafter in the capital just like other daimyo cum nobles. Again showing willingness to eliminate Kagoshima's administrative authority over Ryukyu, two months later, Ijichi directed Shuri to close the Ryukyu House in Kagoshima and to recall its officials there. More significantly, he decreed that tribute taxes, which Ryukyu had sent to Kagoshima for centuries, were now to be paid to the Finance Ministry of the central government. Finally, in the summer of 1873, the government directed that the Ministry of Home Affairs and not the Foreign Ministry should thereafter supervise affairs of the Ryukyu domain.[8]

---

8. Endō and Gotō, *Ryūkyū shobun teikō*, 17–35.

In the eyes of central government leaders in Tokyo and officials in Kagoshima, Ryukyu had ceased to be a kingdom under Kagoshima's rule, and instead, under the administrative authority of Tokyo, had become the southern border of Japan. The more complete incorporation of Ryukyu into the Japanese nation-state, termed the "disposition of Ryukyu," turned out to be a more protracted process involving the severing of the kingdom's tribute ties with the Qing, as well as extended negotiations between Meiji, Ryukyuan, Qing, and Western leaders. A complete discussion of those events is beyond the scope of this study,[9] which takes as its ending point the year 1873. By then, one point had been resolved (on the Japanese side, at least): Satsuma's agency vis-à-vis Ryukyu, held since the early seventeenth century, was, with Kagoshima's blessing, now firmly in the hands of the central Meiji authority.

Immediately following the Restoration, the Tsushima leadership pressed for reform in relations with Korea. Ōshima Tomonojō lobbied Meiji leaders, preoccupied with subduing the pro-Tokugawa opposition, to place relations with Korea at the top of their agenda. With the assistance of Kido, he engineered an imperial commission and higher court rank for Sō Yoshiakira, who was designated the court's representative in diplomatic duties with the Chosŏn Kingdom. Soon after, Ōshima presented a memorial to the imperial court describing the reforms advocated by his domain's leaders. He called for the termination of the Sō family's private ties with Chosŏn, as well as revision of existing relations that were "harmful" to Tsushima and the Japanese state because they were based upon the Sō's status as a vassal to the Chosŏn court. He also pushed for direct imperial control of commercial and diplomatic contacts with Korea. Stressing again that policy toward Japan's neighbor should be guided by "benevolence and might," Ōshima urged that a punitive invasion of Korea be launched if Chosŏn leaders failed to respond to Japanese overtures.[10]

---

9. For discussions of the "disposition of Ryukyu" and events in Ryukyu/Okinawa in the late nineteenth century see, Okinawa-ken kyōiku iinkai, ed., *Tsūshi*, 47–59; Smits, *Visions of Ryukyu*, 143–49; also several chapters in Gabe and Kuwabara, ed., *Ezo-chi to Ryūkyū*.

10. Kim, *The Last Phase of the East Asian World Order*, 116–17; Ishikawa, "Meiji ishinki ni okeru Tsushima-han no dōkō," 2.

In the summer of 1868, Ōshima met with members of the recently established Foreign Ministry, and reached an agreement whereby the Sō would stop using the official seals, received from the Chosŏn court, that had been affixed to all diplomatic correspondences with Korea for centuries. Under the new plan, Tsushima would instead use Yoshiakira's new Japanese court rank and the name of the Japanese emperor in all documents. Existing protocol maintained parity between the shogun and the Chosŏn king, partly by avoiding references to the Japanese emperor in official documents. Therefore, by using the title of emperor, the Japanese would place the Chosŏn king in an inferior position. Ōshima realized that these measures would anger Chosŏn officials and lead them to suspend trade and the annual stipends of rice. He therefore again memorialized the court, requesting a large stipend of aid to fill the expected shortfall in rice supplies. The court replied that it was sympathetic to Tsushima's plight but lacked the funds to provide such aid.[11]

Despite the rejection, Ōshima and the Tsushima leadership pushed ahead. Early in 1869, they informed Chosŏn officials of the collapse of the *bakufu* and the restoration of imperial rule. To demonstrate loyalty to the imperial court, Tsushima officials signed the documents with Yoshiakira's new court rank and used a seal of office issued by the Japanese court. As expected, Chosŏn officials bitterly reproached Tsushima for this break with protocol and refused to accept the documents. As Ōshima had also predicted, Korea suspended the official trade and the annual shipments of rice. Over the next year, relations between Tsushima and Chosŏn officials remained tense. Ōshima and several envoys traveled to the Japan House and attempted to negotiate a settlement. Due in part to Korean suspicions that Tsushima representatives were colluding with Westerners, the situation remained at an impasse.[12]

When the imperial court ordered all daimyo to return their land and population registers to the emperor in the summer of 1869, Yoshiakira abdicated his position as lord and became the governor of the Izuhara domain, the new name for the lands previously controlled by the Sō,

---

11. Kim, *The Last Phase of the East Asian World Order*, 116–17.
12. Kim, *The Last Phase of the East Asian World Order*, 117–23; Choe, *The Rule of the Taewŏn'gun*, 146–47.

although the term "Tsushima domain" was still commonly used.[13] The order also spelled the theoretical end of the Sō's role as intermediary in relations with Korea. Nonetheless, a still-disorganized Foreign Ministry was not ready to assume control of diplomatic ties, so Yoshiakira and Tsushima officials continued to supervise day-to-day operations. Ōshima and other Tsushima leaders maintained their appeals both for reform in relations with the Chosŏn Kingdom and financial aid for Tsushima. Stating that they still wished to move away from the domain's dependence upon trade and stipends from Korea, Tsushima officials asked for another grant to augment the slowdown in trade. The court, apparently now in a better financial position, responded by providing lands in Kyushu valued at 35,000 *koku*.[14]

Although these lands provided a steady source of new income for the domain, the Tsushima leadership still felt that it required more funds to invigorate the domain economy. Consequently, domain leaders explored other economic enterprises, attempting to earn revenue from the sale of domain products, and if trade were restored, goods imported from Korea as well. The domain required capital for these endeavors, but because of Tsushima's mountain of debts, Osaka and Tokyo merchants refused to offer loans. Domain officials in Osaka therefore took a step explored to a limited degree in previous decades: establishing direct ties with Western merchants. The domain secured a loan of 30,000 Mexican dollars from a British merchant to purchase a steamship, which the domain then leased to a transport firm. Through this arrangement, Tsushima hoped to pay off the loan and make an additional profit. In the end, the scheme failed and the domain eventually sold the steamship to a private transport line. Over the next two years, Tsushima representatives engaged in a reckless pattern of borrowing from Western merchants to pay off interest on previous debts. By mid-1871, the domain had not paid any of the principal on a staggering 359,000 yen in new debts to several Western merchants. Furthermore, the domain still owed nearly 700,000 yen in old debts to domestic

---

13. Two months later, Yoshiakira also changed his name to Shigemasa but for continuity, I will continue to refer to him as Yoshiakira. I will also use the designation "Tsushima domain" instead of "Izuhara domain."

14. Ishikawa, "Meiji ishin-ki ni okeru Tsushima-han no dōkō," 5.

merchant houses, giving it the third highest level of debt among all domains. Despite the domain's long history of trade and commerce, Tsushima officials proved painfully inept in building new commercial enterprises in the years following the Restoration.[15]

Meanwhile, in late 1869, the Meiji leadership became more assertive in diplomatic relations with Korea, dispatching Sada Hakubō to Tsushima and the Japan House to investigate the state of relations with the Chosŏn Kingdom. The Foreign Ministry subsequently sent a string of envoys to Tsushima and Korea with the goal of first removing the Sō as the intermediary. In the clan's place, Meiji leaders hoped to institute central government control, and in turn, conduct relations with Chosŏn based upon Western-style treaties and diplomatic practices. Tsushima leaders supported these moves but made little progress in the negotiations because the Korean side still stubbornly refused even to hear the proposals of the Meiji officials. In the autumn of 1870, a frustrated Yoshiakira requested to be officially relieved of his role as the diplomatic intermediary. He stressed that Tsushima's dependence upon the Chosŏn Kingdom was damaging national prestige and saw little value in continuing to dispatch Tsushima officials to Korea, given that all recent missions had ended in failure. In a frank admission, Yoshiakira also suggested that there was little hope of achieving reform because some Tsushima merchants and officials at the Japan House were colluding with Chosŏn officials to sabotage reform initiatives. He argued, therefore, that the Sō's role had to be eliminated in order to implement reform in Japanese-Korean relations. Once again, we see the strong desire of Tsushima leaders to abandon the established system and institute central government control.[16]

A Foreign Ministry delegation, headed by Yoshioka Kōki, arrived at the Japan House in early 1871 to find the Koreans obstinate. Yoshioka had to wait for nearly six months simply to meet with a Chosŏn representative, who then refused even to consider his proposals. As a result, he came to support Yoshiakira's plan for removing the Sō as the intermediary in Japanese-Korean relations, concluding that the Sō's

---

15. Nagasaki kenshi henshū iinkai, ed., *Nagasaki kenshi, hanseihen*, 1176–80; Tabohashi, "Meiji ishin-ki ni okeru Tsushima-han zaisei oyobi hansai ni tsuite," 110–17.
16. Ishikawa, "Meiji ishin-ki ni okeru Tsushima-han no dōkō," 9–10.

involvement provided Chosŏn officials with a tool to manipulate relations with Japan. In the summer of 1871, Hirotsu Hironobu, a member of Yoshioka's party, sent a report to the Foreign Ministry, urging for the quick elimination of the Sō's diplomatic position. Yet Hirotsu realized that such a move would also bring a definitive end to all trade and rice shipments from Korea, for centuries an economic lifeline for the denizens of Tsushima. Therefore, he advised that the Meiji government should provide Tsushima with 10,000 *koku* of rice to augment the loss of revenue that would result when ties were officially severed. The Foreign Ministry accepted these recommendations and ordered Yoshiakira to come to Tokyo. Two days after he arrived in the seventh month of 1871, the Meiji leadership announced that all domains would be dissolved, replaced by prefectures under more direct control of the central government. As part of this process, Yoshiakira ceased to be the governor of the Tsushima domain and accepted the post of assistant foreign minister. Fortunately for Tsushima, the Meiji government did more than provide a stipend of rice. It assumed the debts of all former domains, including Tsushima's enormous unpaid sums to domestic and Western merchants. On advantageous terms, the Sō house's long history as intermediary in Japanese-Korean relations officially came to an end.[17]

Although the leaders of the involved parties had agreed upon this change, it nonetheless took time to be implemented on the ground. Some Tsushima merchants attempted to protect their privileged commercial positions with Korean merchants. Chosŏn officials, hoping to retain the existing system, encouraged them by providing food and provisions. Eventually, in the fall of 1872, Assistant Foreign Minister Hanabusa Yoshimoto arrived in Pusan on a warship accompanied by two platoons of infantry. He forced most of the Tsushima merchants to return home and renamed the Japan House, the "Japanese Mission." Although the Foreign Ministry continued to use Yoshiakira as an envoy, thereafter control of relations with Korea now rested firmly in the hands of the Meiji government.[18]

---

17. Ishikawa, "Meiji ishin-ki ni okeru Tsushima-han no dōkō," 10–12; Kim, *The Last Phase of the East Asian World Order*, 159–63.

18. Kim, *The Last Phase of the East Asian World Order*, 164–65.

The 1873 debate among Meiji leaders over the proposed invasion of Korea therefore had little to do with Tsushima, which largely through the initiative of its leaders had now ceded its agency in foreign relations to the Meiji central government. Although Ōshima and other Tsushima leaders had advocated an invasion for a decade, there was little connection between Ōshima's proposal and the 1873 plan. Indeed, Kido, another early invasion advocate and a close ally of Ōshima, opposed the 1873 initiative, asserting that instead of a punitive military expedition against the Chŏson Kingdom, Meiji leaders should focus on the "proper management of domestic affairs."[19] For Ōshima and Kido, an invasion of Korea was no doubt less appealing given that Tsushima had achieved the goal of relinquishing its agency in foreign relations to the Meiji regime.

The Meiji leadership subsequently used military force to establish state-to-state ties with Korea based upon Western-style diplomacy and free trade. In 1876, Chosŏn and Japanese officials signed the Treaty of Kanghwa, which ended all vestiges of Tsushima's intermediary relationship and allowed Japanese merchants to engage in Western-style free trade at Pusan. The treaty also permitted Japanese ships to survey Korean coastal waters and granted Japanese consular jurisdiction in Pusan and other ports to be opened at a later date.[20] With the elimination of the Sō's role and the closing of the Japan House, Tsushima now also served as a definitive border of the Japanese nation-state. The Meiji government would later fortify the island, a step that *bakufu* leaders had refused to take.

In 1876, the Meiji regime now firmly held all agency in Japanese foreign relations, and as such could move to recast relations with neighboring East Asian states based upon the tenets of international relations. For example, in 1880, it completed the transition from early modern East Asian practices to Western-style international relations in Japanese-Korean relations with the establishment of a Japanese legation in Seoul.[21]

---

19. Kido, *The Diary of Kido Takayoshi*, vol. 2, 370–71.
20. Gaimūshō, comp., *Dai Nihon gaikō monjo*, vol. 12, 114–19.
21. Kim, *The Last Phase of the East Asian World Order*, 351.

Rather than attempting to hold on to their agency in foreign relations, Satsuma and Tsushima leaders ceded power to the new central Meiji regime. For their part, Tsushima officials welcomed centralization as a path to allow the domain to finally escape its weak economy. Consequently, their support for reform overcame resistance offered by a handful of merchants at the Japan House. In much the same way, the leadership of the Satsuma domain, and later Kagoshima prefecture, supported the Meiji government's assumption of control over Ryukyu. Although Satsuma leaders made fewer proposals to revise the established system before the Restoration, commercial opportunism energized the domain and led Godai Tomoatsu and others to create a burgeoning domestic and foreign trade network that helped make the established system of trade through Ryukyu obsolete. As a result, Kagoshima officials were amenable to revising established practices and transforming Ryukyu into the defined southern border of the Japanese nation-state.

Similarly, after the fall of the Tokugawa regime, Meiji leaders and merchants did not seek to maintain vestiges of the pre-1868, China-centered system of foreign trade conducted through Nagasaki. Instead, trade with China and later Korea at Nagasaki and other major Japanese ports expanded under the auspices of the treaty port system.[22] Yet importantly, Japan began to greatly expand its exports to, and imports from, Western states. A major reason for this was the fact that the nascent foundations of industrialization, which had appeared in Western nations in the early nineteenth century, had finally created the economic prowess that allowed European nations and the United States to become centers of manufacturing that definitively surpassed China. While China and Europe shared roughly 30 percent of the world's overall manufacturing output around 1830, Europe had surged by 1870 to well over 50 percent, with China dropping under 20 percent. This "gap," as Robert Marks terms it, continued to accelerate in the closing

---

22. For one account of how Japanese trade with China and Korea developed in the late 1870s and especially the 1880s, see Furuta, "Inchon Trade," 71–95. Shipments to China and other East Asian ports of export mainstays of the late Edo period, such as camphor and marine products, continued in the remaining decades of the nineteenth century. For a study of a Chinese merchant house in Nagasaki involved in these and other trades, see Zhu Delan, *Nagasaki kashō bōeki no shiteki kenkyū*.

decades of the nineteenth century, with Europe accounting for 60 percent of the world's industrial output and the United States grabbing 20 percent. By 1900, China contributed only about 7 percent of the global manufacturing total.[23]

Because of this manufacturing power and the related rise in gross domestic product (GDP) of Western nations, consumers in the United States, for example, enjoyed larger personal incomes that allowed them not only to buy more goods but also become more selective and sophisticated in their purchases. For one, Americans of all classes began to buy a wide variety of imported and domestically produced decorated pottery and porcelain, which became keepsakes in American homes.[24]

Japan moved to meet the demand of Western consumers most prominently by exporting raw silk, which came to account for 44 percent of Japan's total exports. The Meiji government also began to develop green tea as an export product, tailoring it specifically for the American and later Canadian markets, where tea drinkers often chose their green tea based upon its preparation before packaging.[25] Over the next three decades, Japanese producers, in conjunction with Western export firms, aggressively marketed Japanese tea to North American consumers, who came to drink 90 percent of Japan's tea exports. Japanese tea competed with Chinese, Taiwanese, and later Ceylonese varieties, first in the United States and later in Canada.[26]

The trades in silk and tea illustrate how a significant portion of Japanese foreign trade had transitioned to direct Japanese-Western trade by the early 1870s, a situation in contrast to just a decade earlier, when Japanese and Western merchants still focused on Japanese-Chinese trade. Western nations were also producing in greater amounts goods that the Japanese wanted, such as manufactured cotton and woolen goods, which amounted to 67 percent of total imports in 1872.[27] The profound

---

23. Marks, *The Origins of the Modern World*, 123–25.

24. Blaszczyk, *Imagining Consumers*, 60.

25. Labels placed upon packages of Japanese tea on the American market often distinguished how the tea had been fired, the process to remove moisture before packaging. The tea was fired in either a basket or a large pan. For a selection of these labels, see Ide, *Ranji*, 66–112.

26. Sugiyama, *Japan's Industrialization in the World Economy*, 140–69.

27. Ibid., 65.

political changes of the Meiji Restoration and the opening of more Japanese ports to foreign trade—for example, Hyōgo (Kobe) in 1868—certainly help to explain this situation, but the global context must also be taken into account. Japan engaged in greater trade with Western nations after 1870 because global commercial changes made that engagement more possible and profitable than ever before.

The consolidation of foreign relations authority into the hands of the central Meiji government created an environment, not present decades earlier, to develop veritable national ideologies of foreign relations. With the elimination of local agency, Meiji leaders could truly act on a national scale and include individual Japanese in the project of embracing international relations. This was part of a larger program whereby Japanese ceased to be merely subjects in a feudal state and became instead citizens, with vested interests in national enterprises of the new nation-state.[28] In this environment, prominent intellectuals debated how Japan's expanding foreign trade should be conducted, contesting, for example, the merits of protective tariffs to achieve a balance of

imports and exports. In these debates, we find a desire to cultivate an individual connection to foreign trade, and by implication, the national Meiji-era themes of "rich country, strong army" (*fukoku kyōhei*) and "civilization and enlightenment" (*bunmei kaika*). Arguing against tariffs and hoping to allay concerns over the growing imbalance of imports to exports, Tsuda Mamichi wrote in January 1875:

As the lower classes invariably wax enthusiastic over what their rulers admire, the people in our empire are coming on the whole gradually to admire foreign ways, to wear foreign caps and clothes, and to construct foreign houses. Almost all the homes have come to depend upon foreign imports for household appliances ranging from such items as glass, mirrors, pictures, chairs, and tables to cakes, wines, and other edibles. Such are the reasons why the excess

---

28. In a famous essay, Maruyama Masao argues that true ideals of national consciousness were not possible during the Edo period because the common people "were permitted to exist only to serve and feed the samurai." Maruyama, "National Consciousness Under Tokugawa Feudalism," 328.

of imports over exports has reached the large sum of Yen 8 million each year.[29]

Moreover, some early Meiji intellectuals developed the idea, alluded to in the Charter Oath, that Tokugawa officials acted selfishly and to the great detriment of the Japanese people in foreign relations, particularly in previous decades. Writing in December 1874, Sugi Kōji asserted that Tokugawa officials did not appreciate the importance of balanced foreign trade and instead were "aimlessly controlled by foreign nations."[30] The irony in this attack is that throughout much of the Edo period, *bakufu* leaders had pursued foreign trade in order to protect both the Nagasaki merchant community and to uphold the greater social good of maintaining imports of medicinal products. In the new environment of the Meiji period, however, there was no place for such positive interpretations of the fallen Tokugawa regime. Yet while he blamed *bakufu* officials, Sugi stressed that "all people of the nation were guilty" of contributing to the past failures, thereby also cultivating—in a negative but equally powerful way—a sense of personal involvement in the process of creating a nation-state that would embrace the ideals of international relations.[31]

All told, Japan in the early 1870s could now have its foreign relations guided by ideologies such as "rich country, strong army" and "civilization and enlightenment" because a single entity, the Meiji government, effectively controlled foreign relations and its leaders were intent on building popular participation in its policies. More than during the Edo period, intellectuals became an integral part of the process of cultivating national ideologies related to foreign relations. Men like Tsuda and Suji contributed to building an ideology of a Japan actively and positively engaged with the outside world by trumpeting Western ideals and railing against the alleged evils of the fallen *bakufu*. They asserted that Tokugawa leaders, concerned only with staying in power, had woefully managed Japan's interactions with the outside world. By creating

---

29. Tsuda Mamichi, "On the Trade Balance" in Braisted, trans., *Meiroku zasshi*, issue 26 (January 1875), 325–26.
30. Sugi Kōji, "On Reforming Trade," in Braisted, trans., *Meiroku zasshi*, issue 24 (December 1874), 306.
31. Ibid.

such a negative image of Tokugawa policies, they could present Meiji policies in a contrasting positive light. In other words, they could suggest to the new citizenry that Japan would embark upon a new era of "civilization and enlightenment" unlike the dark bygone days of the *bakufu*. In short, the intellectuals could work in conjunction with the strong Meiji leadership to create new ideologies predicated on the idea that intercourse with the outside world was positive for Japan. As Carol Gluck demonstrated in her comprehensive study, Meiji leaders and prominent intellectuals developed these and other ideologies through heated discourse and political competition over the course of the Meiji period.[32]

The point here is not to wholly dismiss the role of intellectuals and discourse on foreign relations in the Edo period; rather, it is to consider that prominent Edo-period intellectuals could not contribute to the development of a national ideology of foreign relations because in the Edo-period polity there was little popular participation and more importantly, no single actor creating coherent national policies. Instead, the *bakufu*, Satsuma, and Tsushima, each with competing and complementary agendas, together conducted Japan's foreign relations. When the Tokugawa regime fell and the two remaining actors, Satsuma and Tsushima, ceded their agency to the Meiji government, the new national, Meiji leadership could define anew Japan's engagement with the outside world based upon evolving national ideologies and the tenets of international relations—tenets that Japan still embraces today.

---

32. Gluck, *Japan's Modern Myths*, 6–10.

Reference Matter

Works Cited

Japanese, Chinese, and Korean personal names are listed surname first, except in the case of Western-language publications, where they follow the order given in the text.

List of Abbreviations

DNIS   Dai Nihon ishin shiryō [Historical records of the Meiji Restoration of Japan]
DNISK Dai Nihon ishin shiryō kōhon [Manuscript of historical records related to the Meiji Restoration of Japan]
IC   Izuhara chōshi [The history of Izuhara town]
KK   Kagoshima kenshi [The history of Kagoshima prefecture]
RGKM   Ryūkyū gaikoku kankei monjo [Documents relating to the foreign relations of Ryukyu]
TI   Tsūkō ichiran [A compendium of foreign relations]
TIZ   Tsūkō ichiran zokushū [A compendium of foreign relations, supplemental]

Akamine Seiki. *Daikōkai jidai no Ryūkyū* [Ryukyu in the great age of voyages]. Naha: Okinawa taimuzusha, 1988.

Amenomori Hōshū. *Hōshū gaikoku kankei shiryō shokanshū* [A collection of Hōshū's historical papers related to foreign relations]. *Amenomori Hōshū zensho* [The complete papers of Amenomori Hōshū]. Vol. 3. Suita: Kansai Daigaku shuppanbu, 1982.

Appleby, John H. "Ginseng and the Royal Society." *Notes and Records of the Royal Society of London* 37.2 (March 1983): 121–45.

Arai Eiji. *Kinsei kaisanbutsu keizaishi no kenkyū* [An economic history of marine products in the early modern period]. Tokyo: Meicho shuppan, 1988.

———. *Kinsei kaisanbutsu bōekishi no kenkyū* [The history of the marine product trade in the early modern period]. Tokyo: Yoshikawa kōbunkan, 1973.

Arano Yasunori. *Kinsei Nihon to higashi Ajia* [Early modern Japan and East Asia].Tokyo: Tōkyō Daigaku shuppankai, 1988.

Auslin, Michael. *Negotiating with Imperialism: The Unequal Treaties and the Culture of Japanese Diplomacy.* Cambridge, MA: Harvard University Press, 2004.

Batten, Bruce L. *To the Ends of Japan: Premodern Frontiers, Boundaries, and Interactions.* Honolulu, HI: University of Hawai'i Press, 2003.

Bayly, C. A. *The Birth of the Modern World, 1780–1914.* Oxford, UK: Blackwell Publishing, 2004.

———."'Archaic' and 'Modern' Globalization in the Eurasian and African Arena, ca. 1750–1850." In *Globalization in World History,* ed. A. G. Hopkins, 45–72. New York: W.W. Norton, 2002.

Beasley, W.G. *The Meiji Restoration.* Stanford, CA: Stanford University Press, 1972.

———, ed. and trans. *Select Documents on Japanese Foreign Policy, 1853–1868.* London: Oxford University Press, 1955.

Berridge, Geoff, and Alan James. *A Dictionary of Diplomacy.* Houndmills, Basingstoke, Hampshire, UK: Palgrave Macmillan, 2003.

Blaszczyk, Regina Lee. *Imagining Consumers: Design and Innovation from Wedgwood to Corning.* Baltimore, MD: Johns Hopkins University Press, 2000.

Blussé, Leonard. *Visible Cities: Canton, Nagasaki, and Batavia and the Coming of the Americans.* Cambridge, MA: Harvard University Press, 2008.

Blussé, Leonard, and W. G. J. Remmelink, eds. *The Deshima Diaries: Marginalia, 1700–1740.* Tokyo: Japan-Netherlands Institute, 1992.

———, eds. *The Deshima Diaries: Marginalia 1740–1800.* Tokyo: Japan-Netherlands Institute, 2004.

Bolitho, Harold. "The Tempō Crisis." In *Cambridge History of Japan*, vol. 5 *The Nineteenth Century*, ed. Marius B. Jansen, 116–67. Cambridge, UK: Cambridge University Press, 1989.

Bōnotsu-machi kyōdoshi hensan iinkai, ed. *Bōnotsu-machi kyōdoshi* [The local history of Bōnotsu town]. 2 vols. Kagoshima: Bōnotsu-machi, 1969.

Braisted, William R., trans. Meiroku zasshi: *Journal of the Japanese Enlightenment.* Cambridge, MA: Harvard University Press, 1976.

Breen, John. "The Imperial Oath of April 1868: Ritual, Politics, and Power in the Restoration." *Monumenta Nipponica* 51.4 (Winter 1996): 407–29.

Chaiklin, Martha. *Cultural Commerce and Dutch Commercial Culture: The Influence of European Material Culture on Japan, 1700–1850.* Leiden: CWNS, 2003.

Choe, Ching Young. *The Rule of the Taewŏn'gun, 1864–1873: Restoration in Yi Korea.* Cambridge, MA: East Asian Research Center, Harvard University, 1972.

Cowan, C. D, ed. "Early Penang and the Rise of Singapore, A Selection of the Manuscript Records of the East India Company over the Period, 1805–1832." *Journal of the Malayan Branch of the Royal Asiatic Society* 23.2 (March 1950): 3–210.

Craig, Albert. *Chōshū in the Meiji Restoration.* Cambridge, MA: Harvard University Press, 1967.

Cribb, R. B. *Historical Atlas of Indonesia.* Honolulu, HI: University of Hawai'i Press, 2000.

"Dai Nihon ishin shiryō kōhon" [Manuscript of historical materials related to the Meiji Restoration of Japan]. Document collection in archives of Historiographical Institute (Shiryō hensanjo), University of Tokyo.

Dalby, Liza Crihfield. *Geisha.* Berkeley, CA: University of California Press, 1983.

Davidson, James W. *The Island of Formosa: Past and Present.* New York: Macmillan & Co., 1903. Reprint, Taipei: SMC Publishing Inc., 1992.

Donkin, R. A. *Dragon's Brain Perfume: A Historical Geography of Camphor.* Boston: Brill, 1999.

Drake, Fred W. *China Charts the World: Hsu Chi-Yü and His Geography of 1848.* Cambridge, MA: East Asian Research Center, Harvard University, 1975.

Duus, Peter. *Modern Japan.* Second edition. New York: Houghton Mifflin Company, 1998.

———, ed. *The Japanese Discovery of America, A Brief History with Documents.* Boston, MA: Bedford Books, 1997.

Earns, Lane Robert. "The Development of Bureaucratic Rule in Early Modern Japan: The Nagasaki Bugyō in the Seventeenth Century." Ph.D. diss., University of Hawai'i at Mānoa, 1987.

Elisonas, Jurgis. "The Inseparable Trinity: Japan's Relations with China and Korea." Chap. In *The Cambridge History of Japan*, vol. 4, *Early Modern Japan*, ed. John W. Hall, 235–300. Cambridge, UK: Cambridge University Press, 1991.

Endō Tatsu and Gotō Kenshin. *Ryūkyū shobun teikō Meiji 4-nen–dō 12-nen* [An overview of the disposition of Ryukyu, 1871–79]. Tokyo: Naimushō, 1879.

Ericson, Mark D. "The Bakufu Looks Abroad, the 1865 Mission to France." *Monumenta Nipponica* 34.4 (Winter 1979): 383–407.

Eskildsen, Robert. "Of Civilization and Savages: The Mimetic Imperialism of Japan's 1874 Expedition to Taiwan." *American Historical Review* 107.2 (April 2002): 388–418.

Flershem, Robert G. "Some Aspects of Japan Sea Shipping and Trade in the Tokugawa Period, 1603–1867." *Proceedings of the American Philosophical Society* 110.3 (June 1966): 182–226.

Flershem, Robert G., and Yoshiko N. Flershem, "Nakano Family Documents, Satsuma-Chōshū, 1856–66." *Monumenta Nipponica* 26.1–2 (1971): 1–15.

Flynn, Dennis, and Arturo Giráldez. "Cycles of Silver: Global Economic Unity through the Mid-Eighteenth Century." *Journal of World History* 13.2 (Fall 2002): 391–428.

Fortune, Robert. *Yedo and Peking: A Narrative of a Journey to the Capitals of Japan and China.* London: John Murray, 1863.

Fox, Grace. *Britain and Japan, 1858–1883.* Oxford, UK: Oxford University Press, 1969.

Frank, Andre Gunder. *ReOrient: Global Economy in an Asian Age.* Berkeley, CA: University of California Press, 1998.

Fry, Howard T. *Alexander Dalrymple (1737–1808) and the Expansion of British Trade.* London: Frank Cass & Company, 1970.

Fukuse Kōichirō. "Ryūkyū-kan ni miru Satsuryū kankei" [Satsuma-Ryukyu relations as seen through the Ryukyu House]. *Kagoshima rekishi kenkyū* (May 1998): 45–50.

Furuta, Kazuko. "The Inchon Trade: Japanese and Chinese Merchants and the Shanghai Network." In *Commercial Networks in Modern Asia,* ed. Shinya Sugiyama and Linda Grove, 71–95. Richmond, Surrey, UK: Curzon, 2001.

Gabe Masao and Kuwabara Masato, ed., *Ezo-chi to Ryūkyū* [Ezo and Ryukyu]. Tokyo: Yoshikawa kōbunkan, 2001.

Gaimūshō [Foreign Ministry of Japan], comp. *Dai Nihon gaikō bunsho* [Diplomatic documents of Japan]. 73 vols. Tokyo: Nihon kokusai kyōkai, 1936–63.

Geertz, Clifford. *An Interpretation of Cultures.* New York: Basic Books, 1973.

Gluck, Carol. *Japan's Modern Myths: Ideology in the Late Meiji Period.* Princeton, NJ: Princeton University Press, 1985.

Greene, D. C. "Correspondence between William II of Holland and the Shogun of Japan, A.D. 1844." *Transactions of the Asiatic Society of Japan* vol. 34.3 (October 1906): 99–131.

Hall, John W. *Tanuma Okitsugu (1719–1788): Forerunner of Modern Japan.* Cambridge, MA: Harvard University Press, 1955.

———. "Notes on Early Ch'ing Copper Trade with Japan." *Harvard Journal of Asiatic Studies* 12:3–4 (December 1949): 444–61.

Hamashita, Takeshi. "Tribute and Treaties: Maritime Asia and Treaty Port Networks in the Era of Negotiation, 1800–1900." In *The Resurgence of East Asia: 500, 150, and 50 Year Perspectives,* ed. Giovanni Arrighi, Takeshi Hamashita, and Mark Selden, 17–50. New York: Routledge, 2003.

———. "The Interregional System in East Asia in Modern Times," In *Network Power: Japan and Asia,* ed. Peter J. Katzenstein and Takashi Shiraishi, 113–35. Ithaca, NY: Cornell University Press, 1997.

———. *Chōkō shisutemu to kindai Ajia* [Modern Asia and the tribute system]. Tokyo: Iwanami shoten, 1997.
Haraguchi, Izumi. "The Influence of the Civil War in the U.S. on the Meiji Restoration in Japan" *South Pacific Study* 16.1 (1995): 130–31.
Haraguchi Izumi and Nagayama Shūichi, et al. *Kagoshima-ken no rekishi* [The history of Kagoshima prefecture]. Tokyo: Yamakawa shuppansha, 1999.
Haraguchi Torao. *Kagoshima-ken no rekishi* [The history of Kagoshima prefecture]. Tokyo: Yamakawa shuppansha, 1973.
———. *Bakumatsu no Satsuma* [Satsuma in the *bakumatsu* period]. Tokyo: Chūō kōronsha, 1966.
Hashiguchi Kanefuru, et al. *Sappan shōkei hyakuzu: kaihen* [One hundred views of the Satsuma domain: the coastline], 1815. Unpublished illustrated scroll in collection of Historiographical Institute, University of Tokyo.
Hawks, Francis L. *Narrative of the Expedition of an American Squadron to the China Seas and Japan Performed in the Years 1852, 1853, 1854 under the Command of Commodore M. C. Perry.* 3 vols. Washington, DC: Beverley Tucker, Senate Printer, 1856.
Hayashi Akira, ed. *Tsūkō ichiran* [A compendium of foreign relations]. 8 vols. Tokyo: Kokusho kankōkai, 1913. Reprint, Osaka: Seibundō shuppan, 1967.
Haycox, Stephen. *Alaska: An American Colony.* Seattle, WA: University of Washington Press, 2002.
Heard Family Collection. Baker Library Historical Collections, Harvard Business School.
Hesselink, Reinier H. "The Assassination of Henry Heuksen." *Monumenta Nipponica* 49.3 (Autumn 1994): 331–51.
Hevia, James L. *Cherishing Men From Afar: Qing Guest Ritual and the Macartney Embassy of 1793.* Durham, NC: Duke University Press, 1995.
Higashibaba, Ikuo. *Christianity in Early Modern Japan: Kirishitan Belief and Practice.* Leiden: Brill, 2001.
Hino Seisaburō. *Bakumatsu ni okeru Tsushima to Ei-Ro* [England, Russia, and Tsushima in the *bakumatsu* period] Tokyo: Tōkyō Daigaku shuppankai, 1968.
Honma Sadao. "Aizu-han yōtashi Adachi-ke ni tsuite: bakumatsu Nagasaki no ninjin bōeki-shō" [The Adachi clan, purveyors for the Aizu domain: ginseng traders in Nagasaki in the *bakumatsu* period]. *Nagasaki dansō* 69 (1986): 55–108.
Hoover, William Davis. "Godai Tomoatsu (1836–1885), An Economic Statesman of Early Meiji Japan." Ph.D. diss., University of Michigan, 1973. Ann Arbor, MI: University Microfilms, 1977.

Hopkins, A. G. "Globalization: an Agenda for Historians." In *Globalization in World History*, ed. A. G. Hopkins, 1–11. New York: W. W. Norton & Company, 2002.

Howe, Christopher. *The Origins of Japanese Trade Supremacy: Development and Technology in Asia from 1540 to the Pacific War*. Chicago, IL: University of Chicago Press, 1996.

Howell, David. *Capitalism From Within, Economy, Society, and the State in a Japanese Fishery*. Berkeley, CA: University of California Press, 1995.

———. *Geographies of Identity in Nineteenth-Century Japan*. Berkeley, CA: University of California Press, 2005.

Hyŏn Myŏng-ch'ŏl [Hyon Myonchoru]. "Bunkyū gannen Tsushima-han no ihō undō ni tsuite" [The transfer request of the Tsushima domain in 1861]. *Nihon rekishi* 536 (January 1993): 69–87.

Ide, Nobuko. *Ranji: The Roots of Modern Japanese Commercial Design*. Tokyo: Dentsū, 1993.

Imamura Tomo. *Ninjin-shi* [A history of ginseng]. 7 vols. Keijō [Seoul]: Chōsen fōtokufu senbaikyoku, 1934–40.

Inaba Masatsugu. *Meiji kenpō seiritsushi* [The history of the creation of the Meiji constitution]. Tokyo: Yūhikaku, 1960.

Innes, Robert LeRoy. "The Door Ajar: Japan's Foreign Trade in the Seventeenth Century." 2 vols. Ph.D. diss., University of Michigan, 1980. Ann Arbor, MI: University Microfilms International, 1984.

Ishida Chihiro. "Edo jidai no sarasa yunyū: Oranda-sen no hakusai-hin o chūshin toshite" [The import of calico (*sarasa*) in the Edo period: an examination of goods imported on Dutch ships]. In *Kowatari sarasa to wasarasa* [Old imported calico and Japanese calico], ed. Nezu bijutsukan, 73–81. Tokyo: Nezu bijutsukan, 1993.

Ishii Kenji. *Edo kaiun to bezaisen* [The *bezai* ships and marine transport in the Edo period]. Tokyo: Nihon kaiji kōhō kyōkai, 1988.

Ishii, Ryōsuke. *Japanese Legislation in the Meiji Era*. Trans. William J. Chambliss. Cultural History of the Meiji Era 10. Tokyo: Pan-Pacific Press, 1958.

Ishii Takashi. *Bakumatsu bōekishi no kenkyū* [A study of trade in the *bakumatsu* period]. Tokyo: Nihon hyōronsha, 1944.

Ishikawa Hiroshi. "Meiji ishin-ki ni okeru Tsushima-han no dōkō" [The stance of the Tsushima domain during the Meiji Restoration]. *Rekishigaku kenkyū* 709 (April 1998): 1–17.

Ishin shiryō hensan jimukyoku, ed. *Dai Nihon ishin shiryō* [Historical records of the Meiji Restoration of Japan]. 19 vols. Tokyo: Meiji shoin, 1938–43.

Iwakura Ichirō, ed., *Sasshū Yamakawa baisen kikigaki* [Notes on the *baisen* ships of Satsuma's Yamakawa port]. Artist Museum Series 16. Tokyo: Maruei kabushiki gaisha, 1938.

Iwao, Seiichi. "Japanese Foreign Trade in the 16th and 17th Centuries." *Acta Asiatica* 30 (1976): 1–18.

———."Edo jidai no satō bōeki nitsuite" [The sugar trade in the Edo period]. *Nihon gakushiin kiyō* 31.1 (March 1973): 1–34.

Iwata, Masakazu. *Ōkubo Toshimichi: The Bismarck of Japan.* Berkeley, CA: University of California Press, 1964.

Izuhara chōshi henshū iinkai, ed. *Izuhara chōshi* [The record of Izuhara town] 3 vols. Izuhara: Izuhara-chō, 1998.

Jansen, Marius B. *The Making of Modern Japan.* Cambridge, MA: The Belknap Press of Harvard University Press, 2000.

———. *China in the Tokugawa World.* Cambridge, MA: Harvard University Press, 1992.

———. *Sakamoto Ryōma and the Meiji Restoration.* Princeton, NJ: Princeton University Press, 1961.

Japan Weekly Mail. 16 November 1872.

Kagoshima-ken. *Kagoshima kenshi* [The history of Kagoshima prefecture]. 7 vols. Tokyo, 1940.

Kagoshima-ken ishin shiryō hensanjo and Kagoshima-ken rekishi shiryō sentā Reimeikan. *Kagoshima-ken shiryō, kyūki zatsuroku. kōhen 6, furoku; 1.* Kagoshima: Kagoshima-ken, 1986.

Kagoshima-ken rekishi shiryō sentā Reimeikan. *Reimeikan jōsetsu tenji zuroku* [An illustrated guide to the permanent exhibits at the Reimeikan Musuem]. Kagoshima: Kagoshima-ken, 1996.

Kamiya Nobuyuki. *Taikun gaikō to higashi Ajia* ["Great Prince" diplomacy and East Asia]. Tokyo: Yoshikawa kōbunkan, 1997.

Katsu Yasuyoshi. *Kaishū zenshū* [The complete works of Katsu Kaishū]. 10 vols. Ed. Kaishū zenshū kankō kai. Tokyo: Kaizōsha, 1927–29.

———. *Kaikoku kigen* [The origins of the opening of the country]. 3 vols. Tokyo: Kunaishō zōhan, 1893.

Kasutani Kenichi. "Naze Chōsen tsūshin-shi wa haishi sareta ka: Chōsen shiryō o chūshin ni" [Why were Korean embassies to Edo ended? A view through Korean documents]. *Rekishi hyōron* 355 (November 1979): 8–23.

Keene, Donald. *The Japanese Discovery of Europe, 1720–1830.* Revised edition. Stanford, CA: Stanford University Press, 1994.

Kerr, George H. *Okinawa: The History of an Island People.* Revised edition. Boston, MA: Tuttle Publishing, 2000.

Kido Takayoshi. *The Diary of Kido Takayoshi*, 3 vols. Trans. Sidney Devere Brown and Akiko Hirota. Tokyo: University of Tokyo Press, 1983–86.

Kido Takayoshi and Tsumaki Chūta. *Kido Takayoshi monjo* [The papers of Kido Takayoshi]. 8 vols. Tokyo: Nihon shiseki kyōkai, 1929–31.

Kim, Key-Hiuk. *The Last Phase of the East Asian World Order: Korea, Japan, and the Chinese Empire, 1860–1882*. Berkeley, CA: University of California Press, 1980.

Kimura Naoya. "Bakumatsu no Nitchō kankei to seikanron" [Plans to invade Korea and Japanese-Korean relations in the *bakumatsu* period]. *Rekishi hyōron* 516 (April 1994): 26–37.

———. "Bunkyū sannen Tsushima-han enjo yōkyū undō ni tsuite" [Concerning the aid request of Tsushima in 1863]. In *Nihon zenkindai no kokka to taigai kankei* [Foreign relations and the state in premodern Japan], ed. Tanaka Takeo, 703–33. Tokyo: Yoshikawa kōbunkan, 1987.

King, C.W. and G. Tradescant Lay. *Notes of the Voyage of the Morrison from Canton to Japan*, vol 1 in *The Claims of Japan and Malaysia upon Christendom: Exhibited in Notes of Voyages Made in 1837, from Canton, in the Ship Morrison and Brig Himmaleh, Under the Direction of the Owners*. 2 vols. New York: E. French, 1839.

Knaap, Gerrit, and Heather Sutherland. *Monsoon Traders: Ships, Skippers, and Commodities in Eighteenth-Century Makassar*. Leiden: KITLV Press, 2004.

Kōshaku Shimazu-ke henshūjo. *Sappan kaigunshi* [The history of the navy of the Satsuma domain] 3 vols. Tokyo: Sappan kaigunshi kankōkai, 1928–29.

Krusenstern, A. J. von. *Voyage Round the World in the Years 1803, 1804, 1805, and 1806*. Trans. Richard Belgrave Hoppner. London: John Murray, 1813. Reprint, Tenri Central Library, 1973.

Kuroda Yasuo. "Kōka-ki no Ryūkyū gaikō jiken to Satsuma-han" [The Satsuma domain and diplomatic maneuvers in Ryukyu during the Kōka period]. In *Kaikoku to kindaika* [Modernization and the opening of the country], ed. Nakamura Tadashi, 116–39. Tokyo: Yoshikawa kōbunkan, 1997.

LaFeber, Walter. *The Clash: A History of U.S.-Japan Relations*. New York: W. W. Norton, 1997.

Lal, Brij V. and Kate Fortune. *The Pacific Islands: An Encyclopedia*. Honolulu, HI: University of Hawai'i Press, 2000.

Lamb, Alastair, comp. and ed. "British Missions to Cochin China: 1788–1822," *Journal of the Malayan Branch Royal Asiatic Society* 34 parts 3&4 (September 1961): 1–248.

Langsdorff, Georg Heinrich von. *Voyages and Travels in Various Parts of the World, During the Years 1803, 1804, 1805, 1806, 1807*. Vol. 2. London: Henry Colburn, 1814.

Lensen, G.A. *The Russian Push Toward Japan: Russo-Japanese Relations, 1697–1875*. Princeton, NJ: Princeton University Press, 1959.
Lewis, James B. *Frontier Contact Between Chosŏn Korea and Tokugawa Japan*. London: RoutledgeCurzon, 2003.
Li, Tana. *Nguyễn Cochinchina: Southern Vietnam in the Seventeenth and Eighteenth Centuries*. Studies on Southeast Asia, no. 23. Ithaca, NY: Southeast Asia Program Publications, Cornell University, 1998.
Macknight, C. C. *The Voyage to Marege': Macassan Trepangers in Northern Australia*. Carlton, Victoria: Melbourne University Press, 1976.
Maehira Fusaaki. "Higashi Ajia no kaigai jōhō to Ryūkyū rūto, Ahen sensō go no Chūgoku jōsei o megutte" [The Ryukyu route and information from East Asia: the situation in China after the Opium War]. In *Kaikoku to kindaika* [Modernization and the opening of the country], ed. Nakamura Tadashi, 140–55. Tokyo: Yoshikawa kōbunkan, 1997.
———. "Kinsei Nihon no kyōkai ryōiki: Ryūkyū no shiten o chūshin toshite" [The territorial boundaries of early modern Japan: focusing on the perspective of Ryukyu]. In *Rettōshi no minami to kita* [North and south in the history of the island chain]. Vol. 1 of *Kinsei chiikishi fōramu* [Forum on early modern regional history], ed. Maehira Fusaaki and Kikuchi Isao, 3–15. Tokyo: Yoshikawa kōbunkan, 2006.
———. "Ryūkyū no kaigai jōhō to higashi Ajia: 19-seiki no Chūgoku jōsei o megutte" [East Asia and overseas information received through Ryukyu: the situation in nineteenth-century China]. In *Kinsei Nihon no kaigai jōhō* [Overseas information and early modern Japan], ed. Iwashita Tetsunori and Maehira Fusaaki, 95–112. Tokyo: Iwata shoin, 1997.
———. "Ryūkyū ōkoku ni okeru kaisanbutsu bōeki: sangokyō kaiiki no shigen to kōeki" [Trade in marine products in the Ryukyu Kindgom: commerce and natural resources in a coral maritime region]. In *Kaijin no sekai* [The world of maritime peoples], ed. Akimichi Tomoya, 219–36. Tokyo: Dōbunkan, 1998.
Marks, Robert. *The Origins of the Modern World: A Global and Ecological Narrative*. Lanham, MD: Rowman and Littlefield, 2002.
Maruyama, Masao. "National Consciousness under Tokugawa Feudalism." In *Studies in the Intellectual History of Tokugawa Japan*, trans. Mikiso Hane, 327–40. Princeton, NJ: Princeton University Press, 1974.
Matsudaira Sadanobu. *Uge no hitokoto, shugyōroku* [The memoirs of Matsudaira Sadanobu]. Ed. Matsudaira Sadamitsu. Tokyo: Iwanami shoten, 1969.
Matsumae chōshi henshūshitsu, ed. *Matsumae chōshi nenpyō* [A chronology of the history of Matsumae town] Matsumae: Matsumae-chō, 1997.
———, ed. *Matsumae chōshi tsūsetsu-hen* [The history of Matsumae town, general history]. 2 vols. Matsumae: Matsumae-chō, 1984–93.

Matsuura Rei. "Bakumatsu-ki no tai Chōsen ron: dōmei ron to seikanron" [Proposals relating to Korea during the *bakumatsu* period: plans for an alliance of Japan and Korea and plans to conquer Korea]. *Rekishi kōron* 57 (August 1980): 43–49.
Mazumdar, Sucheta. *Sugar and Society in China: Peasants, Technology, and the World Market*. Cambridge, MA: Harvard University Asia Center, 1998.
McCann, James C. *Maize and Grace: Africa's Encounter with a New World Crop, 1500–2000*. Cambridge, MA: Harvard University Press, 2005.
Medzini, Meron. *French Policy in Japan During the Closing Years of the Tokugawa Regime*. Cambridge, MA: East Asian Research Center, Harvard University, 1971.
Mintz, Sidney W. *Sweetness and Power: The Place of Sugar in Modern History*. New York: Penguin Books, 1986.
Mitani Hiroshi. *Escape from Impasse: The Decision to Open Japan*. Trans. David Noble. Tokyo: The International House of Japan, 2006.
Mitsui bunko, ed. *Kinsei kōki ni okeru shuyō bukka no dōtai* [The dynamics of key prices in the late early modern period]. Revised edition. Tokyo: Tōkyō Daigaku shuppankai, 1989.
Miyagi Eishō. *Ryūkyū shisha no Edo nobori* [Ryukyuan embassies to Edo]. Tokyo: Daiichi shobō, 1982.
Miyashita Saburō. *Nagasaki bōeki to Ōsaka: yunyū kara sōyaku e* [Osaka and the Nagasaki trade: from the import to the production of medicines] Osaka: Seibundō, 1997.
Miyazato Gennojō and Sawada Nobuto, eds. *Kaijō-ō Hamazaki Taiheiji den* [A biography of Hamazaki Taiheiji, "King of The Seas"]. Kagoshima: Hamazaki Taiheiji-ō kenshōkai, 1934.
Mody, N. H. N. *A Collection of Nagasaki Colour Prints and Paintings; Showing the Influence of Chinese and European Art on That of Japan*. Rutland, VT: C. E. Tuttle Co., 1969.
Mori Katsuhiko. "Minami Kyūshū ni okeru Tōjin-machi ni kansuru oboegaki" [Notes on Chinese merchants villages in southern Kyushu]. *Kagoshima keidai ronshū* 36.3 (October 1995): 127–38.
Nagasaki kenshi henshū iinkai, ed. *Nagasaki kenshi, taigai kōshōhen* [The history of Nagasaki prefecture: interactions with the outside world]. Tokyo: Yoshikawa kōbunkan, 1985.
———, ed. *Nagasaki kenshi, hansei-hen* [The history of Nagasaki prefecture: domain governments]. Tokyo: Yoshikawa kōbunkan, 1973.
———, ed. *Nagasaki kenshi, shiryō-hen* [The history of Nagasaki prefecture: historical documents] 4 vols. Tokyo: Yoshikawa kōbunkan, 1963–66.
Nagasaki shiyakusho, ed. *Nagasaki sōsho* [Documents of Nagasaki]. 2 vols. Reprint edition. Tokyo: Hara shobō, 1968. Originally published 1926.

———. *Nagasaki shishi* [The history of Nagasaki city]. 6 vols. Nagasaki: Nagasaki shiyakusho, 1948.
Nagazumi, Yōko. "From Company to Individual Company Servants: Dutch Trade in Eighteenth-Century Japan." In *On the Eighteenth Century as a Category of Asian History: Van Leur in Retrospect*, ed. Leonard Blussé and Femme Gaastra, 147–72. Brookfield, VT: Ashgate, 1998.
———. *Kinsei shoki no gaikō* [Diplomacy at the beginning of the early modern period]. Tokyo: Sōbunsha, 1990.
———, ed. *Tōsen yushutsunyūhin sūryō ichiran, 1637–1833* [The volume of exports and imports on Chinese ships, 1637–1833]. Tokyo: Sōbunsha, 1987.
———. "Tsūshō no kuni kara tsūshin no kuni e" [From a trading state to a diplomatic state]. *Nihon rekishi* 458 (July 1986): 43–61.
Nakai, Kate Wildman. *Shogunal Politics, Arai Hakuseki and the Premises of Tokugawa Rule*. Cambridge, MA: Council on East Asian Studies, Harvard University, 1988.
Nakamura, Ellen Gardner. *Practical Pursuits: Takano Chōei, Takahashi Keisaku, and Western Medicine in Nineteenth-Century Japan*. Cambridge, MA: Harvard University Asia Center, 2005.
Nakamura Tadashi. *Kinsei Nagasaki bōekishi no kenkyū* [The history of trade in Nagasaki during the early modern period]. Tokyo: Yoshikawa kōbunkan, 1988.
———. "Nagasaki kaisho Tenpō kaikakuki no shomondai: sakoku taisei hōkai katei no ichi sokumen" [The various problems confronting the Nagasaki clearing-house during the Tenpō Reform period: one view of the course of the collapse of the closed country policy]. *Shien* 115 (1978): 65–94.
Nakamura, Tetsuo. "Relationship of Overseas Chinese in Japan to Modern China: A Focus on the Archives of Taiyihao in Nagasaki, Japan." In *Searching the Historical Roots of Overseas Chinese in Kobe Through the Documents of Taiyihao*, ed. Nakamura Tetsuo, 23–30. Kobe: privately published research report, 2007.
Niigata shishi hensan kinseishi bukai, ed. *Niigata shishi, shiryōhen, kinsei* [The history of Niigata city, historical documents 2, early modern]. 2 vols. Niigata: Niigata-shi, 1990.
Nishikawa Takeomi, "Keiō-ki no bakufu bōeki seisaku to Yokohama, bakufu to Satsuma-han no dōkō to chūshin ni" [Yokohama and the *bakufu*'s trade policy in the Keiō period: focusing on the activities of the *bakufu* and the Satsuma domain]. *Yokohama kaikō shiryōkan kiyō* 12 (March 1995): 33–45.
Nomura Noboru. *Kinsei gyoson shiryō no kenkyū: Ōsaka-wan engan gyoson gakujutsu chōsa hōkoku* [Research of documents from early modern fishing villages: a report of a scientific survey of fishing villages on the coast of Osaka Bay]. Tokyo: Sanseidō shuppan, 1956.

Notehelfer, F. G. "Looking for the Lost: Westerners in 19th-Century Japan." In *Japan and Its Worlds: Marius B. Jansen and the Internationalization of Japanese Studies*, ed. Martin Collcutt, Mikio Katō, and Ronald P. Toby, 175–85. Tokyo: I-House Press, 2007.

———, ed. *Japan Through American Eyes, The Journal of Francis Hall: Kanagawa and Yokohama 1859–1866*. Princeton, NJ: Princeton University Press, 1992.

Ogawa Kuniharu. "Tsushima-han no tawaramono seisan to tōsei" [The regulation and production of marine products by the Tsushima domain]. *Nihon rekishi* 296 (January 1973): 53–73.

Ōishi Ken'ichi. *Konbu no michi* [The journey of kelp]. Tokyo: Daiichi shobō, 1987.

Ōishi Shinzaburō. *Tanuma Okitsugu no jidai* [The Tanuma Okitsugu period]. Tokyo: Iwanami shoten, 1992.

Okinawa-ken kyōiku iinkai, ed. *Tsūshi* [A historical overview]. Vol. 1 of *Okinawa kenshi* [The history of Okinawa prefecture]. Naha: Okinawa-ken kyōiku iinkai, 1977.

Osa Setsuko. "Tsushima-tō Sō-shi seikei no seiritsu" [The establishment of the Sō clan on the island of Tsushima]. *Nihon rekishi* 208 (September 1965): 42–53.

Paske-Smith, M. *Western Barbarians in Japan and Formosa in Tokugawa Days, 1603–1868*. Kobe: J. L Thompson & Co., 1930.

Paul, Huibert. "De Coningh on Deshima: *Mijn Verblijf* in Japan, 1856" *Monumenta Nipponica* 32.3 (Autumn 1977): 347–64.

Phipps, John. *A Practical Treatise on the China and Eastern Trade: Comprising the Commerce of Great Britain and India, Particularly Bengal and Singapore, with China and the Eastern Islands*. Calcutta: Baptist Mission Press, 1835.

Pineau, Roger, ed. *The Personal Journal of Commodore Matthew C. Perry*. Washington, DC: Smithsonian Institution Press, 1968.

Pluvier, Jan M. *Historical Atlas of South-East Asia*. New York: E. J. Brill, 1995.

Pomeranz, Kenneth. *The Great Divergence: Europe, China, and the Making of the Modern World Economy*. Princeton, NJ: Princeton University Press, 2000.

Ravina, Mark. *Lord and Lordship in Early Modern Japan*. Stanford, CA: Stanford University Press, 1999.

Reid, Anthony. "Global and Local in Southeast Asian History." *International Journal of Asian Studies* 1.1 (January 2004): 5–21.

———. "Chinese Trade and Southeast Asian Economic Expansion in the late 18th and early 19th Centuries: An Overview." In *Water Frontier: Commerce and the Chinese in the Lower Mekong Region, 1750–1880*, ed. Nola Cooke and Li Tana, 19–34. Lanham, MD: Rowman and Littlefield, 2004.

Ren Hongzhang [Nin Kōshō]. *Kinsei Nihon to Nitchū bōeki* [Early modern Japan and Japanese-Chinese trade]. Tokyo: Rokkō shuppan, 1988.

Rezanov, Nikolai. *Nihon taizai nikki, 1804–1805* [Diary of a sojourn in Japan, 1804–1805]. Trans. Ōshima Mikio. Tokyo: Iwanami shoten, 2000.

Roshia shisetsu Rezanofu raikō emaki [Picture scroll of Russian envoy Rezanov's visit to Nagasaki], 1805. Unpublished illustrated scroll in the archives of the Historiographical Institute, University of Tokyo.

"Ryūkyū gaikoku kankei monjo" [Documents relating to the foreign relations of Ryukyu]. Document collection in archives of the Historiographical Institute, University of Tokyo.

Saitō, Osamu. "Scenes of Japan's Economic Development and the Longue Durée." In *Silkworms, Oil and Chips, Proceedings of the Economics and Economic History Section of the Fourth International Conference of Japanese Studies, Paris, September 1985*, ed. Erich Pauer, 15–28. Bonn: European Association for Japanese Studies, 1986.

Sakai, Robert K. "Shimazu Nariakira and the Emergence of National Leadership in Satsuma." In *Personality in Japanese History*, ed. Albert M. Craig and Donald H. Shively, 209–33. Berkeley, CA: University of California Press, 1970.

———. "The Ryukyu (Liu-Ch'iu) Islands as a Fief of Satsuma." In *The Chinese World Order*, ed. John K. Fairbank, 112–34. Cambridge, MA: Harvard University Press, 1968.

Sakai Seiichi. *Toyama-ken no rekishi* [The history of Toyama prefecture]. Tokyo: Yamakawa shuppansha, 1970.

Sansom, George. *A History of Japan, 1615–1867*. Stanford, CA: Stanford University Press, 1963.

Scheuerman, William. "Globalization." Stanford Encyclopedia of Philosophy http://plato.stanford.edu/entries/globalization/ [accessed 17 July 2009].

Shibahara Takuji. *Kaikoku* [The opening of the country]. Nihon rekishi [Japanese history] 23. Tokyo: Shōgakukan, 1975.

Shim Ki-jae [Shimu Kije]. "Bakumatsu-ki no bakufu no Chōsen seisaku to kikō no henka" [*Bakufu* policy concerning Korea in the *bakumatsu* period and the mechanisms of change in Korean-Japanese relations]. *Shirin* 77.2 (March 1994): 100–130.

Shimada, Ryuto. *The Intra-Asian Trade in Japanese Copper by the Dutch East India Company during the Eighteenth Century*. Boston, MA: Brill, 2006.

Shin Tsushima tōshi henshū iinkai. *Shin Tsushima-tōshi* [A new history of the island of Tsushima]. Tsushima: Shin Tsushima tōshi henshū iinkai, 1964.

Shinzato Keiji, Taminato Tomoaki, and Kinjō Seitoku. *Okinawa-ken no rekishi* [The history of Okinawa prefecture]. Tokyo: Yamakawa shuppansha, 1972.

Shio Teruo. *Konbu o hakonda kitamaebune: konbu shokubunka to kusuriuri no roman* [The *kitamae* ships that transported kelp: the story of medicine peddling and the culture of kelp consumption]. Kanazawa: Hokkoku shinbunsha, 1993.

Shirota Kichiroku. *Tsushima no shominshi* [A chronicle of the people of Tsushima]. Fukuoka: Ashi shobō, 1989.

Shōko Shūseikan. *Shimazu-ke omoshiro rekishikan* 2: *Shūseikan jigyō-hen* [The intriguing historical hall of the Shimazu clan 2: the enterprises of the Shūseikan]. Kagoshima: Shūseikan, 1998.

Smith, Kerry. "Selling the *Fire Dart* and Other Adventures in Business: Augustine Heard and Company in Japan." Unpublished essay.

Smits, Gregory. *Visions of Ryukyu: Identity and Ideology in Early-Modern Thought and Politics*. Honolulu, HI: University of Hawai'i Press, 1999.

Suematsu Kenchō. *Bōchō kaitenshi* [The epoch-making changes in the Suō and Nagato domains]. 12 vols. Tokyo: Tōkyō kokubunsha, 1911–20.

Sugiyama Shinya. *Meiji ishin to Igirisu shōnin: Tomasu Gurabā no shōgai* [English merchants and the Meiji Restoration: the life of Thomas Glover]. Tokyo: Iwanami shinsho, 1993.

———. *Japan's Industrialization in the World Economy, 1859–1899*. London: The Athlone Press, 1988.

———. "Thomas B. Glover: A British Merchant in Japan, 1861–70." *Business History* 26.2 (1984): 115–38.

Tabohashi Kiyoshi. *Kindai Nissen kankei no kenkyū* [A study of modern Japanese-Korean relations]. 2 vols. Keijō [Seoul]: Chōsen sōtōkufu, Chūsūin, 1940. Reprint, Munetaka shobō, 1972.

———. "Meiji ishin-ki ni okeru Tsushima-han zaisei oyobi hansai ni tsuite" [Domain debts and the financial situation of the Tsushima domain in the Meiji Restoration period]. *Seikyū gakusō* 16 (May 1934): 97–117.

Tagliacozzo, Eric. "A Necklace of Fins: Marine Goods Trading in Maritime Southeast Asia, 1780–1860." *International Journal of Asian Studies* 1.1 (January 2004): 23–48.

Taigai kankeishi sōgō nenpyō henshū iinkai, ed. *Taigai kankeishi sōgō nenpyō* [A general chronology of the history of foreign relations]. Tokyo: Yoshikawa kōbunkan, 1999.

Takano Chōei zenshū kankōkai, ed. *Takano Chōei zenshū* [The complete works of Takano Chōei]. 4 vols. Mizusawa: Takano Chōei zenshū kankōkai, 1930.

Takase Tamotsu. *Kaga-han ryūtsūshi no kenkyū* [Research on the history of transport and distribution networks in the Kaga domain]. Toyama: Katsura shobō, 1990.

Takayanagi Shinzō and Ishii Ryōsuke, ed., *Ofuregaki Tenpō shūsei* [Compilation of official proclamations from the Tenpō period (1830–1841)]. 2 vols. Tokyo: Iwanami shoten, 1958.

Tanabe Mokei and Obara Hazan. *Nagasaki jitsuroku taisei, seihen* [The authentic complied records of Nagasaki: main volumes]. Vol. 16. Ed. Niwa Kankichi and Morinaga Taneo. Nagasaki: Nagasaki bunkensha, 1973.

Tanaka Akira. *Bakumatsu ishinshi no kenkyū*. [A study of the history of the *bakumatsu* and Restoration periods]. Tokyo: Yoshikawa kōbunkan, 1996.

———, ed. *Kaikoku: Nihon kindai shisō taikei* [The opening of the country: a compendium of modern Japanese thought]. Vol. 1. Tokyo: Iwanami shoten, 1991.

———. "Bakumatsu Satchō bōeki no kenkyū" [A study of trade between Satsuma and Chōshū in the *bakumatsu* period]. *Shigaku zasshi* 69.3 (February 1960): 54–84 and 69.4 (March 1960): 29–51.

Tanaka, Takeo, with Robert Sakai. "Japan's Relations with Overseas Countries." In *Japan in the Muromachi Age*, ed. by John Whitney Hall and Toyoda Takeshi, 159–78. Berkeley, CA: University of California Press, 1977.

Tashiro Kazui. "Bakumatsu-ki Nitchō shibōeki to Wakan bōeki shōnin: yunyū yon hinmoku no torihiki o chūshin ni" [Private Japanese-Korean trade and merchants at the Japan House in the *bakumatsu* period: a focus on transactions in four imports]. In *Kaikoku* [The opening of the country], ed. Inoue Katsuo, 171–95. Tokyo: Yoshikawa kōbunkan, 2001.

———. *Edo jidai Chōsen yakuzai chōsa no kenkyū* [The survey of Korean medicinal plants in the Edo period]. Tokyo: Keiō Gijuku Daigaku shuppankai, 1999.

———. "Kinsei kōki Nitchō bōekishi kenkyū josetsu" [An introduction to the history of Japanese-Korean trade in the latter part of the early modern period]. *Mita gakkai zasshi* 79.3 (August 1986): 14–29.

———. *Kinsei Nitchō tsūkō bōekishi no kenkyū* [A study of early modern Japanese-Korean commercial intercourse]. Tokyo: Sōbunsha, 1981.

———. "Tsushima-han's Korean Trade, 1684–1710." *Acta Asiatica* 30 (1976): 85–105.

———. "Tsushima-han no Chōsen yushutsu dō chōtatsu ni tsuite—bakufu no dō tōsei to Nissen dō bōeki no suitai" [The Tsushima domain's procurement of copper for export to Korea—the *bakufu*'s regulation of copper and the decline of Japanese-Korean trade in copper]. *Chōsen gakuhō* 66 (January 1973): 141–208.

Toby, Ronald P. *State and Diplomacy in Early Modern Japan: Asia in the Development of the Tokugawa Bakufu*. Stanford, CA: Stanford University Press, 1991.

Tokunaga Kazuyoshi. "Satsuma-han Tōtsūji ni tsuite" [Chinese translators of the Satsuma domain]. *Nantō shigaku* 51 (May 1998): 30–53.

———. "Satsuma-han no Chōsen tsūji nitsuite" [Korean translators of the Satsuma Domain]. *Reimeikan chōsa kenkyū hōkoku* 8 (1994): 18–33.

Tōkyō Teikoku Daigaku bungakubu, shiryō hensangakari, ed. *Dai Nihon shiryō* [Historical documents of Japan]. 359 volumes. Tokyo: Shiryō hensanjo, 1901–.

Tōkyō-to Edo Tōkyō hakubutsukan. *Sankin kōtai: kyodai toshi Edo no naritachi* [The system of alternate residence: the creation of the Edo metropolis]. Tokyo: Tōkyō-to Edo Tōkyō hakubutsukan, 1997.

Tomiyama Kazuyuki. *Ryūkyū ōkoku no gaikō to ōken* [Royal authority and diplomacy of the Ryukyu Kingdom]. Tokyo: Yoshikawa kōbunkan, 2004.

Tomiyama Kazuyuki and Takara Kurayoshi. *Ryūkyū Okinawa to kaijō no michi* [Maritime routes of Ryukyu and Okinawa]. Tokyo: Yoshikawa kōbunkan, 2005.

Totman, Conrad. *Early Modern Japan*. Berkeley, CA: University of California Press, 1993.

———. *Politics in the Tokugawa Bakufu, 1600–1843*. Berkeley, CA: University of California Press, 1988.

———. *The Collapse of the Tokugawa Bakufu, 1862–1868*. Honolulu, HI: University of Hawai'i Press, 1980.

Tregonning, K. C. *The British in Malaya: The First Forty Years, 1786–1826*. Tuscon, AZ: University of Arizona Press, 1965.

Tsukuda Takashi. "Ajia ni okeru ryō to sen: gyūhi ryūtsū o tegakari toshite" [The good and the lowly in Asia: taking the trade in cowhides as a clue]. In *Ajia no naka no Nihonshi I: Ajia to Nihon* [Japanese history in an Asian context, vol. I: Japan and Asia], ed. Arano Yasunori, Ishii Masatoshi and Murai Shōsuke, 249–83. Tokyo: Tōkyō Daigaku shuppankai, 1992.

Tsuruta Kei. *Tsushima kara mita Nitchō kankei* [Japanese-Korean relations from the perspective of Tsushima]. Tokyo: Yamakawa shuppansha, 2006.

———. "The Establishment and Characteristics of the 'Tsushima Gate.'" *Acta Asiatica* 67 (1994): 30–48.

———. "Man'en gannen, Tsushima-han ni yoru Chōsen e no shikoku tsūshō kokuchi ikken" [The first year of the Man'en period (1860), the Tsushima domain's report to Korea concerning the commercial treaties]. In *19-seiki no sekai to Yokohama* [Yokohama and the 19th-century world], ed. Yokohama kaikō shiryōkan, Yokohama kinseishi kenkyūkai, 79–100. Tokyo: Yamakawa shuppankai, 1993.

———. "Tenpō-ki no Tsushima-han zaisei to Nitchō bōeki" [Japanese-Korean trade and the finances of the Tsushima domain in the Tenpō period]. *Ronshū kinsei* 8 (May 1983): 60–79.

Tsurumi Yoshiyuki. *Namako no me* [Through the eyes of sea cucumbers]. Tokyo: Chikuma shobō, 1990.
Tsuzuki, Chushichi. *The Pursuit of Power in Modern Japan, 1825–1995*. New York: Oxford University Press, 2000.
Uehara Kenzen. *Sakoku to han bōeki: Satsuma-han no Ryūkyū mistu bōeki* [The closed country policy and domain trade: the smuggling in Ryukyu conducted by the Satsuma domain]. Tokyo: Yaedake shobō, 1981.
———. "Bakumatsu Satsuma-han no tai Okinawa seisaku" [The Okinawa policy of the Satsuma domain in the *bakumatsu* period]. *Chihōshi kenkyū* 115 (February 1972): 9–19.
Vaporis, Constantine N. "Samurai and Merchant in Mid-Tokugawa Japan: Tani Tannai's Record of Daily Necessities (1748–54). *Harvard Journal of Asiatic Studies* 60.1 (June 2000): 205–27.
Wakabayashi, Bob Tadashi. *Anti-Foreignism and Western Learning in Early Modern Japan: The New Theses of 1825*. Cambridge, MA: Council on East Asian Studies, Harvard University, 1986.
Wakamatsu Masashi. "Nagasaki tawaramono o meguru shokubunka no rekishiteki tenkai" [The historical development of the dietary culture of sea cucumbers and abalone]. *Kyōto Sangyō Daigaku Nihon bunka kenkyūjo kiyō* 1 (March 1996): 128–60.
———. "Sendai hanryō ni okeru Nagasaki tawaramono no seisan shūka [The collection and production of marine products for the Nagasaki market in the Sendai domain]. In *Kinsei Nihon no seikatsu bunka to chiiki shakai* [Regional societies and lifestyles of early modern Japan], ed. Watanabe Nobuo, 309–34. Tokyo: Kawade shobō shinsha, 1995.
Waley-Cohen, Joanna. "China and Western Technology in the Late Eighteenth Century." *American Historical Review* 98.5 (December 1993): 1525–44.
Walker, Brett L. *The Conquest of Ainu Lands: Ecology and Culture in Japanese Expansion, 1590–1800*. Berkeley, CA: University of California Press, 2001.
Warren, James Francis. *The Sulu Zone, 1768–1898: The Dynamics of External Trade, Slavery, and Ethnicity in the Transformation of a Southeast Asian Maritime State*. Singapore: Singapore University Press, 1981.
Weaver, William Woys. *Sauer's Herbal Cures: America's First Book of Botanic Healing, 1762–1778*. New York: Routledge, 2001.
Wigen, Kären. *The Making of a Japanese Periphery, 1750–1920*. Berkeley, CA: University of California Press, 1995.
Williams, Eric. *Capitalism and Slavery*. Chapel Hill, NC: University of North Carolina Press, 1994.
Wolff, Derek. "Notes from the Periphery: Satsuma Identities in Early Modern and Modern Japan." Ph.D. diss. University of Chicago, 2003.

Wright, Mary Clabaugh. "The Adaptability of Ch'ing Diplomacy, The Case of Korea." *Journal of Asian Studies* 17.3 (May 1958): 363–81.

Yamamoto Hirofumi. *Tsushima-han Edo garō: kinsei Nichō gaikō o sasaeta hitobito* [The chief ministers of the Tsushima domain in Edo: the men who supported Japanese-Korean relations in the early modern period]. Sensho mechie 38. Tokyo: Kōdansha, 1995.

Yamawaki Teijirō. *Kinsei Nihon no iyaku bunka* [The medicinal culture of early modern Japan]. Tokyo: Heibonsha, 1995.

———. *Nagasaki no Tōjin bōeki* [Trade with Chinese merchants in Nagasaki]. Tokyo: Yoshikawa kōbunkan, 1964. Reprint, 1995.

———. *Nukeni: sakoku jidai no mitsu bōeki* [Smuggling: secret trade during the closed country period]. Tokyo: Nihon keizai shimbunsha, 1965.

Yanai Kenji, ed. *Tsūkō ichiran zokushū* [A compendium of foreign relations, supplemental]. 5 vols. Osaka: Seibundō shuppan, 1967–73.

Yano Kenichi. *Awabi* [Abalone]. Tokyo: Hōsei Daigaku shuppankyoku, 1989.

Yokoyama Yoshinori. "Japan and Ryukyu in the Bakumatsu Period as Seen in Overseas Sources." *Acta Asiatica* 93 (2007): 41–57.

———. "Nihon kaikoku to Ryūkyū" [Ryukyu and the opening of Japan] In *Atarashii kinseishi 2, kokka to taigai kankei* [A new history of the early modern period 2: the state and foreign relations], ed. Sone Yuji and Kimura Naoya, 365–430. Tokyo: Shin jinbutsu ōraisha, 1996.

Yoshinaga Akira. "Kokusan kaisho shihō no seiritsu to tenkai" [The methods for establishing and developing clearing-houses for domain products]. In *Kyūshū to seisan ryūtsū* [Kyushu and transport networks], ed. Fujino Tamotsu, 3–37. Tokyo: Kokusho kankōkai, 1986.

Zhu Delan [Shu Tokuran]. *Nagasaki kashō bōeki no shiteki kenkyū* [A historical examination of the trade conducted by Chinese merchants in Nagasaki]. Tokyo: Fuyō shobō, 1997.

Zhu Henian [Shu Kakunen]. *Hōshi Ryūkyū zukan* [An illustrated scroll of the Ryukyu investiture mission]. Unpublished illustrated scroll held by the Okinawa Prefectural Museum.

Zuckerman, Larry. *The Potato: How the Humble Spud Rescued the Western World*. New York: North Point Press, 1998.

Index

Page numbers in italics indicate figures or maps

abalone, 55, 80, 83, 90, 122–24; trade controls on, 16, 124–25, 178; clearing-house for, 89, 92–93. *See also* marine products
Abe Masahiro, 146–47, 157; Nariakira and, 158–62, 168; Tsushima and, 168–69; trade policies of, 180
Abe Masatō, 224
Actaeon (British ship), 175, 207, 208
Ainu, 20, 21*n*31, 90, 97–98
Aizawa Seishisai, 9
Alaska, 100–102
Alcmène (French ship), 152, 155–56
Alcock, Rutherford, 178, 195, 208, 212, 216*n*20
alum, 40, 56, 88, 89
Amami islands, *3*, 70, 74, 95, 118, 127–28, 167, 237
Amenomori Hōshū, 60, 63–65, 68, 104–5, 169
Amerindians, 95; silver mining by, 13; ginseng exports by, 74, 75
Andō Nobumasa, 212
Arai Eiji, 182–83
Arai Hakuseki, 62–63, 67, 71, 87

Arano Yasunori, 14–16
Armenian traders, 81
aroma therapy, 88, 119, 120
Ashikaga *bakufu*, 30–32
Asō Bay (Tsushima), *5*, *209*, 210, *211*, 215
Auslin, Michael, 10

bakufu. See Tokugawa shogunate
Balambangan, *15*, 81–82
Barrow, John, 82–83
Batten, Bruce, 74*n*1
Bayly, C. A., 17, 18
Beasley, W. G., 188–89
Bellecourt, Gustave Duchesne de, 191
Benyowsky, Baron Moritz Aladar von, 102
Bettelheim, Bernard Jean, 156
Biddle, James, 169
bird's nests, 81, 83, 122
Borneo, *15*; mines in, 79; natural camphor from, 88, 120.
Boshin War, 233
Britain. *See* United Kingdom
Buddhism, 32, 120

camphor: artificial Borneo type of, 88, 120, 132; natural Borneo variety of, 88, 94, 120; Japanese exports of, 94, 197, 199, 246*n*22; medicinal uses of, 94, 120

castaways, 46, 98, 110, 238

Charter Oath, 235–36, 249

China: Edo Japan and, 1–2; foreign relations model of, 7; silver reserves of, 13, 34; manufacturing output of, 16, 114, 246–47; Nagasaki trade with, 16–17, 32–34, 49, 107–9, 133–34, 183–84, 205; British trade with, 17–18, 81–83, 114, 147–48; tribute system of, 19, 30; Ryukyu tribute missions to, 34–39, 130, 136, 153, 158, 186–87, 240; Taiping Rebellion in, 153, 174, 183–84, 186, 215, 220. *See also* Ming Empire; Qing Empire

Chinese Residence, in Nagasaki, 20, 33, 55–56, 57, 79, 133–34

Chōshū, 187–89, 196, 202; Satsuma and, 186, 187, 196, 202–4, 230, 233, 235–36; Tsushima and, 211, 217–19, 228; Meiji Restoration and, 230, 235, 236

Chosŏn Kingdom, 5; Tsushima trade with, 7, 20–21, 39–42, 45, 135–36, 140–41, 207–8, 214–16, 240–45; pirates and, 30–31, 41; Japan House in, 39–42, 43, 45–46, 171, 175, 215, 225; rice exports of, 40–41, 141, 170, 172, 241, 244; prostitution in, 42; embassy missions of, 43–44, 104–6; *bakufu* protocol with, 44; anti-Christian campaign in, 47–48; silk exports by, 51; sea cucumbers from, 92–93, 141; cowhides from, 93, 141; Satsuma and, 135–36; Western visits to, 207; proposed Japanese invasions of, 226–27, 240, 245; Western clashes with, 231–32; Chinese tribute system and, 236–37; Meiji relations with, 240–45

Christianity, 13, 32, 152–53; campaigns against, 14, 32, 47–49, 156–57, 207; in Korea, 231–32

cinnabar, 88, 89, 138

Collinson, Peter, 75

Commutation Act (1784), 82

Confucianism, 96, 103, 156–57, 224

copper trade, 178, 181, 196; Chinese, 54, 78–79; Korean, 55, 109; restrictions on, 78–79; for Dutch silver, 84; silver and, 142–43; by Westerners, 183–84

corvée labor, 26–27

cosmopolitanism, "globalized," 14

cotton, 179, 187; Japanese imports of, 19, 247; Korean, 40; trade association for, 86; U.S. Civil War and, 196

Coxinga. *See* Zheng Chenggong

currency, 34, 76–78; gold as, 16, 34, 59, 76, 84–89, 109; Chinese, 54; Korean, 55; *bakufu* manipulations of, 59–68; Mexican dollars as, 60, 182*n*12; Tsushima and, 62; Ryukyuan, 192; counterfeit, 196–97. *See also* silver

"Dai Nihon ishin shiryō kōhon" (*DNISK*), 159*n*24

Dai Viet. *See* Vietnam

Dalyrmple, Alexander, 81–82

Đàng Trong, kingdom of (Cochin China), 15, 82–83

Date Munenari, 161, 162

Dejima, 49, 55, 125, 133, 181

Donker Curtius, Jan, 191

Drake, Fred W., 1

Dutch East India Company (VOC), 2, 14, 53; Nagasaki factory of, 20, 42, 49, 56, 107–8, 133; Tokugawa Ieyasu and, 32; *bakufu* protocol with, 44; Edo visits by, 44, 45, 104, 106; limiting trade with, 63; medicinal products from, 76; Sulawesi and, 80–81; silver trade by, 84; Napoleonic wars and, 98–99, 108, 133, 147; Russian trade and, 101; Matsudaira and, 107–8; demise of, 133. *See also* Netherlands
Dutch Supplementary Treaty (1857), 181–82

Ebihara Sōnojo, 156
Emishi, 188
engagement. *See* guarded engagement
English East India Company, 17–18, 81–83, 88, 100–101
entrepôt model, 16, 18, 81–82, 125–28
Ezo, 2, 20, 99; marine products of, 90, 97, 113, 123; Russian trade with, 98, 102–3, 110–11; civil war in, 236

Fiji, 122
Fillmore, Millard, 163
fisheries. *See* marine products
Flershem, Robert, 129
Flynn, Dennis, 80
Forcade, Theodore Augustin, 152
foreign relations: Tokugawa shogunate and, 2–12, 20–24, 42–48, 103–11, 200–206; early modern East Asian structure of, 7; during Ashikaga period, 30–32
Fortune, Robert, 179
France: Ryukyu trading missions of, 152–57, 163–66, 169, 191, 201–4; sericulture in, 179, 184–85; Japanese goods at exposition in, 201–3; Korean reprisals by, 231–32
Franciscan missionaries, 32. *See also* Christianity
Franklin (U.S. ship), 108
Fuchū. *See* Izuhara
Fukuyama. *See* Matsumae
fur trade, 98, 100, 112, 131
Fuzhou, *15*, 38–39, 130, 153, 157, 166–67, 186–87

Geertz, Clifford, 11
General Sherman (U.S. ship), 231
ginseng: Korean, 40, 59, 61–62, 118; Japanese, 50, 68–70, *69*, 75, 86, 91–92, 118, 121; grading of, 74, *119*; North American, 74–75, 118
Giráldez, Arturo, 80
globalization, 12–19, 75; nation-states and, 6–7; reaction against, 14–16, 47–52, 68–71; sugar trade and, 95–96
Glover, Thomas, 194, 198
Gluck, Carol, 250
Godai Hidetaka, 154–56
Godai Tomoatsu, 194, 200–204, 246
gold, xvi, 16, 34, 59, 76, 84–89, 109. *See also* currency
Goshkevich, Iosif Antonovich, 213
Gotō Islands, *33*
Gower, S. J., 199
guarded engagement, 73–74; local impact of, 89–97; Matsudaira reforms and, 102–7; presentation of, 110–15

Hakata silk goods, 140
Hall, Francis, 212*n*13
Hall, John W., 103
Hamashita, Takeshi, 18–19, 236–37

Hamazaki family, 129–30
Hanabusa Yoshimoto, 244
Handa Keitōji, 137
Harris, Townsend, 167
Hayashi Shihei, 102
Heard, Augustine, 198–200
Herbert, John, 82
herring, 90, 97, 129
Heusken, Henry, 189
Hevia, James, 114
Higuchi Kennosuke, 217, 230
Hijikata Katsumasa, 134, 136
Hirata Ōe, 229–30
Hirayama Yoshitada, 232–33
Hirotsu Hironobu, 244
Hokkaido. *See* Ezo
Holland. *See* Netherlands
Honda Toshiaki, 9
Hong Kong, *15*, 148, 163
Hoover, William, 200–201
Hope, James, 212–13
Hosokawa clan, 30
Howell, David, 21*n*31, 97

Ichiki Shirō, 166–67
Ii Naosuke, 188, 189, 208
Ijichi Sadaka, 237–39
Ijichi Sueyasu, 117
Imari porcelain, 140
Imozaki (Tsushima), *5, 211*
indigo, 187
industrialization, 10, 18, 246–47; mercantilism and, 103; proto-, 117–18, 139, 140
international law, 6, 235–36
international relations, 6, 7, 10–11, 23–24; explanation of, 6; Meiji period adoption of, 235–50
investiture missions: Ming, 36, *37, 38*; Qing, 38, 51, 106–7, 193–94
Iriomote, *3*, 97
Ishigaki, *3*, 97

Ishii Ryōsuke, 235
Itakura Katsukiyo, 220, 222, 224, 226–27
Iwashita Masahira, 203
Izuhara (Tsushima), *5*, 28, *41,*169, 170, 175, 211, 213, 217, 228, 230, 241–42

Japan House in Pusan, 39–46, *43*, 171, 175, 215, 225, 243, 244
Jardine, Matheson & Company, 198, 199
Java, 14, *15*, 70, 80, 108, 133; sugar from, 118; British takeover of, 133. *See also* Dutch East India Company
Jesuits, 32. *See also* Christianity

Kagoshima, 28, *33*; harbor of, *35*, 239; Ryukyu House in, *35*, 239; Shūseikan factory in, 166, 194; mint of, 192, 194; British attack on, 194–95; Meiji reforms involving, 237–40, 246. *See also* Satsuma
Kaitsu Zenkurō, 175–76
Kikaijima, *3*, 95
Kamchatka Peninsula, 97–99, *99*, 102
Kanagawa Treaty (1854), 163–65
Kanghwa, Treaty of (1876), 245
Katsu Kaishū, 220–24
Katsui Gohachirō, 217, 227–31
kelp, 16, 80, 122–24; exports of, 55, 90, 183, 189; clearing-house for, 89; regional cuisines with, 123. *See also* marine products
Kerama Islands, *3*
Kido Takayoshi, 202–3, 211, 218–22, 224, 225; on international law, 235–36; Ōshima Tomonojō and, 240, 245

Kim, Key-Hiuk, 232
Kimura Naoya, 221*n*32
King, C. W., 151
kokutai, 160*n*26
Kōmei (emperor), 188
Korea. *See* Chosŏn Kingdom
Krusenstern, Adam Johann von, 100–101
Kudō Heisuke, 87–88, 102
Kumejima, *3*
Kuril Islands, 20, 97–99, *99*, 102
Kuroda Narihiro, 161, 162
Kuroda Naritaka, 133–34
Kuze Hiromasa, 136
Kyushu, 2, *5*; Christians of, 13, 32, 47–49, 207; castle towns of, *33*; Chinese communities of, 46; leather workers from, 94

LaFeber, Walter, 10
Langsdorff, Georg Heinrich von, 101–2, 111–12
Laxman, Adam, 98, 110–11
leather goods, 76, 214; Tsushima and, 93–94, 109, 141, 144, 223; Russian trade in, 99
Lewis, James B., 41–42
licorice, 158

Macartney, Lord, 82–83, 114
marine products, 73–74, 80–84, 122–24; Chinese trade in, 16, 18, 55, 205, 246*n*22; kelp as, 16, 55, 80, 89, 90, 123, 183, 189; shark fins as, 16, 55, 70, 83, 89, 123, 187; Tokugawa monopoly on, 16, 103, 124, 183–84; Penang's trade in, 82, 122; clearing-houses for, 89, 92–93; from Ezo, 90, 97, 113, 123; trade restrictions on, 124–25, 178, 181; value of, 182–83. *See also* abalone; sea cucumbers

Marks, Robert, 246–47
Maruyama Masao, 248*n*28
Mataram, 14, *15*
Matsudaira Sadanobu, 92, 98, 103–10, 137, 145
Matsumae, 20–21, 90, *99*; Russian trade with, 97–98, 102–3, 110–11; shelling of foreign ships by, 150–51
Matsumoto Hidemochi, 103
Matsuura Rei, 221*n*32
medicinal products, 20, 49, 117–19, 196; Chinese trade in, 17, 51, 76, 148, 158, 179; from Korea, 50; research on, 68; China root as, 76, 158; skullcap root as, 76, 93, 132, 141, 144–45, 148, 158; Kudō Heisuke on, 87–88; trade restrictions on, 87–88, 116–17, 132, 158; smuggling of, 88, 116–17; Matsudaira on, 108; camphor as, 94, 120. *See also specific types, e.g.*, ginseng
medicine: humoral, 17, 19; Western, 19
Meiji, Emperor, 236, 238, *239*
Meiji government, 230, 234, 235; Charter Oath of, 235–36, 249; international relations and, 235–50
mercantilism, 84, 103
Ming Empire: tribute system of, 30; pirates and, 31–32; Tokugawa Ieyasu and, 32–34; investiture missions of, 36, *37*, 38; Ryukyu Kingdom and, 36; silk trade and, 36–38, 51
missionaries, 10; on Ryukyu, 152–53, 156–57, 191; in Korea, 231–32. *See also* Christianity
Mitani Hiroshi, 147
Miyako Islands, *3*
Mizoguchi Katsuyuki, 211

Mizuno Tadakiyo, 220
Mizuno Tadakuni, 121–22, 137, 138, 139, 147, 158
Montblanc, Charles Comte de, 201–3
Mōri clan, 217–18, 224
Mōri Takachika, 211
Morrison (U.S. ship), 150–51
Mukōyama Kōson, 225

Nagasaki, *33, 77*, 133–39, 151; Chinese trade at, 16–17, 32–34, 49, 107–9, 133–34, 183–84, 205, 246; Chinese Residence in, 20, *33*, 55–56, *57, 79*, 133–34; Dutch factory at, 20, 42, 49, 56, 107–8, 133; growth of, 32–34; clearing-house of, *33*, 56–59, *57*, 86, 109, 133–34; defense of, 65; Russian delegation to, 98–100, 110–13, *113*; Matsudaira's trade reforms and, 107–10; Marine Product Office at, *125*; Satsuma and, 133–39, 190, 203; Ryukyu trade and, 158–60; British trade in, 178–79, 195; trade initiatives at, 181–83; Meiji reforms involving, 246
Naha. *See* Okinawa
Nakamura, Ellen, 69–70
Nakamura Tadashi, 84–85
Nakamura Tetsuo, 184*n*17
Nakano Hanzaemon, 187
Namamugi incident (1862), 189, 192, 194
Napoleonic Wars, 98–99, 108, 133, 147
Napoleon III, 203
Narahara Kogoro, 237–38
narwhal tusks, 118–19
nation-state model, 6–7
Neale, Edward St. John, 194, 195

Netherlands, 145–46; Ryukyu trading ventures by, 166, 191–92; treaties with, 181–82. *See also* Dutch East India Company; Java
Niigata, 129–30, 138–39, 148, 180
Nimure Sahei, 187
Nisshinkan school, 224, 229
Nonoyama Kanehiro, 214–16, 223
North America, 12, 80; ginseng from, 74–75, 118; Russian outposts in, 100–102

Oda Nobunaga, 32
Ogiwara Shigehide, 61
Oguri Tadamasa, 211–12, 214
Ōishi Kenichi, 123
Okhotsk (trading post), 99, 100
Okinawa, *3*, 35; Western visits to, 151, 156–57; Perry's visits to, 163–65. *See also* Ryukyu
Okinoerabu, *3*
Ōkubo Tadazane, 134–36, 143, 147
Ōkubo Toshimichi, 154, 237
opium trade, 18, 82, 122
Opium War, 146–48, 150, 155, 162
Ōshima Tomonojō, 198, 217–27, 231–33; Kido Takayoshi and, 240, 245; Meiji reforms and, 240–42
Ōuchi clan, 30, 31
Ōura Norinosuke, 217, 228–30
Ōura Sakubei, 228–29

Parkes, Harry, 195
pearls, 81
Penang, *15*, 82, 88, 122
Perry, Matthew C., 8, 146; LaFeber on, 10; Ryukyu visits by, 163–65; Japanese trade policies after, 180–86
Philippines, *15*, 47, 100

Phipps, John, 122
piracy: Korea and, 30–32, 41; Taiwan and, 51; Satsuma and, 200
Pomeranz, Kenneth, 16
porcelain, 13, 81, 98, 100, 138, 140, 166, 247
Portuguese merchants, 14, 31–32, 50; ban of, 49–50, 65
Posadnik (Russian ship), 209–13
prostitution: in Korea, 42; in Japan, 56, 116–17, 124
Pryun, Robert, 216*n*20

Qianlong (emperor), 114
Qing Empire, *15*, 114; tribute system of, 30, 130, 137, 153, 236–37, 240; investiture missions of, 51, 106–7, 138, 193–94; maritime prohibitions of, 51, 52; Taiwan and, 70; British trade and, 114, 146–48; Opium War and, 146–48, 150, 155, 162. *See also* China

rapeseed oil, 50, 127, 129, 140, 196, 197, 202
Raven (British ship), 210
Ravina, Mark, 7–8
Reid, Anthony, 13–14
Rezanov, Nikolai, *57*, 98–100, 110–12, *113*, 125
Richardson, C. L., 189, 192, 194–95
Roches, Léon, 184–85
Roze, Pierre-Gustave, 231–32
Russia: Tsushima outpost of, *5*, 208–12, *211*, 217–18, 233; trade ventures of, 9, 97–102, 110–13, 145, 147
Russian American Company, 100–102
Ryukyu-Netherlands Treaty (1855), 191

Ryukyu House: in Kagoshima, *35*, 239; in Fuzhou, 38, 167, 186
Ryukyu: island chain of, *3*; Shō family of, 7, 35–36, 153; Satsuma and, 20, 34–39, 45–47, 74, 95–96; Chinese tribute of, 34–39, 130, 136, 153, 158, 186–87, 240; Satsuma tribute of, 35, 51, 95, 107, 239; Chinese investiture missions to, 36, *37*, 38, 51, 106–7, 138, 193–94; *bakufu* diplomatic protocol with, 44; embassy missions of, 45, 106–7; Christianity on, 47–48; sugar cane farming on, 74, 75, 95, 127–28; tsunami of 1771 on, 97; Edo diplomatic visits from, 45, 106, 137; smuggling in, 127–31, 151, 162; famine in, 131; Western trade with, 136, 151–59, 163–64, 189–92, 201–4; Tokugawa aid for, 138; Nagasaki trade and, 158–60; trade agreements with, 164–66; currency of, 192; Meiji reforms involving, 237–40, 246; "disposition" of, 240

Sabine (French ship), 156–57
Sada Hakubō, 243
Sai On, 96
Saigō Takamori, 154, 237
Saitō Osamu, 117–18
Sakai, Robert, 162–63
Sakhalin, 20, *99*, 208
Sanjō Sanetomi, 229, 231
sankin kōtai, 26, 193
Sasu Iori, 168–69, 208–10, 212, 216–17
Satsuma, 21–24; Chinese trade at, 2; Ryukyu trade and, *3*, 20–21, 34–39, 45–47, 74, 95–96; corvée labor from, 26–27; samurai of, 28, 127; castle town of, 28, *33*, 35; Ryukyu

tribute to, 35, 51, 95, 107, 239; Ryukyu embassy missions to, 45, 106–7; Chinese community of, 46–47; silver policies and, 66–68, 77–78; eighteenth-century economy of, 94–97; sugar trade and, 95, 127–28, 187–88, 202; Matsudaira's trade reforms and, 109–10; entrepôt of, 125–32; debts of, 126; Nagasaki and, 133–39, 190, 203; Korean trade and, 135–36; shelling of ships by, 150–51; Western visits to Ryukyu and, 151, 154–59, *155*; divisions within, 159–62; Western trade policies and, 186–200, 201–6; indigo crop of, 187; British attacks against, 193–96; Chōshū and, 186, 187, 196, 202–4, 230, 233, 235–36; mining company in, 201; at Paris Exposition, 202–4; Meiji reforms involving, 230, 235, 236–38, 246; during civil war, 236. *See also particular cities, e.g.*, Kagoshima

sea cucumbers, 55, 80–81, 83, 122; trade restrictions on, 16, 124–25, 178; clearing-house for, 89, 90, 92–93; from Korea, 92–93, 141; uses of, 123–24. *See also* marine products

seaweed. *See* kelp

seclusion: ideology of, 4, 8–12, 18, 111; Chinese policy of, 114

Sekigahara, Battle of, 25, 34

sericulture, 50, 68, 70–71, 75, 91, 100, 110; European, 179, 184–85, 205. *See also* silk goods

shark fins, 55, 70, 83, 123, 187; Tokugawa monopoly on, 16; clearing-house for, 89. *See also* marine products

Shell and Repel Order, 9, 150–51

Shibata Takenaka, 201–2

Shimada, Ryuto, 78

Shimazu clan, 27, 38, 45–47; Kagoshima and, 28; Shō family and, 35–36; Sō clan and, 42–43; Ryukyu and, 45, 107, 136; Korean trade and, 135–36; Ii assassination and, 189; Amami islands and, 237

Shimazu Hisamitsu, 162, 167, 186–96, *192*, 204, 222

Shimazu Iehisa, 34–35

Shimazu Mitsuhisa, 50

Shimazu Nariakira, 154, 159–62, 174, 188; as daimyo, 162–68; trade policies of, 164–68, 191; portrait of, *165*; death of, 167, 186; Taiwan and, 167

Shimazu Narioki, 154–56, 160–63, 169

Shimazu Tadayoshi, 167, 186, 195, 237

Shimazu Yura, 162

ships, steam-powered, 150, 166, 188, 194, 197–200

Shiraishi Shōichirō, 187

Shō family, 7, 35–36; as Qing vassals, 51, 107, 138, 153

Shō Hō, 36, 50–51

Shō Nei, 36

Shō Tai, 238, 239

Shō Tei, 189

Shūseikan factory, 166, 194

Siam, 52

silk goods, 13, 19, 49–52, 140, 179, 184–86; Ryukyu trade in, 36–38, 50; Tsushima trade in, 39–40; value of, 182–83; smuggling of, 197. *See also* sericulture

silver, 84–89; American mining of, 13, 80; Chinese reserves of, 13, 34; Japanese reserves of, 16, 34, 49;

Japanese restrictions on, 52–59, 76–78; in Mexican dollar, 60, 182*n*12; copper and, 142–43. *See also* currency
Singapore, 15, 18, 122
skullcap root, 76, 93, 132, 141, 144–45, 148, 158. *See also* medicinal products
Smith, Kerry, 199
Smits, Gregory, 96
smuggling, 54, 56, 74, 133, 180, 197; of medicinal products, 87, 116–17; Ryukyu, 127–31, 151, 162
Sō clan, 7, 47; Kyushu fiefs of, 27, 33, 228; Korean trade with, 31, 39–42, 45, 135–36, 208, 240–45; rice on Kyushu lands of, 40; Shimazu clan and, 42–43; Satsuma competition and, 135–36; proposed transfer of, 209–10, 212, 214, 215, 217
Sō Shigemasa, 242*n*13
Sō Yoshiakira, 218, 220, 228, 230, 240–44
Sō Yoshiaya, 211.
Sō Yoshinari, 50
Sō Yoshinojō, 217–18
Sō Yoshiyori, 169–72, 174–75, 207, 210, 212, 216–17
South America, 12–13, 80
Spain: American silver mines of, 13, 80; Asian ventures of, 31–32, 47; missionaries from, 32, 47
sugar cane farming, 50, 68, 70, 74, 75, 95–96, 127–28
sugar trade, 13, 118, 136–37, 187–88, 196, 197, 202
Sugi Kōji, 249
Sugimura Naoki, 91–92
Sulawesi (Celebes), 15, 80–81
sulfur, 30, 38, 187
Suyama Totsuan, 60

Tada Shōzō, 217, 229.
Taiping Rebellion, 153, 174, 183–84, 186, 215, 220
Taiwan, 15, 36, 70, 167, 220; pirates of, 51; Japanese expedition against, 238
Takano Chōei, 120
Takarajima, 3, 152.
Takasugi Shinsaku, 202
Takebe Seian, 69–70
Takemoto Masaaki, 224
Tanegashima, 3
Tang Dynasty, 220
Tanuma Okitsugu, 87–89, 102–3, 121
Tashiro Kazui, 8, 51–52, 53, 143
tea, 17, 82, 100; Japanese exports of, 19, 55, 179, 182–83, 247; trade association for, 86
tin, 38, 40, 55, 65, 82, 83, 196
tobacco, 86, 196, 197, 202
Toba-Fushimi, battle of, 233
Toby, Ronald, 8, 42, 111
Tokara islands, 3, 152.
Tokugawa Akitake, 203
Tokugawa Hidetada, 47–49
Tokugawa Ieharu, 104
Tokugawa Iemochi, 207, 223
Tokugawa Ienari, 106
Tokugawa Ienobu, 62, 66
Tokugawa Ietsugu, 62
Tokugawa Ieyasu, 20, 25–26, 43; anti-Christian decrees by, 32; trading policies of, 32–34; monetary system of, 34; death of, 47
Tokugawa Ieyoshi, 138–39, 160
Tokugawa shogunate: foreign relations of, 2–12, 20–24, 42–48, 103–11, 200–206; feudal aspects of, 8, 26–28; "seclusionism" of, 4, 8–12, 18, 111; Anti-Christianity campaigns of, 14, 32, 47–49, 207; administrative organization

of, 26–27; trade policies of, 49–51, 73–115, 180–86; Nagasaki clearing-house and, 56–59; currency manipulations by, 59–68; defense policies of, 64–65; decline of, 185–86; civil war and, 236
Tokugawa Tsunayoshi, 59, 66
Tokugawa Yoshimune, 8, 49–50, 64, 68, 70
Tokugawa Yoshinobu, 232–33
Tokunoshima, *3*
Tomiyama Kazuyuki, 36
Totman, Conrad, 32, 85–86
Toyotomi Hideyoshi, 20, 32
Tsuda Mamichi, 248–49
Tsukada Takashi, 93–94
Tsushima, 5, 21–24, 139–45; Asō Bay of, *5, 209*, 210, *211, 215*; Russian occupation of, *5*, 208–12, *211*, 217–18, 233; Korean trade with, 7, 20, 39–42, 45, 135–36, 140–41, 207–8, 214–16, 240–45; Sō clan of, 7, 31, 39; Izuhara on; *5, 28, 41*,169–70, 175, *211*, 213, 217, 228, 230, 241–42; samurai of, 28; piracy and, 31, 41; Korean rice exports to, 40–41, 141, 170, 172, 241, 244; Korean embassy missions and, 44, 104–6; castaways on, 46; silk trade of, 50–53; silver policies and, 59–65, 76–77; defense role of, 64, 65; strategic position of, 64, 208; whaling industry of, 93; leather goods from, 93–94, 109, 141, 144, 223; Matsudaira's trade reforms and, 109; Satsuma competition with, 135–36; Western visits to, 151, 168–76, 207–10; Chōshū and, 211, 217–19, 228; factional rivalry on, 227–31; international relations and, 236, 242–43; Meiji reforms involving, 236, 237, 240–46. *See also* Sō clan

Uehara Kenzen, 54, 138, 158
Uemura Kyūhachirō, 116–17
United Kingdom: Chinese trade with, 17–18, 81–83, 114, 147–48; East India Company of, 17–18, 81–83, 88, 100–101; sugar trade of, 95–96; takeover of Java by, 133; Opium War of, 146–48, 150, 155, 162; Nagasaki trade ventures by, 178–79, 195; Satsuma attack by, 193–96; plans for Tsushima treaty port by, 216.
U.S.-Japan Treaty of Amity and Commerce (1858), 163–65
U.S.-Japan Treaty of Friendship (1854), 163–65

Van Reed, Eugene, 198–99
Van Valkenburg, Robert, 232
Vereenigde Oost-Indische Compagnie (VOC). *See* Dutch East India Company
Vietnam, 14, *15*; mines in, 79; British-Chinese trade and, 82–83

Wakabayashi, Bob, 9
Waley-Cohen, Joanna, 114
Walker, Brett L., 21*n*31
wax, 196, 202
whalebone fertilizer, 187
whaling ships, 23, 93, 118–19, 152; Ryukyu visits by, 150, 152; Tsushima visits by, 170–71, 214
Wigen, Kären, 70–71
William II (Dutch king), 146
Wolff, Derek, 47
wool, 17, 19, 53, 99, 179, 247

Xu Jiyu, 1–2

Yaeyama Islands, *3*, 97
Yakushima, *3*
Yamada Hōkoku, 220, 222, 225
Yamakawa (port), 128, *155*, 156
Yonaguni, *3*, 97
Yoshikawa Saemon, 168–69
Yoshioka Kōki, 242–43

Zeniya Gohei, 131
Zheng Chenggong, 51
Zhoushan Islands, 1, *15*
Zongli Yamen, 236
Zusho Shōzaemon, 126–30, 168; Western visits to Ryukyu and, 154–58; Narioki and, 160–63

Harvard East Asian Monographs
(*out-of-print)

*1. Liang Fang-chung, *The Single-Whip Method of Taxation in China*
*2. Harold C. Hinton, *The Grain Tribute System of China, 1845–1911*
 3. Ellsworth C. Carlson, *The Kaiping Mines, 1877–1912*
*4. Chao Kuo-chün, *Agrarian Policies of Mainland China: A Documentary Study, 1949–1956*
*5. Edgar Snow, *Random Notes on Red China, 1936–1945*
*6. Edwin George Beal, Jr., *The Origin of Likin, 1835–1864*
 7. Chao Kuo-chün, *Economic Planning and Organization in Mainland China: A Documentary Study, 1949–1957*
*8. John K. Fairbank, *Ching Documents: An Introductory Syllabus*
*9. Helen Yin and Yi-chang Yin, *Economic Statistics of Mainland China, 1949–1957*
 10. Wolfgang Franke, *The Reform and Abolition of the Traditional Chinese Examination System*
 11. Albert Feuerwerker and S. Cheng, *Chinese Communist Studies of Modern Chinese History*
 12. C. John Stanley, *Late Ching Finance: Hu Kuang-yung as an Innovator*
 13. S. M. Meng, *The Tsungli Yamen: Its Organization and Functions*
*14. Ssu-yü Teng, *Historiography of the Taiping Rebellion*
 15. Chun-Jo Liu, *Controversies in Modern Chinese Intellectual History: An Analytic Bibliography of Periodical Articles, Mainly of the May Fourth and Post-May Fourth Era*
*16. Edward J. M. Rhoads, *The Chinese Red Army, 1927–1963: An Annotated Bibliography*
*17. Andrew J. Nathan, *A History of the China International Famine Relief Commission*
*18. Frank H. H. King (ed.) and Prescott Clarke, *A Research Guide to China-Coast Newspapers, 1822–1911*
*19. Ellis Joffe, *Party and Army: Professionalism and Political Control in the Chinese Officer Corps, 1949–1964*
*20. Toshio G. Tsukahira, *Feudal Control in Tokugawa Japan: The Sankin Kōtai System*
*21. Kwang-Ching Liu, ed., *American Missionaries in China: Papers from Harvard Seminars*
*22. George Moseley, *A Sino-Soviet Cultural Frontier: The Ili Kazakh Autonomous Chou*
 23. Carl F. Nathan, *Plague Prevention and Politics in Manchuria, 1910–1931*

Harvard East Asian Monographs

*24. Adrian Arthur Bennett, *John Fryer: The Introduction of Western Science and Technology into Nineteenth-Century China*
*25. Donald J. Friedman, *The Road from Isolation: The Campaign of the American Committee for Non-Participation in Japanese Aggression, 1938–1941*
*26. Edward LeFevour, *Western Enterprise in Late Ching China: A Selective Survey of Jardine, Matheson and Company's Operations, 1842–1895*
 27. Charles Neuhauser, *Third World Politics: China and the Afro-Asian People's Solidarity Organization, 1957–1967*
*28. Kungtu C. Sun, assisted by Ralph W. Huenemann, *The Economic Development of Manchuria in the First Half of the Twentieth Century*
*29. Shahid Javed Burki, *A Study of Chinese Communes, 1965*
 30. John Carter Vincent, *The Extraterritorial System in China: Final Phase*
 31. Madeleine Chi, *China Diplomacy, 1914–1918*
*32. Clifton Jackson Phillips, *Protestant America and the Pagan World: The First Half Century of the American Board of Commissioners for Foreign Missions, 1810–1860*
*33. James Pusey, *Wu Han: Attacking the Present Through the Past*
*34. Ying-wan Cheng, *Postal Communication in China and Its Modernization, 1860–1896*
 35. Tuvia Blumenthal, *Saving in Postwar Japan*
 36. Peter Frost, *The Bakumatsu Currency Crisis*
 37. Stephen C. Lockwood, *Augustine Heard and Company, 1858–1862*
 38. Robert R. Campbell, *James Duncan Campbell: A Memoir by His Son*
 39. Jerome Alan Cohen, ed., *The Dynamics of China's Foreign Relations*
 40. V. V. Vishnyakova-Akimova, *Two Years in Revolutionary China, 1925–1927*, trans. Steven L. Levine
 41. Meron Medzini, *French Policy in Japan During the Closing Years of the Tokugawa Regime*
 42. Ezra Vogel, Margie Sargent, Vivienne B. Shue, Thomas Jay Mathews, and Deborah S. Davis, *The Cultural Revolution in the Provinces*
 43. Sidney A. Forsythe, *An American Missionary Community in China, 1895–1905*
*44. Benjamin I. Schwartz, ed., *Reflections on the May Fourth Movement.: A Symposium*
*45. Ching Young Choe, *The Rule of the Taewŏngun, 1864–1873: Restoration in Yi Korea*
 46. W. P. J. Hall, *A Bibliographical Guide to Japanese Research on the Chinese Economy, 1958–1970*
 47. Jack J. Gerson, *Horatio Nelson Lay and Sino-British Relations, 1854–1864*
 48. Paul Richard Bohr, *Famine and the Missionary: Timothy Richard as Relief Administrator and Advocate of National Reform*
 49. Endymion Wilkinson, *The History of Imperial China: A Research Guide*
 50. Britten Dean, *China and Great Britain: The Diplomacy of Commercial Relations, 1860–1864*
 51. Ellsworth C. Carlson, *The Foochow Missionaries, 1847–1880*
 52. Yeh-chien Wang, *An Estimate of the Land-Tax Collection in China, 1753 and 1908*
 53. Richard M. Pfeffer, *Understanding Business Contracts in China, 1949–1963*
*54. Han-sheng Chuan and Richard Kraus, *Mid-Ching Rice Markets and Trade: An Essay in Price History*
 55. Ranbir Vohra, *Lao She and the Chinese Revolution*
 56. Liang-lin Hsiao, *China's Foreign Trade Statistics, 1864–1949*

Harvard East Asian Monographs

*57. Lee-hsia Hsu Ting, *Government Control of the Press in Modern China, 1900–1949*
*58. Edward W. Wagner, *The Literati Purges: Political Conflict in Early Yi Korea*
*59. Joungwon A. Kim, *Divided Korea: The Politics of Development, 1945–1972*
60. Noriko Kamachi, John K. Fairbank, and Chūzō Ichiko, *Japanese Studies of Modern China Since 1953: A Bibliographical Guide to Historical and Social-Science Research on the Nineteenth and Twentieth Centuries, Supplementary Volume for 1953–1969*
61. Donald A. Gibbs and Yun-chen Li, *A Bibliography of Studies and Translations of Modern Chinese Literature, 1918–1942*
62. Robert H. Silin, *Leadership and Values: The Organization of Large-Scale Taiwanese Enterprises*
63. David Pong, *A Critical Guide to the Kwangtung Provincial Archives Deposited at the Public Record Office of London*
*64. Fred W. Drake, *China Charts the World: Hsu Chi-yü and His Geography of 1848*
*65. William A. Brown and Urgrunge Onon, translators and annotators, *History of the Mongolian People's Republic*
66. Edward L. Farmer, *Early Ming Government: The Evolution of Dual Capitals*
*67. Ralph C. Croizier, *Koxinga and Chinese Nationalism: History, Myth, and the Hero*
*68. William J. Tyler, tr., *The Psychological World of Natsume Sōseki*, by Doi Takeo
69. Eric Widmer, *The Russian Ecclesiastical Mission in Peking During the Eighteenth Century*
*70. Charlton M. Lewis, *Prologue to the Chinese Revolution: The Transformation of Ideas and Institutions in Hunan Province, 1891–1907*
71. Preston Torbert, *The Ch'ing Imperial Household Department: A Study of Its Organization and Principal Functions, 1662–1796*
72. Paul A. Cohen and John E. Schrecker, eds., *Reform in Nineteenth-Century China*
73. Jon Sigurdson, *Rural Industrialism in China*
74. Kang Chao, *The Development of Cotton Textile Production in China*
75. Valentin Rabe, *The Home Base of American China Missions, 1880–1920*
*76. Sarasin Viraphol, *Tribute and Profit: Sino-Siamese Trade, 1652–1853*
77. Ch'i-ch'ing Hsiao, *The Military Establishment of the Yuan Dynasty*
78. Meishi Tsai, *Contemporary Chinese Novels and Short Stories, 1949–1974: An Annotated Bibliography*
*79. Wellington K. K. Chan, *Merchants, Mandarins and Modern Enterprise in Late Ching China*
80. Endymion Wilkinson, *Landlord and Labor in Late Imperial China: Case Studies from Shandong by Jing Su and Luo Lun*
*81. Barry Keenan, *The Dewey Experiment in China: Educational Reform and Political Power in the Early Republic*
*82. George A. Hayden, *Crime and Punishment in Medieval Chinese Drama: Three Judge Pao Plays*
*83. Sang-Chul Suh, *Growth and Structural Changes in the Korean Economy, 1910–1940*
84. J. W. Dower, *Empire and Aftermath: Yoshida Shigeru and the Japanese Experience, 1878–1954*
85. Martin Collcutt, *Five Mountains: The Rinzai Zen Monastic Institution in Medieval Japan*
86. Kwang Suk Kim and Michael Roemer, *Growth and Structural Transformation*

Harvard East Asian Monographs

87. Anne O. Krueger, *The Developmental Role of the Foreign Sector and Aid*
*88. Edwin S. Mills and Byung-Nak Song, *Urbanization and Urban Problems*
89. Sung Hwan Ban, Pal Yong Moon, and Dwight H. Perkins, *Rural Development*
*90. Noel F. McGinn, Donald R. Snodgrass, Yung Bong Kim, Shin-Bok Kim, and Quee-Young Kim, *Education and Development in Korea*
*91. Leroy P. Jones and Il SaKong, *Government, Business, and Entrepreneurship in Economic Development: The Korean Case*
92. Edward S. Mason, Dwight H. Perkins, Kwang Suk Kim, David C. Cole, Mahn Je Kim et al., *The Economic and Social Modernization of the Republic of Korea*
93. Robert Repetto, Tai Hwan Kwon, Son-Ung Kim, Dae Young Kim, John E. Sloboda, and Peter J. Donaldson, *Economic Development, Population Policy, and Demographic Transition in the Republic of Korea*
94. Parks M. Coble, Jr., *The Shanghai Capitalists and the Nationalist Government, 1927–1937*
95. Noriko Kamachi, *Reform in China: Huang Tsun-hsien and the Japanese Model*
96. Richard Wich, *Sino-Soviet Crisis Politics: A Study of Political Change and Communication*
97. Lillian M. Li, *China's Silk Trade: Traditional Industry in the Modern World, 1842–1937*
98. R. David Arkush, *Fei Xiaotong and Sociology in Revolutionary China*
*99. Kenneth Alan Grossberg, *Japan's Renaissance: The Politics of the Muromachi Bakufu*
100. James Reeve Pusey, *China and Charles Darwin*
101. Hoyt Cleveland Tillman, *Utilitarian Confucianism: Chen Liang's Challenge to Chu Hsi*
102. Thomas A. Stanley, *Ōsugi Sakae, Anarchist in Taishō Japan: The Creativity of the Ego*
103. Jonathan K. Ocko, *Bureaucratic Reform in Provincial China: Ting Jih-ch'ang in Restoration Kiangsu, 1867–1870*
104. James Reed, *The Missionary Mind and American East Asia Policy, 1911–1915*
105. Neil L. Waters, *Japan's Local Pragmatists: The Transition from Bakumatsu to Meiji in the Kawasaki Region*
106. David C. Cole and Yung Chul Park, *Financial Development in Korea, 1945–1978*
107. Roy Bahl, Chuk Kyo Kim, and Chong Kee Park, *Public Finances During the Korean Modernization Process*
108. William D. Wray, *Mitsubishi and the N.Y.K, 1870–1914: Business Strategy in the Japanese Shipping Industry*
109. Ralph William Huenemann, *The Dragon and the Iron Horse: The Economics of Railroads in China, 1876–1937*
*110. Benjamin A. Elman, *From Philosophy to Philology: Intellectual and Social Aspects of Change in Late Imperial China*
111. Jane Kate Leonard, *Wei Yüan and China's Rediscovery of the Maritime World*
112. Luke S. K. Kwong, *A Mosaic of the Hundred Days:. Personalities, Politics, and Ideas of 1898*
*113. John E. Wills, Jr., *Embassies and Illusions: Dutch and Portuguese Envoys to K'ang-hsi, 1666–1687*
114. Joshua A. Fogel, *Politics and Sinology: The Case of Naitō Konan (1866–1934)*
*115. Jeffrey C. Kinkley, ed., *After Mao: Chinese Literature and Society, 1978–1981*
116. C. Andrew Gerstle, *Circles of Fantasy: Convention in the Plays of Chikamatsu*

Harvard East Asian Monographs

117. Andrew Gordon, *The Evolution of Labor Relations in Japan: Heavy Industry, 1853–1955*
*118. Daniel K. Gardner, *Chu Hsi and the "Ta Hsueh": Neo-Confucian Reflection on the Confucian Canon*
119. Christine Guth Kanda, *Shinzō: Hachiman Imagery and Its Development*
*120. Robert Borgen, *Sugawara no Michizane and the Early Heian Court*
121. Chang-tai Hung, *Going to the People: Chinese Intellectual and Folk Literature, 1918–1937*
*122. Michael A. Cusumano, *The Japanese Automobile Industry: Technology and Management at Nissan and Toyota*
123. Richard von Glahn, *The Country of Streams and Grottoes: Expansion, Settlement, and the Civilizing of the Sichuan Frontier in Song Times*
124. Steven D. Carter, *The Road to Komatsubara: A Classical Reading of the Renga Hyakuin*
125. Katherine F. Bruner, John K. Fairbank, and Richard T. Smith, *Entering China's Service: Robert Hart's Journals, 1854–1863*
126. Bob Tadashi Wakabayashi, *Anti-Foreignism and Western Learning in Early-Modern Japan: The "New Theses" of 1825*
127. Atsuko Hirai, *Individualism and Socialism: The Life and Thought of Kawai Eijirō (1891–1944)*
128. Ellen Widmer, *The Margins of Utopia: "Shui-hu hou-chuan" and the Literature of Ming Loyalism*
129. R. Kent Guy, *The Emperor's Four Treasuries: Scholars and the State in the Late Chien-lung Era*
130. Peter C. Perdue, *Exhausting the Earth: State and Peasant in Hunan, 1500–1850*
131. Susan Chan Egan, *A Latterday Confucian: Reminiscences of William Hung (1893–1980)*
132. James T. C. Liu, *China Turning Inward: Intellectual-Political Changes in the Early Twelfth Century*
*133. Paul A. Cohen, *Between Tradition and Modernity: Wang T'ao and Reform in Late Ching China*
134. Kate Wildman Nakai, *Shogunal Politics: Arai Hakuseki and the Premises of Tokugawa Rule*
*135. Parks M. Coble, *Facing Japan: Chinese Politics and Japanese Imperialism, 1931–1937*
136. Jon L. Saari, *Legacies of Childhood: Growing Up Chinese in a Time of Crisis, 1890–1920*
137. Susan Downing Videen, *Tales of Heichū*
138. Heinz Morioka and Miyoko Sasaki, *Rakugo: The Popular Narrative Art of Japan*
139. Joshua A. Fogel, *Nakae Ushikichi in China: The Mourning of Spirit*
140. Alexander Barton Woodside, *Vietnam and the Chinese Model: A Comparative Study of Vietnamese and Chinese Government in the First Half of the Nineteenth Century*
*141. George Elison, *Deus Destroyed: The Image of Christianity in Early Modern Japan*
142. William D. Wray, ed., *Managing Industrial Enterprise: Cases from Japan's Prewar Experience*
*143. T'ung-tsu Ch'ü, *Local Government in China Under the Ching*
144. Marie Anchordoguy, *Computers, Inc.: Japan's Challenge to IBM*
145. Barbara Molony, *Technology and Investment: The Prewar Japanese Chemical Industry*
146. Mary Elizabeth Berry, *Hideyoshi*

Harvard East Asian Monographs

147. Laura E. Hein, *Fueling Growth: The Energy Revolution and Economic Policy in Postwar Japan*
148. Wen-hsin Yeh, *The Alienated Academy: Culture and Politics in Republican China, 1919–1937*
149. Dru C. Gladney, *Muslim Chinese: Ethnic Nationalism in the People's Republic*
150. Merle Goldman and Paul A. Cohen, eds., *Ideas Across Cultures: Essays on Chinese Thought in Honor of Benjamin L Schwartz*
151. James M. Polachek, *The Inner Opium War*
152. Gail Lee Bernstein, *Japanese Marxist: A Portrait of Kawakami Hajime, 1879–1946*
*153. Lloyd E. Eastman, *The Abortive Revolution: China Under Nationalist Rule, 1927–1937*
154. Mark Mason, *American Multinationals and Japan: The Political Economy of Japanese Capital Controls, 1899–1980*
155. Richard J. Smith, John K. Fairbank, and Katherine F. Bruner, *Robert Hart and China's Early Modernization: His Journals, 1863–1866*
156. George J. Tanabe, Jr., *Myōe the Dreamkeeper: Fantasy and Knowledge in Kamakura Buddhism*
157. William Wayne Farris, *Heavenly Warriors: The Evolution of Japan's Military, 500–1300*
158. Yu-ming Shaw, *An American Missionary in China: John Leighton Stuart and Chinese-American Relations*
159. James B. Palais, *Politics and Policy in Traditional Korea*
*160. Douglas Reynolds, *China, 1898–1912: The Xinzheng Revolution and Japan*
161. Roger R. Thompson, *China's Local Councils in the Age of Constitutional Reform, 1898–1911*
162. William Johnston, *The Modern Epidemic: History of Tuberculosis in Japan*
163. Constantine Nomikos Vaporis, *Breaking Barriers: Travel and the State in Early Modern Japan*
164. Irmela Hijiya-Kirschnereit, *Rituals of Self-Revelation: Shishōsetsu as Literary Genre and Socio-Cultural Phenomenon*
165. James C. Baxter, *The Meiji Unification Through the Lens of Ishikawa Prefecture*
166. Thomas R. H. Havens, *Architects of Affluence: The Tsutsumi Family and the Seibu-Saison Enterprises in Twentieth-Century Japan*
167. Anthony Hood Chambers, *The Secret Window: Ideal Worlds in Tanizaki's Fiction*
168. Steven J. Ericson, *The Sound of the Whistle: Railroads and the State in Meiji Japan*
169. Andrew Edmund Goble, *Kenmu: Go-Daigo's Revolution*
170. Denise Potrzeba Lett, *In Pursuit of Status: The Making of South Korea's "New" Urban Middle Class*
171. Mimi Hall Yiengpruksawan, *Hiraizumi: Buddhist Art and Regional Politics in Twelfth-Century Japan*
172. Charles Shirō Inouye, *The Similitude of Blossoms: A Critical Biography of Izumi Kyōka (1873–1939), Japanese Novelist and Playwright*
173. Aviad E. Raz, *Riding the Black Ship: Japan and Tokyo Disneyland*
174. Deborah J. Milly, *Poverty, Equality, and Growth: The Politics of Economic Need in Postwar Japan*
175. See Heng Teow, *Japan's Cultural Policy Toward China, 1918–1931: A Comparative Perspective*

Harvard East Asian Monographs

176. Michael A. Fuller, *An Introduction to Literary Chinese*
177. Frederick R. Dickinson, *War and National Reinvention: Japan in the Great War, 1914–1919*
178. John Solt, *Shredding the Tapestry of Meaning: The Poetry and Poetics of Kitasono Katue (1902–1978)*
179. Edward Pratt, *Japan's Protoindustrial Elite: The Economic Foundations of the Gōnō*
180. Atsuko Sakaki, *Recontextualizing Texts: Narrative Performance in Modern Japanese Fiction*
181. Soon-Won Park, *Colonial Industrialization and Labor in Korea: The Onoda Cement Factory*
182. JaHyun Kim Haboush and Martina Deuchler, *Culture and the State in Late Chosŏn Korea*
183. John W. Chaffee, *Branches of Heaven: A History of the Imperial Clan of Sung China*
184. Gi-Wook Shin and Michael Robinson, eds., *Colonial Modernity in Korea*
185. Nam-lin Hur, *Prayer and Play in Late Tokugawa Japan: Asakusa Sensōji and Edo Society*
186. Kristin Stapleton, *Civilizing Chengdu: Chinese Urban Reform, 1895–1937*
187. Hyung Il Pai, *Constructing "Korean" Origins: A Critical Review of Archaeology, Historiography, and Racial Myth in Korean State-Formation Theories*
188. Brian D. Ruppert, *Jewel in the Ashes: Buddha Relics and Power in Early Medieval Japan*
189. Susan Daruvala, *Zhou Zuoren and an Alternative Chinese Response to Modernity*
*190. James Z. Lee, *The Political Economy of a Frontier: Southwest China, 1250–1850*
191. Kerry Smith, *A Time of Crisis: Japan, the Great Depression, and Rural Revitalization*
192. Michael Lewis, *Becoming Apart: National Power and Local Politics in Toyama, 1868–1945*
193. William C. Kirby, Man-houng Lin, James Chin Shih, and David A. Pietz, eds., *State and Economy in Republican China: A Handbook for Scholars*
194. Timothy S. George, *Minamata: Pollution and the Struggle for Democracy in Postwar Japan*
195. Billy K. L. So, *Prosperity, Region, and Institutions in Maritime China: The South Fukien Pattern, 946–1368*
196. Yoshihisa Tak Matsusaka, *The Making of Japanese Manchuria, 1904–1932*
197. Maram Epstein, *Competing Discourses: Orthodoxy, Authenticity, and Engendered Meanings in Late Imperial Chinese Fiction*
198. Curtis J. Milhaupt, J. Mark Ramseyer, and Michael K. Young, eds. and comps., *Japanese Law in Context: Readings in Society, the Economy, and Politics*
199. Haruo Iguchi, *Unfinished Business: Ayukawa Yoshisuke and U.S.-Japan Relations, 1937–1952*
200. Scott Pearce, Audrey Spiro, and Patricia Ebrey, *Culture and Power in the Reconstitution of the Chinese Realm, 200–600*
201. Terry Kawashima, *Writing Margins: The Textual Construction of Gender in Heian and Kamakura Japan*
202. Martin W. Huang, *Desire and Fictional Narrative in Late Imperial China*
203. Robert S. Ross and Jiang Changbin, eds., *Re-examining the Cold War: U.S.-China Diplomacy, 1954–1973*
204. Guanhua Wang, *In Search of Justice: The 1905–1906 Chinese Anti-American Boycott*

Harvard East Asian Monographs

205. David Schaberg, *A Patterned Past: Form and Thought in Early Chinese Historiography*
206. Christine Yano, *Tears of Longing: Nostalgia and the Nation in Japanese Popular Song*
207. Milena Doleželová-Velingerová and Oldřich Král, with Graham Sanders, eds., *The Appropriation of Cultural Capital: China's May Fourth Project*
208. Robert N. Huey, *The Making of 'Shinkokinshū'*
209. Lee Butler, *Emperor and Aristocracy in Japan, 1467–1680: Resilience and Renewal*
210. Suzanne Ogden, *Inklings of Democracy in China*
211. Kenneth J. Ruoff, *The People's Emperor: Democracy and the Japanese Monarchy, 1945–1995*
212. Haun Saussy, *Great Walls of Discourse and Other Adventures in Cultural China*
213. Aviad E. Raz, *Emotions at Work: Normative Control, Organizations, and Culture in Japan and America*
214. Rebecca E. Karl and Peter Zarrow, eds., *Rethinking the 1898 Reform Period: Political and Cultural Change in Late Qing China*
215. Kevin O'Rourke, *The Book of Korean Shijo*
216. Ezra F. Vogel, ed., *The Golden Age of the U.S.-China-Japan Triangle, 1972–1989*
217. Thomas A. Wilson, ed., *On Sacred Grounds: Culture, Society, Politics, and the Formation of the Cult of Confucius*
218. Donald S. Sutton, *Steps of Perfection: Exorcistic Performers and Chinese Religion in Twentieth-Century Taiwan*
219. Daqing Yang, *Technology of Empire: Telecommunications and Japanese Expansionism, 1883–1945*
220. Qianshen Bai, *Fu Shan's World: The Transformation of Chinese Calligraphy in the Seventeenth Century*
221. Paul Jakov Smith and Richard von Glahn, eds., *The Song-Yuan-Ming Transition in Chinese History*
222. Rania Huntington, *Alien Kind: Foxes and Late Imperial Chinese Narrative*
223. Jordan Sand, *House and Home in Modern Japan: Architecture, Domestic Space, and Bourgeois Culture, 1880–1930*
224. Karl Gerth, *China Made: Consumer Culture and the Creation of the Nation*
225. Xiaoshan Yang, *Metamorphosis of the Private Sphere: Gardens and Objects in Tang-Song Poetry*
226. Barbara Mittler, *A Newspaper for China? Power, Identity, and Change in Shanghai's News Media, 1872–1912*
227. Joyce A. Madancy, *The Troublesome Legacy of Commissioner Lin: The Opium Trade and Opium Suppression in Fujian Province, 1820s to 1920s*
228. John Makeham, *Transmitters and Creators: Chinese Commentators and Commentaries on the Analects*
229. Elisabeth Köll, *From Cotton Mill to Business Empire: The Emergence of Regional Enterprises in Modern China*
230. Emma Teng, *Taiwan's Imagined Geography: Chinese Colonial Travel Writing and Pictures, 1683–1895*
231. Wilt Idema and Beata Grant, *The Red Brush: Writing Women of Imperial China*
232. Eric C. Rath, *The Ethos of Noh: Actors and Their Art*

Harvard East Asian Monographs

233. Elizabeth Remick, *Building Local States: China During the Republican and Post-Mao Eras*
234. Lynn Struve, ed., *The Qing Formation in World-Historical Time*
235. D. Max Moerman, *Localizing Paradise: Kumano Pilgrimage and the Religious Landscape of Premodern Japan*
236. Antonia Finnane, *Speaking of Yangzhou: A Chinese City, 1550–1850*
237. Brian Platt, *Burning and Building: Schooling and State Formation in Japan, 1750–1890*
238. Gail Bernstein, Andrew Gordon, and Kate Wildman Nakai, eds., *Public Spheres, Private Lives in Modern Japan, 1600–1950: Essays in Honor of Albert Craig*
239. Wu Hung and Katherine R. Tsiang, *Body and Face in Chinese Visual Culture*
240. Stephen Dodd, *Writing Home: Representations of the Native Place in Modern Japanese Literature*
241. David Anthony Bello, *Opium and the Limits of Empire: Drug Prohibition in the Chinese Interior, 1729–1850*
242. Hosea Hirata, *Discourses of Seduction: History, Evil, Desire, and Modern Japanese Literature*
243. Kyung Moon Hwang, *Beyond Birth: Social Status in the Emergence of Modern Korea*
244. Brian R. Dott, *Identity Reflections: Pilgrimages to Mount Tai in Late Imperial China*
245. Mark McNally, *Proving the Way: Conflict and Practice in the History of Japanese Nativism*
246. Yongping Wu, *A Political Explanation of Economic Growth: State Survival, Bureaucratic Politics, and Private Enterprises in the Making of Taiwan's Economy, 1950–1985*
247. Kyu Hyun Kim, *The Age of Visions and Arguments: Parliamentarianism and the National Public Sphere in Early Meiji Japan*
248. Zvi Ben-Dor Benite, *The Dao of Muhammad: A Cultural History of Muslims in Late Imperial China*
249. David Der-wei Wang and Shang Wei, eds., *Dynastic Crisis and Cultural Innovation: From the Late Ming to the Late Qing and Beyond*
250. Wilt L. Idema, Wai-yee Li, and Ellen Widmer, eds., *Trauma and Transcendence in Early Qing Literature*
251. Barbara Molony and Kathleen Uno, eds., *Gendering Modern Japanese History*
252. Hiroshi Aoyagi, *Islands of Eight Million Smiles: Idol Performance and Symbolic Production in Contemporary Japan*
253. Wai-yee Li, *The Readability of the Past in Early Chinese Historiography*
254. William C. Kirby, Robert S. Ross, and Gong Li, eds., *Normalization of U.S.-China Relations: An International History*
255. Ellen Gardner Nakamura, *Practical Pursuits: Takano Chōei, Takahashi Keisaku, and Western Medicine in Nineteenth-Century Japan*
256. Jonathan W. Best, *A History of the Early Korean Kingdom of Paekche, together with an annotated translation of* The Paekche Annals *of the* Samguk sagi
257. Liang Pan, *The United Nations in Japan's Foreign and Security Policymaking, 1945–1992: National Security, Party Politics, and International Status*
258. Richard Belsky, *Localities at the Center: Native Place, Space, and Power in Late Imperial Beijing*
259. Zwia Lipkin, *"Useless to the State": "Social Problems" and Social Engineering in Nationalist Nanjing, 1927–1937*

260. William O. Gardner, *Advertising Tower: Japanese Modernism and Modernity in the 1920s*
261. Stephen Owen, *The Making of Early Chinese Classical Poetry*
262. Martin J. Powers, *Pattern and Person: Ornament, Society, and Self in Classical China*
263. Anna M. Shields, *Crafting a Collection: The Cultural Contexts and Poetic Practice of the Huajian ji 花間集 (Collection from Among the Flowers)*
264. Stephen Owen, *The Late Tang: Chinese Poetry of the Mid-Ninth Century (827–860)*
265. Sara L. Friedman, *Intimate Politics: Marriage, the Market, and State Power in Southeastern China*
266. Patricia Buckley Ebrey and Maggie Bickford, *Emperor Huizong and Late Northern Song China: The Politics of Culture and the Culture of Politics*
267. Sophie Volpp, *Worldly Stage: Theatricality in Seventeenth-Century China*
268. Ellen Widmer, *The Beauty and the Book: Women and Fiction in Nineteenth-Century China*
269. Steven B. Miles, *The Sea of Learning: Mobility and Identity in Nineteenth-Century Guangzhou*
270. Lin Man-houng, *China Upside Down: Currency, Society, and Ideologies, 1808–1856*
271. Ronald Egan, *The Problem of Beauty: Aesthetic Thought and Pursuits in Northern Song Dynasty China*
272. Mark Halperin, *Out of the Cloister: Literati Perspectives on Buddhism in Sung China, 960–1279*
273. Helen Dunstan, *State or Merchant? Political Economy and Political Process in 1740s China*
274. Sabina Knight, *The Heart of Time: Moral Agency in Twentieth-Century Chinese Fiction*
275. Timothy J. Van Compernolle, *The Uses of Memory: The Critique of Modernity in the Fiction of Higuchi Ichiyō*
276. Paul Rouzer, *A New Practical Primer of Literary Chinese*
277. Jonathan Zwicker, *Practices of the Sentimental Imagination: Melodrama, the Novel, and the Social Imaginary in Nineteenth-Century Japan*
278. Franziska Seraphim, *War Memory and Social Politics in Japan, 1945–2005*
279. Adam L. Kern, *Manga from the Floating World: Comicbook Culture and the Kibyōshi of Edo Japan*
280. Cynthia J. Brokaw, *Commerce in Culture: The Sibao Book Trade in the Qing and Republican Periods*
281. Eugene Y. Park, *Between Dreams and Reality: The Military Examination in Late Chosŏn Korea, 1600–1894*
282. Nam-lin Hur, *Death and Social Order in Tokugawa Japan: Buddhism, Anti-Christianity, and the Danka System*
283. Patricia M. Thornton, *Disciplining the State: Virtue, Violence, and State-Making in Modern China*
284. Vincent Goossaert, *The Taoists of Peking, 1800–1949: A Social History of Urban Clerics*
285. Peter Nickerson, *Taoism, Bureaucracy, and Popular Religion in Early Medieval China*
286. Charo B. D'Etcheverry, *Love After* The Tale of Genji: *Rewriting the World of the Shining Prince*

Harvard East Asian Monographs

287. Michael G. Chang, *A Court on Horseback: Imperial Touring & the Construction of Qing Rule, 1680–1785*
288. Carol Richmond Tsang, *War and Faith:* Ikkō Ikki *in Late Muromachi Japan*
289. Hilde De Weerdt, *Competition over Content: Negotiating Standards for the Civil Service Examinations in Imperial China (1127–1279)*
290. Eve Zimmerman, *Out of the Alleyway: Nakagami Kenji and the Poetics of Outcaste Fiction*
291. Robert Culp, *Articulating Citizenship: Civic Education and Student Politics in Southeastern China, 1912–1940*
292. Richard J. Smethurst, *From Foot Soldier to Finance Minister: Takahashi Korekiyo, Japan's Keynes*
293. John E. Herman, *Amid the Clouds and Mist: China's Colonization of Guizhou, 1200–1700*
294. Tomoko Shiroyama, *China During the Great Depression: Market, State, and the World Economy, 1929–1937*
295. Kirk W. Larsen, *Tradition, Treaties and Trade: Qing Imperialism and Chosŏn Korea, 1850–1910*
296. Gregory Golley, *When Our Eyes No Longer See: Realism, Science, and Ecology in Japanese Literary Modernism*
297. Barbara Ambros, *Emplacing a Pilgrimage: The Ōyama Cult and Regional Religion in Early Modern Japan*
298. Rebecca Suter, *The Japanization of Modernity: Murakami Haruki between Japan and the United States*
299. Yuma Totani, *The Tokyo War Crimes Trial: The Pursuit of Justice in the Wake of World War II*
300. Linda Isako Angst, *In a Dark Time: Memory, Community, and Gendered Nationalism in Postwar Okinawa*
301. David M. Robinson, ed., *Culture, Courtiers, and Competition: The Ming Court (1368–1644)*
302. Calvin Chen, *Some Assembly Required: Work, Community, and Politics in China's Rural Enterprises*
303. Sem Vermeersch, *The Power of the Buddhas: The Politics of Buddhism During the Koryŏ Dynasty (918–1392)*
304. Tina Lu, *Accidental Incest, Filial Cannibalism, and Other Peculiar Encounters in Late Imperial Chinese Literature*
305. Chang Woei Ong, *Men of Letters Within the Passes: Guanzhong Literati in Chinese History, 907–1911*
306. Wendy Swartz, *Reading Tao Yuanming: Shifting Paradigms of Historical Reception (427–1900)*
307. Peter K. Bol, *Neo-Confucianism in History*
308. Carlos Rojas, *The Naked Gaze: Reflections on Chinese Modernity*
309. Kelly H. Chong, *Deliverance and Submission: Evangelical Women and the Negotiation of Patriarchy in South Korea*
310. Rachel DiNitto, *Uchida Hyakken: A Critique of Modernity and Militarism in Prewar Japan*

Harvard East Asian Monographs

311. Jeffrey Snyder-Reinke, *Dry Spells: State Rainmaking and Local Governance in Late Imperial China*
312. Jay Dautcher, *Down a Narrow Road: Identity and Masculinity in a Uyghur Community in Xinjiang China*
313. Xun Liu, *Daoist Modern: Innovation, Lay Practice, and the Community of Inner Alchemy in Republican Shanghai*
314. Jacob Eyferth, *Eating Rice from Bamboo Roots: The Social History of a Community of Handicraft Papermakers in Rural Sichuan, 1920–2000*
315. David Johnson, *Spectacle and Sacrifice: The Ritual Foundations of Village Life in North China*
316. James Robson, *Power of Place: The Religious Landscape of the Southern Sacred Peak (Nanyue 南嶽) in Medieval China*
317. Lori Watt, *When Empire Comes Home: Repatriation and Reintegration in Postwar Japan*
318. James Dorsey, *Critical Aesthetics: Kobayashi Hideo, Modernity, and Wartime Japan*
319. Christopher Bolton, *Sublime Voices: The Fictional Science and Scientific Fiction of Abe Kōbō*
320. Si-yen Fei, *Negotiating Urban Space: Urbanization and Late Ming Nanjing*
321. Christopher Gerteis, *Gender Struggles: Wage-Earning Women and Male-Dominated Unions in Postwar Japan*
322. Rebecca Nedostup, *Superstitious Regimes: Religion and the Politics of Chinese Modernity*
323. Lucien Bianco, *Wretched Rebels: Rural Disturbances on the Eve of the Chinese Revolution*
324. Cathryn H. Clayton, *Sovereignty at the Edge: Macau and the Question of Chineseness*
325. Micah S. Muscolino, *Fishing Wars and Environmental Change in Late Imperial and Modern China*
326. Robert I. Hellyer, *Defining Engagement: Japan and Global Contexts, 1640–1868*

LaVergne, TN USA
26 January 2010
171183LV00004BA/1/P